PHENOMENOLOGY OR DECONSTRUCTION?

For Jill, Ken, Alison and Elsie
with love

PHENOMENOLOGY OR DECONSTRUCTION?

The Question of Ontology in Maurice Merleau-Ponty, Paul Ricœur and Jean-Luc Nancy

Christopher Watkin

EDINBURGH UNIVERSITY PRESS

© Christopher Watkin, 2009

Transferred to digital print 2013

Edinburgh University Press Ltd
22 George Square, Edinburgh

Typeset in Sabon
by Servis Filmsetting Ltd, Stockport, Cheshire, and
printed and bound by CPI Group (UK) Ltd
Croydon, CR0 4YY

A CIP record for this book is available from the British Library

ISBN 978 0 7486 3759 1 (hardback)

The right of Christopher Watkin
to be identified as author of this work
has been asserted in accordance with
the Copyright, Designs and Patents Act 1988.

Contents

Acknowledgements	vii
Abbreviations	ix
Introduction	1
1. Maurice Merleau-Ponty: Perception	13
1.1 Contact	14
1.2 Facticity/Essence	17
1.3 The Enrootedness of Perception in the Body	20
1.4 The Enrootedness of Perception in the World	24
1.5 Towards an Indirect Ontology	28
1.6 Conclusion	32
2. Maurice Merleau-Ponty: Language	45
2.1 Expression	45
2.2 Language, Figure and Ground	47
2.3 The Mute Call of the World	51
2.4 From Silence to Language	57
2.5 Beyond the Question of 'Contact'	63
3. Paul Ricœur: Selfhood	76
3.1 Fragments	77
3.2 Commitment	87
3.3 Justification	96
4. Paul Ricœur: Justice	106
4.1 Justice and Space	109
4.2 Justice and Commitment	115
4.3 Justice and Fragmentation	119
4.4 Justice and Love	124

5. Jean-Luc Nancy: Sense ... 136
  5.1 Opening ... 138
  5.2 Presence ... 143
  5.3 Contact ... 147
  5.4 The Decision: Between Good and Evil ... 153

6. Jean-Luc Nancy: Plurality ... 169
  6.1 Corpus ... 170
  6.2 The Singular Plural ... 177
  6.3 Arbitration ... 185

Concluding Remarks ... 203

Bibliography and Further Reading ... 211
Index ... 263

Acknowledgements

Fragments of a much earlier version of Chapter 4 of this book were published in *Transforming Philosophy and Religion: Love's Wisdom* (Indiana University Press, 2008), and fragments of Chapter 6 were marshalled to serve a different argument in an article that appeared in *Paragraph* in 2007.

There are a number of people to whom I want to give special thanks for their help in writing this book. Martin Crowley guided me expertly through the process of drafting the original PhD, and I am deeply grateful for his insight and availability at every stage. The doctoral research was made possible by funding from the Arts and Humanities Research Council (UK). It was Martin and Ian James who first suggested that I combine Merleau-Ponty, Ricœur and Nancy, and I am grateful to Ian for providing both critical comment and personal encouragement at key stages along the way. Occasional conversations with Gerald Moore also helped to clarify some ideas, for which I am thankful. Special thanks must be reserved for my father, Kenneth Watkin, who heroically proof-read the entire manuscript with a scrupulous attention to detail more than once, and on one occasion in the middle of a raging cold. The wider gratitude I bear to my parents for making this book possible is beyond words. All remaining faults are, inevitably, my own.

Abbreviations

WORKS BY MERLEAU-PONTY

EM	'Eye and Mind'
EP	*Éloge de la philosophie*
HAL	'Husserl aux limites de la phénoménologie'
HAL	*Husserl at the Limits of Phenomenology*
I	'Un inédit de Maurice Merleau-Ponty'
IPP	*In Praise of Philosophy*
N	*La Nature: Notes de cours au Collège de France*
N	*Nature: Course Notes from the Collège de France*
NC	*Notes de cours au Collège de France 1958–1959 et 1960–1961*
ŒE	*L'Œil et l'esprit*
P2	*Parcours deux, 1951–1961*
PM	*La Prose du monde*
PP	*Phénoménologie de la perception*
PP	*Phenomenology of Perception*
PPE	*Psychologie et pédagogie de l'enfant: cours de Sorbonne 1949–1952*
PrP	*Le Primat de la perception*
PrP	'The Primacy of Perception and Its Philosophical Consequences'
PW	*The Prose of the World*
RC	*Résumés de cours au Collège de France 1952–1960*
S	*Signes*
S	*Signs*
SB	*The Structure of Behaviour*
SC	*La Structure du comportement*
SNS	*Sens et non-sens*
SNS	*Sense and Nonsense*

TFL	*Themes from the Lectures at the Collège de France 1952–1960*
VI	*Le Visible et l'invisible*
VI	*The Visible and the Invisible*

WORKS BY RICŒUR

A	*Autrement*
AJ	*Amour et justice*
CC	*La Critique et la conviction*
CC	*Critique and Conviction*
CFP	'La cité est fondamentalement périssable'
CI	*Le Conflit des interprétations*
CI	*The Conflict of Interpretations*
COR	*The Course of Recognition*
CRR	'Contingence et rationalité dans le récit'
DC	'Le dialogue des cultures'
DDH	*Déclaration des droits de l'homme*
DIEF	*De l'Interprétation. Essai sur Freud*
FP	*Freud and Philosophy*
HT	*History and Truth*
HV	*Historie et vérité*
J	*The Just*
J1	*Le Juste, 1*
J2	*Le Juste, 2*
JM	'Justice et marché'
L1	*Lectures 1*
L2	*Lectures 2*
L3	*Lectures 3*
LJ	'Love and Justice'
LQN	'Life in Quest of Narrative'
MPCH	'La métaphore et le problème central de l'herméneutique'
MV	*La Métaphore vive*
NR	*La Nature et la règle*
OA	*Oneself as Another*
PR	*Parcours de la reconnaissance*
ROJ	*Reflections on the Just*
RM	*The Rule of Metaphor*
SCA	*Soi-même comme un autre*
SC	'Le sujet convoqué'
SE	*The Symbolism of Evil*
SyM	*Le Symbolique du mal*

TA	*Du Texte à l'action*
TA	*From Text to Action*
TN1	*Time and Narrative 1*
TR1	*Temps et récit 1*
WMUT	*What Makes Us Think?*

WORKS BY NANCY

ACST	*Au Ciel et sur la terre*
Asc	'Ascoltando'
AE	*A l'Écoute*
AFI	*Au Fond des images*
All	*Allitérations*
BSP	*Being Singular Plural*
C	*Corpus*
CA	*La Communauté affrontée*
CD	*La Communauté désœuvrée*
CMM	*La Création du monde, ou, la mondialisation*
Con	'Conloquium'
Com	*La Comparution*
Cor	'Corpus'
CWG	*The Creation of the World, or, Globalization*
DDC	*La Déclosion: déconstruction du christianisme, 1*
DDC	*Dis-enclosure: The Deconstruction of Christianity*
DI	'Dies irae'
EEP	*Être, c'est être perçu*
EF	*L'Évidence du film*
EF	*The Experience of Freedom*
EL	*L'Expérience de la liberté*
ES	*Ego sum*
ESP	*Être singulier pluriel*
EsEP	'L'Espèce d'espace pensée'
FH	'Finite History'
FT	*A Finite Thinking*
GOI	*The Ground of the Image*
I	*L'Intrus*
IC	*L'Impératif catégorique*
IC	*The Inoperative Community*
M	*Les Muses*
M	*The Muses*
MD	'Mad Derrida'
NMT	*Noli me tangere*

OBIC	'Of Being-in-Common'
OP	*L'Oubli de la philosophie*
P	'Passage'
PD	*La Pensée dérobée*
PDD	*Le Portrait (dans le décor)*
PF	*Une Pensée finie*
Poids	*Le Poids d'une pensée*
PV	*Le Partage des voix*
SCP	*Sur le commerce des pensées*
SM	*Le Sens du monde*
SV	'Sharing Voices'
SW	*The Sense of the World*
TEP	'Tout est-il politique?'
TP	'Technique du présent: essai sur On Kawara'
UJ	*Un Jour, les dieux se retirent…*
VPC	*Visitation (de la peinture chrétienne)*

Introduction

As a philosophical movement at the forefront of contemporary thought, phenomenology might be thought to have had its day. Since Edmund Husserl recast the term in his 1901 *Logische Untersuchungen* from earlier Hegelian and Kantian usage,[1] it has come to be employed mainly as a yardstick against which to size up other features in the contemporary philosophical landscape, features that are themselves considered to be post-phenomenological. Terms such as 'intuition' and 'reduction' retain the faint nostalgic glow of a simpler age, when meaning was given to consciousness and the philosopher could go about her business secure in the knowledge that, if certain rigorous procedures were followed, the world and its contents would inexorably surrender their treasures to consciousness. Husserl himself is now very much a philosopher's philosopher, studied less in his own right and more as a figure whom it is necessary to have encountered if one is to grapple with more recent thinkers. Furthermore, the clutch of philosophers whose thought could be classed as 'phenomenological' – Heidegger, Sartre and Merleau-Ponty, to complete the quartet chosen for a recent multi-volume study[2] – have, if not faded from view, then at least been eclipsed by the shooting stars of Foucault, Deleuze, Lacan and, above all, given his close engagement with phenomenological themes, Derrida, whose decisive contributions still dictate the terms of the debate.

Of all the claims to have upset the phenomenological applecart, Derridean deconstruction is hailed with the greatest fanfare. Studying phenomenology today is more often than not a means to the end of coming to grips with Derrida's reading of Husserl in early works such as his introduction to Husserl's *Origin of Geometry*,[3] *La Voix et le phénomène*[4] and *L'Écriture et la différence*.[5] The subtitle of a recent introduction to Derrida's thought, *From Phenomenology to Ethics*,[6] rather makes the point. Phenomenology is a staging post en route to more fertile philosophical pasture. However, it is also noticeable that the phenomenological holds an abiding interest for many, not least in its relation to deconstructive thought.[7] Add to this a sprinkling of infrequent yet tantalising references in the secondary literature to 'phenomenological deconstruction'[8] or 'deconstructive phenomenology'[9] and it seems that phenomenology, if it ever went away, is back with a decisive contribution to make on the contemporary philosophical scene. It is out of the conviction that the phenomenological, however it is finally to be understood, does indeed have an important place in contemporary continental philosophical debates that this book has been written. Specifically, in the following pages we set out from the nostalgic premise that the phenomenological notion of a meaningful world is, perhaps naively, worth another look.

This book does not set out to be about deconstruction, or about Derrida, and to the extent that Derrida's work is repeatedly evoked and discussed below, it is used to probe and pose questions to other philosophers. Derrida's readings of the phenomenological tradition are required reading for any contemporary treatment of the topic, and they will be used to press for and provoke responses from the thinkers whose work we shall be considering. Thus, while we have attempted at all points to deal fairly with Derrida and render a sympathetic and adequate account of his thought, it will be understood that we have done so only to the extent that a detour via the problems he raises brings the phenomenological responses to those problems into relief, and no more. In other words, we have not attempted to do justice to Derrida's thought in its own terms.

What follows can be read as an extended meditation on the 'relation between phenomenology and deconstruction', though none of those five words can remain unchallenged. It is always a difficult task to plot the history of thought in terms of the relations between different traditions or schools, but the task can scarcely be more delicate then in the case of the relation between phenomenology and deconstruction. Delicate, but crucial. Not only has the Derridean 'critique' of phenomenology determined in large part its contemporary reception, but the question of the relation of phenomenology and deconstruction is a matter of great importance for the future direction of Continental thought, as we shall argue below. However, any attempt to discern the contours of the relation between phenomenology and deconstruction immediately encounters the difficulty that both terms lack a discernible – or at any rate widely accepted and broadly unproblematic – definition, though the reasons for the lack of consensus are different in each case. For phenomenology the issue is complicated by a broad spectrum of divergent

Introduction

philosophies and philosophers all having hailed from the phenomenological stable, whereas in the case of deconstruction we are not dealing with a philosophy *as such* at all, for reasons to be explored below. So before we can continue, the somewhat nebulous terms 'phenomenology' and 'deconstruction' each require some minimal elucidation.

Perhaps the nearest we can come to a general statement about phenomenology is that 'la phénoménologie au sens large est la somme des variations de l'œuvre husserlienne et des hérésies issues de Husserl,'[10] and such a broad definition leaves us with a cohort of phenomenological thinkers united only by family resemblances. 'Deconstruction' provides us with problems which, while they are of a different nature, nonetheless lead to similar difficulties. Whereas the problem with phenomenology resides in deciding what, and who, is to 'count' as phenomenological and who/what should define 'the phenomenological', with deconstruction the problem is in an inability to identify anything that is *properly* 'deconstructive'. Deconstruction is not a method or a process in its own right. Derrida's deconstruction of phenomenology, which is predominantly a deconstruction of Husserl, claims neither to add nor to take away from Husserl's own thought. Derrida argues, rather, that Husserl claims too much for himself, that 'la constitution de l'autre et du temps renvoient la phénoménologie à une zone dans laquelle son « principe des principes » (selon nous son principe *métaphysique: l'évidence originaire* et la présence de la chose elle-même en personne) est radicalement mis en question.'[11] Though there is here neither the space nor the necessity to engage in a detailed analysis of Derrida's early texts on Husserl, his relation to phenomenology can well be characterised as one of ambivalence.[12] Phenomenology for Derrida is a critique of metaphysics, which he defines in *Limited Inc* as 'le projet de remonter « stratégiquement », idéalement, à une origine ou à une « priorité » simple, intacte, normale, pure, propre, pour penser *ensuite* la dérivation, la complication, la dégradation, l'accident etc.'[13] But phenomenology, notes Derrida, 'n'a critiqué la métaphysique en son fait que pour la restaurer'.[14] Derrida is similarly suspicious of intuition; there can be no return to the things themselves because 'la chose même se dérobe toujours'.[15]

In pursuing phenomenology's inability to adhere to its own principles, we could argue that Derrida is doing nothing more than being more radically, and truly, phenomenological than Husserl.[16] But this is a misleading characterisation, for he is not merely suggesting that phenomenology happens to be deficient, but that it is constitutively so, that it is impossible for phenomenology to be self-consistent. The only truly phenomenological thing to do would therefore be to acknowledge the ill-foundedness of phenomenology. Derrida, we might say, is at the limit of the phenomenological. This by no means indicates, however, that he thinks we should discount phenomenological thinkers; Husserl and Heidegger are two philosophers belonging to the space of repetition 'dans lequel nous sommes compris, pré-compris, auquel nous sommes déjà destinés et qu'il s'agirait de penser, non pas *contre* Husserl ou Heidegger, bien sûr ce serait un peu simple, plutôt *à partir* d'eux, et sans doute autrement.'[17] Indeed, though he notes inconsistencies in Husserl, Derrida by no means urges a disregard for Husserlian phenomenology. John D. Caputo, friend of the late Derrida and deconstructive practitioner, notes that 'Derrida better than anyone has shown us the ambiguity of this text [Caputo is referring to Husserl's writing in general: CW] and unearthed the radical, more deconstructive side of Husserl'.[18]

A sustained effort to recover a nuanced reading of Derrida's Husserl is made by Leonard Lawlor in his *Husserl and Derrida*, where he suggests that 'Derrida's philosophy – his deconstruction – is continuous with Husserl's phenomenology.'[19] For Derrida 'il faut passer par elle [the transcendental reduction: CW] pour ressaisir la différence',[20] and John Sallis in a similar vein talks of the 'closure' of metaphysics as 'a matter of preparing a displacement of phenomenology from within, a displacement by the very force of its appeal to the things themselves, hence a displacement that would be at the same time a radicalising of phenomenology itself'.[21] The value of evoking these interventions as we embark on our study is to challenge the hasty assumption that equates the Derridean denunciation of the 'metaphysics of presence' in Husserl with an adequate reading of the relation between phenomenology and deconstruction.

Having briefly sketched the difficulties inherent in using the terms 'phenomenology' and 'deconstruction', we now come to the problematic copula 'and'. The relation of phenomenology 'and' deconstruction has recently excited a flurry of critical activity, with volumes and articles by Hugh Silverman[22] and David Wood,[23] in addition to the aforementioned works by Cumming, Lawlor[24] and Sallis. Robert Denoon Cumming for his part is quite clear: Derrida is not a phenomenologist.[25] Silverman is more circumspect, suggesting in the preface to *Inscriptions* that Derrida (and Foucault) 'mark out the place signified by the intersection of phenomenology and structuralism, albeit not reducible to either',[26] while Sallis writes of an 'interplay' between phenomenological research and deconstruction.[27] It is our contention that such characterisations of the relationship are misleading, suggesting as they do that 'phenomenology' and 'deconstruction' can be plotted in relation to each other on some putative philosophical topography, and that the distance separating them can be calculated. We cannot speak of some 'place' 'between' them, and we need to search for a different and better way of articulating the relation.[28] Given that Derrida's disagreements with Husserl are made in the name of phenomenology, it is by no means clear that 'phenomenology and deconstruction' is not a tautology, an idea we shall investigate further below.

In addition to this need to interrogate the copula, two further errors are to be avoided. The first is the mistake of seeking to relate phenomenology and deconstruction in terms of an arbitrary historical progression. Cumming tends in this direction when he claims to be writing 'the history of phenomenology and of *its aftermath*, deconstruction',[29] and Martin Jay seems to follow the same route when he cites Derrida as a 'salient example' of the generation of French philosophers that 'fashioned itself as post-phenomenological and took special pleasure in deriding the concept of "lived experience" '.[30] Although the term 'post-phenomenological' may be used here *about* Derrida, we search for the term in vain in his own writing. It is in fact incorrect to say that he fashions himself as post-phenomenological, much less that he is a 'salient example' of post-phenomenology.

While it is wrong to draw too crisp a historical demarcation between phenomenology and deconstruction, it is equally misguided to account for deconstruction as a matter of internal phenomenological housekeeping. The relation is not best treated by applying to it some simplifying periodisation. Responding to a question from Richard Kearney as to what is to be done after deconstruction, Derrida emphatically replies:

> Your question started with the phrase 'after deconstruction', and I must confess I do not understand what is meant by such a phrase. Deconstruction is not a philosophy or a method, it is not some phase, a period or a moment. It is something which is constantly at work and was at work before what we call 'deconstruction' started, so I cannot periodise. For me there is no after deconstruction . . .[31]

By this logic, for Derrida there is no 'before deconstruction' either. Deconstruction never arrives, – it is at work long before what we call 'deconstruction' became known as such – but the recognition that (for example) Husserl's notion of presence self-deconstructs does nonetheless have fresh philosophical implications. Philosophically speaking, with deconstruction something *has* happened. Something new, we now see, needs to be taken into account. But we cannot know *ab initio* what that 'something' is, what sort of 'account' needs to be taken, or how the encounter is to be thought, calculated and assimilated. Deconstruction never signs off and it never clocked in, and it is precisely the problem of doing justice to that which has not happened *as such*, which is not an event within the history of phenomenology, something that resists designation as 'encounter' or 'critique' or 'disagreement' – it is precisely this problem that we shall have to address. Taking account or taking the measure of the relation between deconstruction and phenomenology is an infinite task, demand and responsibility.

The encounters staged in the studies which follow explore the resources in the thought of three philosophers for thinking the ontological in a way that precisely does seek to take account of the questions and problems that deconstruction raises, while from time to time also throwing questions and problems back to Derrida. Through interrogating the relation of meaning and the world we shall be asking whether there is a phenomenology which is not amenable to deconstruction, or which accounts (*per impossibile*) for deconstruction. We are not asking what is left 'after' deconstruction, but what sort of ontological claims can be made when deconstruction has (not) happened.

We propose to investigate the issues sketched above through readings of the work of three thinkers who, while it is not unreasonable to claim that their work can in each case be characterised as to some extent phenomenological, are nonetheless far (to say the least) from being straightforwardly Husserlian. Maurice Merleau-Ponty, Paul Ricœur and Jean-Luc Nancy have been chosen in order to avoid the twin pitfalls indicated by Robert Cumming in the first of his four volumes on phenomenology and deconstruction:

> Most of the applauded ventures in the history of philosophy today do not do justice to the problems of the relations between philosophers, either because they cover too many philosophers to get down to details about their relations, or because they stick to an individual philosopher, subordinating his relations to other philosophers to the exposition of his.[32]

The reasons for the particular choice of Merleau-Ponty, Ricœur and Nancy are threefold. Pragmatically speaking, much more work has already been undertaken on Derrida's relation to Husserl than to these three thinkers, and so we are in part redressing a critical deficit. It is an important deficit to address because, given that these three writers are far from straightforwardly Husserlian, we cannot simply read over – it is an obvious point but needs to be made – from Derrida's engagement with Husserl to assume that the relation of deconstruction with Merleau-Ponty, Ricœur and Nancy will be some minor variation of it.

Secondly, thematically speaking these three thinkers have been chosen in order to allow us to elaborate a phenomenological ontology that has not yet sufficiently been brought to critical attention.[33] We will use the three writers to think the ontological differently to the position that draws Derrida's fire in his reading of Husserl. In addition to this, it is important for our purposes that all three thinkers assimilate phenomenology only ever in relation to other philosophical ideas and doctrines, which means that their work will allow us to see the phenomenological in various guises – to caricature for the sake of brevity: existential phenomenology in the case of Merleau-Ponty, hermeneutic phenomenology for Ricœur and, in what must remain a provisional nomenclature at this stage, deconstructive phenomenology for Nancy – thus better understanding its possibilities and limits.

Thirdly, and strategically speaking, the choice is prompted by a desire to situate Nancy more adequately than has hitherto been achieved in the landscape of contemporary philosophy.[34] On the way, we will also see marked affinities between all three thinkers that are often obscured by the vicissitudes of their critical reception. We claim no necessary progression from Merleau-Ponty through Ricœur to Nancy such that no other constellation of thinkers could have been chosen. Neither do we set out with the aim of telling the story of late twentieth- and early twenty-first-century phenomenology (or even philosophy), but rather of staging a series of related encounters between each of the three thinkers and the deconstructive concerns and responsibilities that Derrida sets forth.

Merleau-Ponty's shadow looms ever larger in contemporary philosophical debates. Relatively neglected in the decades following his sudden death in 1961, Merleau-Ponty scholarship has in recent years taken on a new purpose with landmark volumes by Gary Madison,[35] Renaud Barbaras,[36] Martin Dillon[37] and Françoise Dastur,[38] with Derrida himself staging a long overdue encounter in *Le Toucher*.[39] Partly as a result of this renewed interest, and partly through a new engagement with aspects of Merleau-Ponty's thought previously shrouded in critical neglect, his philosophy is increasingly being used both to question deconstruction[40] and to talk about an opening and delimiting of phenomenology in a deconstructive register.[41] Given wider concerns in French thought, it is not surprising that Merleau-Ponty's understanding of the body has generated much interest,[42] whereas his work on language acquisition and visual art has been relatively underreceived by philosophers.

Although Merleau-Ponty has before now been described as engaging in deconstruction,[43] it is no aim of the studies below to discover in him a Derridean *avant la lettre*, but rather to bring Merleau-Ponty and Derrida into a dialogue which will lead to a better understanding of the complexity of Merleau-Ponty's ontological position. In the first chapter we shall argue that, from his early work on Gestalt psychology in *La Structure du comportement* through to the 'cosmology of the visible' in

Le Visible et l'invisible, Merleau-Ponty develops an ontology that cannot be subsumed as a Husserlian footnote. Through examining Derrida's reading of Merleau-Ponty in *Le Toucher* and the latter's work on an indirect or 'diplopic' ontology, we shall be able to see how Merleau-Ponty can respond to some of Derrida's questions, on the way being confronted with the readerly problem of the ambiguity of Merleau-Ponty's own texts. The second chapter will turn to Merleau-Ponty's work on language, both the Sorbonne lectures on language acquisition and the philosophy of language in *La Prose du monde*. We will argue that the relation of meaning ('le sens') and world ('le monde') is thought by Merleau-Ponty in terms of a model not accounted for by a deconstructive reading, and that the world can indeed be said to be meaningful, providing that this phrase is correctly understood.

The work of Paul Ricœur has never enjoyed the fashionable interest that now surrounds Merleau-Ponty studies, though it is to be hoped that his sad death in 2005 will continue to occasion a stocktaking in the coming years that will go at least some way to remedying this critical lapsus. Never part of the Parisian avant-garde, Ricœur's philosophy is nevertheless an unavoidable milestone in twentieth-century French thought, and its breadth alone means that a Ricœurean encounter is virtually inevitable for the student of phenomenology, structuralism or psychoanalysis in twentieth-century France. Add to this his masterly study of the 'hermeneutics of the self' in *Soi-même comme un autre*, the two volumes of collected essays on justice, his work on memory, history and forgetting and the late *Parcours de la reconnaissance*, and we see a rich and varied philosophical corpus still substantially waiting to be discovered by many.

In Chapter 3 we will focus on Ricœur's work on the self in order to elaborate an understanding of selfhood that can respond to some of the worries Derrida voices in relation to Cartesian and Heideggerean notions of subjectivity. Examining Ricœur's understanding of narrative we shall ask whether it can achieve the ontological 'openness' which Derrida seeks. At stake in this chapter are two issues: the relation between 'life' and 'narrative' and the question of the coherence of heterogeneous discourses into a meaningful synthesis. The latter problem, crucial to the difference between Ricœur and Derrida, is further pursued in the fourth chapter as we turn to Ricœur's incisive though under-received work on justice. Following Ricœur through his readings of John Rawls, Michael Walzer, Luc Boltanski and Laurent Thévenot, we see how he rethinks justice in ways that do not refute deconstructive readings but operate *otherwise* than them. The two chapters build towards sketching a relation in which Ricœur neither succumbs to the 'metaphysics of presence' nor pulls the props out from under Derrida.

Their relation, it is argued, is less antagonistic than productive, though never settled or stable.

The reception of Jean-Luc Nancy's work has, until recently, been preoccupied in the main with the question of community, but while this is indeed an important motif in Nancy's earlier writings, such a focus does not do justice to the breadth of the concerns with which his more recent work deals, where a different set of figures – consideration, constellation, cosmos, fragmentation – comes to the fore. Though recent publications are going some way to rebalancing this lopsided reception of Nancy, these motifs, which we could group under the umbrella term of the (a)cosmological, have passed more or less under the critical radar.[44] In the fifth chapter we explore, via the themes of openness, presence and contact in Nancy, just how his thought responds to Derrida's uneasiness with his ontological language. By highlighting similarities with and differences from Merleau-Pontean and Ricœurean thought, we will see both the uniqueness of Nancy's position in the contemporary philosophical landscape and the difficulties his thought needs to face. We will interrogate Nancy's ontological language and elucidate the nature of his ontological claims, drawing conclusions about the ethical imperative in his thought and its relation to Derridean responsibility. The chapter will culminate in a consideration of a question which cuts to the heart of Nancy's ontological position: whether a decision can ever be retrospectively validated as good or condemned as bad. In the sixth and final chapter we will turn to motifs of fragmentation and incommensurability, with particular reference to Nancy's notions of 'corpus' and the 'singulier pluriel' ('singular plural'). The chapter will question how, within Nancy's thought, we can 'calculate the incalculable', whether that be in terms of arbitrating between competing political systems, measuring the senses against each other, or comparing and evaluating the relation between the different arts. With the problem of calculating the incalculable we arrive at the very heart of what is at stake in the relation 'between' phenomenology and deconstruction.

Gathering together the insights and clarifications accumulated over six studies, we will conclude by suggesting ways to think about the relation of phenomenology and deconstruction which avoid the pitfalls sketched above. In addition to and in dialogue with these concerns, we will show how our thinking about this relation can be put to use in finding fresh, distinctive and powerful ways to think about the philosophically crucial problems of alterity and coherence. Finally, at the end of the series of studies we will suggest a way to understand the ontological that neither repeats nor rebuts the Derridean position, but thinks ontology otherwise. It is an understanding that will bring us closer to seeing what form a 'deconstructive phenomenology' might take. So as we begin, the tantalising question is posed: to what extent can we speak of a 'phenomenological deconstruction', or a 'deconstructive phenomenology', and what, if there is such a thing, might be its characteristics?

NOTES

1. Kant first uses the term in his *Metaphysische Anfangsgründe der Naturwissenschaft*: 'The *fourth* chapter, however, determines matter's motion or rest merely in relation to the mode of representation or *modality*, and thus as appearance of the outer senses, and is called phenomenology' (Kant, 'Metaphysical Foundations of Natural Science' 191). Hegel's *Phaenomenologie des Geistes* was published in 1807.
2. See Cumming, *Phenomenology and Deconstruction*.
3. See *Introduction à L'Origine de la géométrie de E. Husserl*; *Edmund Husserl's 'Origin of geometry': an introduction*.
4. See *La Voix et le phénomène*; *Speech and Phenomena*.
5. See 'Genèse et structure' in *L'Écriture et la différence* 229–51; '"Genesis and Structure" and phenomenology' in *Writing and Difference* 154–68.
6. Howells, *Derrida: Deconstruction from Phenomenology to Ethics*.
7. Witness, for example, Lawlor, *Derrida and Husserl*; Howells, *Derrida*; Cumming, *Phenomenology and Deconstruction*; McKenna and Joseph (eds), *Derrida and Phenomenology*; Moran, *Introduction to Phenomenology*; Reynolds, *Merleau-Ponty and Derrida*.
8. Ihde, *Experimental Phenomenology: An Introduction* 107; Evans, 'Phenomenological Deconstruction: Husserl's Method of Abbau'.
9. Wood, *The Step Back*; Vahabzadeh, *Articulated Experiences: Toward a Radical Phenomenology of Contemporary Social Movements* 5.
10. Ricœur, *A l'École de la phénoménologie* 9; 'in the broad sense phenomenology is both the sum of Husserl's work and the heresies issuing from it' (*Husserl: An Analysis of his Philosophy* 6).
11. Derrida, *L'Écriture et la différence* 244; 'the constitution of the other and of time refers phenomenology to a zone in which its "principle of principles" (as we see it, its *metaphysical* principle: *the original self-evidence* and presence of the thing itself in person) is radically put into question' (*Writing and Difference* 164).
12. It is an ambivalence reflected in the secondary literature. While François-David Sebbah argues in a recently published *Companion to Phenomenology and Existentialism* that 'it is not without legitimacy that we invite him [Derrida: CW] to this "family reunion"' (Sebbah, 'French Phenomenology' 51), Leonard Lawlor argues that 'one can of course continue to call these new kinds of investigations phenomenological, but, I think, that name does not acknowledge that a threshold has been crossed, that something has come to an end, and that we are starting to do something else' (Lawlor, *Thinking Through French Philosophy* 150).

Introduction

13. Derrida, *Limited Inc* 174; 'the enterprise of returning "strategically", in idealisation, to an origin or to a "priority" seen as simple, intact, normal, pure, untainted (i.e. presence), in order *then* to conceive of derivation, complication, deterioration, accident, etc.' (Derrida, *Limited Inc* 236; translation altered).
14. 'La Forme et le vouloir-dire: Note sur la phénoménologie du langage' 277; 'Phenomenology has criticised metaphysics as it is in fact only in order to restore it' (*Speech and Phenomena* 107).
15. Derrida, *La Voix et le phénomène* 117; 'the thing itself always escapes' (*Speech and Phenomena* 104).
16. This position, taken by Vincent Descombes when he characterises Derrida's work as 'the radicalisation of phenomenology' (*Modern French Philosophy* 136), is shared by Lawlor, who suggests that 'whether one follows Derrida's or Deleuze's critique of phenomenology – both have been extremely important for me – what one is doing is following the phenomenological reduction as far as one absolutely can, so far that phenomenology finds itself transformed into something else, something non-phenomenological' (Lawlor, *Thinking Through French Philosophy* 150).
17. Derrida, *Du Droit à la philosophie* 516; 'in which we are contained, preunderstood, for which we are already destined and that we are to think not *against* Husserl or Heidegger – that would of course be rather simple – but rather *beginning with* them, and doubtless otherwise' (author's translation).
18. Caputo, *Radical Hermeneutics* 4.
19. Lawlor, *Derrida and Husserl* 11.
20. Derrida, *La Voix et le phénomène* 92; 'it is necessary to pass through the transcendental deduction in order to grasp the difference' (*Speech and Phenomena*, 82; translation altered).
21. Sallis, *Delimitations* x.
22. Silverman's work on the relation of deconstruction and phenomenology is scattered throughout a number of books. See *Inscriptions*; 'Merleau-Ponty and Derrida: Writing on Writing'; *Textualities*; Silverman (ed.), *Philosophy and Non-Philosophy Since Merleau-Ponty*; Silverman and Ihde (eds), *Hermeneutics and Deconstruction*.
23. Wood, *The Step Back*.
24. Leonard Lawlor has generated a prodigious output on this subject in recent years. In addition to his *Derrida and Husserl*, see *Imagination and Chance: The Difference Between the Thought of Ricoeur and Derrida*; 'Phenomenology and Metaphysics: Deconstruction in *La Voix et le phénomène*'; and 'Verflechtung: The Triple Significance of Merleau-Ponty's Course Notes on Husserl's *The Origin of Geometry*'.
25. Cumming, *Phenomenology and Deconstruction*, vol. 1, 20. In a similar vein, Dermot Moran rashly argues that Derrida portrays himself as having 'gone beyond both phenomenology and philosophy' (Moran, *Introduction to Phenomenology* 436).
26. Silverman, *Inscriptions* x.
27. Sallis, *Delimitations* 77.

28. Silverman is not insensitive to these concerns, qualifying the 'place between' in terms of 'the slashes, the borders, the belonging-together of alternatives' (*Textualities* 2), yet he persists in his use of the term 'between'.
29. Cumming, *Phenomenology and Deconstruction*, vol. 1, 4; author's italics. The characterisation of deconstruction as an 'aftermath' and the possessive 'its' are equally problematic here.
30. Jay, 'The Lifeworld and Lived Experience' 91.
31. In Kearney and Dooley (eds), *Questioning Ethics* 65.
32. Cumming, *Phenomenology and Deconstruction* vol. 1, 15.
33. A book by Renaud Barbaras (*De l'Être du phénomène: sur l'ontologie de Merleau-Ponty* (translated as *The Being of the Phenomenon*) and a PhD thesis by Matthew A. Daigler ('Paul Ricœur's Hermeneutic Ontology: Between Aristotle and Kant') are notable exceptions.
34. Ian James' *The Fragmentary Demand: An Introduction to the Philosophy of Jean-Luc Nancy* goes a long way to redressing this deficit and is particularly helpful on the relation of Nancy and Merleau-Ponty. In what follows I will be adding to and nuancing James' work. The relation of Nancy and Ricœur and of Merleau-Ponty and Ricœur have, as yet, not been brought to light in a similarly clear way.
35. *The Phenomenology of Merleau-Ponty: A Search for the Limits of Consciousness.*
36. *De l'Être du phénomène.*
37. *Merleau-Ponty's Ontology.*
38. *Chair et langage.*
39. Derrida, *Le Toucher, Jean-Luc Nancy*; *On Touching – Jean-Luc Nancy*.
40. See Dillon, *Semiological Reductionism*. Although Dillon's sallies against Derrida are often ill-conceived, his use of Merleau-Ponty is nevertheless notable.
41. See John Sallis, *Delimitations*.
42. A by no means exhaustive list of recent articles includes Brodsky, 'Cezanne Paints: "Whole Body" Practices and the Genre of Self-portrayal'; Cassam, 'Representing Bodies'; Matthews, 'Merleau-Ponty's body-subject and psychiatry'; Finlay, 'The Body's Disclosure in Phenomenological Research'; Kelly, 'Merleau-Ponty on the Body'; Krasner, 'Doubtful Arms and Phantom Limbs: Literary Portrayals of Embodied Grief'; Vasterling, 'Body and Language: Butler, Merleau-Ponty and Lyotard on the Speaking Embodied Subject'; and Wynn, 'The Early Relationship of Mother and Pre-infant: Merleau-Ponty and Pregnancy'.
43. '. . . it is never a matter of sheer sensible content devoid of synthetic connection and over against it an activity of synthesis that would compose the full perceptual object from that content. Rather, the effect of Merleau-Ponty's analysis is to deconstruct the very distinction between synthetic form and sensible content' (Sallis, *Delimitations* 80).
44. Jeffrey S. Librett's article 'The Practice of the World: Jean-Luc Nancy's Liminal Cosmology' is a notable exception.

1. *Maurice Merleau-Ponty: Perception*

Homme, libre penseur! te crois-tu seul pensant
Dans ce monde où la vie éclate en toute chose?
Des forces que tu tiens ta liberté dispose,
Mais de tous tes conseils l'univers est absent.

Gérard de Nerval, 'Vers dorés'[1]

In recent years, two trends have coincided in French thought. First, a number of authors have taken it upon themselves to assess the relation of deconstruction and phenomenology, and secondly in the same period a renewed and growing interest has been shown in the work of Maurice Merleau-Ponty.[2] The two tendencies are by no means independent, for Merleau-Ponty's work is often cited in relation to deconstructive concerns, either as a precursor[3] or as an antagonist.[4] It appears that the moment has come to assess, if not settle, the ontological accounts between Merleau-Ponty and deconstruction.

A text which by any reckoning constitutes one of the most decisive interventions in this debate is Jacques Derrida's *Le Toucher: Jean-Luc Nancy*. In *Le Toucher*, Derrida stages the most significant of his engagements with Merleau-Ponty's thought, both in terms of its length – he devotes an entire chapter, 'Tangente III', to a discussion of Merleau-Ponty, in addition to a number of references elsewhere in the text – and its subject matter – he sets out in an extended series of readings his main concerns with Merleau-Ponty's thought. This makes *Le Toucher* a privileged text for considering the relation of Merleau-Ponty's phenomenology to deconstruction.

While some have chosen to cast the relation of phenomenology and deconstruction as a *querelle d'école*, an internal case of philosophical housekeeping, and others herald in deconstruction the end of phenomenology, a careful reading of 'Tangente III' reveals that both these positions oversimplify what is at stake. In this chapter we offer an alternative reading of the Merleau-Pontean account of perception, one that takes its lead from Merleau-Ponty's own interpretation of Gestalt psychology and the elaboration, in his later work, of an indirect or 'diplopic' ontology which, it will be argued, does not belong to what Derrida calls the 'metaphysics of presence'.

1.1 CONTACT

It is to say the least remarkable that, before the publication of *Le Toucher* in 2000, Derrida had undertaken no extended discussion of Merleau-Ponty's thought. Before this overdue engagement, Derrida's references to Merleau-Ponty are broad and, on the whole, disparaging.[5] *Le Toucher* is a text which ranges over the philosophical history of tactility from Aristotle to Nancy, exploring the motif of touch in terms of the possibility of contact with alterity, either in terms of the 'external world' or other people. The evocation of 'contact' is understood by Derrida as a metaphysical claim to the immediate proximity of alterity,[6] which he dismisses as a metaphysical impossibility, for 'je se touche en s'espaçant, en perdant le contact avec soi, justement à se toucher.'[7] For Derrida, contact is always also non-contact, 'con-tact comme contact interrompu.'[8]

It is notable that, in the course of a close and trenchant reading of Merleau-Ponty's philosophy in *Le Toucher*, Derrida witnesses a certain readerly malaise, finding the interpretation of Merleau-Ponty 'une chose à la fois passionnante et difficile, mais aussi parfois irritante ou décevante'.[9] Derrida ascribes this reaction to the juxtaposition in Merleau-Ponty's texts (and above all in *Le Visible et l'invisible*) of, on the one hand, phenomenological statements with which he strongly disagrees and, on the other hand, indications of a phenomenology that receives a broad, if not unconditional, Derridean welcome.

Turning first to the Merleau-Ponty with whom Derrida disagrees, the Derridean misgivings focus on two interrelated 'confusions': the relation between touching one's own body and seeing another person, and the relation between the senses, primarily touch and sight. He fails to see how Merleau-Ponty can claim that:

> Ma main droite *assistait* à l'avènement du toucher actif dans ma main gauche. *Ce n'est pas autrement* que le corps d'autrui s'anime devant moi, quand je serre la main d'un autre homme ou quand seulement je le regarde.[10]

Even leaving aside the punning 'humainisme' ('humanualism') that he detects in the anthropological privilege of the hand in Merleau-Ponty's discussion of touch, Derrida protests that Husserl, whom Merleau-Ponty claims to be glossing, would never have signed up to this 'ce n'est pas autrement'. Rather than orientating Husserl towards taking more audacious account of the other, Derrida argues, this interpretation 'risque d'aboutir au résultat exactement inverse. On risque de reconstituer un intuitionnisme de l'accès immédiat à l'autre, aussi originaire que mon accès à mon propre le plus propre'.[11] The 'ce n'est pas autrement' risks, in negating the difference between touching one's hand and touching the hand of another (never mind 'merely looking' at them), negating also the difference between self and other, reducing the other person to the same quality of otherness as one's own hand: that is to say, to an alterity very much less 'other' than Derrida would like. We risk, he warns, reappropriating the alterity of the other more certainly, more blindly and more violently than ever.[12]

The second confusion Derrida finds in Merleau-Ponty's writing is between touch and sight. In *Signes* Merleau-Ponty claims that 'je vois que cet homme là-bas voit, *comme* je touche ma main gauche en train de toucher ma main droite'.[13] In addition to finding it impossible to justify this 'comme', Derrida is alarmed at the conclusions which Merleau-Ponty is quick to build upon its shaky foundations, for it becomes indispensable to the Merleau-Pontean 'ontology of the sensible' and to what Derrida understands to be a Merleau-Pontean notion of (dualistic) incarnation, 'la « mienne » et, sans limite, celle de la chair du monde'.[14] The metaphysical shades summoned by the notion of incarnation have not been exorcised to Derrida's satisfaction. The two confusions amount to the collapsing, on Merleau-Ponty's part, of two irreducible Husserlian differences: (1) the difference between originary and direct intuition of my body ('corps propre') touching itself and (2) the indirect appresentation that gives me access to other people, with both of these also confused with the difference between sight and touch. Add to this both an 'exorbitant privilege' of vision in Merleau-Ponty[15] and the claim that 'il me semble que *l'expérience visuelle est plus vraie que l'expérience tactile*',[16] and it becomes clear why Derrida would feel a deconstructive responsibility to disrupt these unwarranted confusions and privileges.

These worries on Derrida's part are indicative of a broader concern in *Le Toucher* with a (disingenuous) philosophical desire for 'full' or 'immediate' presence which he sees it as his task to expose:

> nous essayons . . . d'identifier un intuitionnisme constitutif de la philosophie même, du geste qui consiste à philosopher – et même du processus d'idéalisation qui consiste à retenir le toucher dans le regard pour assurer à celui-ci le plein de présence immédiate requis par toute ontologie ou par toute métaphysique.[17]

Precisely whether such immediate presence *is* indeed required by *every* ontology and metaphysics, and in our immediate context by

Merleau-Ponty's ontology, it is the business of this chapter to question. The starting point for our consideration of the Derridean claim that every ontology requires immediate presence is given by Derrida himself, when he claims that 'malgré toutes les différences qui séparent le discours que je tiens à l'instant d'un discours de style husserlien . . . je lui trouve plus d'affinité avec celui que Husserl maintient obstinément au sujet de l'apprésentation . . . qu'avec celui d'un *certain* Merleau-Ponty'.[18] Derrida is closer to Husserl than is *a certain* Merleau-Ponty, a curious choice of words upon which Derrida expands, albeit fleetingly, as he discusses more briefly *another* Merleau-Ponty with whom he finds a much greater degree of affinity, a Merleau-Ponty with 'une insistance croissante sur l'inadéquation à soi, sur la non-coïncidence, sur la déhiscence, la fission, l'interruption, l'inachèvement et la béance du corps visible, le hiatus, l'éclipse, l'inaccessibilité de cette plénitude ou de cette réversibilité sensible qui reste toujours *imminente*'.[19] This other Merleau-Ponty is implicitly commended for 'l'originalité du traitement de l'invisible, d'un invisible non intelligible ou idéal mais d'un invisible qui, pour être *à même* le visible ne serait pas « l'invisible comme un autre visible "possible", ou un "possible" visible pour un autre »',[20] in other words for precisely avoiding, in the way he talks about the relation between the visible and the invisible, the perils of dualistic incarnation with which Derrida has trouble elsewhere in 'Tangente III'. Derrida's treatment of this 'other Merleau-Ponty' echoes certain aspects of Jean-Luc Nancy's thought with which he deals, of course, at length elsewhere in *Le Toucher*.

Derrida's palpable exasperation – 'passionnante . . . difficile . . . irritante . . . décevante'[21] – at what he considers to be the contradictory nature of these two Merleau-Pontys leaves him ambivalent:

> Faut-il en créditer le philosophe, comme je suis le plus souvent tenté de le faire, ou au contraire regretter qu'il n'ait pas pu procéder à une reformalisation plus puissante de son discours pour thématiser et penser la loi sous laquelle il se plaçait ainsi, *préférant* toujours, au bout de compte, *en fait*, la « coïncidence » . . . à la non-coïncidence.[22]

The question is, frustratingly, left hanging. While Derrida has opened a fascinating vein of Merleau-Ponty interpretation in *Le Toucher*, we must now take the bait of his observations and ask whether there *are* in fact two Merleau-Pontys and, if not, how the two aspects of Merleau-Ponty's thought which Derrida identifies might be brought together. It is not uncommon to refer to contradictions or inconsistencies in Merleau-Ponty's work,[23] but it is high time to ask whether that common observation does not read Merleau-Ponty against the grain of his own ideas and miss something of the subtlety of what he is doing. Given Derrida's characterisation of the two Merleau-Pontys, the problem of reading Merleau-Ponty here represents the relation of deconstruction and phenomenology *en abyme*.

It is possible, indeed imperative, to build a case in support of Merleau-Ponty that is sensitive to the Derridean caution while not completely accepting its reading. This chapter will lay out such a response by interrogating the notion of meaning as contact, upon which the ontological suspicion relies. We shall argue that it is possible to claim that the world is meaningful without having to rely on any notions of incarnation or dualistic thinking. Any argument in support of Merleau-Ponty will be required to deal, therefore, not with outright refutation but with a sceptical questioning: how could we know if the meaning we *think* we find is not, in fact, manufactured by us? On what basis could a claim to have stumbled across meaning in the world be substantiated, for surely it would require verification from a position outside human subjectivity, the imprimatur of a 'view from nowhere'. Or perhaps not. It is by exploring how Merleau-Ponty thinks the question of 'contact' and the related issues of alterity and the coherence of the visible that we shall begin to see how his thought complicates any attempt crisply to delineate the relation of phenomenology and deconstruction.

1.2 FACTICITY/ESSENCE

In discussing possible responses to the concerns raised by Derrida, it is not our intention to argue that Merleau-Ponty proleptically and presciently rebuts Derrida's arguments, but rather that he elaborates his ontological commitment in a way that is only obliquely addressed by 'Tangente III'. The metaphysics of presence which Derrida impugns sits ill with Merleau-Ponty's ontology, especially as it is elaborated in his later work. Merleau-Ponty can sustain the claim, we will argue, that the world is meaningful, provided that we understand what that claim implies and what it does not.

Before broaching the question of intramundane meaningfulness itself, it is instructive to note how Merleau-Ponty deals with the alternative. To hold that the world has no role in determining meaning, he maintains, resolves to idealism and implies a detached subject:

> car admettre un naturalisme et l'enveloppement de la conscience dans l'univers des *blosse Sachen* à titre d'événement, c'est précisément poser comme premier le monde théorétique auquel elles appartiennent, c'est un idéalisme extrême. (RC 112–13)[24]

The demand for a constituting subjectivity, argues Merleau-Ponty, calls for and is inextricable from a world affirmed to be, or assumed to be, bare of meaning.[25] In opposition to this extreme idealism, Merleau-Ponty proposes that self and world are inextricable in the constitution of sense, an unanalysable Gestalt in which meaning emerges in the interaction of self and world, while remaning reducible to neither.

The terms in which the question of meaning is posed for the early Merleau-Ponty (that is to say, the Merleau-Ponty before *Le Visible et l'invisible* and *L'Œil et l'esprit*) are 'fact' or 'facticity' and 'essence', echoing the scholastic motifs of the *an sit*: *whether* something is (existence) and the *quid sit*: *what* something is (essence).[26] The first way in which Merleau-Ponty problematises this distinction between fact and essence is by renouncing the vain quest for knowledge of an ab-solute or pure essence apart from phenomenality. The fundamental metaphysical fact, he insists in 'Le métaphysique dans l'homme' (SNS 102–49/SNS 83–98), is a double sense of the *cogito*, that I am sure that there is being, but only on the condition that I do not seek another sort of being than being-for-me (SNS 114/SNS 93). In Renaud Barbaras' pithy formulation, being for Merleau-Ponty is the being *of the phenomenon*.[27] In *Phénoménologie de la perception* he frames the argument in still more strident terms, insisting that to ask oneself whether the world is real is to fail to understand what one is asking (PP 396/PP 144), and 'il ne faut donc pas se demander si nous percevons vraiment un monde, il faut dire au contraire: le monde est ce que nous percevons' (PP xi).[28]

This must by no means be understood as a retreat into solipsistic reverie. It would be so only if Merleau-Ponty maintained the dichotomy of fact and essence and if self, world and meaning were not intertwined. *That* the world exists is for Merleau-Ponty undeniable, providing of course that we understand the world as the world-for-me, the phenomenality of the world. But that does not mean that I understand or can give an account of the world:

> « Il y a un monde », ou plutôt « il y a le monde », de cette thèse constante de ma vie je ne puis jamais rendre entièrement raison. Cette facticité du monde est ce qui fait la *Weltlichkeit* du *Welt*, ce qui fait que le monde est monde. (PP xii)[29]

This, for Merleau-Ponty, is not simply a claim to the facticity of the world completely divorced from the question of its essence, however, for essentiality encroaches onto facticity. David Michael Levin helps us to understand this by drawing a contrast with the Lévinasian 'il y a'/'there is'.[30] In Lévinas, the 'il y a' of brute Being is indeterminate and content-free, an absolute other beyond calculation. For Merleau-Ponty however, brute being is not chaotic and inscrutable, but more like the Heraclitean notion of nature 'under the spell of the *logos*', with a certain incipient – though by no means definitive – synthetic form.[31] It is indeterminate, but only relatively so, a proto-meaningfulness as opposed to a meaningless facticity. Concomitantly, the experience of the 'il y a' is not one of abject horror as it is for Lévinas, but of Heraclitean *thaumazein*, astonished incomprehension at being confronted with the incipient *logos*. The world-for-me is always already 'pregnant' (a term to which we shall have occasion to return) with form, structure and meaning.

Facticity never appears for me without this pregnant, indeterminate essence, and so the question of essence cannot be evoked a posteriori, as if it were a second stage in an argument of which the first move is to establish brute facticity. Essence is 'ni au-dessus, ni au-dessous des apparences, mais à leur jointure, elle est l'attache qui relie secrètement une expérience à ses variantes' (VI 153).[32] In the terms that come to characterise Merleau-Ponty's investigation in the later work, the invisible (essence) is the invisible *of* the visible (the sensible world), encrusted in the joints of the visible, and there is no dualism of fact and essence.

In addition to the fact/essence dichotomy being an a posteriori abstraction from a primary meaningfulness, the claim that the world is meaningful rests on two further moves on Merleau-Ponty's part, one concerning the body and one concerning the world. We cannot say that facticity is given to the perceiver from the world (that the perceiver is merely a passive *re*ceiver), nor that essentiality is projected upon the world by the perceiver (that the perceiver is, in this respect, merely an active *con*ceiver). That distinction is, in its turn, abstractive and a posteriori. Meaningfulness must be understood in terms of a strictly irreducible mutuality of self and world, and Merleau-Ponty's argument for this mutuality is two-pronged: perception is anchored (1) in the body and (2) in the world. This is what guards both against an exclusively passive theory of perception as reception and an overactive understanding of perception as conception:

> L'esprit qui perçoit est un esprit incarné, et c'est l'enracinement de l'esprit *dans son corps* et *dans son monde* que nous avons cherché d'abord à rétablir, aussi bien contre les doctrines qui traitent la perception comme le simple résultat de l'action des choses extérieures sur notre corps, que contre celles qui insistent sur l'autonomie de la prise de conscience. (I 402; author's emphasis)[33]

We shall take these two arguments – the rootedness of the perceiving mind in the body and in the world – in turn, in order to explore how Merleau-Ponty's understanding of meaning in terms of an intertwining and mutuality of world and body escapes the binaries upon which Derrida's intervention will, in turn, be shown to rely.

1.3 THE ENROOTEDNESS OF PERCEPTION IN THE BODY

The possibilities afforded by Merleau-Ponty's understanding of the body for any staging of an encounter between his phenomenology and deconstruction are not lost on Merleau-Ponty scholars. Jack Reynolds in his *Merleau-Ponty and Derrida* asserts that 'a thorough thematisation of the body might have induced a somewhat different deconstruction, and perhaps one more along the lines of the later philosophy of Merleau-Ponty',[34] and David Michael Levin inveighs against a 'biologism' that 'ignores the phenomenological body of meaningful experience' and refuses to recognise that 'the human body has – is – an order of its own.'[35] The body, in belonging both to the perceived world and to the perception of the world, can be adequately described in terms of neither aspect alone. Given that 'tout mouvement de mes yeux – bien plus, tout déplacement de mon corps – a sa place dans le même univers visible que par eux je détaille' (VI 175)[36] any phenomenology of perception must acknowledge the 'indivision de cet être sensible que je suis et de tout le reste qui se sent en moi' (VI 309).[37]

We must not assume, furthermore, that the body acts like a Husserlian transcendental subjectivity: the consciousness that constitutes the world. That division is precluded, once more as a result of the overlapping or intertwining of perceiver and perceived in the body. In the lecture course 'Nature et logos: Le corps humain' (N 263–354),[38] Merleau-Ponty emphasises that the body straddles the nature/culture divide, and expression lies half way between *physis* and *logos*. As the *Nichturpräsentierbarkeit* of the *Nichturpräsentierten* – that is: the figuration of the invisible in the visible (N 271/N 209) – the body is both in the world and that which gives access to things in the world. For Merleau-Ponty there is no passively received worldly meaning, and there is nothing outside expression, for 'l'expression n'est pas une des curiosités que l'esprit peut se proposer d'examiner, elle est son existence en acte' (S 127).[39] Perception always already stylises (PM 83/PW 59). Nevertheless, and this is where Merleau-Ponty's thought antagonises Derrida's anti-ontological bent, he can still claim that it is mute Being which itself comes to show forth its own meaning' (ŒE 87/EM 188). To understand how this is so, we turn now to examine the relation of the biological and the historical in the body's perception of worldly meaningfulness.

Hubert and Stuart Dreyfus helpfully distinguish in Merleau-Ponty three different ways in which corporeality contributes to an understanding of meaning. Assuming that 'the basic structure of the body is not up for interpretation',[40] Dreyfus and Dreyfus argue for a facticity of the perceptual world based on corporeality. There are 'three ways our bodies determine what shows up in our world', each stage having a different balance of 'givenness' and 'constitution'. The three ways are (1) innate structures, (2) general acquired skills and (3) specific cultural skills. To explain, Dreyfus and Dreyfus take the example that, to Western human beings, a chair affords sitting. In terms of innate structures, this is because 'we have the sort of bodies that get tired and that bend backwards at the knees'; in terms of general acquired skills this is because 'chairs can only solicit once we have learned to sit', and in terms of specific cultural skills, 'only because we Western Europeans are brought up in a culture where one sits on chairs, do chairs solicit us to sit on them.'[41]

So my favourite armchair's affordance of sitting is neither a given nor a purely contingent fact; it is neither received nor conceived and it can be accounted for neither in purely biological nor in purely historical terms. Each of these discourses (biological, historical and cultural, though this list is not exhaustive) must be called upon to account for an aspect of the chair's affordance of sitting. The point here is not that chairs share an essence of sit-onable-ness, but that any adequate explanation of their function is incomplete if it does not take into account both the facticity of the human body and any number of historico-cultural accretions. Merleau-Ponty's embodied philosophy splits the horns of the historicism/biologism dilemma. Levin, once again, calls the order of the body (what Dreyfus and Dreyfus term 'innate structures') an 'immanent *logos* of the flesh'[42] and, provided that we understand this in terms of the Heraclitean *logos* of incipient meaningfulness (as opposed to a notion of the *logos* in terms of ready-made meanings in which things participate), this is an accurate characterisation.

The role Merleau-Ponty gives to the body in perception also helps us to respond to some of Derrida's worries in *Le Toucher*. Merleau-Ponty does not understand the body as a simple unity, which would by that token be ripe for deconstruction. On the contrary, our body acquaints us with a type of unity that is not a matter of subsumption under a law (PP 175/*PP* 150), and though there is an imminence (with an 'i') of touched and touching, the circle never closes in self-presence. Neither the body nor perceptual experience is ever gathered under a concept; their coherence is fragile and untheorisable:

> il y a une idéalité rigoureuse dans les expériences qui sont des expériences de la chair : les moments de la sonate, les fragments du champ lumineux, adhèrent l'un à l'autre par une *cohésion sans concept*, qui est du même type que la cohésion des parties de mon corps, ou celle de mon corps et du monde. (VI 199; author's emphasis)[43]

The body is irreducibly open. The body itself, furthermore, is not a given but an inextricable mutuality of the biological and the historical, as much a human creation as a natural artefact. It is not to a physical object that the body is to be compared, but to a work of art (PP 176/*PP* 150).

Merleau-Ponty seeks to articulate this inextricability of 'fact' and 'essence' through the notion of 'style'. There is no dichotomy of bodily perception and bodily expression because perception is always already expressive, poetic and creative; as we have seen already, 'la perception déjà stylise' (PM 83).[44] Merleau-Ponty would agree here with Derrida, contra Husserl, that we have no access to a pure or pre-schematised world of meanings, no reduction *to* meaning. Perception, Merleau-Ponty claims in 'Le langage indirect et les voix du silence', must be poetry, 'c'est-à-dire qu'elle réveille et reconvoque en entier notre pur pouvoir d'exprimer, au-delà des choses déjà dites ou déjà vues' (S 84).[45] The 'style' of existence is expressed in the body, again with no gulf between perception and expression:

> Le corps . . . n'est pas où il est, il n'est pas ce qu'il est – puisque nous le voyons secréter en lui-même un « sens » qui ne lui vient de nulle part, le projeter sur son entourage matériel et le communiquer aux autres sujets incarnés. (PP 230)[46]

In short all perception, and all action which presupposes it, indeed every human use of the body, is already primordial expression (PM 110/*PW* 78). 'Style' is a notion larger than the perceived or the expressed alone, and indeed the categories of perception and expression can only be understood as a posteriori abstractions from a poetic, participatory engagement of coping in a meaningful body-world manifold.

The uses to which bodily intertwining are put in the secondary literature are, it has to be said, sometimes forced, and the responses to Derridean deconstruction upon which they are based misguided. Jack Reynolds takes the example of a master chess player, whose decisions in the context of a game can be made quickly, even while occupied with another mental task, with negligeable loss of proficiency. Following Dreyfus and Dreyfus, and with an eye to the Derridean understanding of the decision (which we shall discuss at length in the coming chapters), Reynolds ventures that 'the aporetic difference between that which prepares for a decision and the instantiation of the decision itself can be largely effaced. The aporia is eased by mastering a technique'.[47] Reynolds' argument here is won in his choice of example, for the chess move is not amenable to comparison with the Derridean decision. 'How do I reach checkmate?' is not a question requiring a decision of the same order as 'what is just?', 'to whom should I give?' It may well be that the 'aporia' of decision can be minimised in the context of a game of chess with its given rules and aims, but this proves nothing in the case of gift-giving, justice or hospitality with their competing and incommensurable claims and responsibilities. Computers can convincingly win complicated chess games; they cannot convincingly decide complicated legal cases.

Furthermore, restricting the openness of undecidability through habit does not challenge the aporia of the decision in Derrida, for it is precisely that irreducible undecidability that the aporia is ensuring in the first place. The decision must be impossible, otherwise it would limit what Derrida seeks to preserve as a limitless responsibility. It would turn the decision into a technology, 'la simple application d'un savoir ou d'un savoir-faire'.[48] The decision for Derrida needs to be undecidable in order to avoid the reliance on mechanical, unthinking, reflexive decision-making which would pay little attention to the singularity of the case, a calculability that Reynolds seems to want to argue is an improvement on Derrida's position. All that Reynolds' 'embodied decisionmaking' can do is restrict the openness of undecidability, the very openness that Derrida labours hard to maintain. Habit is precisely what Derrida needs to suspend in the decision. Reynolds is not correcting Derrida, but simply reiterating the position against which the latter's understanding of the decision militates in the first place.

It gets us nowhere to suggest that Merleau-Ponty's 'chiasmic account of embodiment, and his emphasis on the body-subject's propensity to seek an equilibrium within its environment, better accounts for the "possible" side of the aporias that Derrida describes.'[49] Derrida accounts quite adequately for such 'possibility' himself in terms of calculation and convention. It is wrong to suggest that 'habitual behaviour can alter and sometimes even recuperate the aporetic framework that Derrida discerns',[50] for the aporia is nothing if not that which cannot be recuperated. No, this is not the point at which Merleau-Ponty can be brought in to help us better understand how phenomenology might respond to deconstruction's questions. It is wrong to use Merleau-Ponty's account of corporeality to ground decision-making or eliminate the aporia of the decision. This does not mean, however, that corporeality is unable to help us mediate fact and essence. We must be clear not only *that* Merleau-Ponty's understanding of enrootedness is to be employed in his encounter with Derrida, but *how* it is to be employed, and in order to explore the latter point more adequately we turn now to the relation of meaning and world.

1.4 THE ENROOTEDNESS OF PERCEPTION IN THE WORLD

The second way in which Merleau-Ponty thinks the enrootedness of perception is in the world. Meaning is always a function of the irreducible manifold of body and world. It is important to recognise that this is incompatible with an information-theoretical understanding of meaning as a datum transmitted from the object itself to the percipient herself, where the two are separated by a gulf or abyss. Rather, we must acknowledge that meaning emerges from the self–world Gestalt and does not map onto the code–decode and sender-receiver model of transactional communication. Meaning is *shared* between body and world in the same way that (as we shall shortly see) it is shared between figure and ground, and an attempt to locate it exclusively in one or the other will inevitably traduce this relation which cannot be analysed into the quantifiable contribution of each abstracted element. From his earliest work, Merleau-Ponty seeks to capture this idea of irreducibility in the notion of 'comportement' ('behaviour'), which is neither objective nor subsumable under the cogito.

In coping with the world, there is a compound of the world and of ourselves that precedes reflection (VI 295/VI 102), and once more we must avoid here the mistake of assuming an originary dichotomy of self and world. On the contrary, 'il ne faut plus que je me pense *dans le monde* au sens de la spatialité ob-jective, ce qui revient à m'autoposer et à m'installer dans l'*Ego uninteressiert*' (VI 276).[51] I am not only *in* the world, according to Merleau-Ponty, but also *of* it (N 164/N 121): 'celui qui voit en est et y est' (VI 134).[52] This does not suggest a consciously cognisable or totalisable relation, however. The world is not what I think, but what I live through, and I am open to it and have no doubt that I am in communication with it, but I do not possess it, for it is inexhaustible (PP xii/*PP* xvi–xvii). This irreducible relation is evident in Merleau-Ponty's writing as early as *La Structure du comportement*. Arguing against the mechanising tendencies of a behaviourism that reduces experience into a system of inputs and outputs, Merleau-Ponty maintains that perception is irreducibly structured as a Gestalt of figure and ground.

The evocation of Gestalt in no way amounts to suggesting that worldly meaning is mathematisable. Indeed, in *La Structure du comportement* Merleau-Ponty is arguing against precisely this sort of reification of perceptual order, such as that found in the early behaviourism of J. B. Watson,[53] according to which specific mental phenomena are the reflex caused by the firing of specific, localisable nerve endings, where reflex is 'l'opération d'un agent physique ou chimique défini sur un récepteur localement défini, qui provoque, par un trajet défini, une réponse définie' (SC 7).[54] Merleau-Ponty rejects the logic of cause and effect in favour of a 'circular causality' (SC 13/SB 15) between body and environment. John Sallis articulates well the way in which the Gestalt for Merleau-Ponty is not the imposition of order on the formless content of perception. We quote him here at length:

> ... it is never a matter of sheer sensible content devoid of synthetic connection and over against it an activity of synthesis that would compose the full perceptual object from that content. Rather, the effect of Merleau-Ponty's analysis is to deconstruct the very distinction between synthetic form and sensible content. Instead of an external correlation of form and content, his analysis uncovers at every level a sensible content that is already informed – or, more precisely, a sensible fragment that is already installed within a horizonal structure and through that structure already engaged in synthesis ... [This is] a shift of the horizonal structures into the very core of the content in such a way that there virtually ceases to be any merely presented content.[55]

Sallis goes on to characterise Merleau-Ponty's thought in terms strikingly similar to those more commonly employed to describe Derrida's relation to phenomenology. He notes how 'this second shift, *deconstructing* the distinction between horizonal structures and the intuitively presented, proves so radical as to *turn phenomenology against itself*, against its founding injunction. And it is equally a *turning against metaphysics*, a shift by which phenomenology is *driven to the very edge of metaphysics*.'[56]

The distinctiveness of a Gestalt understanding of meaning is that it is the structure or form of the world that is meaningful, not some ideational essence infusing inert matter with sense, for it is in virtue of the structure and arrangement of the world that meaning and existence are inextricable one from the other:[57]

> Ce qu'il y a de profond dans la Gestalt d'où nous sommes partis, ce n'est pas l'idée de signification, mais celle de structure, la jonction d'une idée et d'une existence indiscernables, l'arrangement contingent par lequel les matériaux se mettent devant nous à avoir un sens, l'intelligibilité à l'état naissant. (SC 223)[58]

The meaningfulness of form (structure, pattern) is basic and irreducible, and Merleau-Ponty uses the term *comportement* to describe this irreducible form-matter manifold as it relates to human action. The term breaks disciplinary boundaries, such that 'un nouveau genre d'analyse, fondé sur le *sens* biologique des comportements s'impose à la fois à la psychologie et à la physiologie' (SC 19),[59] and it amounts to a profound criticism of the *Gestalttheorie* from which Merleau-Ponty is nevertheless drawing inspiration, for the Gestaltists, while affirming the primacy of structure, conceive it in a realist fashion, reducing all forms to physical forms, in contrast to which Merleau-Ponty understands that 'by revealing "structure" or "form" as irreducible elements of being' he has again thrown into question the classical alternative between 'existence as thing' and 'existence as consciousness' and 'established a communication between, and a mixture of, objective and subjective.'[60] Meaning as order is understood to be immanent in the world.[61]

In *Phénoménologie de la perception* Merleau-Ponty develops the critique of the behaviourist's idea that the perceiving subject is the passive recipient of a data stream of atomised sensations, in the process subsuming the Humean category of sensation under the broader notion of perception.[62] It is simply not the case that we construct the world out of intrinsically meaningless raw and disconnected sensations. On the contrary, 'une figure sur un fond est la donnée sensible la plus simple que nous puissions obtenir . . . Le « quelque chose » perceptif est toujours au milieu d'autre chose, il fait toujours partie d'un « champ »' (PP 10).[63] The perceptual field is not composed of constitutive 'parts' waiting to be actively related into a Gestalt; the Gestalt is irreducible. Such an understanding does not fall prey to the charge of totalisation, for the Gestalt is never closed, the perception never complete. In fact, 'toute perception n'est perception de quelque chose qu'en étant aussi relative imperception d'un horizon ou d'un fond, qu'elle implique mais ne thématise pas' (RC 12).[64] To adopt Merleau-Ponty's own terms from *Phénoménologie de la perception,* the Gestalt is neither 'empiricist' nor 'intellectualist' (idealist), but an inextricable melange of both.

In *Le Visible et l'invisible*, this relation will be understood in terms of an ontology *of* the visible (VI 182/VI 140) in which the invisible is not separate from the visible but encrusted in its joints. If meaning is a function of form and structure, then meaning and matter are inextricable, and 'il faut comprendre que c'est la visibilité même qui comporte une non-visibilité' (VI 295).[65] Merleau-Ponty's account of meaning is not incarnational, but rather what we might venture to call 'excarnational': Meaning emerges in the folds of the world, from within the structure of its unatomisable ripples and forms. The passing of sensible objects under our gaze or through our hands is 'comme un langage que s'enseignerait lui-même, où la signification serait sécrétée par la structure même des signes, et c'est pourquoi l'on peut dire à la lettre que nos sens interrogent les choses et qu'elles leur répondent' (PP 369).[66] There is no ideational home of meaning alien to sensible experience; excarnational meaningfulness does not rely on a principle or concept to govern meaning, it harbours no dualistic echoes, and by that token it avoids the paralysing dichotomy of the 'given' and the 'constituted':

> Une chose n'est pas donc effectivement *donnée* dans la perception, elle est reprise intérieurement par nous, reconstituée et vécue par nous en tant qu'elle est liée à un monde dont nous portons avec nous les structures fondamentales et dont elle n'est qu'une des concrétions possibles. (PP 377)[67]

This trajectory of thought also leads Merleau-Ponty to an understanding of form in nature. In his 1959–60 Collège de France lectures on 'Nature et Logos: Le corps humain' he develops a structural understanding of being in relation to organisms in the natural world, emphasising the necessity of understanding an organism or animal as a whole in its environment, and not as a sum of microscopic, punctual parts or events. The animal is a '« phénomène-enveloppe », macroscopique, que l'on n'engendre pas à partir des éléments' (N 275).[68] This appeal to form in nature does not require the introduction of a second element or space outside, behind or otherwise elsewhere than the meaning-world manifold; Merleau-Ponty does not need to reinstate dualistic incarnation by introducing a supplement to the *phénomène-enveloppe*, for he maintains that it is *both* merely the sum of its parts *and also* a transcendent entity (N 204/N 153):

> les diverses parties de l'animal ne sont pas intérieures les uns aux autres. Il faut éviter deux erreurs: placer derrière les phénomènes un principe positif (idée, essence, entéléchie) et ne pas voir du tout de principe régulateur. (N 206–7)[69]

It is not the case that another principle suspends the normal functioning of physico-chemical laws in order to establish the structure of the *phénomène-enveloppe*, yet it is the case that physico-chemical laws are by themselves inadequate to explain that structure:

> L'organisme ne se définit pas par son existence ponctuelle; ce qui existe au-delà, c'est un *thème*, un *style*, toutes ces expressions cherchant à exprimer non une participation à une existence transcendante, mais à une structure d'ensemble. (N 239; author's emphasis)[70]

A multiplicity of discourses is required to account for its existence, and no one discourse alone is adequate. The organism exists as relationship, not as substance; it burgeons forth between its 'elements', and totality is 'partout et nulle part' (N 240).[71] This totality is not simply 'given' in the natural world, and neither is it a perceptual illusion. Structure is originary, and the holistic *phénomène-enveloppe* is a nondualistic response to the 'idée cartésienne de la décomposition du complexe en simple, qui exclut toute considération de la composition comme réalité originale' (N 124).[72] We must not, insists Merleau-Ponty, count form and structure as any less 'real' than the smallest divisions of matter: 'La notion de réel n'est pas forcément liée à celle d'être moléculaire. Pourquoi n'y aurait-il pas de l'être molaire?' (N 209).[73] This is a radical challenge to the notion of self-present and immediate punctual identity.

1.5 TOWARDS AN INDIRECT ONTOLOGY

As the figure-ground structure is primary for Merleau-Ponty, so too is its meaningfulness. Matter is pregnant with its form (PrP 42/*PrP* 12) not pregnant with a meaning dualistically divorced from its own structure but with an always-already meaningful distribution of folds, forms and structures; 'il faut reconnaître ... avant la subsomption du contenu sous la forme, la « prégnance » symbolique de la forme dans le contenu' (PP 337).[74] Again:

> soit une tache blanche sur un fond homogène. Tous les points de la tache ont en commun une certaine « fonction » qui fait d'eux une « figure ». La couleur de la figure est plus dense et comme plus résistante que celle du fond; les bords de la tache blanche lui « appartiennent » et ne sont pas solidaires du fond pourtant contigu; la tache paraît posée sur le fond et ne l'interrompt pas. *Chaque partie annonce plus qu'elle ne contient et cette perception élémentaire est donc déjà chargée d'un sens.* (PP 9; author's emphasis)[75]

Once more what we have here is an invisible *of* the visible.

But what is meant by 'sens' here? Certainly not one pole of a dichotomy of matter and meaning; there is no incarnational haunting of certain material substances by ideal significance. It is for Merleau-Ponty the structure or order of the world that is meaningful, and it is in virtue of structure and order that meaning and existence are inextricable one from the other. In *Le Visible et l'invisible* the interweaving of the questions of meaning and order is given expression in terms of a 'cosmology of the visible':

> Je révoque en doute la perspective évolutionniste, je la remplace par une cosmologie du visible en ce sens que, considérant l'endotemps et l'endospace, il n'y a plus pour moi de question des origines, ni de limites, ni de séries d'événements allant vers une cause première, mais un seul éclatement d'Être qui est à jamais. (VI 313)[76]

'Cosmology of the visible' does not mean that the visible can be abstractly and precisely charted on some kosmotheoretic *mappa mundi*, nor that every object in the field of vision is equally determinable. Cosmos is not the antonym of chaos here, just as *être* and *néant* for Merleau-Ponty are not dichotomised as they are for Sartre. So to claim that for Merleau-Ponty 'the universe is in fact not a chaos but a *cosmos*, that is a Totality, a Great Whole which is well structured and which, consequently, is intelligible (chaos being by definition unintelligible)',[77] is to pass over the important way in which the world exists for Merleau-Ponty in a tension between cosmos and chaos, order and disorder, and how, like the 'elements' of a perceptual Gestalt, these poles are a posteriori abstractions from a more originary complex.

The 'intelligibility in the nascent state' (SC 223/SB 207) of the body-world manifold adumbrates what, in *Le Visible et l'invisible*, Merleau-Ponty will later call an 'empirical pregnancy':

> La « prégnance empirique » . . . consiste à définir chaque être perçu par une structure ou un système d'équivalences autour duquel il est disposé, et dont le trait du peintre, – la ligne flexueuse, – ou le balayage du pinceau est l'évocation péremptoire. Il s'agit de ce λογοσ qui se prononce silencieusement dans chaque chose sensible, en tant qu'elle varie autour d'un certain type de message, *dont nous ne pouvons avoir idée que par notre participation charnelle à son sens*, qu'en épousant par notre corps sa manière de « signifier » – ou de ce λογοσ proféré dont la structure interne sublime notre rapport charnel au monde. (VI 257–8; author's emphasis)[78]

By the term 'empirical pregnancy' Merleau-Ponty is suggesting that there is worldly meaningfulness, but that it stops short of giving any worldly meanings. It is inchoate, indeterminate and therefore not a presentation or gift of meaning but an invitation to participate in meaning.[79] This pregnancy is also a 'promiscuity', a term Merleau-Ponty uses to describe the overlap of the visible and the invisible, rejecting a dualism of exteriority and interiority in favour of an 'empiètement de tout sur tout, être de promiscuité' (VI 282).[80]

Meaningful 'contact' between percipient and perceived, if we understand it in terms of the relative presences and absences of the Gestalt with its reliefs and folds, is made not with objects or substances, and not in terms of any full or immediate presence of worldly meanings to the subject, but laterally, and in terms, once more, of 'style'. For Merleau-Ponty the other is there for us not with the frontal evidence of a thing, but installed crosswise to ('installé en travers de') our thought (S 259/S 159). This refusal of alterity fixed in the gaze is important in understanding how Merleau-Ponty's ontology cannot be straightforwardly deconstructed.

'Contact' must not be understood in terms of immediacy and communion, but promiscuity, the Gestalt and the mutuality of body and world. In other words, the world with which there is contact is not 'un pur objet de pensée sans fissure et sans lacune, mais comme le style universel auquel participent tous les êtres perceptifs' (I 404),[81] not an object in my field of vision of which I can be directly aware, but the style of all vision, that by virtue of which vision is possible and that by virtue of which the question of contact can be posed in the first place; the world is that which affords a style, a manner of being in the world. Style is not itself the object of perception, 'car je ne le regarde pas comme on regarde une chose, je ne le fixe pas en son lieu, mon regard erre en lui comme dans les nimbes de l'Être, je vois selon ou avec lui plutôt que je ne le vois' (ŒE 23).[82] As such, we cannot speak of style in terms of a metaphysics of presence; it is not something that can be immediately present to the percipient, but is rather the index of an indirect ontology.

Style is not a nominal assertion of meaning but an adverbial manner of existing:[83]

> J'ai reçu avec l'existence une manière d'exister, un style. Toutes mes actions et mes pensées sont en rapport avec cette structure, et même la pensée d'un philosophe n'est qu'une manière d'expliciter sa prise sur le monde, cela qu'il est. (PP 519)[84]

Similarly, 'tout style est la mise en forme des éléments du monde qui permettent d'orienter celui-ci vers une de ses parts essentielles' (S 87).[85] As in the case of the Gestalt, the meaningfulness of style is primarily as a structuring of experience:

> Je dis que je sais une idée lorsque s'est institué en moi le pouvoir d'organiser autour d'elle des discours qui donnent sens cohérent, et ce pouvoir même ne tient pas à ce que je le posséderais par devers moi et le contemplerais face à face, mais à ce que j'ai acquis un certain style de pensée. (S 99)[86]

Furthermore, it is style that accounts for the meaning of the world:

> Il suffit que, dans le plein des choses, nous ménagions certains creux, certaines fissures – et dès que nous vivons nous le faisons, – pour faire venir au monde cela même qui lui est le plus étranger: *un sens* . . . Il y a style (et de là signification) dès qu'il y a des figures et des fonds, une norme et une déviation, un haut et un bas, c'est-à-dire dès que certains éléments du monde prennent valeur de dimensions selon lesquelles désormais nous mesurons tout le reste. (PM 85; M-P's emphasis)[87]

So worldly meaning is to be understood cosmologically, as a web of irreducible relations; it is in the structure of the perceived world that meanings are discerned, meanings that are 'incrustées à ses jointures' (VI 152).[88] For the Merleau-Ponty of *Phénoménologie de la perception*, the body operates a patterning ('mise en forme') of the world (PP 220/PP 189), and like the notion of 'forme' in *La Structure du comportement*, style is what makes any signification possible (PM 81/PW 58). This forming, this pre-conceptual generality (PM 63/PW 44), plays a central role in understanding, for 'comprendre n'est pas constituer dans l'immanence intellectuelle, . . . comprendre est saisir par coexistence, latéralement, *en style*' (VI 239).[89]

The ontology that is indicated through these notions of pregnancy, Gestalt and style is indirect, and must remain indirect if it is to remain ontological:

> Le style comme généralité pré-conceptuelle – généralité du « pivot » qui est pré-objective, et qui fait la *réalité* du monde . . . Cette rationalité non constituée de la chose-pivot . . . n'est possible que si la chose est non frontale, objet, mais ce qui mord sur moi et sur quoi je mords par mon corps, si la chose est, elle aussi, donnée en saisie indirecte, latérale. (PM 63)[90]

Merleau-Ponty's indirect ontology is an ontological 'diplopia' (double vision), 'une ontologie prédialectique qui découvrirait dans l'être même un porte-à-faux ou un mouvement' (RC 128).[91] The philosopher is called to occupy alternately two ontological positions, each of which excludes and invites the other (RC 127/TFL 90): an ontological parallax. Like the relation of figure and ground, this ontology cannot be reified, completed or contemplated; it is dispersed, always incomplete in itself and yet calling for its completion, while at the same time denying that possibility. Merleau-Ponty develops the notion of ontological diplopia from the work of Maurice Blondel, as that of which 'on ne peut attendre la réduction rationnelle après tant d'efforts philosophiques, et dont il ne pourrait être question que de prendre possession entière, comme le regard prend possession des images monoculaires pour en faire une seule vision' (RC 127).[92] This diplopia holds together two approaches to nature, one that puts the accent on its determinability and transparency while the other underlines its irreducible facticity. Although no synthesis is possible, the duality is itself unstable. Its instability is no bar to its philosophical usefulness, however. On the contrary, for the task of philosophy is to elaborate a concept of being such that its contradictions, neither accepted nor transcended, still have their place (RC 128/TFL 90).

Marcel Gauchet draws out the implications of this diplopia in suggesting that 's'organisant dans la diplopie, la métaphysique n'y est pas purement et simplement enfermée . . . la métaphysique est dérivée à partir et autour de la diplopie, et par là elle est fondamentalement historique, répétition dans la différence.'[93] Repetition in difference here is vanishingly close to Derridean *différance*, though Merleau-Ponty's distortion retains a level of tension between the gathering and scattering of sense that is not present in Derridean dissemination. Indeed in this ontological diplopia Merleau-Ponty moves to the very limit of phenomenology, as John Sallis notes when he determines that for Merleau-Ponty's ontology 'the question is that of a *differential* shift, of a shift which would decisively install difference within what one would previously have called, but could no longer simply call, the thing itself'.[94]

By the time he drafted the working notes for *Le Visible et l'invisible*, Merleau-Ponty's ontological diplopia had become *surréflexion* (hyper-reflection): a reflection which, in reflexively reflecting on its own status, forecloses the myth of absolute reflection (in other words, the very reflection on the closure of absolute refection opens that closure, in supplementing its circularity with yet more reflection, like the young artist who ruins a canvas by adding too many over-deliberative 'final touches') and thwarts any dialectical synthesis of reflection and its object (VI 69/VI 46). Although it is interesting to note that Jean-François Lyotard dates the necessity of an operation such as deconstruction back to Merleau-Ponty's hyper-reflection,[95] Merleau-Ponty's own ontological diplopia can only superficially be compared with Derrida's resistance to the ontological. We may be able to make the minimal comment that 'both hyper-reflection and deconstruction point towards the necessity of a philosophical proposition containing contrary elements within it (and do not seek an ultimate synthesis of these differences)',[96] but it is a step too far to suggest that they are not in opposition but can 'supplement and enrich one another'.[97] The rhetoric of reciprocation is misleading here. The relation between the sort of ontological affirmation found in Merleau-Ponty and Derrida's suspension of the ontological is not mutual; as we shall discuss at length in Chapter 3, Derrida's thought *haunts* the ontological.

1.6 CONCLUSION

We have seen that Merleau-Ponty's move beyond the fact/essence dichotomy in relation to the body and the world, along with his evocation of ontological 'style' and the pregnancy and promiscuity of the figure-ground relation, all make for an 'excarnational' ontology that does not conform to Derrida's metaphysics of presence. It is now time to take the ideas and terms around which the discussion in this chapter has turned, and consider how they might be brought to bear on the problems which Derrida highlights in *Le Toucher*, particularly the problem of the 'two Merleau-Pontys'. In so doing we return once more to the question of 'contact' by paying attention to the style of Derrida's own reading of the Merleau-Pontean corpus. The guiding ideas of inchoate pregnancy and diplopia are peculiarly suited to describing how Merleau-Ponty argues philosophy should be read, and not least to reading his own philosophy.

For Merleau-Ponty the reader of philosophy proceeds like a baby learning a language through initiation into its tones and rhythms – '. . . je commence à comprendre une philosophie en me glissant dans la manière d'exister de cette pensée, en reproduisant le ton, l'accent du philosophe' (PP 209)[98] – and the ambiguity of Merleau-Ponty's own thinking must be read, like his ontology, *indirectly*:

> Comme le monde perçu ne tient que par les reflets, les ombres, les niveaux, les horizons entre les choses, qui ne sont pas des choses et qui ne sont rien, qui au contraire délimitent seuls les champs de variation possible dans la même chose et le même monde, – de même l'œuvre et la pensée d'un philosophe sont faites aussi de certaines articulations entre les choses dites, à l'égard desquelles il n'y a pas dilemme de l'interprétation objective et de l'arbitraire, puisque ce ne sont pas là des *objets* de pensée, puisque, comme l'ombre et le reflet, on les détruirait en les soumettant à l'observation analytique ou à la pensée isolante. (S 260–1)[99]

If it is true that 'l'idée du chiasme et de *l'Ineinander*, c'est . . . l'idée que toute analyse qui démêle rend inintelligible' (VI 316),[100] then this is nowhere truer than in the case of reading Merleau-Ponty's own philosophy. This is Merleau-Ponty's 'double parole'.[101]

What, then, are we to make of Derrida's disquiet at the 'confusion' or ambiguity in Merleau-Ponty's thought?[102] We would like to suggest a reading of this ambiguity that follows the guidelines Merleau-Ponty himself sets out (and that thereby reads against the grain of the Derridean construal), namely that the ambiguity in Merleau-Ponty's thought is to be understood as fidelity to a diplopic lived experience which is itself ambiguous and self-contradictory. Claude Lefort comes close to articulating this insight when he suggests that Merleau-Ponty's ideas only signify because of what shows through between the lines: dimensions, directions, articulations and hinges.[103] This is close to the Gestalt or *phénomène-enveloppe* understanding of molar, as opposed to molecular, reality. Understanding is not a matter of immediate contact, or indeed of its lack. In fact, immediate contact would ruin this model of recognition, of 'style' and of 'form', that relies on indeterminacies and equivocations of meaning in the call of the to-be-interpreted:

> « Comprendre », c'est ressaisir l'intention totale . . . l'unique manière d'exister qui s'exprime dans les propriétés du caillou, du verre ou du morceau de cire, dans tous les faits d'une révolution, dans toutes les pensées d'un philosophe. . . . tout a un sens, nous retrouvons sous tous les rapports la même structure d'être. (PP xiii–xiv)[104]

It may well be that the ambiguities and indeterminacies in Merleau-Ponty's own thought, especially the texts left unfinished at his sudden death in 1961, are to be received less as a problem for the interpreter and more as an indication of the 'spirit' and 'style' of his *œuvre*, not that which, reified in some a posteriori abstraction, exhibits supposed contradictions, but that which, like ontological diplopia, demands to be interpreted and yet resists final, totalising interpretation.[105]

The deliberate and expressly single-minded faithfulness of Derrida's reading of Merleau-Ponty's philosophy *à la lettre* in *Le Toucher* means that he necessarily neglects its 'spirit' or 'style', the meaning carried by its structure and 'contradictions' in the form of a demand, and so he misses, in his preoccupation with what he perceives to be an immediacy of contact in Merleau-Ponty's argument, the wider notion of contact which the latter carefully establishes. Derrida is right to draw worried attention to certain sentences in Merleau-Ponty which seem to suggest immanentist self-presence, but only because he, Derrida, does not simply stop there. His approach is commendable because he goes on to take such sentences as an invitation to engage in participative dialogue with the whole of Merleau-Ponty's work, for the Merleau-Pontean corpus does not present the reader with a ready-made interpretation; it beckons on, invites, calls to further reading, and it is precisely the incoherencies, the tensions and deformations, the lacunae, that issue this solicitation.[106]

Merleau-Ponty is faithful to the *style* of the world, not to atomised objects within it (which would in fact not be faithfulness at all). As for Derrida's reading of Merleau-Ponty, it is certainly close, the examples precise, the reasoning tight. Yet a preoccupation with understanding the question of contact in terms of self-presence leads Derrida to atomise Merleau-Ponty and at best to privilege a 'certain' reading to the detriment of other possible readings with which the text is pregnant, at worst to suggest (as others have before and after him) that Merleau-Ponty's thought is self-contradictory. But in a further twist Derrida is reproducing, in the style of his own reading, the very model of which he is wary when he sees it at work in Merleau-Ponty, for what is Derrida doing if not perceiving on the pregnant ground of Merleau-Ponty's writings an interpretational figure, one of a number of figures that could emerge from this ground, namely the relative presence of the 'immanentist' Merleau-Ponty at the expense of the relative absence of other Merleau-Pontys? We should approach Merleau-Ponty's philosophy along the lines of the famous remark that he himself cites from Auguste Rodin, that 'les vues instantanées, les attitudes instables pétrifient le mouvement', and instead we should search for a mutual confrontation of incompossibles to shake us from 'une rêverie zénonienne sur le mouvement' (ŒE 78).[107] This is a risk.[108] It requires a certain interpretive commitment, a hermeneutical creativity which responds to the text always in the name of remaining faithful to the constitutive indeterminacy, the mutually informing interweaving of presence and absence that characterise our being in the world. This is the lesson we have learned from Merleau-Ponty's indirect ontology, and yet it remains incomplete and open to the charge of staggering naivety, for as yet it discounts the ontological role of language, and therefore also discounts the major preoccupation of most of Continental thought over the past half century. Such a naivety is by no means inevitable, however, for Merleau-Ponty develops a sophisticated understanding of the relation of ontology and language. We need to understand how his ontological claims can respond to the deconstructive understanding of this relation, and it is to this task that we now turn.

NOTES

1. 'Man, freethinker! Do you believe yourself to be alone in thinking | In this world where life's splendour | Bursts forth in everything? | Your freedom has its power | – But you leave the universe out of the conversation' (Gérard de Nerval, 'The golden verses').
2. See the Introduction for relevant bibliography.
3. This position is forcefully held by John Sallis in *Delimitations*.
4. The lineaments of this position are ably sketched in Martin Dillon's *Semiological Reductionism*.
5. See, for example, Derrida's verdict in 'The time of a thesis' that 'I still see phenomenology today as a discipline of incomparable rigour . . . Not – especially not – in the versions proposed by Sartre or by Merleau-Ponty, . . . but rather in opposition, or without them' (Derrida, 'The Time of a Thesis: Punctuations' 38). Derrida also cites Merleau-Ponty in his *Introduction à l'Origine de la géométrie de E. Husserl* 71, 116–18, 122 (*Edmund Husserl's 'Origin of geometry': an introduction* 77, 111–13, 116), in *De la Grammatologie* 155 n4, 219 n6 (*Of Grammatology* 340 n6, 335 n4), and in 'Force et signification', in *L'Écriture et la différence*, 22 (*Writing and Difference* 11). In addition, he makes reference to Merleau-Ponty in *Mémoires d'aveugle* (*Memoirs of the Blind*) and *Voyous* (*Rogues*).
6. Derrida does not distinguish between proximity and presence in this respect, but evokes elsewhere 'la valeur de proximité, c'est-à-dire de présence en général' (Derrida, *Marges* 151); 'the value of proximity, that is, of presence in general' (*Margins* 127).
7. Derrida, *Le Toucher* 47; 'I self-touches spacing itself out, losing contact with itself, precisely in touching itself' (*On Touching* 34).
8. Derrida, *Le Toucher* 78; 'con-tact as interrupted contact' (*On Touching* 62).
9. Derrida, *Le Toucher* 238; 'a thing at once passionately exciting and difficult, yet also irritating or disappointing at times' (*On Touching* 211).
10. Derrida, *Le Toucher* 216, quoting Merleau-Ponty's 'Le philosophe et son ombre' (S 259–95); 'The Philosopher and His Shadow' (S 159–81); 'My right hand *was present* at the advent of my left hand's active sense of touch. *It is in no different fashion* that the other's body becomes animate before me when I shake another man's hand or just look at him' (*On Touching* 190, quoting Merleau-Ponty, S 138).
11. Derrida, *Le Toucher* 218; 'there is a risk of the exact opposite resulting. One runs the risk of reconstituting an intuitionism of immediate access to

the other, as originary as my access to my own most properly proper' (*On Touching* 191).
12. Derrida, *Le Toucher* 218; *On Touching* 191.
13. *Le Toucher* 223, JD's emphasis, quoting S 215; 'I see that this man over there sees, *as* I touch my left hand while it is touching my right' (*On Touching* 197, quoting *S* 170).
14. Derrida, *Le Toucher* 223; ' "my own," as well as the incarnation of the flesh of the world' (*On Touching* 197).
15. Derrida, *Le Toucher* 227; *On Touching* 201. Derrida is quoting Françoise Dastur, 'Monde, chair, vision' ('World, Flesh, Vision').
16. Derrida, *Le Toucher* 233, quoting PP 270 n1, JD's emphasis; 'it seems to me that *visual experience is truer than tactile experience*' (*On Touching* 206, quoting *PP* 234 n1).
17. Derrida, *Le Toucher* 138; 'we endeavour to identify an intuitionism constitutive of philosophy itself, of the gesture of thought that consists in philosophising – and even of the idealisation process that consists of retaining the sense of touch within sight so as to ensure for the glancing eye the fullness of immediate presence required by every ontology or metaphysics' (*On Touching* 120).
18. Derrida, *Le Toucher* 218, JD's emphasis; 'despite all the differences separating the discursive way in which I am holding forth at this moment from a discourse in Husserl's style . . . I do find this way to have more affinities with the discourse that Husserl obstinately holds to on the subject of appresentation . . . than with the one of a *certain* Merleau-Ponty' (*On Touching* 192).
19. Derrida, *Le Toucher* 239; 'an increasing insistence on self-inadequation, non-coincidences, dehiscences, fissions interruptions, incompletion, and the visible body openly gaping, as well as hiatuses, eclipses, the inaccessibility of this plenitude or this reversibility, this pure, sensible reflexivity, which always remains *imminent*' (*On Touching* 212; translation altered). It is a failure fully to take account of this 'second' Merleau-Ponty that leads Leonard Lawlor to overemphasise the differences between Derrida and a certain Merleau-Ponty, whom he takes to be Merleau-Ponty *tout court*. While '*différance*'s structure is supplementary . . . the structure of the flesh is circular' (Lawlor, *Thinking Through French Philosophy* 48) he argues, and 'while for Merleau-Ponty being is homogeneous, relatively continuous, and undivided, writing for Derrida is heterogeneous, relatively discontinuous, and divided' (Lawlor, *Thinking Through French Philosophy* 60).
20. Derrida, *Le Toucher* 234; 'the original way in which he treats the invisible, an invisible that is not intelligible or ideal, but an invisible that would not – though *right at* the visible – be "the invisible as the *other* visible 'possible' or a 'possible' visible for an other" ' (*On Touching* 207).
21. Derrida, *Le Toucher* 228; 'exciting . . . difficult . . . irritating . . . disappointing' (*On Touching* 211).

22. Derrida, *Le Toucher* 239, JD's emphasis; 'Shall we give the philosopher credit for this, as I am most often tempted to do, or, on the contrary, regret that he was unable to proceed to a more powerful reformalisation of his discourse in order to thematise and think the law under which he was thus placing himself – always, *in fact*, and all things considered, *preferring* "coincidence" . . . to "noncoincidence"?' (*On Touching* 211; translation altered).
23. See, for example, Simon Glendinning's *In the Name of Phenomenology*. Although Glendinning argues that 'the ongoing strength and coherence of phenomenology as a force within the contemporary philosophical culture is to be explained not by what Maurice Merleau-Ponty called the "unity" of its "manner of thinking" but by what he perhaps somewhat more faithfully called its "unfinished nature"' (p. 5), he seems unwilling to extend the same insight to his discussion of Merleau-Ponty himself, in the course of which he treats only *Phénoménologie de la perception*, not touching on *Le Visible et l'invisible* or any other of Merleau-Ponty's later texts, and limits himself merely to indicating 'a series of contradictory assertions' (p. 121) in that text.
24. 'For to acknowledge a naturalism and the envelopment of consciousness in the universe of *blosse Sachen* as an occurrence, is precisely to posit the theoretical world to which they belong as primary, which is an extreme form of idealism' (*TFL* 80).
25. This point is well made by Renaud Barbaras in 'De la parole à l'Être' 197.
26. The Scholastics also distinguished 'qualia sit', the value or worth of something, but this will not concern us until the chapters on Ricœur.
27. See Renaud Barbaras, *De l'Être du phénomène*.
28. 'We must not, therefore, wonder whether we really perceive a world, we must instead say: the world is what we perceive' (*PP* xvi).
29. '"There is a world", or rather: "There is the world"; I can never completely account for this ever-reiterated assertion in my life. This facticity of the world is what constitutes *die Weltlichkeit der Welt*' (*PP* xvii).
30. See D. M. Levin, 'Justice in the Flesh'.
31. For an influential reading of the Heraclitean *logos* along these lines, see Heidegger and Fink, *Heraclitus Seminar*.
32. 'neither above nor beneath the appearances, but at their joints; it is the tie that secretly connects an experience to its variants' (*VI* 116).
33. 'The mind that perceives is an incarnate mind, and it is the enrootedness of the mind *in its body* and *in its world* that we have first sought to restore, both against the doctrines that treat perception as the mere result of the action of exterior things on our body, and against those which insist on the autonomy of conscious apprehension' (author's translation).
34. Reynolds, *Merleau-Ponty and Derrida* 54.
35. Levin, 'Justice in the Flesh' 35.

36. 'every movement of my eyes – even more, every displacement of my body – has its place in the same visible universe that I itemise and explore with them' (*VI* 134).
37. 'indivision of this sensible Being that I am and all the rest which feels itself in me' (*VI* 255).
38. 'Nature and Logos: The Human Body' (*N* 201–84).
39. 'expression is not one of the curiosities that the mind may propose to examine but is its existence in act' (*S* 79).
40. Dreyfus and Dreyfus, 'The Challenge of Merleau-Ponty's Phenomenology of Embodiment for Cognitive Science' 103. We shall return to this assumption in our discussion of Jean-Luc Nancy's notion of *corpus*.
41. Dreyfus and Dreyfus, 'The Challenge of Merleau-Ponty's Phenomenology of Embodiment for Cognitive Science' 104.
42. Levin, 'Justice in the Flesh' 35.
43. 'There is a strict ideality in experiences that are experiences of the flesh: the moments of the sonata, the fragments of the luminous field, adhere to one another with a *cohesion without concept*, which is of the same type as the cohesion of the parts of my body, or the cohesion of my body with the world' (*VI* 152, author's emphasis).
44. 'perception already stylises' (*PW* 59).
45. 'that is, it must completely awaken and recall our sheer power of expressing beyond things already said or seen' (*S* 52).
46. 'The body . . . is not where it is, nor what it is – since we see it secreting in itself a "significance" which comes to it from nowhere, projecting that significance upon its material surrounding, and communicating it to other embodied subjects' (*PP* 197).
47. Reynolds, *Merleau-Ponty and Derrida* 94.
48. Derrida, *L'Autre Cap* 46; 'the simple application of a knowledge or know-how' (*The Other Heading* 45).
49. Reynolds, *Merleau-Ponty and Derrida* 174.
50. Reynolds, *Merleau-Ponty and Derrida* 193.
51. 'I must no longer think myself in the world in the sense of the ob-jective spatiality, which amounts to autopositing myself and installing myself in the *Ego uninteressiert*' (*VI* 227).
52. 'he who sees is of it and is in it' (*VI* 100).
53. See Watson, *Behaviorism*. Watson characterises his project thus: 'Psychology, as the behaviourist views it, is a purely objective experimental branch of natural science. Its theoretical goal is the prediction and control of behaviour' (J. B. Watson, 'Psychology as the Behaviorist Views It', *Psychological Review* 20 (1913) 158).
54. 'the action of a defined physical or chemical agent on a locally defined receptor which evokes a defined response by means of a defined pathway' (*SB* 9).
55. Sallis, *Delimitations* 80. This is what Luce Irigaray fails to take into account when she suggests that 'Merleau-Ponty voudrait que ce soit la

vision qui ferme – et ouvre – mon corps, y compris dans la réversibilité du visible. Que l'horizon m'achève dans un réseau, un vêtement, une peau, que nous nous donnons, nous tissons, sans cesse pour vivre, pour naître' (Luce Irigaray, *Éthique de la différence sexuelle* 163); 'Merleau-Ponty would want it to be vision which closes – and works – my body, including the reversibility of the visible. And for the horizon to perfect me in a network, a garment, a skin, which we give ourselves, which we weave unceasingly in order to live, to be born' (*An Ethics of Sexual Difference* 175). In suggesting that 'chez Merleau-Ponty, le monde se retourne sur lui-même' (*Ethique* 169); 'in Merleau-Ponty's view, the world turns back on itself' (*Ethics* 181), she is misunderstanding the dehiscence of meaning in the world, about which more below.
56. Sallis, *Delimitations* 81; author's emphasis.
57. Merleau-Ponty does acknowledge a distinction between 'forme' and 'structure', though the difference is not always respected in his writing: 'Meili distingue dans la perception la *forme* (mélodie, rythme) et la *structure* (liens précis des détails les uns par rapport aux autres). La perception enfantine parvient souvent à saisir la forme, mais rarement la structure de l'objet' (PPE 194); 'Meili distinguishes in perception the *form* (melody, rhythm) and the *structure* (precise links among the details, from one to the other). Infantile perception often succeeds in grasping the form, but rarely the structure of an object' (author's translation).
58. 'What is profound in the notion of 'Gestalt' from which we started is not the idea of signification but that of *structure*, the joining of an idea and an existence which are indiscernible, the contingent arrangement by which materials begin to have meaning in our presence, intelligibility in the nascent state' (*SB* 207).
59. 'a new kind of analysis, founded upon the biological *meaning* of behaviour, imposes itself at the same time on psychology and physiology' (*SB* 21; translation altered). It is therefore misleading to attempt to co-opt the figure/ground structure as a tool for understanding deconstruction, suggesting that 'Derrida is doing something of a standard phenomenological reading in his play upon margins and the like'. It is not the case that the Derrida who 'draws our attention to features that are there, but are usually taken at most as background, secondary, or unimportant features' is engaging in a 'phenomenological technique' (Ihde, *Consequences of Phenomenology* 192).
60. Dillon, *Merleau-Ponty's Ontology* 254 n47.
61. 'Le grand mérite de la psychologie de la forme est la mise en évidence de l'idée de *structuration*, c'est-à-dire un ordre qui n'est pas surajouté aux matériaux, mais qui leur est immanent et qui se réalise par leur organisation spontanée' (PPE 195); 'The great merit of form psychology is in clarifying the idea of *structuration*, an order that is not added over and above the material, but that is immanent to it and is realised by its spontaneous organisation' (author's translation).

62. 'Ce qu'on appelle sensation n'est que la plus simple des perceptions . . .' (PP 279); 'What is called sensation is only the most rudimentary of perceptions' (PP 241).
63. 'A figure on a background is the simplest sense-given available to us . . . The perceptual "something" is always in the middle of something else, it always forms part of a "field" ' (PP 4). David Morris argues that 'the first unit of perception is not even a figure-on-a-ground (as Merleau-Ponty argues) but a thing-in-a-place' (Morris, *The Sense of Space* 113), but this is imprecise because the figure may not be a thing, as in the case of a hallucination or an optical illusion.
64. 'every perception is the perception of something solely by way of being at the same time the relative imperception of a horizon or background which it implies but does not thematise' (TFL 4).
65. 'One has to understand that it is the visibility itself that involves a non-visibility' (VI 247).
66. 'as a language which would teach itself, and in which the meaning would be secreted by the very structure of the signs, and this is why it can literally be said that our senses question things and that things reply to them' (PP 319; translation altered).
67. 'A thing is, therefore, not actually *given* in perception, it is internally taken up by us, reconstituted and lived by us, in so far as it is bound up with a world, the basic structures of which we carry with us, and of which it is merely one of many possible concrete forms' (PP 326; translation altered).
68. 'It is the macroscopic "envelopment-phenomenon" that we do not engender from elements' (N 213).
69. 'The diverse parts of the animal are not interior to each other. We must avoid two errors: placing behind the phenomena a positive principle (idea, essence, entelechy) and not seeing the regulative principle at all' (N 155; translation altered).
70. 'The organism is not defined by its punctual existence; what exists beyond is a theme, a style, all these expressions striving to express not a participation in a transcendental existence, but but a structure of the whole' (N 183; translation altered).
71. 'Totality is . . . everywhere and nowhere' (N 183).
72. 'the Cartesian idea of the decomposition of the complex into the simple that excludes all consideration of composition as original reality' (N 89).
73. 'The notion of the real is not necessarily linked to that of molecular being. Why would there not be molar being?' (N 157).
74. 'We must recognise . . . anterior to any subsuming of content under form, the symbolical "pregnancy" of form in content' (PP 291).
75. 'Let us imagine a white patch on a homogeneous background. All the dots in the patch have a certain "function" in common, that of forming themselves into a "shape". The colour of the shape is denser, and as it were more resistant than that of the background; the edges of the white patch

"belong" to it, and are not part of the background although they adjoin it: the patch appears to be placed on the background and does not break it up. *Each part announces the expectation of more than it contains, and this elementary perception is therefore already charged with meaning*' (PP 3–4; translation altered).
76. 'I call the evolutionist perspective into question. I replace it with a cosmology of the visible in the sense that, considering endotime and endospace, for me it is no longer a question of origins, nor limits, nor of a series of events going to a first cause, but one sole explosion of Being which is forever' (VI 265).
77. Madison, *The Phenomenology of Merleau-Ponty* 292.
78. ' "empirical pregnancy" . . . consists in defining each perceived being by a structure or a system of equivalencies about which it is disposed, and of which the painter's stroke – the flexuous line – or the sweep of the brush is the peremptory evocation. It is a question of that λογοσ that is pronounced silently in each sensible thing, inasmuch as it varies around a certain type of message, *which we can have an idea of only through our carnal participation in its sense*, only by espousing by our body its manner of "signifying" – or of that λογοσ uttered whose internal structure sublimates our carnal relation with the world' (VI 207–8; author's emphasis).
79. Merleau-Ponty's figure/ground understanding of meaning fulfils John Sallis' requirements for a 'phenomenological attending' that 'must exercise thorough reticence to allow the horizon its reserve, must discern it in the texture of experience without detaching it from that texture and transforming it into something simply present' (Sallis, *Delimitations* 78).
80. 'encroachment of everything upon everything, a being by promiscuity' (VI 234).
81. 'a pure object of thought without crack and without gap, but like the universal style in which all perceiving beings participate' (author's translation).
82. 'for I do not look at it as I do at a thing; I do not fix it in its place. My gaze wanders in it as in the halos of Being. It is more accurate to say that I see according to it, or with it, than that I *see it*' (EM 164).
83. Hugh Silverman attempts to draw parallels between Merleau-Ponty's style as a way of being in the world and Derridean *écriture*. For Merleau-Ponty, style is 'an indirect language that conditions writing itself', while for Derrida, writing is 'the inscription of difference between speech and writing, word and concept, the sensible and the intelligible.' See Silverman, 'Merleau-Ponty and Derrida: Writing on Writing', 135. Silverman concludes that 'the style of writing is the signature event of expression. The writing of style is the differential marking of expression as "signature event" ' (p. 138), but we should not allow the proximity of the Merleau-Pontean and Derridean positions to mask the ontological gulf that separates them.

84. 'I . . . have received, with existence, a manner of existing, a style. All my actions and thoughts stand in relationship to this structure, and even a philosopher's thought is merely a way of making explicit his hold on the world, what he is' (PP 455).
85. 'All style is that giving form to elements of the world which permits the orientation of these elements towards one of the essential parts of the form' (S 54).
86. 'I say that I know an idea when the power to organise discourses which make coherent sense around it has been established in me; and this power itself does not depend on my alleged possession and face-to-face contemplation of it, but upon my having acquired a certain style of thinking' (S 91).
87. 'It is sufficient that we shape in the manifold of things certain hollows, certain fissures – and we do this the moment we are alive – to bring into the world that which is strangest to it: *a meaning* . . . Style exists (and hence signification) as soon as there are figures and backgrounds, a norm and a deviation, a top and a bottom, that is, as soon as certain elements of the world assume the value of dimensions to which subsequently all the rest relate' (PW 61).
88. 'encrusted in its joints' (VI 114).
89. 'to comprehend is not to constitute in intellectual immanence, . . . to comprehend is to apprehend by coexistence, laterally, by the style' (VI 188).
90. 'Style as pre-conceptual generality – generality of the "axis" which is pre-objective and creates the *reality* of the world . . . This nonconstituted rationality of the thing-axis . . . is only possible if the thing is nonfrontal, object, but what bites into me, and what I bite into through my body, if the thing is, itself too, given through an indirect grasp, lateral' (PW 45).
91. 'a predialectical ontology would become possible in an ontology which reveals in being itself an overlap or movement' (TFL 91).
92. 'after so much philosophical effort we cannot expect to bring to a rational reduction and which leaves us with the sole alternative of wholly embracing it, just as our gaze takes over monocular images to make a single vision out of them' (TFL 90).
93. Marcel Gauchet, 'Le lieu de la pensée' 26 n23; 'Metaphysics, though it is organised in diplopia, is not purely and simply enclosed there . . . metaphysics is derived from and around diplopia, and for that reason it is fundamentally historical, repetition in difference' (author's translation).
94. Sallis, *Delimitations* 83.
95. Gasché, *Inventions of Difference* 30.
96. Reynolds, *Merleau-Ponty and Derrida* xv.
97. Reynolds, *Merleau-Ponty and Derrida* xv.
98. 'I begin to understand a philosophy by feeling my way into its existential manner, by reproducing the tone and accent of the philosopher' (PP 179).
99. 'Just as the fixed world endures only through the reflections, shadows, levels and horizons between things (which are not things and are not

nothing, but on the contrary mark out by themselves the fields of possible variation in the same thing and the same world), so the works and thoughts of a philosopher are also made of certain articulations between things said. There is no dilemma of objective interpretation or arbitrariness with respect to these articulations, since they are not *objects* of thought since (like shadow and reflection) they would be destroyed by being subjected to analytic observation isolating thought' (S 160).

100. 'the idea of chiasm and *Ineinander* is on the contrary the idea that every analysis that disentangles renders unintelligible' (VI 268).

101. I adopt the term 'double parole' ('double speaking') from Maurice Blanchot's short article on Merleau-Ponty entitled 'Le discours philosophique'. Blanchot writes, 'Le philosophe . . . est toujours l'homme d'une double parole: il y a ce qu'il dit et qui est important, intéressant, nouveau et propre à prolonger l'interminable discours, mais derrière ce qu'il dit, il y a quelque chose qui lui retire la parole, ce *dis-cours* précisément sans droit, sans signes, illégitime, mal venu, de mauvais augure et, pour cette raison, obscène, et toujours de déception ou de rupture et, en même temps, passant par-delà tout interdit, le plus transgressif, le plus proche du Dehors intransgressible' (Blanchot 'Le « Discours Philosophique »' 2); 'The philosopher . . . is always a man who speaks double: there is what he says, which is important, interesting, new and apt to prolong the unending discourse, but behind what he says, there is something that takes away his speech, this *dis-course* precisely without right, without signs, illegitimate, ill timed, a bad omen and, for this reason, obscene, and always a disappointment or a rupture and, at the same time, passing through every proscription, the most transgressive, the closest to the intransgressible Outside' (author's translation). It is this illegitimate discourse of rupture and disappointment (the disappointment of being unable to reconcile ontological diplopia) that the problem of inconsistency in Merleau-Ponty brings to light.

102. Derrida is not alone in indicating this confusion. 'From Sartre's perspective, Merleau-Ponty jumps around inconsistently, so there is no reliable relational continuity to his analysis. There is a problem of direction here, which presumably explains why Sartre finds it difficult to get his "bearings" in the *Phenomenology of Perception*' (Cumming, *Phenomenology, and Deconstruction*, vol. 1, 175, quoting Paul Arthur Schilpp, *The Philosophy of Jean-Paul Sartre*, The Library of Living Philosophers, vol. 16 (La Salle, IL: Open Court, 1981), 44). One of the few writers apart from Derrida to be sensitive to the 'diplopia' of the Merleau-Pontean corpus is Vincent Descombes who, in *Modern French Philosophy*, notes that 'Merleau-Ponty's work is open to a double reading. A new "philosophy of consciousness", as it was called, could as readily be found there as an attempt to surpass this type of philosophy' (p. 68).

103. See Lefort, 'Philosophie et non-philosophie' 101–2.

104. 'to "understand" is to grasp the total intention . . . the unique mode of existing expressed in the properties of the pebble, the glass or the piece of wax, in all the events of a revolution, in all the thoughts of a philosopher . . . everything has a meaning, and we shall find this same structure of being underlying all relationships' (*PP* xviii, xix; translation altered).

105. Thus in relation to Husserl's legacy, Merleau-Ponty comments that 'quand Husserl termine sa vie, il y a un impensé de Husserl qui est bel et bien à lui et qui pourtant ouvre sur tout autre chose' (S 260); 'At the end of Husserl's life there is an unthought-of element in his works which is wholly his and yet opens out onto something else' (*S* 160). It is an 'unthought' which is not possessed by the philosophy which it haunts, and the philosopher can only indirectly bequeath it to others.

106. François Heidsieck sees this more clearly than most: 'le contenu de la pensée [de Merleau-Ponty] ne peut être abstrait de la modalité même du discours. Cette modalité, ou si l'on veut son style, ne constitue donc pas une méthode dont on pourrait épuiser les axiomes' (Heidsieck, *L'Ontologie de Merleau-Ponty* 43); 'the content of the thought [of Merleau-Ponty] cannot be abstracted from the very modality of the discourse. This modality, or if you will its style, thus does not constitute a method the axioms of which could be exhaustively stated' (author's translation).

107. 'the instantaneous glimpses, the unstable attitudes, petrifying the movement . . . a Zenonian reverie on movement' (*EM* 185). This argument is also made by Rudi Visker in *Truth and Singularity* 167.

108. Marc Richir notes that, with the later, fragmentary Merleau-Ponty we have to 'prendre nos responsabilités, interpréter plus librement au risque de l'infidélité' (Richir, 'Le sens de la phénoménologie dans *Le Visible et l'invisible*' 135); 'shoulder our responsibilities, interpret more loosely at the risk of infidelity' (author's translation).

2. Maurice Merleau-Ponty: Language

In the first chapter we asked if, in the light of the questions Derrida raises in *Le Toucher*, we can still speak, phenomenologically, about a worldly meaningfulness. We saw that, although Derrida's worries about what Merleau-Ponty means by 'presence' and 'intuitionism' do provide cause for concern, there is 'another' Merleau-Ponty (to whom Derrida alludes but does not explore at any length) who is not prey to the same accusations. We also began to see that Derrida's reading rests substantially on a particular understanding of the notion of 'contact' as immediate proximity, which it is by no means clear that Merleau-Ponty shares. In this chapter we return to the latter problem, this time not from the angle of perception but from that of language. It is in his thinking about the relation of language and the world that Merleau-Ponty is closest to Derridean concerns,[1] and in turning to Merleau-Ponty's philosophy of language we shall argue that, contrary to Derrida's assumption, Merleau-Ponty's construal of the relationship of language and the ontological need not be reductively violent. Deploying the two key motifs of being 'in the interrogative mode' and the call and response structure of world and language, we shall show how what Merleau-Ponty calls the 'work of expression' offers an alternative to deconstruction's abyss between subject and world, and we shall begin to interrogate deconstructive questioning itself in order to explore possible phenomenological responses to it.

2.1 EXPRESSION

With the building blocks of the Gestalt, style and Merleau-Ponty's indirect, diplopic ontology in place, we are able now to consider linguistic expression and its relation to perception, a thesis which, for James Edie at least, 'stands at the centre of Merleau-Ponty's work', but that presents 'almost insuperable problems'.² Indeed, language is as fundamental to Merleau-Ponty's phenomenological enterprise in both *Phénoménologie de la perception* and *Le Visible et l'invisible* as it is to Derrida's grammatology:

> Pour avoir l'idée de « penser » (dans le sens de la « pensée de voir et de sentir »), pour faire la « réduction », pour revenir à l'immanence et à la conscience . . . il est nécessaire d'avoir des mots (VI 222; M-P's ellipsis)³

> C'est à propos du langage qu'on verrait le mieux comment il ne faut pas et comment il faut revenir aux choses mêmes. (VI 164)⁴

In recent years, attention has been drawn to the proximity of Merleau-Ponty and Derrida on the question of language in comparisons of Merleau-Ponty's newly published course notes on Husserl's *Ursprung der Geometrie* with Derrida's early work on the same text.⁵ Both Merleau-Ponty's Notes and Derrida's Introduction stress that geometry, or indeed any ideal object, cannot be fully constituted without inscription, and in a piece written before he read Merleau-Ponty's course notes, Derrida himself attests to an affinity between the ideas of the late Merleau-Ponty and his own:

> Le sens doit attendre d'être dit ou écrit pour s'habiter lui-même et devenir qu'à différer de soi il est: le sens. C'est ce que Husserl nous apprend à penser dans *L'Origine de la géométrie*. L'acte littéraire retrouve ainsi à sa source son vrai pouvoir. Dans un fragment du livre qu'il projetait de consacrer à *L'Origine de la vérité*, Merleau-Ponty écrivait: « La communication en littérature n'est pas simple appel de l'écrivain à des significations qui feraient partie d'un *a priori* de l'esprit humain: bien plutôt elle les y suscite par entraînement ou par une sorte d'action oblique. Chez l'écrivain la pensée ne dirige pas le langage du dehors: l'écrivain est lui-même comme un nouvel idiome qui se construit . . . » « Mes paroles me surprennent moi-même et m'enseignent ma pensée » disait-il ailleurs.⁶

Despite these strong affinities, Leonard Lawlor threatens to overstrain the comparison when he glosses the Merleau-Pontean observation 'Vrai pensée husserlienne: homme, monde, langage sont enchevêtrés, *verflochten*' (HAL 50)⁷ by suggesting that 'a thick identity exists there, which truly contains difference', judging that 'nothing could sound more Derridean'.⁸ It is true that the late Merleau-Ponty and the early Derrida are remarkably close when they discuss identity and difference, but Derrida would surely not be content with the statement that identity 'truly *contains* difference'. *Différance* is not contained; it is precisely that which cannot be contained and which makes exhaustive containment impossible. 'Are we supposed to think, now, in light of these "new" Notes,' Lawlor continues, 'that Derrida's philosophy somehow continues that of Merleau-Ponty? In light of these Notes, I think we have to answer this question with a "yes".'[9] In the light of these notes and their wider context in the thought of Merleau-Ponty and Derrida, this author thinks we have to answer with a less decisive, but more accurate, 'yes . . . and no'.

One major difference is that for Merleau-Ponty, language has a flesh – in 'Sur la phénoménologie du langage' (S 136–58),[10] he discusses the quasi-corporeity of the signifier (S 142/S 88) – and with the coming of expression 'c'est comme si la visibilité qui anime le monde sensible émigrait, non pas hors de tout corps, mais dans un autre corps moins lourd, plus transparent, comme si elle changeait de chair, abandonnant celle du corps pour celle du langage' (VI 200).[11] Linguistic expression is on a continuum with perceptual experience; there is a flesh of the body and a flesh of language, and the visibility in which invisible sense is encrusted (as we saw in the previous chapter) has the same structure of promiscuity and pregnancy in the case of language.

Nevertheless, the expressivity of language draws on 'un langage tacite . . . que la peinture parle à sa façon' (S 75),[12] and whereas painting can yield a silent science (ŒE 82/EM 186) and a conceptless opening upon things (ŒE 43/EM 172) where it is not a case of speaking of space and light, but making space and light speak (ŒE 59/EM 178), by contrast, 'que le langage soit la présomption d'une accumulation totale, c'est certain' (S 132).[13] In short, language speaks, and the voices of painting are the voices of silence (S 130/S 81). Should we expect, in the light of this contrast, a totalising, recuperating theory of language in Merleau-Ponty? A language from which the 'world' and its supposed meanings derive? Not at all, for reasons that take up once more the threads we have so far been tracing: the figure/ground relation, the cosmology of the visible and the inextricable intertwining of subject and world.

2.2 LANGUAGE, FIGURE AND GROUND

In *Phénoménologie de la perception*, expression and language are related as figure to ground:

> Une fois le langage formé, on conçoit que la parole puisse signifier comme un geste sur le fond mental commun . . . la clarté du langage s'établit sur un fond obscur. (PP 217–19)[14]

The Gestalt relationship remains in *La Prose du monde*, where *parole* signifies by raising figures on the ground of language:

> nous appelons parole le pouvoir que nous avons de faire certaines choses convenablement organisées . . . à mettre en relief . . . les significations qui traînent à l'horizon du monde sensible. (PM 199)[15]

As in Merleau-Ponty's avoidance of the *néant/être* binary in his account of perception, so also in language this Gestalt structure entails that meaning is never absolute, nor ever absent. Meaningful forms always appear on a ground of indeterminacy, and indeed it is this indeterminacy, characteristic of all natural languages, that makes meaning possible at all. One important implication of this structure is that indeterminacy is no impediment to the communication of meaning, but rather the principle of its productivity: 'la signification n'est jamais qu'une tendance' (VI 129).[16] As with the untotalisable boundaries of the perceptual Gestalt, like the visual field, the individual's linguistic field ends in vagueness (PM 46/PW 32). The presence and absence of meaning are indivisible, and communication is always intertwined with the uncommunicated.[17] This is far from the dichotomous understanding of meaning propounded by deconstruction in which, Derrida argues in his introduction to Husserl's *Origine de la géométrie*, it must either descend from some heavenly *topos ouranios* (the Platonic place of ideas, representative and true, adequate to itself) or be a product of history, its historicity being intrinsic and essential.[18] This is like the biologism/historicism binary we borrowed from David Levin in the previous chapter; in each case Merleau-Ponty wants to split the horns of the dilemma in an inextricable and unanalysable mutuality.

For Merleau-Ponty, it is as misguided to alienate language from the world as it is to conflate the two:

> la philosophie n'est pas un lexique, elle ne s'intéresse pas aux « significations des mots », elle ne cherche pas un substitut verbal du monde que nous voyons, elle ne le transforme pas en chose dite, elle ne s'installe pas dans l'ordre du dit ou de l'écrit, comme le logicien dans l'énoncé, le poète dans la parole ou le musicien dans la musique. Ce sont les choses mêmes, du fond de leur silence, qu'elle veut conduire à l'expression. (VI 18)[19]

Precisely how the 'things themselves' are 'brought to expression' we shall leave until the section below entitled 'From Silence to Language'. For now we note that, mirroring the primacy of perception over contemplation, language here is conceived according to a dimension which is neither that of the concept nor of essence, but of existence (PM 56/PW 40). It is an understanding not reliant on the Saussurean presence of the concept in the sign,[20] while maintaining language use (*parole*) and language as system (*langue*) in a mutually dependent relation. A misreading of Saussure? If so, then, *felix culpa*! For Merleau-Ponty's reading opens the way for a fresh appropriation of Saussure, and one that challenges poststructuralist assumptions about the primacy of the contemplative attitude and philosophical language over the everyday. For Merleau-Ponty there are no conventional signs, 'il n'y a que des paroles dans lesquelles se contracte l'histoire de toute la langue, et qui accomplissent la communication sans aucune garantie, au milieu d'incroyables hasards linguistiques' (PP 219).[21]

This primacy of language *use* (*parole*), with its irreducibly meaningful 'style' of tones, cadences and rhythms, over language *analysis* (*langue*) plays a crucial role in Merleau-Ponty's argument for an understanding of meaning in terms of style, whereas Derrida's suspicion of the ideology nesting in claims to 'straightforward' or 'commonsense' meanings commits him to affirming the primacy of philosophical over everyday language, where 'ordinary' language finds its place only within a philosophical framework:

> Or la 'langue usuelle' n'est pas innocente ou neutre. Elle est la langue de la métaphysique occidentale et elle transporte non seulement un nombre considérable de présuppositions de tous ordres, mais des présuppositions inséparables, pour peu qu'on y prête attention, nouées en système.[22]

This sort of suspicion necessitates the elevation of the self-reflexive, cautious language of philosophy to the paradigm for all language. The problem with this from a Merleau-Pontean point of view, however, is that the system is being taken for that which it systematises; philosophical language is retrojected as an *archē* of all language in a metaphysical fiat. For Merleau-Ponty in contrast, language in use, language as expression, resists decomposition into a linguistic datum open to contemplation and by means of which 'contact' can (or cannot) be secured with the world. This characterisation is inadequate not least because expression is irreducibly corporeal:

> Quand je parle, je ne me représente pas des mouvements à faire: tout mon appareil corporel se rassemble pour rejoindre et dire le mot comme ma main se mobilise d'elle-même pour prendre. (PM 28)[23]

The final clause here refers to Merleau-Ponty's notion of gesture. In an attempt to restore to the act of speaking its true physiognomy (PP 211/PP 181), Merleau-Ponty resists the analytic decomposition of gesture into a dichotomy of motion and meaning. If the gesture becomes the object of direct attention, it loses its signifying power. Gestures 'ne s'accomplissent pas sans quelque négligence' (PM 162; quoting Jean Paulhan),[24] for language, like ontology, is encountered indirectly. Language 'se dérobe à qui le cherche et se donne à qui l'avait renoncé' (PM 163).[25] Language will not yield itself to the contemplative analyst with the lepidopterist's net and pin. Unatomisable phrases, not single words, constitute the linguistic gesture, and such a gesture is not isolable from its linguistic context, the Gestalt in which it appears. Such a refusal of the primacy of the contemplative attitude means that in the vast majority of cases even if each word, according to the dictionary, has a great number of meanings, we go straight to the one which fits a given sentence (PM 32/PW 22).

The attempt to make logic do duty for use will overstretch the former and betray the latter. An epistemology which asserts – contrary to their order in experience – the primacy of contemplation over use will always end in a suspension and deferral of epistemology, not as a result of anything to do with what may or may not be known, but as a result of its own internal tensions and instability. By contrast, for Merleau-Ponty:

> la parole, celle que je profère ou celle que j'entends, est prégnante d'une signification qui est présente dans la texture même du geste linguistique, au point qu'une hésitation, qu'une altération de la voix, le choix d'une syntaxe suffit à la modifier, et cependant jamais contenue en lui, toute expression m'apparaissant toujours comme une trace, nulle idée ne m'étant donnée qu'en transparence, et tout effort pour fermer la main sur la pensée, qui habite la parole, ne laissant entre nos doigts qu'un peu de matériel verbal. (S 144)[26]

Such meaningfulness cannot be represented propositionally; if it is fixed or contemplated, it disappears. But the assumption that 'normal language' is not innocent or neutral, that it must be violent, forces Derrida's hand, for he must now consider all language to be reductive, foundational and party to the metaphysics of presence.

Contrary to the conclusion to which some have jumped, this is not to claim Derrida to be saying that 'there is nothing but language, and that language is nothing but a differential system of slippage and dissemination.'[27] 'Text' for Derrida is not limited to linguistic structure, but extends to symbolic systems in whatever form (cultural, social, institutional . . .). Rather than a pantextualism or a 'meaningless play', Derrida's privileging of philosophical discourse issues in an aporia of structure and meaning. Derrida is not a nihilist at this point, but a mystic of sorts, holding the faith that pleromatic meaning, the messianic, will have arrived, but that it never arrives and never has arrived, and it is certainly not inherent in structure. Since meaning is metaphysical (and given that all language is metaphysically violent), Derrida is left not with meaningless, nihilistic play, but an aporia of system and the Impossible, an asymmetrical duality necessitated by the inaugural move of branding all language metaphysical. It is this that Martin Dillon fails to take into account in his reading of Derrida's 'semiological reductionism', according to which any rejection of foundations leads to scepticism and nihilism.[28] Dillon's Derrida is all system, and there is no accounting for the Impossible, the Undeconstructable, or Justice. As a result, he regrettably characterises deconstruction, under the umbrella categories of 'post-hermeneutic skepticism' and 'semiological reductionism', as 'a position that defends no position, but attacks from whatever vantage point is expeditious at the moment.'[29] The air of *Semiological Reductionism* is thick with the demons of 'nihilism' (undefined by Dillon) and 'relativism' (left relatively vague), an atmosphere in which the deconstructive imperative to responsibility is conspicuous by its absence.

Rather than using Merleau-Ponty to attack Derrida on this point, or vice versa, we would do well to acknowledge their proximity (though not their identity). For Derrida, language is violent, but it is also subject to *différance*: it is open and non-totalisable. This double ('diplopic', we might venture) understanding of language bears striking resemblance to Merleau-Ponty's insistence that language both reduces quickly to meaningless material when contemplated but indicates an excess of meaning over what it can contain when it is used. The difference is that, for Merleau-Ponty, the irreducible excess of meaning is a function of the pregnancy of worldly meaningfulness, whereas for Derrida it is a product of aleatory *différance* and related to what meaning there may be only aporetically.

2.3 THE MUTE CALL OF THE WORLD

In the same way that he showed the visible and the invisible to be in a relation of encroachment, Merleau-Ponty problematises any absolute distinction between language, meaning and world. Creativity cannot be isolated and treated as autonomous from sedimentation which, far from being the obscurity which truth needs to dispel, is the very tissue of its manifestation:

> ce que nous pouvons avoir de vérité ne s'obtient pas contre l'inhérence historique, mais par elle. Superficiellement pensée, elle détruit toute vérité; pensée radicalement, elle fonde une nouvelle idée de la vérité. (S 178)[30]

This can be the case because meaning emerges structurally, from expressive gesture as a whole, at the intersection of a number of gestures (S 131/S 81). 'Contact' is not on the level of the single word and the individual thing but of the semantic Gestalt and the world; it takes place in the gaps between words, as the cosmos-chaos tension of language, in the hollows of space, time and signification they mark out (S 123/S 76). This interplay of sedimentation and innovation short-circuits the dichotomy of natural and conventional signs. No sign can ever be univocally natural and none exclusively conventional for:

> il est impossible de superposer chez l'homme une première couche de comportements que l'on appellerait 'naturels' et un monde culturel ou spirituel

> fabriqué. Tout est fabriqué et tout est naturel chez l'homme, comme on voudra dire, en ce sens qu'il n'est pas un mot, pas une conduite qui ne doive quelque chose à l'être simplement biologique – et qui en même temps ne se dérobe à la simplicité de la vie animale. (PP 220–1)[31]

There is nothing untouched by text; there is nothing reducible to text.

A further, and crucial, difference between Merleau-Ponty's and Derrida's account of language is that for Merleau-Ponty, world and language are related in a dialectic of call and response, where the world announces itself in terms of a call to interpretation, the recognition that 'there is' (il y a) something meaningful that affords interpretation. It is important to distinguish between this recognition of the to-be-interpreted and the work of interpretation or expression itself, because it is on the former that Merleau-Ponty's arguments for empirical pregnancy and worldly meaningfulness hang, and it is also this recognition in wonderment, which precedes understanding, to which Derrida's reading fails to do justice. The recognition of the world as 'to-be-interpreted' is not an indicative 'contact' with the world that informs (a pinpointing of the *quid sit* of worldly meaning), but an interrogative call that de-forms (an *an sit* that, like the Heraclitean *logos*, is always already pregnant with meaningfulness) and demands an interpretive response. We recognise *that* the world affords meaning without (yet) knowing *what* such meaning(s) might be. Like the beginning of Vinteuil's little phrase in Proust's *Un Amour de Swann*[32] that implicitly suggests the form of its own completion, it is a pregnancy of meaningfulness rather than the presence of meaning:

> La prégnance est ce qui, dans le visible, exige de moi une juste mise au point, en définit la justesse. Mon corps obéit à la prégnance, il lui « répond », il est ce qui se suspend à elle, chair répondant à chair. (VI 259)[33]

This call is not itself a determinate meaning, nor does it prescribe a determinate meaning, such that we could say that sense resides in the world regardless of who is there to apprehend it, any more than we could say that Beethoven's Ninth is 'in' the hi-fi as opposed to 'in' the CD or 'in' the mind of the listener; in both cases we should say that the form of the in-form-ation is in none of these alone and in all together, for meaningfulness understood in terms of form emerges in the Gestalt of subject and world. The question of contact changes as we take fuller account of the situation within which the question itself arises.

The world is not experienced as full of self-present objects with objective meanings with which contact is made, but rather in terms of the call of a to-be-interpreted, a burgeoning forth or dehiscence of meaningfulness soliciting a response, and the response to this solicitation is not grasping or completion but astonishment, puzzlement and further questioning:

> Montrer que ces notions [*En marge*: prégnance, Gestalt, phénomène] représentent une prise de contact avec l'être comme il y a pur. On assiste à cet événement par lequel il y a quelque chose. Quelque chose plutôt que rien et ceci plutôt qu'autre chose. On assiste donc à l'avènement du positif: ceci plutôt qu'autre chose. (VI 256)[34]

The response to this call is not one that affirms the meaning of the world or that posits its being; for Merleau-Ponty the world exists in the interrogative mode (VI 139/*VI* 103) and the interrogative is 'le mode propre de notre rapport avec l'Être' (VI 168).[35] By understanding being in the interrogative mode, Merleau-Ponty is not suggesting the prelude to the closure of meaning in a definitive answer to the interrogation. Merleau-Pontean interrogation dispossesses the questioner of the control of his discourse, making him pass continually from the loss of sense to its re-opening.[36] We might even say that it puts it under erasure. It is not the formal scholastic *quaestio*, nor a sceptical exercise of methodical and hyperbolic doubt, but the open and dynamic *interrogatio*: a question open to a possible response[37] and a question that invites a response.

As Hugh Silverman notes, 'Merleau-Pontean interrogation . . . not only places meaning in the space of difference, it animates a questioning that places what is to be interpreted (or interrogated) in the interrogative mode.'[38] In this way, Merleau-Ponty's thought resists the category of full and immediate presence which the Derridean reading seems to find in it. In other words, in putting language in the interrogative it also puts its own ontology under erasure. Silverman also makes the important distinction between putting into question and putting into doubt.[39] Interrogation is neither doubt nor affirmation, but opens the possibility of both. In his short article on Merleau-Ponty entitled 'Le « discours philosophique »', Maurice Blanchot characterises the Merleau-Pontean interrogative as a way of negotiating the difference of the said and the unsaid (we might say the speakable and the unspeakable):

> Le philosophe cherche un compromis en maintenant son discours manifeste (afin qu'il ne trahisse pas trop le discours latent ou clandestin) en position interrogative: interroger, rechercher, c'est s'exclure des privilèges du langage affirmatif, c'est-à-dire établi, parler au-delà de la parole, l'ouvrir et la tenir en suspens; langage d'interrogation, cependant capable de devenir à son tour inquisiteur, ayant sa technique, ses habitudes quasi institutionnelles, ses élégances et toujours anticipant sur une réponse, ne pouvant durer qu'à ce prix.[40]

This double potential of interrogation, resisting direct affirmation but also capable of turning inquisitor, is indicative of the tension that David

Wood identifies when he notes that 'our continuing debt to the unthematised and the impossibility of finally discharging that debt is one of the central motifs of phenomenology.'[41] It is also, in the various guises of the gift, hospitality and justice, one of the abiding features of Derrida's thought.[42] So Hugh Silverman is incorrect to suggest that the relation between interrogation and deconstruction is that 'the former presupposes the latter' because 'at issue in interrogation is the logic of visibility; at issue in deconstruction is the logic of supplementarity.'[43] In interrogation, what is at stake is the logic of supplementarity *as* the logic of visibility.

In accordance with the call and response structure of meaning we understand sense as neither simply projected onto, nor passively received from, the world. In his 1949–50 Sorbonne lecture course on language acquisition in children (PPE 9–88), Merleau-Ponty stresses that before understanding individual words, a child first learns the rhythm of a language, gaining an 'attunement' prior to understanding in the pre-linguistic babbling communication between parent and child. It is not thought or concept that is primary in the acquisition of language, but rhythm and corporeal vibration, not an indicative proposition but the space of a to-be-interpreted.[44] Allied to the dynamic of 'style' we encountered in the previous chapter, this 'attunement' to language is also explored in Merleau-Ponty's evocation of the Humboldtian notion of *innere Sprachform*, the reflection in language of a culture's perspective on the world even down to the level of the distribution of accents, inflections and the use of the article (PPE 65). The *innere Sprachform* is language's interrogative response to the world and itself a 'to-be-interpreted'; it both responds to the world's empirical pregnancy and is itself pregnant with meaning. The child is content to note the *relations* of words, 'leur récurrence, la manière dont ils se fréquentent, s'appellent ou se repoussent, et constituent ensemble une mélodie d'un style défini' (PM 46),[45] and it is 'style' that mediates thought and words:

> Entre le langage, somme de mots, et la pensée, s'interpose une couche de significations qui supposent un certain rapport avec lui. C'est cette espèce de pensée dans le langage, non explicite, qui constitue le *style*. (PPE 65)[46]

Once more, this is not meaning that can be contemplated or rendered in philosophical propositions, but indirect, oblique meaningfulness. 'Style' here is not to be understood as an extra-linguistic essence which descends into language, possessing and ventriloquising it, nor as a merely aleatory linguistic quirk. The mind does govern language, but not in a latter-day ontological dualism:

Tout le langage est l'esprit; il n'est pas une mélodie verbale qui ne suppose de vigilance intellectuelle. Mais l'esprit qui gouverne le langage n'est pas l'esprit pour soi, c'est paradoxalement un esprit qui ne se possède qu'en se perdant dans le langage. (PPE 66–7)[47]

The 'mind' in question is the form – we might say the cosmos – of spoken language.[48] The manner in which language emerges from tone, gesture and style is construed by Merleau-Ponty not as a move from chaos to cosmos and *logos*, but in terms of a transition *within* the *logos*, of which he identifies two moments. The *logos endiathetos*[49] is a worldly to-be-interpreted, that which 'ne contient aucun mode d'expression et qui pourtant les appelle' (VI 223–4).[50] Linguistic meaning on the other hand is characterised in terms of the *logos proforikos*, or 'spoken *logos*'. The use of the term *logos* in both cases should alert us to Merleau-Ponty's rejection of the dichotomising of experience and language (and *a fortiori* the need to establish 'contact' between them), for he understands them both as moments of an enlarged dynamic of call and response in which we admit an original text (perception itself) which carries its meaning within itself, and set over against it that of memories (PP 29/PP 21). In fact, *logos endiathetos* and *logos proforikos* are themselves in a relation of call and response. The *logos endiathetos* calls for ('appelle') the *logos proforikos*, and the *logos proforikos* bespeaks or names ('appelle') the *logos endiathetos*; one order (the figure-ground cosmology of the perceived world) calls for another (the figure-ground structure of *parole*). The *logoi* exist in a collaborative but always incomplete mutual implication, neither one dominating or controlling the other. Merleau-Ponty's *logoi* are neither to be confused with each other nor distinguished to such an extent that meaning is dualistically exiled from the world and caught in a web of language.

We must understand that Merleau-Ponty accounts for worldly meaningfulness by elaborating a polysemy of the *logos*. Linguistic meaning is but one manifestation of meaningfulness, and it is reliant on gestural meaning, which itself is an expressive response to the call of Gestalten that emerge in the irreducible mutuality of body and world. At no point can meaning be isolated in language or in the body. This polysemy highlights one important area where Merleau-Ponty's philosophy disagrees with Derrida's, for in *La Voix et le phénomène* Derrida subverts the Husserlian distinction between natural and conventional signs by speaking of the sign in general. It is not our intention here to use Merleau-Ponty to reinstate the natural/conventional dichotomy – indeed we have already seen how he subverts it himself – but it is important to recognise that he does it differently from Derrida, who prefers to collapse the difference and refer instead to signs in general.

Merleau-Ponty sees the polysemy of *sens* as crucial to his account of the relation of meaning and world:

> Si nous ne considérons que le *sens conceptuel et terminal* des mots, il est vrai que la forme verbale – exception faite des désinences – semble arbitraire. Il n'en serait plus ainsi si nous faisions entrer en compte le *sens émotionnel* du mot, ce que nous avons appelé plus haut son *sens gestuel*, qui est essentiel par exemple dans la poésie. On trouverait alors que les mots, les voyelles, les phonèmes sont autant de manières de chanter le monde et qu'ils sont destinés à représenter les objets, non pas, comme le croyait la théorie naïve des onomatopées, en raison d'une ressemblance objective, mais parce qu'ils en extraient et au sens propre du mot en expriment l'essence émotionnelle. (PP 218; author's emphasis)[51]

Merleau-Ponty elaborates upon 'emotional' or 'gestural' sense in the following terms:

> La prédominance des voyelles dans une langue, des consonnes dans une autre, les systèmes de construction et de syntaxe ne représenteraient pas autant de conventions arbitraires pour exprimer la même pensée, mais plusieurs manières pour le corps humain de célébrer le monde et finalement de le vivre. (PP 218)[52]

This gestural sense is not amenable to the same modes of analysis as linguistic sense; it is an indirect sense, more implied by the edifice of words than designated by them (S 134/S 83). Gesture signifies not in the indicative but in the interrogative, presenting itself to us as a question, bringing certain perceptual fragments of the world to our notice and inviting our involvement with them (PP 216/PP 185). The point here is simply that the meaning of *parole* is not unidimensional, and no single understanding of meaning can account for the different ways in which it signifies. *Parole* does not signify by virtue of words in isolation from accent, tone, gesture and physiognomy but by all of these together (PP 176/PP 151), and this means that their signification always has a style (PP 212/PP 182) that is intermingled with the world and with perceptual meaningfulness. *Parole* is not a sign; it is a manifold of *sens* that responds, calls, expresses and interprets, and no one of these functions can be abstracted or stand by itself. This manifold of sense is present even in the most abstracted discourses, and like art, like all language, philosophy itself is expression, not only on the level of words, but in terms of 'cette mélodie hérisée de changements de clés, de pointes et de chutes' (PM 42–3);[53] its rhythms and tones are pregnant with meaning.

So we are no longer dealing with the problem of the genesis of *sens tout court*, for there is no pure facticity before the arrival or imposition of *sens*, but always already a sharing of meaning between body and world. It is now the question of the passage, within *logos*, from one 'sense' to another, the sublimation of one sense in another, the resonance of one sense with another. What remains is 'le problème du passage du sens perceptif au sens langagier, du comportement à la thématisation' (VI 227).[54] Nevertheless, this only accounts for the move from the inchoate to the specific, from relatively indeterminate to relatively determinate gestural meaning; it does not yet address the question of the relation of (the order recognised in) language and (the order perceived in) the world. For this we need to look more closely at the relation of call and response.

2.4 FROM SILENCE TO LANGUAGE

In his account of the primacy of language use (*parole*) Merleau-Ponty distinguishes two orders of speech: 'parole parlante',[55] in which signifying intention is in its nascent state, and 'parole parlée'[56] where speech takes up existing sedimented significations without innovation (PP 229).[57] The relation between 'operative' language ('parole parlante') and the world is one of call and response, 'ce langage-là qui ne peut se savoir que du dedans, par la pratique, est ouvert sur les choses, appelé par les voix du silence, et continue un essai d'articulation qui est l'Être de tout être' (VI 168).[58] The 'voices of silence' are formless ('gestaltlos'), or more precisely they have a conspicuous absence of determinate form in the bursting forth of the multiform pregnancy that solicits responsive expression. The silence of the perceived world is not the negation of language but primordial speech, a silent *logos*, and it is never fully surpassed or exhausted in speech. It is not silent in terms of a complete absence of signification, but like empirical pregnancy it is 'sans signification expresse et pourtant riche de sens' (VI 316).[59] Similarly, the silence of perception is exemplified in 'l'objet en fil de fer dont je ne saurais dire ce qu'il est, ni combien de côtés il a etc. et qui pourtant est là' (VI 322).[60]

There is no simple linear progression from (the voices of) silence to (the voice of) language, for silence can only be 'heard' in expression, in a dialectic relation in which 'le langage réalise en brisant le silence ce que le silence voulait et n'obtenait pas' (VI 227).[61] This is far removed from the transactional model of communication. The world silently announces itself as a pregnancy of meaningfulness, the to-be-said of 'une sourde présence qui éveille mes intentions sans se déployer devant elles' (S 145).[62] There is an 'ominal sense' (VI 289/VI 240) – from the Latin *omen*, meaning portent or presage – of experience,[63] and the language user is drawn on by the conviction that the sensible is a treasury full of things for the philosopher to speak (VI 300/VI 252). Language arises in the world, it is 'incrusté dans le visible et y tient sa place' (NC 212),[64] emerging from the Gestalt of body and world with the result that:

> fait et essence ne peuvent plus être distingués, non que, mélangés dans notre expérience, ils soient dans leur pureté inaccessibles et subsistent comme idées-limites au-delà d'elle, mais que l'Être n'étant plus *devant moi*, mais m'entourant et, en un sens, me traversant, ma vision de l'Être ne se faisant pas d'ailleurs, mais du milieu de l'Être, les prétendus faits, les individus spatio-temporels, sont d'emblée montées sur les axes, les pivots, les dimensions, la généralité de mon corps, et les idées donc déjà incrustées à ses jointures. (VI 151–2).[65]

Meaningfulness does not inhere in the world in the absence of any percipient but, in the terms of *Le Visible et l'invisible*, the flesh of the world, the flesh of the body and the flesh of language overlap and interpenetrate.

Should we speak of the call, then, as the 'origin' of language? This question remains unresolved in the work that death never allowed Merleau-Ponty to finish, but it is posed by Jean-Louis Chrétien at the opening of *L'Appel et la réponse*, a work which grapples, though from an overtly theologico-philosophical standpoint, with the same issues of meaning and contact which drive forward Merleau-Ponty's interrogation.[66] Just as Merleau-Ponty refuses any short route to the meaningfulness of experience via an appeal to immediate intuition, so too Chrétien does not allow for an unproblematic return to the 'origin' of the call, for 'nous n'entendons l'appel que dans la réponse, dans une voix par lui altérée, portant à la parole cette altération qui la donne à elle-même comme ne s'appartenant pas.'[67] The world signifies in the creative 'error', the deviation from a norm it disrupts. This is the sense in which the voice can give voice to what calls for its response.[68] The response by no means drowns out, totalises or recuperates the call. On the contrary, 'la parole . . . n'entend qu'en répondant.'[69] Nevertheless, we must not conclude from this intertwining of call and response that there is no innovation possible:

> Ce qui est premier ne résonne pour la première fois que dans notre réponse. L'appel silencieux de la parole, nous ne l'écoutons vraiment qu'en parlant. Et ce qui dans notre parole est originaire n'a rien de créateur, mais, recevant de l'initial son initiative, répond.[70]

There is no dichotomy of (passively) hearing and (actively) responding to the call. Chrétien further complicates the relation of call and response when he suggests that the call 'répond tout autant à ce qu'il appelle. Pour pouvoir inviter quelque chose ou quelqu'un à venir, il faut que déjà ils soient avenus . . . Nous ne pouvons inviter à venir que . . . ce qui appelle notre appel.'[71] Once more, the distinction between activity and passivity, finding and discovering meaning, is rendered problematic. Thinking that we encounter a call, it is already a response that we meet, and the call is neither a phenomenological given nor the foundation of the response. Chrétien explains this in the Merleau-Pontean language of 'l'entrelacs, dans la parole, de l'appel et de la réponse,'[72] developing Merleau-Ponty's idea of that which silence wished to say but could not. Contact is not achieved by looking *through* language to a 'reality' behind or beyond it, nor is it thwarted by the inability so to do. The call is not a call to return to a putative immediacy of signification, for 'la description n'est pas le retour à l'immédiat: on n'y revient pas. Il s'agit simplement de savoir si on se propose de le comprendre' (PrP 77).[73] This attempt to understand experience from within language is the whole problematic of Merleau-Ponty's excarnational philosophy. If Merleau-Ponty resists the philosophical inversion of taking the abstracted idea for the originary experience of the world, he is equally unaccommodating to any attempt that causes us to install pure sensation as an *archē* of experience and to believe that it precedes knowledge (PP 46–7/PP 37). Language is our element, just as water is the element of fishes (S 32/S 17); it is in the air between subjects, which they breathe, but never fully realised in any of them.

Martin Dillon's reading of the relation of language and world in Merleau-Ponty sits ill with these considerations. The question of language is, as Dillon rightly suggests, linked to the issue of foundations, but it is an issue which Dillon polarises by claiming that 'either language is founded on something prior to it which serves as its ground, origin, measure, and referent – or language refers only to itself and any appeal to a foundation which would serve as its ground, origin, or measure is an appeal to onto-theology.'[74] For Dillon, anything else but foundationalism leads to 'rhetorical noise and philosophical silence,' and 'there can be no grounds for espousing one viewpoint rather than another'[75] Quite apart from the opposition of rhetoric and philosophy here– surprising given Merleau-Ponty's own emphasis on rhythm and 'style' and his sustained interest in literary uses of language–it is simply not the case that Dillon's dichotomy of *either* external foundation *or* some sort of undefined relativism exhausts the options available for understanding Merleau-Ponty's delicate articulation of the relation of linguistic and worldly meaning. If perception always already stylises, if the most basic perception is not of an object but a figure on a ground, and if there is a sublimation of meaningful form in gesture and language, then it is quite consistent with Merleau-Ponty's notion of a worldly pregnancy of meaning to hold that 'la clarté du langage s'établit sur un fond obscur, et si nous poussons la recherche assez loin, nous trouverons finalement que le langage, lui aussi, ne dit rien que lui-même, ou que son sens n'est pas séparable de lui' (PP 219).[76] Language speaks only itself, but (and we need to be sensitive to the indirect, ungraspable sense of ontological diplopia here) in it we hear the rhythms and tones of the voices of silence.

Merleau-Ponty indeed holds that language does not conjure up a prelinguistic world, but this by no means leads to the conclusion that he can find no worldly grounds for espousing one viewpoint rather than another, as we shall see shortly. Nor is it to suggest that language is turned irreparably in on itself, for 'c'est l'erreur des philosophies sémantiques de fermer le langage comme s'il ne parlait que de soi: il ne vit que du silence' (VI 165).[77] Meaning is a matter of structures mutually shared (and mutually constituted) between the 'world' and the 'body', not a transaction of meaning beginning with one and ending with the other:

> Une chose n'est donc pas effectivement donnée dans la perception, elle est reprise intérieurement par nous, reconstituée et vécue par nous en tant qu'elle est liée à un monde dont nous portons avec nous les structures fondamentales et dont elle n'est qu'une des concrétions possibles. (PP 377)[78]

Here and elsewhere, Merleau-Ponty is at pains to stress that subject and world are not irreconcilably estranged but that the 'corps-sujet' (*Phénoménologie de la perception*) or the 'chair du corps' (*Le Visible et l'invisible*)[79] is *of* the world, and the world is 'ce en quoi nous sommes, elle est mélange, et non ce que nous contemplons de loin' (N 164).[80] In this context, Foucault's criticism of Merleau-Ponty,[81] that for him expression amounts (paying disproportionate heed to the term's etymology) to no more than *pressing out* the implicit, taking up the tacit meanings pre-inscribed in nature, misses the mark in the same way as does Dillon's *Semiological Reductionism*.[82] For Merleau-Ponty we neither 'press out' any meanings 'implicit' in nature, nor is discourse a practice we impose on things. Merleau-Ponty's theory of language is neither Derridean nor anti-Derridean, neither Foucauldian nor anti-Foucauldian, for it resists the dichotomies that govern their thought. It is otherwise than Derrida and otherwise than Foucault. Similarly, in the light of Merleau-Ponty's evocation of the voices of silence and the distinction between *logos endiathetos* and *logos proforikos*, Gary Madison goes too far in suggesting that Merleau-Ponty is arguing for acting *as if* there were pre-linguistic meaning, all the while knowing there is no such thing. Madison calls on Jean Hyppolite for what he terms an 'excellent way of formulating Merleau-Ponty's own problem':

> Everything happens as if there existed an immediate lived experience which it is a question of expressing, this expression being at once a discovery, in the etymological sense of the term, and an invention, since its expression has not yet been formulated.[83]

This will not do at all as a summary of Merleau-Ponty's thought on the relation of worldly and linguistic meaning though, for there is no 'as if' and no unproblematic 'immediate lived experience'. Perception is not in the mode of the 'as if', a decision to suspend disbelief, but in the mode of the interrogative, a commitment to the possibility of meaning in relation to which suspicion always already stands in relief.[84]

In contradistinction to Madison's reading, but equally short of the mark, is Douglas Low's characterisation of the difference between Merleau-Ponty and Derrida on the question of the pre-linguistic. 'For Merleau-Ponty,' suggests Low, 'perception . . . and language . . . refer to something beyond them that acts as their open-ended support. For Derrida there is no perception and signifiers refer only to other signifiers.'[85] He continues by suggesting that language and ideas are, for Merleau-Ponty, carried by existence, whereas for Derrida it is reversed: language is the vehicle for everything else. This characterisation does not capture the subtlety of Merleau-Ponty's intertwining of language and the world, however, for the meaningful order of the world is not 'beyond' language for Merleau-Ponty, and language carries the world as much as the world language. Further on, Low suggests that, 'unlike most postmodernists who disavow any connection with perception that carries its own meaning . . . Merleau-Ponty clearly finds a visual field replete with meanings – even if these meanings are not fully clear or "rational" in themselves,'[86] but it is not with 'meanings' that the world is 'replete' for Merleau-Ponty, rather it is *pregnant* with meaning*fulness*, with not-yet-meanings, with the to-be-said silence (different from a mere lack of clarity or rationality) of gesture and style.

Such accounts fail, each in their own way, to understand that what is called for in Merleau-Ponty's account is an *effort* of meaning, that 'il y a une Gestalt de la langue, il y a dans le présent vivant de l'exprimé et du non-exprimé, *il y a travail à faire*' (PM, 53; author's emphasis).[87] There is a work of expression irreducible either to the arbitrary 'invention' of meanings or to their 'discovery' in nature (and that Merleau-Ponty has been accused of both should alert us to the fact that, in his thought, something subtler than either is going on):

> Sentir, vivre, la vie sensorielle est comme un trésor, mais qui ne vaut encore rien tant qu'il n'y a pas eu travail, le travail ne consiste pas seulement d'ailleurs, à 'convertir en mots' le vécu; il s'agit de *faire parler* ce qui est senti. (P2 313)[88]

The 'work' that is required is no violent totalising of an ineffable reality, and reflection does not carry all before it but rather plunges into the world instead of dominating or surveying it (VI 60/VI 39–40). Yes, it is the voice of silence that is heard in language; yes, it is language that speaks. The world calls in its style, and this silent call is heard *in* a response that is nothing but language:

> Il s'agit seulement de rencontrer cette phrase déjà faite dans les limbes du langage, de capter les paroles sourdes que l'être murmure. (PM 11)[89]

Merleau-Ponty is not regressing here to a notion of a world labelled with ready-made sentences, for the speech of the world is dumb. What is 'already made in the limbs of language' is the possibility of innovative expression, the Gestalt-like dialectic of sedimentation and innovation that can respond to an encounter with the unheard-of. Even though the subject is thrust among objects, words still need to be found, to be worked:

> celui qui parle ou qui écrit est d'abord muet, tendu vers ce qu'il veut signifier, vers ce qu'il *va* dire, et . . . soudain le flot des mots vient au secours de ce silence, et en donne un équivalent si juste, si capable de rendre à l'écrivain lui-même sa pensée quand il l'aura oublié, qu'il faut croire qu'elle était déjà parlée dans l'envers du monde. (PM 11)[90]

Again, this is not the 'il faut croire' of acting *as if* the world were speaking, but it is through its sublimation in this work that the world can be approached, not by short-circuiting it with a claim of access to immediate experience. The weight of the 'il faut' is this: in all reasonableness we *must* believe that the voices of silence resonated with sense on the hitherside of the world. But this is no disappointing (because speculative) naivety on Merleau-Ponty's part. Glossing Bergson's claim of the futility of a return to the original given, Merleau-Ponty comments with a Ricœurean turn of phrase that 'cette naïveté, seconde, laborieuse, retrouvée, ne nous fond pas avec une réalité préalable, ne nous identifie pas avec la chose même, sans point de vue, sans symbole, sans perspective . . . l'intuition a besoin d'être comprise . . . Qu'y a-t-il au juste de vraiment intuitif dans l'intuition?' (EP 25).[91]

The fact that meaning is the result of a labour, that it is created, should not be taken to mean that it can be accounted for as *nothing but* this creation. Rather, 'l'être est ce qui exige de nous création *pour que nous en ayons l'expérience*' (VI 251; author's emphasis),[92] and although Being is never spoken directly but always laterally and obliquely, it is still spoken. Contact (as Merleau-Ponty understands it) and creation are by no means antithetical. In fact, 'l'art et la philosophie *ensemble* sont justement, non pas fabrications arbitraires dans l'univers du « spirituel » (de la « culture »), mais contact avec l'Être *justement en tant que créations*' (VI 248; author's emphasis),[93] and institution creates 'le devoir de recommencer autrement et de donner au passé, non pas une survie qui est la forme hypocrite de l'oubli, mais l'efficacité de la reprise ou de la « répétition » qui est la forme noble de la mémoire' (PM 96).[94]

The particular form taken by the 'creation' or 'work' in question is poetic, an expression of the sense of the world:

> les mots, les voyelles, les phonèmes sont autant de manières de chanter le monde et . . . ils sont destinés à représenter les objets, non pas, comme le croyait la théorie naïve des onomatopées, en raison d'une ressemblance objective, mais parce qu'ils en extraient et au sens propre du mot en expriment l'essence émotionnelle. (PP 218)[95]

David Michael Levin identifies 'singing the world' as the third of three moments in the call and response structure of expression, the first of which is attunement and the second conventional language use.[96] For Levin, 'singing the world' is 'a moment when, through radical phenomenological reflection, the ego, deliberately poetising, applies itself to the task of . . . attempting to retrieve a bodily felt sense of its originary attunement to the world and its originary rootedness in the earth.'[97] What Levin omits to say, however, is that this sequence of three moments can only ever be an abstracted reconstruction. Phenomenologically, Levin's second moment is primary, and the movement 'forwards' to the third moment is indistinguishable from a movement 'backwards' towards the first: the impulse to recover attunement simply is the same movement as the singing of the world, and the way to harken to the sense of the world is to pass by the creative work of expression.

Expressive language is self-effacing,[98] but this does not indicate that we have moved 'beyond' language, simply that the juxtaposition of words fades from view as the linguistic Gestalt begins to resonate. It rests on a distinction between direct and indirect language (the latter referring to language in a state of genesis and evoking the structure of sedimentation-innovation) that is not liable to be deconstructed because there is already a reciprocal contamination of the two elements, as we have seen above.

2.5 BEYOND THE QUESTION OF 'CONTACT'

Through an examination of Merleau-Ponty's account of meaning in perception and in language we have seen that the notion of empirical pregnancy does not amount to a claim that meaning can be read off the world, 'pressed out' from it or passively received from a world replete with meanings. It is not meanings that are in the world, but inchoate meaningfulness, and this meaningfulness is not a spirit inhabiting the world's matter but the very form, distribution or structure of the perceived world. Furthermore, we have seen that Merleau-Ponty's claim to worldly meaningfulness does not rely on the figure-ground relation being free of any cultural bias, creation or 'work' on the part of the percipient. For Merleau-Ponty perception and language do not claim to secure immediate contact with a putatively pre-linguistic or pre-cognitive nature, but with culturally sedimented accretions, as 'les significations disponibles, c'est-à-dire les actes d'expression antérieurs établissant entre les sujets parlants un monde commun auquel la parole actuelle et neuve se réfère comme le geste au monde sensible' (PP 217).[99] In expression, worldly meaning is not represented but sublimated. The form of the world is most certainly a creation of the subject, but in the creation something of the worldly dehiscent meaningfulness yet resonates.

In the same way that meaning as form, rhythm and tone is not 'in' the world as a soul might be thought to be 'in' the body, we have already misunderstood Merleau-Ponty if we pose the question in terms of 'meaning in the world'. Meaning is not in the world as opposed to outside it, but it is *of* the world, in the same way that the body is of the world, emerging in relief in its folds and ripples. It is the form of the world that is meaningful, not any isolated object within it, and the corporeo-ideality of the world cannot be atomised. This means that we must be careful to understand the question of 'contact' with the world not according to a model in which meaning is transacted, passing from the world to the subject over an abyss, but according to a mutuality of body and world, where meaning must be located 'everywhere and nowhere'.

This shift from reciprocity to mutuality also has important implications for the way Merleau-Ponty understands the question of alterity. As Rudi Visker rightly argues, the major problem for Merleau-Ponty is not with the other but with the ego. 'The problem of the other is a false problem,' he writes, 'since it supposes having solved what according to Merleau-Ponty has been the major difficulty, ever since the *Phenomenology of Perception*'.[100] Quoting Merleau-Ponty in *Phénoménologie de la perception* saying that 'une pensée qui se contenterait d'exister pour soi, hors des gênes de la parole et de la communication, aussitôt apparue tomberait à l'inconscience, ce qui revient à dire qu'elle n'existerait pas même pour soi' (PP 206),[101] Visker argues that the self-other relation is 'not to be thought as a relation between an I, already in full self-possession, and some Other whose alterity demands that he be granted both the status of an *alter* ego and an alter *ego*,' concluding that 'for such "I" to be there in the first place and at least in some sense to exist "for itself", it will have to grow out of the perception of the other.'[102] Merleau-Ponty thinks the relation of self and other primarily as a relation of mutuality, not of reciprocity; it is 'best encountered as an interaction between two or more people in which the lives of all participants are irretrievably altered'.[103]

Against the charge that mutuality risks eliding the alterity of the other, and to adumbrate a discussion which will come to the fore in the chapters on Ricœur and Nancy, we merely suggest here that in respecting the *otherness* of the other, Derrida risks not respecting the other at all. If 'tout autre est tout autre' means that 'every other is wholly other', the words can also and irreducibly be read to mean 'every other is every other', every other is as good as any other, said with a shrug of the shoulders. In Merleau-Ponty's own terms, in respecting the otherness of the other, the risk is that we are left with 'une hantise anonyme, sans visage, un autre en général' (VI 100).[104] We shall let Derrida answer this concern in the fourth chapter. For now, it opens up an important question on the road to understanding how our three writers think alterity *otherwise* than in terms of the violent appropriation that Derrida rightly deconstructs.

Moving on for now to consider Merleau-Ponty's account of language we saw that, because language and the world share a common style of dehiscent expressivity, language acts for Merleau-Ponty as a means by which the meaningfulness of the world is shared. The speaking 'I' is situated in/as its body and in/as its language 'non pas comme dans une prison, mais au contraire comme dans un appareil qui le transporte magiquement dans la perspective d'autrui' (PM 29).[105] There is a sharing ('partage') of speech ('parole'), and co-functioning is understood by Merleau-Ponty in terms of prosthesis,[106] where 'mon monde privé a cessé de n'être qu'à moi, c'est maintenant l'instrument dont un autre joue, la dimension d'une vie généralisée qui s'est greffée sur la mienne' (VI 26).[107] For Merleau-Ponty, communicability is not bought at the expense of a reductive violence. Rather, and with distinct fore-echoes of Ricœur's *Soi-même comme un autre*, 'à chaque instant, le langage me rappelle que, « monstre incompréhensible » dans le silence, je suis, au contraire, par la parole, mis en présence d'un autre moi-même' (PM 29).[108]

We then turned to examine the importance of the call/response relation in Merleau-Ponty's understanding of meaning. The world is not posited, its meanings indicatively self-present, but our ontological engagement is in the mode of the interrogative; we are solicited by the dehiscent meaningfulness of the world, not forced passively to receive certain pre-given meanings. Furthermore, the relation of call and response is not straightforward. The call is mute, and only heard resonating in the response. We saw the problems that can arise when language ceases to be a response to the call of the world but becomes an object of contemplation, problems which Merleau-Ponty's gestural account of language avoids.

These observations have been necessary in defending Merleau-Ponty's account of meaning against a Derrida who, while his concern for alterity and the avoidance of metaphysical violence is well placed, allows assumptions about the nature of language to prevent him from engaging fully with what Merleau-Ponty is saying about style and the figure-ground relation. They have also provided a response to the question with which we began: how can Merleau-Ponty justify his argument for empirical pregnancy faced with the haunting question 'How do you know?' To be sure we have arrived at no definitive answer; the only possible response of that sort would come in the form of establishing a position outside Merleau-Ponty's own thought from which to arbitrate his claim. To respond in this way, however, would be a regression to the foundationalism that it is precisely Merleau-Ponty's labour to avoid.

The Derridean call that haunts Merleau-Ponty's philosophy – 'How do you know?' – is the call to lay bare the unwritten law which undergirds the Merleau-Pontean privilege of coincidence over non-coincidence. But how? In terms of Merleau-Ponty's thought itself? That would be circular. In terms of Derrida's own thought? That does nothing but ventriloquise Merleau-Ponty. In terms of a third, disinterested position exterior to both? But where can we find such a divine and impartial standpoint? It is not clear what form any putative response to the question in its own terms might take, if there were such a thing. But perhaps, to reverse Chrétien's delicate interweaving, the response may be heard in the call itself.

This more productive response would be to consider once more (as we did in the first chapter) Derrida's articulation of his disquiet with Merleau-Ponty as, at the same time, a performance of what it is he is questioning. The question does not answer itself, but it does cause us to take a productive detour, for a response to the question cannot be thought independently of a response to the questioner. Simon Critchley sets out the interrelation as follows:

> In Stanley Cavell's terms, it is the very unknowability of the other, the irrefutability of scepticism, that initiates a relation to the other based on acknowledgment and respect. The other person stands in a relation to me that exceeds my cognitive powers, placing me in question and calling me to justify myself.[109]

The Derridean question may be the condition of impossibility of justifying Merleau-Ponty's claim to worldly meaningfulness, but it is also its condition of possibility, for it initiates a dialogue in which both the call to justification, and its response, appear. This is not a threat to phenomenology, for 'to the extent that phenomenology is about reactivation, going "back to the things themselves," phenomenology is precisely the overcoming of the distinction between the old and the "new," and thus a meditation on the very idea of "renewal." Critique is the force that keeps whatever *is* alive' and 'deconstruction . . . is not negative. Destabilisation is required for progress as well.'[110]

The question is a call to respond, a provocation, an invitation: 'justify yourself!' Here, it is what Stanley Cavell calls scepticism – and we are not intending to claim that Derrida can be characterised at all points as a sceptic; that would be to misunderstand the moment of radical affirmation in deconstruction and the constant call to responsibility for the other. So we must elaborate a response to the question 'how do you know?' by approaching it indirectly, as Merleau-Ponty approaches the ontological. We must not vainly attempt Sisyphus-like, to secure a place off limits to the question which, try as we may, sooner or later it will always succeed in haunting, but we must rather take the dynamic of the sceptical provocation itself as the impetus for a response. We must learn from the question as question and begin to think – in response to the appeal 'How do you *know*?' – not in terms of knowledge but in terms of the question as address.

This is a much more fruitful line of inquiry in pursuing the relation of deconstructive and phenomenological thought than seeking to bring 'what' they say into direct contact. Trying to make progress in terms of the latter, Monika Langer is not alone in her gloomy appraisal of the possibility of arbitrating between Merleau-Ponty and 'rival' philosophies, rejecting on principle the possibility of philosophical refutation: 'Merleau-Ponty's only recourse – as he readily acknowledges – is to endeavour to re-awaken his critics to their own experience and induce them to abandon their assumptions by disclosing the plethora of previously incomprehensible phenomena made accessible through his approach.'[111] Some, however, may deem Merleau-Ponty's accounts more unintelligible than those of his 'rivals', appealing perhaps to the plethora of metaphors (pregnancy, flesh, voices of silence . . .) on which his argument floats.

By contrast, in this chapter we have shown how Merleau-Ponty offers an account of meaning that has the flexibility to respond convincingly to Derridean questioning. His rejection of the dichotomy of 'natural' and 'conventional' signs in favour of a worldly split *logos* and a polysemy of meaning irreducible to meaning in general indicates that all language cannot be construed as inevitably violent, and Merleau-Ponty's ontology in the 'interrogative mode' and a dialectic of call and response mean that meaning is neither simply found in the world nor projected

68   *Phenomenology or Deconstruction?*

onto it by language, but sublimated in a work of expression that creates what it discovers. We must conclude that Derrida's questions are not terminal for phenomenological ontology, but they do mean that this ontology must be thought differently. However, in raising the issue of how Merleau-Ponty's philosophy might justify itself in the face of sceptical questioning of its ontological claims, we have begun to pursue the ontological question by appealing to an ontology of the person, arguing that this is the most fruitful way to engage Derrida's questions. We must now follow this through, but we cannot do so in terms of Merleau-Ponty's own tragically curtailed thought. We turn rather to the phenomenologist whose work on selfhood will allow us to explore the ontology of the person more adequately. We turn to Paul Ricœur.

NOTES

1. Hermann Rapaport, commenting on Merleau-Ponty's readings of Heidegger in the 1959 course notes 'La philosophie aujourd'hui' (NC 33–157) judges that: 'Surprisingly compatible with some of Derrida's later readings of Heidegger (Merleau-Ponty explores the notion of the *retrait*), it is, for that time, a remarkable reading that sets the stage, as it were, for a later generation of French Heideggerians of whom Derrida could be counted as one' (Rapaport, *Later Derrida* 145 n2).
2. Edie, *Merleau-Ponty's Philosophy of Language* 41.
3. 'To have the idea of "thinking" (in the sense of the "thought of seeing and of feeling"), to make the "reduction," to return to immanence and to the consciousness of . . . it is necessary to have words' (*VI* 171).
4. 'It is by considering language that we would best see how we are to and how we are not to return to the things themselves' (*VI* 125).
5. See Maurice Merleau-Ponty, *Notes de cours sur L'Origine de la géométrie de Husserl*; Bergo and Lawlor (eds), *Husserl at the Limits of Phenomenology*; Derrida, *Introduction à L'Origine de la géométrie de E. Husserl*.
6. Derrida, 'Force et signification', in *L'Écriture et la différence* 22; 'meaning must await being said or written in order to inhabit itself, and in order to become, by differing from itself, what it is: meaning. This is what Husserl teaches us to think in *The Origin of Geometry*. The literary act thus recovers its true power at its source. In a fragment of a book he intended to devote to *The Origin of Truth*, Merleau-Ponty wrote: "Communication in literature is not the simple appeal on the part of the writer to meanings which would be part of an a priori of the mind; rather, communication arouses these meanings in the mind through enticement and a kind of oblique action. The writer's thought does not control his language from without; the writer is himself like a kind of new idiom, constructing itself." "My own words take me by sur-

prise and teach me what I think," he said elsewhere' (*Writing and Difference* 11).
7. 'True Husserlian thought: man, world, language are interwoven, *verflochten*' (*HAL* 41).
8. Lawlor, *Thinking Through French Philosophy* 63.
9. Lawlor, *Thinking Through French Philosophy* 63.
10. 'On the Phenomenology of Language' (*S* 84–97).
11. 'it is as though the visibility that animates the sensible world were to emigrate, not outside of every body, but into another less heavy, more transparent body, as though it were to change flesh, abandoning the flesh of the body for that of language' (*VI* 153).
12. 'a tacit language . . . that painting speaks in its own way' (*S* 47; translation altered).
13. 'there is no doubt that language is the presumption to a total accumulation' (*S* 81).
14. 'Once language is formed, it is conceivable that speech may have meaning, like the gesture, against the mental background held in common . . . the clearness of language stands out from the obscure background' (*PP* 186–8).
15. 'we call speech our power of making use of certain conveniently organised things . . . to put in relief . . . the significations which trail on the horizon of the sensible world' (*PW* 143).
16. 'signification is only ever a tendency' (*VI* 94; translation altered).
17. 'Pour que quelque chose soit dite, il faut qu'elle ne soit jamais dite absolument' (*PM* 51–2); 'for something to be said, it must not be said absolutely' (*PW* 36).
18. See Derrida, *Introduction à L'Origine de la géométrie de E. Husserl* 69; *Edmund Husserl's Origin of Geometry: An Introduction* 75.
19. 'philosophy is not a lexicon, it is not concerned with "word-meanings," it does not seek a verbal substitute for the world we see, it does not transform it into something said, it does not install itself in the order of the said or of the written as does the logician in the proposition, the poet in the word, or the musician in the music. It is the things themselves, from the depths of their silence, which it wishes to bring to expression' (*VI* 4).
20. For Saussure, a sign is constituted by a concept and sound-image (*Course in General Linguistics* 66), but for Merleau-Ponty there is a level of phonological meaning in language whose very existence such intellectualism does not suspect (see *PP* 179/*PP* 153).
21. 'there are only words into which the history of a whole language is compressed, and which effect communication with no absolute guarantee, dogged as they are by incredible linguistic hazards' (*PP* 188).
22. Derrida, *Positions* 29; 'Now, "everyday language" is not innocent or neutral. It is the language of western metaphysics, and it carries with it not only a considerable number of presuppositions of all types, but also

presuppositions inseparable from metaphysics, which, although little attended to, are knotted into a system' (*Positions* 19).
23. 'When I am actually speaking I do not first *figure* the *movements* involved. My whole bodily system concentrates on finding and saying the word, in the same way that my hand moves of itself toward what is offered to me' (*PW* 19; translation altered).
24. 'gestures . . . are not accomplished without some negligence' (*PW* 116).
25. 'hides from anyone who seeks it and surrenders to anyone who had renounced it' (*PW* 116; translation altered).
26. 'the spoken word (the one I utter or the one I hear) is pregnant with meaning which can be read in the very texture of the linguistic gesture (to the point that a hesitation, an alteration of the voice, or the choice of a certain syntax suffices to modify it), and yet is never contained in that gesture, every expression always appearing to me as a trace, no idea being given to me except in transparency, and every attempt to close our hand on the thought which dwells in the spoken word leaving only a bit of verbal material in our fingers' (*S* 89).
27. Stewart, *Beyond the Symbol Model* 176.
28. Dillon, *Semiological Reductionism* 180.
29. Dillon, *Semiological Reductionism* 185.
30. 'whatever truth we may well have is to be gotten not in spite of but through our historical inherence. Superficially considered, our inherence destroys all truth; considered radically, it founds a new idea of truth' (*S* 109).
31. 'It is impossible to superimpose on man an initial layer of behaviour which one chooses to call "natural", followed by a manufactured cultural or spiritual world. Everything is both manufactured and natural in man, as it were, in the sense that there is not a word, not a form of behaviour which does not owe something to purely biological being – and which at the same time does not elude the simplicity of animal life' (*PP* 189; translation altered).
32. Proust, *À la recherche du temps perdu I* 236–7; *Swann's Way* 612.
33. 'The pregnancy is what, in the visible, requires of me a correct focusing, defines its correctness. My body obeys the pregnancy, it "responds" to it, it is what is suspended on it, flesh responding to flesh' (*VI* 209).
34. 'Show that these notions [pregnancy, Gestalt, phenomenon] represent a getting into contact with being as pure *there is*. One witnesses that event by which there is something. Something rather than nothing and this rather than something else. One therefore witnesses the advent of the positive: this rather than something else' (*VI* 206).
35. 'the proper mode of our relationship with Being' (*VI* 129).
36. This point is well made by Marcel Gauchet, 'Le lieu de la pensée' 29 n30.
37. Interrogation runs the risk of what Waldenfels calls 'interrogativism', an indefinite reiteration of the question, which dogmatically rejects any answer and thereby establishes itself in an absolute and counter-interrogative way.

Maurice Merleau-Ponty: Language

(See Francesco Colli, 'Nell'imminenza della riposta: la responsabilità dell'interrogazione filosofica nell'ultimo Merleau-Ponty' 449).
38. Silverman, *Textualities* 35.
39. Silverman, *Textualities* 36.
40. Blanchot, 'Le « Discours Philosophique »' 3; 'The philosopher seeks a compromise in maintaining his manifest discourse (so that he does not overly betray the latent or clandestine discourse) in an interrogative position: to question, to seek, are to exclude oneself from the privileges of affirmative – or established – language, to speak beyond the spoken word, open it and keep it suspended; the language of interrogation, nonetheless capable of turning inquisitor in its turn, with its technique, its quasi-institutional habits, its elegance and always anticipating a response; this is the only way it can continue' (author's translation).
41. Wood, *The Step Back* 2.
42. This crucial aspect of deconstruction will be discussed at length in the chapters that follow.
43. Silverman, *Textualities* 41.
44. This notion of attunement is remarkably similar to Jean-Luc Nancy's evocation in *Allitérations* of the rhythmical resonance that establishes contact between two dancers before propositional meaning: 'L'autre, là-bas, proche dans son éloignement, tendu, plié, déplié, retentit dans mes jointures. Je ne le perçois proprement ni par les yeux, ni par l'ouïe, ni par le toucher. Je ne perçois pas, je résonne' (All 139); 'The other, over there, near in his distancing, taut, bending, unbending, resounds in my joints. I do not really perceive it with my eyes, nor hearing, nor touch. I do not perceive it, I resonate' (author's translation). We will have occasion to return to this resemblance in our discussion of Nancy.
45. 'their recurrence, the way they associate with one another, evoke or repel one another, and together make up a melody with a definite style' (*PW* 32).
46. 'Between language, a sum of words, and thought, a layer of meanings inserts itself which supposes a certain relation to it. It is this type of thinking in language, not explicit, that constitutes *style*' (author's translation).
47. 'All of language is mind; it is not a verbal melody, which supposes no intellectual vigilance. But the mind that governs language is not the mind per se, it is paradoxically a mind which possesses itself only by losing itself in language' (author's translation).
48. As such, it bears resemblances to the Aristotelian notion of the soul as the 'form' of the body. Once more, and underlining the resonances between them, Nancy will make explicit reference to this notion (All 116).
49. Also 'logos du monde esthétique', 'logos silencieux', or 'logos sauvage', or 'logos perceptif' (*logos* of the aesthetic world, silent *logos*, wild *logos*, perceptual *logos*) in *Phénoménologie de la perception*.
50. 'contains no mode of expression and which nonetheless calls them forth' (*VI* 120). Marc Richir makes a similar division in the *logos* with his evocation of the *logos* 'en blanc' (blank *logos*), which is 'une sorte de

"*musique sans sons*" ou de langage sans traces matérielles . . . une sorte de pur mouvement rythmique' (Richir, *Phénomènes, temps et êtres* 329); 'a sort of "music without sounds" or language without material traces . . . a sort of pure rhythmic movement' (author's translation). Like Merleau-Ponty's 'empirical pregnancy,' *logos* 'en blanc' is the transcendental phenomenological matrix of all concrete language, which constitutes the phenomenological horizon of language, *a priori* indeterminate and indefinitely determinable.

51. 'If we consider only the conceptual and delimiting meaning of words, it is true that the verbal form – with the exception of endings – appears arbitrary. But it would no longer appear so if we took into account the emotional content of the world, which we have called above its "gestural" sense, which is all-important in poetry, for example. It would then be found that the words, vowels and phonemes are so many ways of "singing" the world and that their function is to represent things not, as the naïve, onomatopeic theory had it, by reason of an objective resemblance, but because they extract, and literally squeeze out their emotional essence' (*PP* 187; translation altered).
52. 'The predominance of vowels in one language, or of consonants in another, and constructional and syntactical systems, would not represent so many arbitrary conventions for the expression of one and the same idea, but several ways for the human body to sing the world's praises and in the last resort to live it' (*PP* 187).
53. 'this melody bristling with changes of key, with rises and falls' (*PW* 30; translation altered).
54. 'the problem of the passage from perceptual meaning to linguistic meaning, from behavior to thematisation' (*VI* 176; translation altered).
55. Also 'parole opérante'/'operative word' (*VI* 199/*VI* 154), 'parole originaire'/'originary speech' (*HAL* 56/*HAL* 85), 'parole instituante'/'instituting speech' (*PM* 170/*PW* 121) or 'parole conquérante'/'conquering speech' (*PM* 196/*PW* 141).
56. Also 'parole secondaire'/'secondary speech' (*HAL* 56/*HAL* 85 n120), 'parole empirique, ontique'/'empirical, ontic speech' (*HAL* 57/*HAL* 46) or 'parole instituée'/'speech as an "institution"' (*PP* 214/*PP* 184). For further explanation of these distinctions, see Lawlor, '*Verflechtung*: The Triple Significance of Merleau-Ponty's Course Notes on Husserl's *The Origin of Geometry*' xxxvi n33.
57. 'significant intention is at the state of coming to being' (*PP* 197). In his translation of Phénoménologie de la perception Colin Smith renders 'parole parlante' as 'the word in the speaking' and 'parole parlée' as 'the spoken word'.
58. 'that language that can be known only from within, through its exercise, is open upon the things, called forth by the voices of silence, and continues an effort of articulation which is the Being of every being' (*VI* 126–7).
59. 'without express signification and yet rich in meaning' (*VI* 268).

60. 'the object made of wires of which I could not say what it is, nor how many sides it has, etc. and which nonetheless is there' (*VI* 268).
61. 'language realises, by breaking the silence, what the silence wished and did not obtain' (*VI* 176).
62. 'a mute presence which awakens my intentions without deploying itself before them' (*S* 89).
63. See Bernhard Waldenfels, 'Vérité à faire: Merleau-Ponty's Question Concerning Truth'.
64. 'encrusted in the visible and has its place there' (author's translation).
65. 'Fact and essence can no longer be distinguished, not because, mixed up in our experience, they in their purity would be inaccessible and would subsist as limit-ideas beyond our experience, but because – Being no longer being *before me*, but surrounding me and in a sense traversing me, and my vision of Being not forming itself from elsewhere, but from the midst of Being – the alleged facts, the spatio-temporal individuals, are from the first mounted on the axes, the pivots, the dimensions, the generality of my body, and the ideas are therefore already encrusted in its joints' (*VI* 114).
66. Chrétien, *L'Appel et la réponse* 25; *The Call and the Response* 15.
67. Chrétien, *L'Appel et la réponse* 38; 'We hear the call only in the answer, in a voice that has been altered by it, which utters the very alteration that gives it to itself as not belonging to itself' (*The Call and the Response* 27).
68. See Chrétien, *L'Appel et la réponse* 58.
69. Chrétien, *L'Appel et la réponse* 9; 'speech . . . hears only by responding' (*The Call and the Response*, 1).
70. Chrétien, *L'Appel et la réponse* 16; 'That which is first resonates for the first time in our response. We listen to the silent call of Saying only when we speak. And that which in our speech is originary is devoid of creativity: rather, receiving its initiative from the Initial, it answers' (*The Call and the Response* 6).
71. Chrétien, *L'Appel et la réponse* 15; 'It [the call: CW] also . . . responds to what it calls. The power to invite something or someone to come forth presupposes that they have already come forth. . . . We can only beckon to ourselves . . . what calls upon us to call' (*The Call and the Response* 5).
72. Chrétien, *L'Appel et la réponse* 11; 'mutual intertwining, within speech, of call and response' (*The Call and the Response* 3; translation altered).
73. 'description is not the return to immediate experience; one never returns to immediate experience. It is only a question of whether we are to set about understanding it' (*PrP* 30; translation altered).
74. Dillon, *Semiological Reductionism* 177.
75. Dillon, *Semiological Reductionism* 178.
76. 'the brightness of language stands out from a dull background, and if we carry our research far enough we shall eventually find that language is equally uncommunicative of anything other than itself, and that its meaning is inseparable from it' (*PP* 188; translation altered).

77. 'It is the error of the semantic philosophies to close up language as if it spoke only of itself: language lives only from silence' (*VI* 126).
78. 'A thing is, therefore, not actually *given* in perception, it is internally taken up by us, reconstituted and experienced by us in so far as it is bound up with a world, the basic structures of which we carry with us, and of which it is merely one of the many possible concrete forms' (*PP* 326).
79. 'body-subject' (*PP*) and 'flesh of the body' (*VI*).
80. 'that in which we are, it is a mixture, and not what we contemplate from a distance' (*N* 121).
81. See Foucault, 'Theatricum Philosophicum'.
82. Merleau-Ponty indeed can at times sound most Foucauldian: 'L'homme est une idée historique et non pas une espèce naturelle' (PP 199); 'Man is a historical idea and not a natural species' (*PP* 170).
83. Madison, *The Phenomenology of Merleau-Ponty* 139. Madison is quoting Jean Hyppolite, *Études sur Marx et Hegel* 188.
84. We will deal more adequately with the themes of commitment and suspicion in the chapters on Ricœur.
85. Douglas Beck Low, *Merleau-Ponty's Last Vision* 18.
86. Low, *Merleau-Ponty's Last Vision* 66.
87. 'there is a Gestalt of language, in the living present there is something of the expressed and nonexpressed; *there is work to do*' (*PW* 37; author's emphasis).
88. 'Sensing, living, the sensory life is like a treasure, but still has no value as long as there has been no work, work which does not merely consist in converting lived experience into words; what is felt must be *made to speak*' (author's translation).
89. 'All that is required is to meet the phrase ready made in the limbs of language, to capture the muted language in which being murmurs to us' (*PW* 6; translation altered).
90. 'the writer or speaker is at first mute, straining toward what he wants to convey, toward what he is *going to say*. Then suddenly a flood of words comes to save this muteness and gives it an equivalent so exact and so capable of yielding the writer's own thought to him when he may have forgotten it, that one can only believe that the thought had already been expressed on the underside of the world' (*PW* 6; translation altered).
91. 'this secondary, laborious rediscovered naiveté does not merge us with a previous reality, does not identify us with the thing itself, without any point of view, without symbol, without perspective . . . intuition needs to be understood . . . what precisely is intuitive in intuition?' (*IPP* 18).
92. 'Being is what requires creation of us for us to experience it' (*VI* 197).
93. 'art and philosophy together are precisely not arbitrary fabrications in the universe of the "spiritual" (of "culture"), but contact with Being *precisely as creations*' (*VI* 197; author's emphasis).

94. 'the duty to start over again and to give to the past, not survival, which is the hypocritical form of forgetfulness, but the efficacy of renewal or "repetition", which is the noble form of memory' (*PW* 68).
95. 'the words, vowels and phonemes are so many ways of "singing" the world and . . . their function is to represent things not, as the naïve, onomatopeic theory had it, by reason of an objective resemblance, but because they extract, and literally express their emotional essence' (*PP* 187).
96. Levin, 'Singing the World' 319–36.
97. Levin, 'Singing the World' 327.
98. 'Or, c'est bien un résultat du langage de se faire oublier, dans la mesure où il réussit à exprimer' (PM 15); 'Now, one of the effects of language is to efface itself to the extent that its expression comes across' (*PW* 9).
99. 'Available meanings, in other words former acts of expression, establish between speaking subjects a common world, to which the words being actually uttered in their novelty refer as does the gesture to the perceptible world' (*PP* 186).
100. Visker, *Truth and Singularity* 188.
101. 'a thought limited to existing for itself, independent of the constraints of speech and communication, would no sooner appear than it would sink into the unconscious, which means that it would not exist even for itself' (*PP* 177).
102. Visker, *Truth and Singularity* 188.
103. Reynolds, *Merleau-Ponty and Derrida* 171.
104. 'the other an anonymous, faceless obsession, an other in general' (*VI* 72).
105. 'Rather than imprisoning it, language is like a magic machine for transporting the "I" into the other person's perspective' (*PW* 19).
106. The prosthetic will become a major feature of Nancy's thinking of the body, or *corpus*. See Chapters 5 and 6.
107. 'my private world has ceased to be mine only; it is now the instrument which another plays, the dimension of a generalised life which has grafted itself onto my own' (*VI* 11; translation altered).
108. 'language continuously reminds me that the "incomprehensible monster" that I am when I am silent can, through speech, be brought into the presence of *another myself*' (*PW* 19).
109. Critchley and Mouffe, *Deconstruction and Pragmatism* 32.
110. Wood, *The Step Back* 132.
111. Langer, *Merleau-Ponty's Phenomenology of Perception: A Guide and Commentary* 168.

3. *Paul Ricœur: Selfhood*

> Language most shows a man. Speak, that I may see thee.
>
> Ben Johnson, *Timber*

In the previous two chapters we began to explore how phenomenology might respond to the questions put to it by deconstruction in a way which neither rebuts nor embraces them, but searches within itself for the means to think beyond itself, or at least beyond its hitherto perceived limits and shortcomings. Specifically, we have seen that Merleau-Ponty's ontology, whether elaborated in terms of perception or language, is interrogative and indirect, and as such does not fully fall under the Derridean umbrella of 'le plein de présence immédiate requis par toute ontologie ou par toute métaphysique.'[1] Meaning is not given in Merleau-Ponty's philosophy, arising as it does in an inextricable mutuality of world and body, call and response, perception and expression. However, in the process of recasting the issue of the ontological in an 'interrogative mode' and framing the question of alterity not in terms of reciprocity but in terms of mutuality, the question of the ontology of the person has emerged as a privileged line of inquiry, and in order to explore this further we shall engage the help of Paul Ricœur.

No one has approached the question of selfhood from a phenomenological point of view with more care and incisiveness than Ricœur, and in this chapter we shall see how he responds to the question of selfhood by insisting that the relation of 'life' and 'narrative' must be neither collapsed nor dichotomised. This will lead us to explore how the combination of a 'polysemy of being' and the self as attested, not posited, mean that Ricœur's thought is sensitive to deconstructive concerns, while still maintaining a certain resistance to deconstructive questioning.

Ricœur's work owes a great debt to Merleau-Ponty – whom in *Le Conflit des interprétations* he eulogises as the greatest of the French phenomenologists (CI 243/CI 261) – while it also departs from Merleau-Ponty in a pronounced hermeneutical direction. In the second chapter we noted Merleau-Ponty's move in his later writing towards giving greater weight to the task of interpretation as he identified ever more closely the ontological and the linguistic, and this move is confirmed in Ricœur's work by what he comes to call the graft of the hermeneutic problem onto the phenomenological method (CI 7/CI 3). Ricœur seeks, through this 'graft', to illuminate the meaning of existence, a sense which would express the renewal of phenomenology through hermeneutics (CI 7/CI 3). The manner of existing yielded by this hermeneutics is from start to finish a being-interpreted (CI 15/CI 11).

It will also become clear that Ricœur's approach to ontological questions is vanishingly close to Derrida's at many points, despite the profound differences that separate heremeneutic phenomenology from deconstruction. The two philosophies entertain what Ricœur himself called 'a very complex kind of relationship, between men who are very different and yet very close.'[2] In addition to this clarification we will continue to elaborate, through Ricœur, an ontology *otherwise*, an ontology that does not require the fullness of presence that Derrida needs and cannot have.

3.1 FRAGMENTS

Ricœur's ontology, like Merleau-Ponty's, is indirect, characterised by the motif of the 'long détour' (long detour)[3] which challenges the claim of the early Husserl to seek a scientific, presuppositionless philosophy.

Like Merleau-Ponty's ontology in the interrogative mode, Ricœur raises the ontological question only to postpone any definitive response. His ontology of comprehension (as opposed to an ontology explanation, following the Diltheyan distinction) 'ne saurait être, pour nous qui procédons indirectement et par degrés, qu'un horizon, c'est-à-dire une visée, plus qu'une donnée' (CI 23).[4] In fact, the ontological for Ricœur is cast in the motif of a utopia, a promised land that the philosopher, like Moses, approaches but does not enter (CI 28/CI 24).

Nevertheless, it is a mistake to understand this approach as an inexorably asymptotic approximation to being. On the contrary, as Ricœur explains in an interview with Tamás Tóth, 'most of the Socratic dialogues do not reach the dénouement: as the multiplication of Cézanne's paintings pushes the "object that must be painted" further and further away, the "thing that must be told" becomes more and more distant by the multitude of dialogic approaches.'[5] Nevertheless, this should not be taken to imply that Ricœur's thought resolves to the anti-ontological pole of a dichotomous 'all or nothing' understanding of being, for an implied or truncated ontology is still an ontology (CI 23/CI 19).

Of all the hermeneutic 'detours' which Ricœur takes, it is the elaboration of the four 'objectivities of being' in *Soi-même comme un autre* that will detain us here. In this text, Ricœur seeks to develop a 'hermeneutics of the self' in terms of a fourfold detour via the question 'who?': Who is speaking? Who is acting? Who is recounting about himself or herself? Who is the moral subject of imputation? (SCA 28/OA 16). These four 'objectivities of being' provide the structure of the ten studies which comprise *Soi-même comme un autre*, each of the four corresponding to a different discourse: discursive (studies one and two), practical (studies three and four), narrative (studies five and six) and prescriptive (studies seven to nine), with the final study asking the question 'Which ontology in view?' Like Merleau-Ponty's being in the interrogative mode, the question form is significant in Ricœur's formulation of the four objectivities, for it avoids both the dogmatism of the indicative and the withdrawal of suspension, instead issuing a call and inviting a response.

Ricœur resists an all-too-easy amalgam of the four 'who?' questions, insisting on 'la méthode fragmentaire qui a été constamment la nôtre' (SCA 345)[6] and acknowledging an ultimately irreducible heterogeneity. If the four objectivities of being are not unproblematically unifiable, however, then neither are they incommensurable, for 'cette fragmentation n'est pas telle que nulle *unité thématique* ne la garde de sa dissémination qui reconduirait le discours au silence. En un sens, on peut dire que l'ensemble de ces études a pour unité thématique *l'agir humain*' (SCA 31; PR's emphasis).[7] Ricœur is not suggesting that a detour via the objectivities of being is a temporary stage on the way to arriving, fully and finally, at an integrated and stable subjectivity. Indeed, the 'human action' to which he makes reference here, adopting the Merleau-Pontean motif of the 'I can' (as opposed to the 'I think') is often misunderstood as a claim to unreconstructed subjectivity. It is nothing of the sort, either for Merleau-Ponty or for Ricœur. The 'I' of the Merleau-Pontean 'I can' is no subject and is always inextricable from an irreducible anonymity. As Renaud Barbaras notes, there is always 'one' ('on') in the 'I' ('je').[8] As for Ricœur, the 'unity' of action by no means recuperates the fragmentation of the self among the objectivities of being, as we shall see below when we discuss the polysemy of being.

Borrowing a term first employed in *Temps et récit 1* in relation to the tensional and fragile coherence of narrative *muthos*, Ricœur describes the relation between the objectivities of being as a 'concordance discordante' ('discordant concord'), a tension of dispersal and gathering (SCA 169/OA 142) in which neither concord nor discord cancels out the other. A personal narrative identity is found 'à la croisée de la cohérence que confère la mise en intrigue et de la discordance suscitée par les péripéties de l'action racontée' (PR 153),[9] a fragile balance between the possession and the dispossession of the self.[10] The art of narrative composition – and a fortiori Ricœur's hermeneutics of the self that takes the detour via narrative ('who is recounting?') and is inextricably intertwined in stories[11] – appears as a mediation between the time that passes and slips away, and the form that lasts and remains. The peripeteia figures as a threat to that order, like a crisis of configuration (CRR 136). But 'threat' and 'crisis' do not amount to destruction or overcoming, and we are bound to misunderstand Ricœur's philosophy if we unbalance this fragile tension in either direction.

As this tensional characterisation in terms of 'form' and 'configuration' indicates, the problems raised by Ricœur's hermeneutics of the self are not to be framed in terms of a binary of existence and non-existence, but as a tension of order and disorder. David Wood captures well the dynamic stability of the relation when, in *The Step Back*, he observes that Ricœur 'leaves us with a vision of peace marked by the possibility of ineliminable conflict.'[12] In other words, the notion of selfhood that Ricœur is elaborating through the uneasy tension of the four objectivities of being is not static. It is a dialectic of two modes of identity: identity as sameness in permanence through time (*idem* identity) and identity as selfhood in self-constancy through time (*ipse* identity).

Elaborating the notion of permanence through time using the example of the genetic code, Ricœur notes 'ce qui demeure ici, c'est l'organisation d'un système combinatoire' (SCA 142).[13] It is important to note here that even *idem* identity (constancy over time) is not monolithic and static. It betokens a configurational identity, a constellation of relations that recalls Merleau-Ponty's cosmology of the visible and not an atomistic, irreducible unity of substance. *Ipse* identity – characterised by self-constancy ('le maintien de soi' – SCA 143/OA 165), the making and keeping of promises through time in spite of a lack of permanence through time – will be considered more fully in the second half of this chapter, but it suffices to note here that what is at stake is the possibility of identity emerging (not unproblematically) from the non-self-coincident, from an intertwining of presence and absence. *Ipse* identity must be understood in terms of action and ethics, and so we need to enlarge the scope of the interrogative that enquires after it. While self-identity as sameness (*idem*) can be adequately interrogated with the question 'What?', self-identity of selfhood (*ipseity*) only makes sense as response to the question 'Who?'

The claim that Ricœur makes in *Soi-même comme un autre* is that the narrative operation reconciles identity and diversity, the same categories that Locke took as contraries (SCA 170/OA 143). With *ipse* identity (as with Merleau-Ponty's *phénomène-enveloppe* and equally in his understanding of linguistic meaning) punctual self-presence is not the all-important criterion of identity, and identity itself is not something to be grasped or contemplated: 'dans une philosophie de l'ipséité comme la nôtre, on doit pouvoir dire: la possession n'est pas ce qui compte' (SCA 198).[14] What does matter is the capacity to make and keep promises over time. This has important consequences for our understanding of the relation of Ricœur's thought to Derridean deconstruction. Any disagreement between Ricœur and Derrida at this point is not on the question of multiple or fragmented subjectivities, for both acknowledge a fragmented subject. The question is not 'does the self exist?' but 'does the self cohere?' In '« Il faut bien manger »',[15] Derrida offers fragmented readings of the Heideggerean 'wer?' ('who?') that remain irreconcilable with each other, while the 'who' itself is the singularity that cannot be captured in any form of subjectivity. This fragmentation is by no means a destruction of the subject, however, as Derrida is at pains to point out, emphasising that, 'le sujet est peut-être réinterprété, restitué, réinscrit, il n'est certainement pas « liquidé ». La question « qui ? », notamment chez Nietzsche, y insiste avec beaucoup plus de force.'[16] For Derrida himself, the emphasis on the 'who?' is framed in a way more resistant to ontological discourse:

> For me the great question is always the question who. Call it biographical, autobiographical or existential, the *form* of the question who is what matters to me.[17]

It is through this focus on the *form* of the question who, similar as it is to Ricœur's (and Merleau-Ponty's) preoccupation with configuration and order, that Derrida avoids having to give any determinate content to subjectivity. It is one of a number of instances (we will encounter more in this chapter and the next) where Ricœur and Derrida use similar language in the service of strikingly divergent ends. The question 'who?' ensures for Derrida that 'le rapport à soi ne peut être, dans cette situation, que de différance, c'est-à-dire d'altérité ou de trace.'[18] If for Derrida the subject is dispersed or thrown[19] in language, then also for Ricœur subjectivity is irreducibly linguistic. In *Parcours de la reconnaissance* Ricœur returns to the motif of entanglement in stories, emphasising that, according to Wilhelm Schapp, this entanglement is not secondary, but the principle experience of self-identity (PR 156/COR 104), and it is the identity of the story that makes the identity of the character (SCA 175/OA 148). Furthermore, Derrida agrees with Ricœur that if the subject is storied it is not, for that reason, to be dismissed: 'Le sujet est une fable, tu l'as très bien montré, et ce n'est pas cesser de le prendre au sérieux (il est le sérieux même) que de s'intéresser à ce qu'une telle fable suppose de parole et de fiction *convenue*'.[20] The terms in which Ricœur and Derrida think the self are overwhelmingly similar, but the two understandings of selfhood that emerge are profoundly dissimilar.[21] Both agree that the language in which the subject is fragmented provides no stable identity. The self is not determined in terms of any one discourse, nor exhaustively determined by any number of discourses, and the self as such cannot be named. There is no wedge to be driven between Ricœur and Derrida in terms of the plurivocity of linguistic determinations of subjectivity. The question dividing hermeneutic phenomenology from deconstruction at this point is: on what basis can we claim that the fragments of subjectivity cohere? There are at least three responses that can be made from Ricœur's work.

The first response returns us to the 'call-interrogation' structure so crucial to Merleau-Ponty's ontology. Narrative does not supervene upon an ineffable flux of life violently and *ex nihilo*; it is implicated in a structure of call and response with human action, which constitues a delineated pattern that has to be interpreted according to its inner connections (TA 123/TA 151). The dehiscent notion of being-demanding-to-be-said ('être-à-dire' – echoing the 'to-be-interpreted' that we saw in Merleau-Ponty's thought) appears as early as Ricœur's 1965 'De l'Interprétation' (TA 38/TA 19), and in *Temps et récit 1* Ricœur stresses that an understanding of action must go as far as to recognise in action temporal structures that *call for* narration (TR1 117–18/TN1 59). As we saw with Merleau-Ponty's notions of empirical pregnancy and the voices of silence, the dichotomy of 'action' and 'narrative', of the lived and the expressed, is undermined by the relation of call and response. Discourse does not come about for its own sake (TA 38/TA 19); it wants to bring to language an experience, a way of being in the world, a possible world for the unfolding of one's ownmost possibilities. Action becomes fully action in being supplemented by narrative, and without the call of action or life there would be no narrative. Like world and meaning in Merleau-Ponty's phenomenology of perception, life and narrative mutually encroach upon each other; they are inextricably intertwined, not irreconcilably sundered. Again, and echoing Merleau-Ponty's metaphor of pregnancy, Ricœur claims that life is 'a story in its nascent state' (LQN 29), an inchoate story in the mode of the to-be-told. As in the case of Merleau-Ponty, this does not amount to ready-made meaning or to a univocity of meaning, but to a surplus of meaningfulness that calls forth a creative work of interpretation.

There is an irreducible plurality in Ricœur's narrative identity which does not *impose* beginning, middle and end on an irreducible flux of events. In a manner reminiscent of Merleau-Ponty's figure/ground structure of perception with its 'prégnance de possibles, *Weltmöglichkeit*' (VI 298),[22] for Ricœur 'le dicible' ('the sayable') is in relief against the background of the unsayable from which it arises (DC 66). It is important therefore to realise that the mutual implication of life and narrative does not amount to a claim that life is rational, or that it can be captured without remainder in narrative forms. Ricœur is careful to make the distinction between intelligibility and rationality, and though the world may be intelligible, it is by no means rational:

> J'insiste sur cette différence entre intelligibilité et rationalité. La négliger condamne à refuser au récit toute place dans l'échelle du savoir et à réserver aux seules constructions du narratologue en critique littéraire et de l'historien dans les sciences humaines une dignité épistémologique. (CRR 137)[23]

As we saw in the case of Merleau-Ponty, Ricœur substantiates the claim that the world is meaningful by discerning distinctions in the notion of meaning: not all sense is of the same nature, nor does it all signify in the same way. He too resists Derrida's move of evoking sense 'in general'. This allows Ricœur, once more with echoes of Merleau-Ponty, to split the horns of a troubling dichotomy. It is erroneous to criticise Ricœur's account of the relation of action and narrative as 'referring to a non-linguistic element as if this notion were immediately self-evident,'[24] for 'action' is not a-figurative but (in terms of Ricœur's famous threefold understanding of mimesis in the *Temps et récit* trilogy) *pre*-figurative, being-demanding-to-be-said, not being already said, and the laborious detours of the hermeneutics of selfhood surely imply that existence is not 'immediately self-evident'. With Ricœur, as with Merleau-Ponty, there is a work of expression to be done. Once more, the relation of call and response is irreducible to the dichotomy of being and nothingness, or to a pre-linguistic flux upon which language supervenes and which it construes as rational. Considered in this light, it amounts to a philosophical 'have you stopped beating your wife?' to judge Ricœur's argument according to whether it 'escapes from' or 'collapses into' the clutches of textuality,[25] for his hermeneutics of the self re-inscribes ontology *otherwise* than in terms of the binary of text and a-textual life, of escape and collapse.

Similarly, but in terms of the opposite error, when Ricœur seems to be arguing for 'la condition originairement *langagière* de toute expérience humaine' (TA 33; PR's emphasis),[26] according to which 'le personnage, peut-on dire, est lui-même mis en intrigue' (PR 151),[27] it must not be assumed that this is underpinned by a dichotomous relation of text and world. Ricœur rejects the dichotomy that 'stories are recounted, life is lived' (LQN 25), maintaining that 'stories are recounted, but they are also lived in the mode of the imaginary' (LQN 27), and that 'fiction is only completed in life; life can be understood only through the stories we tell about it' (LQN 31). Once more, David Wood is one of the few critics to discern what is at stake here when he suggests that

> to bridge the apparent gap between narrative and life what we need to do is to rework our sense of each term. Narratives are not just configurations out there; they are completed only in the act of reading. Moreover, life is not simply a biological phenomenon but symbolically mediated. And Ricœur argues that human experience is already riddled with stories in a way that suggests a demand for narrative immanent in experience itself.[28]

More briefly, a second and related response concerns the understanding of presence appropriate to this interweaving of life and narrative. It is perhaps a misunderstanding of the difference that the call/response structure makes to the notion of presence that leads John Caputo to claim that Ricœur attempts to 'block off the radicalisation of hermeneutics and turn it back to the fold of metaphysics.'[29] Ricœur's tensional and fragmented notion of selfhood in the long, indeed interminable, detour via discourses in which it is intertwined confounds the notion of pure presence upon which such a metaphysics relies. We must be sensitive to the fact that the relation of being and language for Ricœur, which frustrates the punctuality of self-presence, cannot be mapped onto a metaphysics of presence.

The third response to be taken into account in appreciating what Ricœur is, and is not, claiming about the coherence of narrative fragments of selfhood is that the self is not open to inspection by the contemplative gaze. Ricœur's self is a relational constellation of discourses and, like the individual benday dots of a newsprint photograph, it loses its coherence if an attempt is made to isolate its elements or contemplate it with abstract rigour. So to attempt to describe the convergence of the objectivities as an 'immense play of reflections or echo soundings, all of which converge back towards an invisible centre and origin situated, as it were, behind us, in the blind spot of knowledge'[30] is to misunderstand the cosmological, tensional nature of the Ricœurean self. The self is not *behind* the variety of discourses Ricœur discusses, but emerges in their midst: it is constellatory. The self is not hidden behind the text but appears in its midst, so to speak, as it is interpreted. When Ricœur evokes the unity of the self, he does so under the rubric of action and the Spinozan *conatus*, or 'l'effort pour persévérer dans l'être' (SCA 365–6),[31] and then only with hesitation: 'it is only recently that I felt allowed to give a name to this overarching problematics. I mean the problem of human capability as the cornerstone of philosophical anthropology . . . I share this concern with Merleau-Ponty' (EHC 280). If the conatus forms the unity of man (SCA 366/OA 316), it is a unity always already comporting an irreducible alterity (as we saw above), a unity lived and not contemplated and which breaks down when it is made the object of philosophical dissection.

We can further understand the tensive cosmology that characterises selfhood for Ricœur if we consider the coherence of his own philosophical work. The dichotomous reading of Ricœur in terms of pre-linguistic 'life' and a violently reductive 'narrative' not only misreads Ricœur's argument in *Soi-même comme un autre* but also fails to take account of the structure of the text itself. It is a profound misconstrual of the work to read it solely as a linear argument, for even a cursory glance at the table of contents will reveal that it is not composed as a series of ten chapters but as a constellation of ten studies. Their interrelation is tensional as well as sequential and progressive: each reflects and informs the others, like, as has often been noted, the studies of a musical composition. Ricœur explicitly draws attention to the fragmentary character of the studies, a fragmentary character that 'récuse la thèse de la *simplicité* indécomposable du Cogito . . . sans céder pour autant au vertige de la *dissociation* du soi poursuivie avec acharnement par la déconstruction nietzschéenne' (SCA 30; PR's emphasis).[32] This is by no means merely a feature of the text imposed by the original Gifford lecture format; in *La Nature et la règle*, the transcript of a series of conversations with neuroscientist Jean-Pierre Changeux, Ricœur again insists on an approach that navigates between the Scylla of monadic unity and the Charybdis of centrifugal dissemination: 'je reste dans la fragmentation, dans la multiplicité des discours' (NR 308).[33]

It is time now to widen our investigation of identity in Ricœur, for the objectivities of being in *Soi-même comme un autre* are only one instance of a sustained strategy that shapes Ricœurean ontology as a problem of coherence and fragmentation. In his work on fragmented discourses Ricœur goes beyond Merleau-Ponty. Specifically, instead of Merleau-Ponty's single ontological element of the flesh, Ricœur's hermeneutic phenomenology gives him the resources to model worldly meaningfulness on the polysemy (neither equivocity nor univocity) of sense that hermeneutics encounters in the text, a more sophisticated position than Merleau-Ponty's evocation of dictionary definitions.[34] The world, always already shot through with symbol, metaphor and narrative, is interpreted not as if concealing one transparent meaning that must be extracted from it – the *Umwelt* of the ostensive references of dialogue – but a plurality of figurative meanings the hermeneut teases out – the *Welt* projected by the non-ostensive references of a text – and for which she provides a criteriology. As well as fragmenting the hermeneutics of the self into four objectivities of being, Ricœur persistently pursues the possibility of fragmenting being itself, and it is this fragmentation which he cites as the means by which he seeks to question the status of a putative metaphysics of presence:

> I have the impression that it (the project of the deconstruction of metaphysics) is a construction destined only to be deconstructed. This means that I am much more interested in the approaches of reconstruction like the possibility of reopening a certain number of issues closed by the Greeks; I think for example of the polysemy of the verb that we developed in Book E2 of the *Metaphysics*, where Aristotle says that the notion of being means many different things like substance, true and false being, potential and actual being, etc.[35]

Where Merleau-Ponty elaborated a polysemy of sense (gestural, operative, linguistic) that allowed him to claim worldly meaningfulness without lapsing into a dichotomy of self-present sense and abyssal non-sense, along with the metaphysics of presence that inevitably follows, Ricœur focuses his attention on the verb 'to be'. From his earliest work, Ricœur sees reduction to univocity as pernicious:

> . . . dès que l'exigence d'une vérité-une entre dans l'histoire comme une tâche de la civilisation, elle est aussitôt affectée d'un indice de violence, car c'est toujours trop tôt qu'on veut boucler la boucle. L'unité réalisée du vrai est précisément le mensonge initial. (HV 200)[36]

The equation of determinate meaning and violence, in his early texts, is a marked foreshadowing of what was later to become a recurring Derridean theme, and Ricœur also approaches more Derridean concerns when he understands Aristotle's polysemy of being in terms of a problem of the plurality of discourses.[37] Ricœur develops his ontology according to a theory of modes or 'spheres of discourse',[38] taking care to give each discourse its due, to meet the requirement that the meaningfulness of a kind of discourse be measured by its own criteria, in an approach that yields a continuous series of figures of the self relative to different cultural contexts of interpretation, with only a family resemblance to each other. Ricœur explains this fragmented approach in a conversation with Richard Kearney:

> Language has lost its original unity. Today it is fragmented not only geographically into different communities but functionally into different disciplines – mathematical, historical, scientific, legal, psychoanalytic and so on. It is the function of a philosophy of language to recognise the specific nature of these disciplines and thereby assign each 'language-game' its due (as

Wittgenstein would have it), limiting and correcting their mutual claims. Thus one of the main purposes of hermeneutics is to refer the different uses of language to different regions of being – natural, scientific, fictional and so on.[39]

Furthermore, given that subjectivity takes the long detour of a range of discourses, if there is a fragmentation of discourses then there is also a fragmentation of subjectivity. Ricœur holds that 'man' is found at the crossover of scientific, moral, juridicial and political discourses: 'C'est à leur point de jonction que pratique théorique et non théorique projettent, *de façon risquée et toujours réversible*, l'horizon de sens par rapport auquel se définit l'humanité de l'homme' (J2 23; author's emphasis).[40] It is the error and crime of totalitarianism to impose one univocal idea of man and of the good (SCA 303/OA 260), for 'no single discourse is capable of encompassing the openness of being that founds the unity of all diverse questioning.'[41] For Ricœur, there is no hierarchy of discourses, and no one discourse can claim to yield an exhaustive account of being. This is why he is suspicious of Jean-Pierre Changeux's evocation of *L'Homme neuronal* in the latter's 1983 bestselling book of that name,[42] for whereas 'neuronal' has a frame of reference within the specialised discourse of cognitive science, 'homme' is plucked from a discourse of phenomenological lived experience. Where the neuroscientist is bold and confident about the possibility of building a bridge between the brain and the mind, the philosopher once more characteristically refuses the short route. Ricœur's main intervention in the debate with Changeux is to argue for the difference and specificity of types and levels of discourse (NR 299/WMUT 269).

Changeux, in a dichotomy that is by now all too familiar, allows only two options for the relation between meaning and the world: either a universe intrinsically empty of meaning and intention (NR 128/WMUT 111) or a universe labelled with pre-given meanings. For Ricœur, Changeux has made the same false move as – unlikely bedfellows indeed – Marx, Nietzsche and Freud before him. What Ricœur in *De l'Interprétation* calls Marxian economism, Nietzschean biologism and Freudian simplistic pansexualism (DIEF 43/FP 32–3) all frame human identity in terms of one privileged discourse: the economic, the biological and the sexual respectively. Far from condemning outright the usefulness of such spheres of discourse, Ricœur is merely pleading for a recognition of their inherent and constitutive limits. In each case the theorist is charged with the crime of totalitarianism, imposing a univocal conception of what he believes to be the new humanity (L1 174). Each discourse should retain control over its own agenda (NR 179/WMUT 179), with its own domain of validity, and not seek to be established as the theoretical *archē* of lived experience itself.

Ricœur's own approach detours via a cluster of discourses, none of which deliver the essence of human identity and all of which need to be kept in uneasy tension with no one discourse at the centre. Each provides not a definition of humanity (for example 'neuronal man'), but in each case it is a partial (in both senses) definition, a metaphor of being human, the metaphoricity of which must not be allowed to collapse into definitional totalitarianism. The different discourses are to signify the opening up of being. Ricœur uses a similar term in *Le Conflit des interprétations*, evoking here not an opening ('éclosion') but an explosion ('éclatement'):

> ce qui fait la spécificité des herméneutiques, c'est précisément que cette *prise* du langage sur l'être et de l'être sur le langage se fait dans des modes différents... Ainsi, le symbolisme, pris à son niveau de manifestation dans des textes, marque l'éclatement du langage vers l'autre que lui-même: ce que j'appelle son *ouverture*; cet éclatement, c'est dire; et dire, c'est montrer. (CI 67–8)[43]

Each discourse bears witness to lived experience, but none can promise (nor could deliver) direct, untheorised or exhaustively complete access to it. Each discourse does not close around being, but opens onto it. Identity is not conferred by the content of any one discourse, nor does it appear at a punctual centre,[44] but it emerges as a function of their uneasy constellation, which allows being to remain the vulnerability of a discourse aware of its own lack of foundation (SCA 34/OA 22). However we finally understand these different ways of relating the discourses, one thing has become clear: it will do neither to say that they are related only in the manner of a constellation of stars seen from earth (by the sheer chance and the fancy of an observer), nor that they are united in and of themselves by some force or power. The nature of the relation will lie somewhere in between these two extremes, neither given nor imposed. It is a relation that follows the contours we began to sketch in the previous chapter, when we considered the interrogative mode and the work of expression.

3.2 COMMITMENT

The ontological for Ricœur is not posited but attested, a difference which has far-reaching implications. With his hermeneutic turn in *Le Symbolique du mal*, Ricœur seeks to justify his approach by casting it as a wager:

> Je parie que je comprendrai mieux l'homme et le lien entre l'être et l'homme et l'être de tous les étants si je suis *l'indication* de la pensée symbolique. Ce pari devient alors la tâche de *vérifier* mon pari et de le ceinturer en quelque

> sorte d'intelligibilité; en retour cette tâche transforme mon pari: en pariant *sur* la signification du monde symbolique, je parie en même temps *que* mon pari me sera rendu en puissance de réflexion dans l'élément du discours cohérent. (SyM 330; PR's emphasis)[45]

The motif of the wager allows Ricœur to develop a way of thinking about the ontological otherwise than in terms of the dichotomy of dogmatism and doubt, which he does by making the important distinction between validation and verification. *Muthos*, the narrative plot, obeys the 'logic of probability' or validation, and not the 'logic of empirical verification' (MPCH 105; author's translation). 'Validation' is a legal term, evoking the uncertainty and qualitative probability of the legal judgement, irreducible either to dogmatism or to scepticism. The distinction is developed in *Soi-même comme un autre*, where the notion of 'attestation' becomes central. Attestation does not deal in facts and substances, being and nothingness, escape from or collapse into textuality, but in testimonies and witnesses, commitments and suspicions.

The logic of attestation is not to be understood as a logic of the probable in contrast to – and therefore by implication weaker than – a putative logic of certainty, for its probability is not determined with respect to an ideal of scientificity (L3 135). Ricœur claims that attestation is of another nature to verification in the sense of logical empiricism, and that we must make a choice between the philosophy of absolute knowledge and the heremeneutics of testimony (L3 139). For Ricœur, validation and attestation are the appropriate terms in which to elaborate an understanding of selfhood, and 'l'attestation garde . . . quelque chose de spécifique, du seul fait que ce dont elle dit l'être-vrai, c'est le soi' (SCA 350).[46] Attestation provides no foundationalist ontological guarantee. Its only ground and support is more attestation, and this exposes it, as we have seen, to its own special fragility (SCA 34/OA 22). It will not bend itself to the Procrustean bed of verification and falsification. Simply because it is not grounded in some putative mechanism of verification, it does not follow that attestation is arbitrary, however, for rather than imposing an inappropriate criterion of (Cartesian) certainty and seeing the ontological collapse again and again into the web of the text, the fragility of the attested self is accompanied by the fragility of attestation, the attestation of the broken cogito with an 'attestation which is itself broken' (SCA 368/OA 318).[47] In *Parcours de la reconnaissance* Ricœur draws a further link between attestation and the self, discerning a close semantic affiliation between attestation and self-recognition ('reconnaissance de soi'), combining the two to give 'reconnaissance-attestation' (PR 140),[48] and in *La Critique et la conviction*, he explains what is at stake in the move from identity as self-sameness to recognition: in the notion of identity there is only the idea of sameness, whereas recognition is a concept that directly integrates otherness and allows a dialectic of the same and the other (CC 96/CC 194).

The important point here is that Ricœurean commitment is no blind and unaccountable faith, no a-rational leap, but rather a spiralling dialectic of commitment and meaning. Taking up the Augustinian motif of 'credo ut intelligam',[49] Ricœur casts the relation of commitment and meaning in terms of the hermeneutic circle: 'Il faut comprendre pour croire, mais il faut croire pour comprendre', going on to explain that 'ce cercle n'est pas vicieux, encore moins mortel; c'est un cercle bien vivant et stimulant' (SyM 327).[50] Commitment here is no *archē*, any more than understanding is. In a comment that goes some way to addressing the concerns raised by Nancy in note 29 to this chapter below, Domenico Jervolino discerns this virtuous circularity (or, better, virtuous 'spirality') in Ricœurean commitment when he comments that, if this commitment is a philosophical act of faith, then it is also a *philosophical* faith,[51] faith seeking understanding that finds retrospective attestation in the meaning that is yielded as a result of the commitment. This faith is not an irrevocable credulity but a provisional suspension of suspicion that opens a space for understanding. It allows the question of being to be asked without having immediately to close it down again. An argument has been put forward which suggests that attestation transgresses Ricœur's avowed philosophical agnosticism, giving 'final priority concerning the other to the domain of belief'.[52] But attestation is no pistic monolith; it is provisional and contingent on the meaning that commitment yields: faith seeking understanding. As such, it is not the case that *final* priority concerning the other is given to the domain of belief, for attestation never closes in on itself in an unbreakable circle. It is no ontological *terminus ad quem*; indeed, without attestation there would be nothing to be agnostic about.

Rather than posing the question in terms of the suspension of agnosticism, it is more acutely rendered as a problem of the same and the other, or more precisely of what quality our 'knowledge' of alterity takes. It is the 'quis custodiet ipsos custodes?' (who will guard the guards?) objection: I cannot attest to anything outside my own perception and judgements, for all that I know, I know through my perception and judgements. Nothing is attested but the attestation itself, and nothing can attest to attestation but more attestation. This is a question which will lead us once more into a consideration of the relation of deconstruction to Ricœur's thought, but before we can undertake that exploration we shall first need to take the detour of considering the place of the ethical in deconstruction, with particular attention paid to the notion of identity. The originary responsibility which motivates deconstruction, to do justice to the other, can be traced back to the call of the other, which is the trace of a trace, an echo twice removed: 'Quelque chose de cet appel de l'autre doit rester non réappropriable, non subjectivable, d'une certaine manière non identifiable, supposition sans suppôt, pour rester *de l'autre*.'[53] The deconstructive 'call' to responsibility cannot be fully determined or identified; instead Derrida speaks of 'ce surcroît de responsabilité qu'appelle ou qui appelle le geste déconstructeur'.[54] Whether the gesture or the responsibility 'came first', who/what calls and who/what is called it is not possible to discern.

The response to the call is an unconditional 'viens!' ('come!'): hospitality to the stranger. Derrida's 'viens!' does not know what it is summoning. It runs 'le risque: que l'autre de la langue se passe dans le pas au-delà de la langue',[55] and the responsibility of deconstruction is a responsibility to take this risk. But if it is a risk, it is also an impossibility, for 'from the moment that I am in relation with the other, with the look, the request, the love, the order, the call of the other, I know that I am able to respond to it only by sacrificing ethics, that is to say, by sacrificing that which obliges me to respond also and in the same way, in the same instant, to all others.'[56] Drucilla Cornell sums up the exercise of this responsibility as the interruption of the true for the sake of the Good, and 'the Good remains as the disruption of ontology that continually reopens the way beyond what "is".'[57] In short: 'Il y a du devoir dans la déconstruction',[58] and in addition to *quis sit* and *an sit*, we are always already dealing with *qualia sit,* a question in an ethical register: what is the value of something?

In being open to the surprise of the stranger, to the unpredictability beyond calculation, it is not accurate to suggest that deconstruction opts 'for chaos, for the undecidable, for the primacy of the flux',[59] or at the very least this is only part – and not the main part – of the story. The aleatory is a means to the end of disrupting totality for the sake of the Good of the untotalisable other, breaking the circuit of sameness. Patrick Bourgeois thinks that Derrida's is 'a thought arbitrary to its core, in which the human act of thinking, grasping, and imagining is left, like a ship in a tumultuous sea with no other control over the sail or rudder except the haphazard capriciousness of the elements',[60] but this misses the ethical impetus for Derrida's use of 'arbitrariness'. Simon Critchley, arguing that deconstruction is a philosophy of hesitation, rightly stresses 'it must be understood that such hesitation is not arbitrary, contingent or indeterminate, but rather, a rigorous, strictly determinate hesitation: the "experience" of undecidability.'[61]

Calculability is not exceeded in a moment of 'anything goes' but in an openness to the other who comes, the alterity which a strict calculability would foreclose. There must be no preconception, no restriction on the possibility of the other's arrival, as Derrida makes succinctly clear in his work on hospitality. For Derrida there is a hospitality of law (immigration laws and so on) and a hospitality of justice. The latter, Absolute hospitality, 'exige que j'ouvre mon chez-moi et que je donne non seulement à l'étranger (pourvu d'un nom de famille, d'un statut social d'étranger etc.) mais aussi à l'autre absolu, inconnu, anonyme, et que je lui *donne lieu*, que je le laisse venir, que je le laisse arriver. . . La loi de l'hospitalité absolue commande de rompre avec l'hospitalité de droit.'[62]

Both the Ricœurean and Derridean positions briefly sketched here have their problems, with which we will deal now in turn. Derrida, for his part, is uneasy with Ricœur's *ipse* identity, which he esteems to be an overconfident bid to control contingency. There is 'une multiplicité de lieux qui ne soient pas sous l'autorité de l'ipse, du soi-même,'[63] he warns, responding at a conference to a paper given the previous day by Ricœur and giving as an example of this multiplicity the act of making a promise to speak at a conference and then contracting a sore throat. But this excess over the authority of the *ipse* is, as we have seen, not foreign to Ricœur's narrative identity but rather constitutive of its irreducible vulnerability and tension of concordance and discordance. The value of the promise for Ricœur is precisely that it prevents the self being reduced to a transcendental subjectivity in full possession of itself. The self can never be posited, present, perfect, if it is structured as a promise which never has the status of epistemic certainty.[64] The sore throat scenario does not invalidate Ricœur's position. A more biting critique would be to pursue the justification for Ricœur's commitment. Richard Cohen, in a defence of Lévinas contra Ricœur's reading in *Autrement*,[65] claims that 'Ricœur posits what he cannot prove. No wonder he will later, in chapter ten [of SCA: CW], rely on the moralistic language of "conscience," "attestation," and "conviction." No evidence supports his optimism, or, rather, equal evidence supports it.'[66]

On the other side, there are also questions to be put to Derrida. The equation of openness and freedom is not unproblematic. Richard Kearney among others identifies a problem with the indeterminability of the origin of the call to responsibility:

> If *tout autre* is indeed *tout autre*, what is to prevent us saying yes to an evil alien as much as to a transcendent God who comes to save and liberate? Is there really no way for deconstruction to discriminate between true and false prophets, between bringers of good and bringers of evil, between holy spirits and unholy ones?[67]

Here we see once more the 'every other is every other' problem we encountered in relation to Merleau-Ponty. Furthermore, the Derridean distinction between the hospitality of law and the hospitality of justice 'undervalues our need to differentiate not just legally but *ethically* between good and evil aliens' which we fail to do 'by relegating the requirement of ethical judgement to a matter of selective and calculating legislation invariably compromised by injustice and violence.'[68]

Let us be clear what argument is being made here, for Derrida is rightly energetic in his rebuttal of a certain reading of unconditional hospitality, arguing against a position (whose position?) that wants to suggest that the decision should be a matter of procedure and calculation alone:

> L'inconditionnalité incalculable de l'hospitalité, du don ou du pardon – par exemple – excède le calcul des conditions comme la justice excède le droit, le juridique et le politique. La justice ne se réduira jamais au droit, à la raison calculatrice, à la distribution nomique, aux normes et aux règles qui conditionnent le droit.[69]

Quite so. Who would want to argue with the notion that we must, in the name of reason, be suspicious from time to time of rationalism?[70] But the point is not that justice should, or could, be reduced to law and calculating reason. The point is that Derrida cannot distinguish between *different* others because, in his well-placed desire not to fore-guess the other to come, he removes otherness *so* far from calculation that no arbitration between (to use Kearney's catchy triumvirate of alterities) strangers, gods and monsters is possible. The question becomes: is there a way to avoid the former danger (a priori restriction) while not being snared in the latter (inability to arbitrate)? The attempt to find just such a way to arbitrate is, we would suggest, a description of Ricœur's project, and with this delicate navigation in mind it is to his notion of attestation that we now return.

We have put off returning to the 'quis custodiet ipsos custodes?' question until now for two reasons: first, to show that Ricœur's is not the only position with ethical questions to which it struggles to respond, and secondly because the response to be investigated here will not seek to answer Derrida from inside a supposed Ricœurean stronghold, but will rather proceed by examining the relation of Ricœur's questionable attestation to Derrida's questionable Absolute (whether it be Absolute hospitality or Absolute justice). The point of this approach is to avoid the strategy which limits itself either to throwing up a Derrida/Ricœur dichotomy in which Ricœur's philosophy emerges as 'a viable and positive alternative to present-day deconstruction',[71] or to decrying Ricœur's 'affirmation' in favour of Derridean suspension. These arguments miss the ethical ground to be gained by considering what happens when the Derridean and Ricœurean positions are brought into relation with each other, without letting either 'deconstruction' or 'phenomenology' immediately trump the other.

It is not the case that, while Ricœur's position is one of untrammelled affirmation, deconstruction can be characterised by limitless suspension and suspicion; even the brief sketch above will suffice to show that this would be a misreading of Ricœur and Derrida alike. Both Ricœur and Derrida practise a suspension: Derrida suspends judgement in the face of the imperative call of the other; Ricœur suspends suspicion in a provisional faith seeking understanding. Neither suspension, furthermore, is indefinite. Derrida's (as we shall shortly see) is broken by the madness of the decision and renewed by the impossibility of the self-presence of Justice; Ricœur's is mediated through hermeneutics and needs constantly to be renewed for, in the words of Paul Celan's 'Aschenglorie', 'Niemand zeugt für den Zeugen.'[72] The pistic, though differently construed, is ineliminable for both Derrida and Ricœur. Derrida commits unconditionally to (the *an sit* of) alterity for the sake of an impossible Justice; Ricœur commits to the meaning (the *quid sit*) to be yielded by the hermeneutic approach for the sake of better situation in being. The two commitments are not so very far apart at this point. Indeed, there is no distance between them at all, not because they are the same, but because their relation is one where the Derridean suspension haunts Ricœurean attestation.

In Ricœur's own thought, the relation between attestation and suspicion (which Ricœur is careful to distinguish from sceptical doubt[73]) is by no means one of mutual exclusivity. In *Soi-même comme un autre*, attestation does not sit on a putative spectrum between escape to a pragmatics of reference and collapse into a semantics of identity. The 'opposite' of attestation is not collapse, and attestation itself does not amount to an 'escape' from the semantic web. Attestation cannot be refuted, only challenged (*récusé*: one of many legal terms Ricœur uses). Suspicion, in turn, does not negate or oppose attestation in a binary logic; it haunts attestation, moving within the space opened by it and threatening to overcome it. There is a kind of uneasy balance between attestation and suspicion (SCA 351/OA 302). More than this, we attest only where there is disagreement between parties who plead against each other and take each other to court (L3 112), and the possibility of invalidation is not secondary but the very touchstone of judgements which rely on the hermeneutics of the witness (L3 113). Suspicion of false testimony does not nullify the true, nor condemn it to some ill-defined relativistic morass, but rather the two are unthinkable without each other. The contamination is reciprocal, for suspension and refusal suppose a moment of affirmation: 'en toute contestation du réel par quoi une valeur surgit dans le monde, une affirmation d'être est envelopée' (HV 399).[74]

Ricœur's commitment to a faith seeking understanding has its parallel in Derrida's thought in the notion of *héritage*. For Derrida, *héritage* is received as a particular sort of gift, a gift passed down (tra-ditio), and which carries with it a responsibility: both a privilege, and an imperative. The responsibility before the imperative is twofold. First, as inheritor of the story of the past I am responsible 'de l'entendre, d'essayer de comprendre d'où elle vient',[75] amounting to an exercise of hyperbolically close reading haunted by the sense of a limitless responsibility which is crucial to deconstruction. Responsibility begins with the recognition of this inheritance, 'dans l'initiative qui revient à prendre connaissance, à lire, à comprendre, à interpréter la règle, et même à calculer'.[76] It is a demand of infinite justice, to pay the debt of limitless attention. It cannot be evaded, for inheritance is not a possession but rather 'l'être de ce que nous sommes est d'abord héritage, que nous le voulions et le sachions ou non.'[77]

This excessive recall of the past is a necessary, but not sufficient, condition of deconstructive responsibility, however, because impossible *justice* (as opposed to calculating *justesse* or precision) is not the call to a legal duty of adequation, to give the pound of flesh, but to a constant reworking of the story of the past, and this is deconstructive responsibility. The inheritance announces itself as inadequate, not as a datum but as a task,[78] and demands absolutely a going beyond itself, a suspension of 'la bonne conscience qui s'arrête dogmatiquement à telle ou telle détermination héritée de la justice.'[79] Thus the impossibility of adequate responsibility to the past in its own terms is the possibility of a response-ability (the very condition of the ability to respond) towards the future. Responsibility lies in the impossibility of responsibility. My responsibility is not to respond to *héritage* with an unthinking 'yes', but proactively to assume it, to keep it breathing by changing it, which is in no way in opposition to reaffirming it: 'Cet héritage, il faut le réaffirmer en le transformant aussi radicalement que ce sera nécessaire.'[80] The response to inheritance must be one of difference without opposition.[81]

Investigating the relation between Ricœur's faith seeking understanding and Derrida's responsibility before *héritage* is instructive both for its clarification of the points of similarity between the two and also for the profound disjunctions which it brings to the fore. They are similar in what they attempt to do in terms of exercising a fidelity which expresses itself precisely as deformation and the refusal of repetition. They are both open to the past and to the future.[82] The profound difference, however, is the way in which this is envisaged. Starting from an aporetic disjunction of singular alterity and structures both societal and linguistic, Derrida has no choice but to figure Justice or the other in terms of incalculable excess, a moment of madness being the only way he can suspend the horizon of calculable predictability.[83] Labouring under no such dichotomy of singularity and structure, however, Ricœur can allow creativity in interpretation to emerge *von unten*, from the imaginative juxtaposition of the 'is-is not' structure of metaphorical or indirect reference, much like Merleau-Ponty's diplopic ontology. Viewed with a Derridean eye, this would be prey to the accusation of never escaping the horizon of the same imposed by the calculability of the justice it evokes, just as the Derridean solution would be hard pressed to defend itself against the accusation that it cannot distinguish between good and bad inheritance.

One way to explore these questions further is to trace the relation between Ricœur and Derrida in terms of a move from an ontology propelled by the question 'what?' to one that forms around the interrogative 'who?',[84] and from the question of 'contact' with an exterior world to the dynamics of call and response. This shift is called for by Ricœur's distinction between *ipse* and *idem* identity, and it adds a further layer of complexity to the move by which Merleau-Ponty negotiates the binary of fact and essence. With Ricœur's hermeneutics of the self and attestatory ontology it is no longer sufficient to work in terms of the difference and overlap between the *an sit*: *whether* something is (existence) and *quid sit*: *what* something is (essence). We need to bring in a third term: *quis sit* or *who* someone is. Neither a fact nor an essence, the hermeneutics of selfhood demands a different approach. This only returns us, however, to the problem of the determinability of alterity. Derrida's own reading of the 'who?' would seem to forestall any progress that this distinction might facilitate:

> Mais qui s'adresse à vous? Comme ce n'est pas un 'auteur', un 'narrateur' ou un 'deus ex machina', c'est un '*je*' qui fait partie à la fois du spectacle et de l'assistance, et qui, un peu comme 'vous', assiste à (subit) sa propre réinscription incessante et violente dans la machinerie arithmétique, un 'je' qui, pur lieu de *passage* livré aux opérations de substitution, n'est plus une singulière et irremplaçable existence, un sujet, une 'vie', mais seulement, entre vie et mort, réalité et fiction etc., une fonction, ou un fantôme.[85]

It is not so much that these assertions rest on the assumption that reality and fiction are dichotomised, but that the 'I' is assumed to have to 'move between' the two, and a fortiori that this movement renders it a mere 'function or phantom'. This position is close to Ricœur inasmuch as he, like Derrida, recognises an inextricability of 'reality' and 'fiction' (though he would not use those terms, preferring 'life' and 'narrative'), but for Ricœur that irreducible entanglement does not reduce the 'I' to a 'mere function'. Why should it? The options Derrida arraigns ('is no longer. . . but only') are neither mutually exclusive nor exhaustive, and do not take account of the Ricœurean self as disciple of the text, which is neither univocally 'some subject of "life"' nor just a 'function or phantom'. In the words of Patrick Bourgeois, 'since the traditional distinction between the "reality" of the historical narrative and the "unreality" of fictional narrative emerges as inadequate to deal with the interweaving of the time of history and the time of fiction, Ricœur passes beyond these categories that he invoked in earlier works.'[86]

3.3 JUSTIFICATION

After circling around the question of arbitrating between Ricœur and Derrida for most of this chapter, we must now come to assess what progress can be made on it. We need not hasten to the conclusion, arrived at by Patrick Bourgeois, that given 'the vast chasm that separates the views of Derrida and Ricœur, stretching even to all-pervasive metaphysical differences', what those differences require is 'a *decision* in favour of one at the expense of the other'.[87] This is a little too rushed, and what is called for is not a precipitous decision but an indirect, oblique consideration of the relation. The motif of the detour is the most appropriate approach to the difficulties posed by the two respective positions.[88] A question like 'How can we know if Ricœur's ontological detour escapes a semantics of identity?' is a question that, if Derrida's fears are to be addressed, cannot be met with a direct argument as to precisely *how* Ricœur's ontology does just that.[89] A definitive answer to the question 'how do you know?' would confirm all Derrida's worst fears. We need to begin from the observation that once suspicion is raised, that suspicion addresses itself *to* someone, even if it is unclear precisely to whom.[90]

Let us recall Simon Critchley's reading of Stanley Cavell's scepticism with which we concluded the previous chapter. Critchley comments, it will be recalled, that 'it is the very unknowability of the other, the irrefutability of scepticism, that initiates a relation to the other based on acknowledgment and respect. The other person stands in a relation to me that exceeds my cognitive powers, placing me in question and calling me to justify myself.'[91] The question ('How do you know?') is, in fact, a call: 'justify yourself!' It is in the act of presenting oneself in response to a call,[92] in the *impossibility* of self-justification in terms of reason and

'Greek ontology', that the sceptic is answered (not refuted or rebutted). The 'here I am' is always already the response to the 'where are you?', the call to responsibility and justification.[93]

This consideration of the dynamics of scepticism suggests a response to the question 'how do you know?' that approaches it obliquely and via detours, not by securing a place off limits from the sceptical question but rather by taking the dynamic of the sceptical provocation itself as the impetus for a response, learning from the provocation *as* provocation, as the appeal 'how do you *know*?' The aim is not to outflank the sceptic, but to listen carefully and respond to her, to take up in good faith the invitation issued by the call to 'justify yourself!' as the imperative to renew the ungrounded attestation of selfhood; the imperative is responded to in terms of the *quis sit*. Furthermore, the very question 'how do you know?' witnesses to the same fragile commitment that characterises Ricœur's attested ontology, and it witnesses to it on the level of the question qua question. The Pyrrhonian 'que sais-je?' is a two-sided coin, and even at this point where we might expect them to be the farthest apart, Ricœur and Derrida are almost vanishingly close.

There is no space between the 'Saying' of the sceptical imperative and the 'said' of its suspension, and so attestation cannot secure itself a niche within the sceptical call, but this is the very basis for a rapprochement between Ricœur and Derrida for, in a similar way to the Cartesian 'ego sum, ego existo', the attestation (of suspicion in Derrida's case, of meaning in Ricœur's) cannot last beyond the duration of its own utterance and needs to be constantly renewed in a dialogue of call and response which performs the problem of its legitimation. An 'adequate' response to the question of justification cannot be found within the philosophy either of Ricœur or Derrida in relation to the other, because in relation to each other their thought precisely amounts to that problem. In performing the problem, however, the relation also perpetuates the dialogue in which attestation and suspicion are held in tension and responsibility is maintained. Without the provocation/convocation of the call to 'justify yourself!' there would be no hermeneutic ontology of the person, no call and response, no 'who?' Scepticism, or more precisely the call to justification, is the condition of possibility of a hermeneutics of selfhood. Suspicion is not an embarrassment to an ontology of the 'who?', but neither is it subsumed as a moment on the way to its *Aufhebung*. Suspicion does destabilise the ontology of attestation, but at the same time it also drives forward the need for ever-renewed attestation.

If Merleau-Ponty's ontology is in the interrogative mode, then Ricœur's ontology is in the attestatory, and if Merleau-Ponty refused to dichotomise *an sit* and *quid sit*, then Ricœur does the same for *quis sit* and *qualia sit*. Ricœur's ontology is irreducibly personal and irreducibly pistic, though selfhood is not monadic and faith is not beyond suspicion (nor suspicion beyond faith). Furthermore, Ricœur's is an ontology reliant on the shifting sands of a range of discourses and a fragile commitment to a meaning to be found in their midst. Little wonder that Ricœur himself should comment:

> Not that I have ever found my ontological feet in any final or absolute sense. It is no accident that the title of the last chapter of *Oneself as Another* is in the form of an interrogation rather than an assertion – 'Towards which Ontology?'[94]

Through our exploration of ontology and selfhood in this chapter we have examined how Ricœur's 'hermeneutics of selfhood' is both ontologically circumspect, evoking a long detour and a journey towards the ontological promised land, and also fragmented into a number of 'objectivities'. Combined with his insistence on a 'polysemy of being' and an attested ontology, Ricœur has shifted the centre of gravity in our ontological investigation to the question of coherence and fragmentation. This is a crucial move because it foregrounds an important new arena of engagement between phenomenology and deconstruction that we shall loosely label the question of the many and the one. What is at stake ontologically between phenomenology and deconstruction is an understanding of coherence and commensurability. This same problem, furthermore, is precisely at the heart of Ricœur's and Derrida's respective treatments of the question of justice, and so continuing our interrogation of the ontological in terms of this question will provide us with a privileged site for observing the interaction of deconstructive and phenomenological concerns. A legal register will also allow us to investigate further the relation of the two problems that have emerged for deconstruction and phenomenology respectively: How can we arbitrate between different witnesses? Who will witness for the witness?

NOTES

1. Derrida, *Le Toucher* 138; 'the fullness of immediate presence required by every ontology or metaphysics' (*On Touching* 120).
2. Ricœur and Raynova, 'All That Gives us to Think: Conversations with Paul Ricœur' 692.
3. The motif of the 'long détour' appears early in Ricœur's work, in *Le Volontaire et l'involontaire* of 1950 (translated as *Freedom and Nature: The Voluntary and Involuntary*, 1966), where the transparency of consciousness is not a given but remains a task to be accomplished. Ricœur

subsequently takes detours via symbol and myth (SM/SE), the unconscious (DI/FP) and narrative (TR1–3/TN1–3).
4. 'can be, for us who proceed indirectly and by degrees, only a horizon, an aim rather than a given fact' (CI 18).
5. Ricœur and Tóth, 'The Graft, the Residue, and Memory: Two Conversations with Paul Ricœur' 660.
6. 'the fragmented method we have continually practiced' (OA 297).
7. 'this fragmentation is not such that no thematic unity keeps it from the dissemination that would lead the discourse back to silence. In a sense, one could say that these studies together have as their thematic unity *human action*' (OA 19; translation altered).
8. Barbaras, *Le Tournant de l'expérience* 118.
9. 'at the intersection of the coherence conferred by emplotment and the discordance arising from the peripeteia within the narrated action' (COR 101).
10. See Greisch, *Paul Ricœur: l'itinérance du sens* 386.
11. In *Soi-même comme un autre* Ricœur develops Wilhelm Schapp's notion that the self is 'in Geschichten verstrickt' ('enchevêtré dans des histoires'/'entangled in stories') (SCA 130/OA 107).
12. Wood, *The Step Back* 20.
13 'what remains here is the organisation of a combinatory system' (OA 117). Such a relational identity is foreshadowed by Merleau-Ponty in his disagreement with Sartre. For Merleau-Ponty, 'je m'emprunte à autrui' (S 201) – 'I borrow myself from others' (S 159) – whereas as Merleau-Ponty characterises Sartre, 'Autrui ou moi, il faut choisir, dit-on' (PP 414) – 'I must choose between others and myself, it is said' (PP 420). This contrast is repeatedly made by Robert Cumming. See, for example, *Phenomenology and Deconstruction*, vol. 1, 171.
14. 'In a philosophy of selfhood like ours, one must be able to say that ownership is not what matters' (OA 168).
15. '« Il faut bien manger »' 269–302; 'Eating Well' 255–87.
16. Derrida, '« Il faut bien manger »' 271; 'the subject can be re-interpreted, re-stored, re-inscribed, it certainly isn't "liquidated." The question "who," notably in Nietzsche, strongly reinforces this point' ('Eating well' 257).
17. From 'I Have a Taste for the Secret' 41. The text is translated from the Italian *Il Gusto del Segreto* (Roma: Laterza, 1997).
18. Derrida, '« Il faut bien manger »' 275; 'The relation to self, in this situation, can only be differance, that is to say alterity, or trace' ('Eating well' 261).
19. Derrida uses the Heideggerean motif of thrownness in relation to subjectivity in his essay on Artaud 'Forcener le subjectile' ('Maddening the subjectile').
20. Derrida, '« Il faut bien manger »' 279. 'The subject is a fable, as you have shown, but to concentrate on the elements of speech and *conventional* fiction that such a fable presupposes is not to stop taking it seriously (it is the serious itself)' ('Eating well' 264).
21. The second half of this chapter will explore the important role of commitment in accounting for this difference in proximity.

22. 'pregnancy of possibles, *Weltmöglichkeit*' (VI 250).
23. 'I insist upon this difference between intelligibility and rationality. If we ignore it, we are condemned to deny stories any place on the scale of knowledge, reserving an epistemological dignity only for the constructions of the narratologist in literary criticism or the historian in the human sciences' (author's translation).
24. LaCapra, 'Who Rules Metaphor?' 26.
25. These terms are used by Venema, 'Am I the Text?' 766.
26. 'it is *language* that is the primary condition of all human experience' (*TA* 16).
27. 'the character, we can say, is him- or herself emplotted' (*COR* 100).
28. David Wood, 'Introduction: Interpreting Narrative', in *On Paul Ricoeur: Narrative and Interpretation* 11.
29. Caputo, *Radical Hermeneutics* 5. A similar argument is made by Jean-Luc Nancy in *Le Partage des voix*, where he accuses Ricœur of employing an ordinary conceptualisation of interpretation ('conceptualité ordinaire de l'interprétation'), gliding over complexities and ambivalences (PV 11/SV 248). On Ricœur's hermeneutic circle – we must understand in order to believe, and believe in order to understand – Nancy comments that this regime of belief is foreign to philosophy (PV 14/SV 213). It will be evident from the argument of this chapter that we consider Nancy to have misunderstood Ricœur on this point, and we shall respond to Nancy's accusation in Chapters 5 and 6 below.
30. Gifford and Gratton, *Subject Matters* 203.
31. 'the effort to persevere in being' (*OA* 316).
32. 'challenges the thesis of the indecomposable *simplicity* of the cogito ... without thereby giving in to the vertigo of the *disintegration* of the self pursued mercilessly by Nietzschean deconstruction' (*OA* 19).
33. 'I remain caught up in fragmentation, in the multiplicity of discourses' (*WMUT* 275).
34. The split reference of Ricœur's metaphor sets an ambiguity at the heart of ontology that is not present for a Merleau-Ponty for whom there is no metaphor between the visible and the invisible (VI 275/VI 221). The point is made by Michaël Foessel in 'La lisibilité du monde. La véhémence phénoménologique de Paul Ricœur' 172.
35. Raynova, 'All That Gives Us to Think' 691.
36. 'as soon as the exigency for a single truth enters into history as a goal of civilisation, it is immediately affected with a mark of violence. For one always wished to tie the knot too early. The *realised* unity of the true is precisely the initial lie' (*HT* 176).
37. See Daigler, 'Paul Ricœur's Hermeneutic Ontology' 191.
38. Ricœur, 'Philosophy and Religious Language', in *Figuring the Sacred* 35. 'Philosophy and Religious Language' was originally published in *Journal of Religion* 54 (1974): 71–85, not translated from a previous French version.

39. Kearney, *On Paul Ricoeur* 124.
40. 'from their point of intersection, theoretical and nontheoretical practices project, *in a risky, always reversible way,* the horizon of meaning in relation to which we define the humanity of human beings' (*ROJ* 16).
41. Ricœur, 'The Problem of the Will and Philosophical Discourse' 283.
42. Changeux, *L'Homme neuronal*; *Neuronal Man*.
43. 'What causes the specific character of various hermeneutics is precisely that this *grasp* of language on being and of being on language takes place according to different modes . . . In this way, symbolism, taken at the level of manifestation in texts, marks the breakthrough of language toward something other than itself – what I call its *opening*. This breakthough is *saying*; and saying is showing' (*CI* 65–6; translation altered).
44. Here Ricœur differs markedly from Daniel Dennett's 'centre of narrative gravity', elaborated in Dennett, 'The Origins of Selves'. For a discussion of the differences between Ricœur and Dennett, see Shaun Gallagher, 'Philosophical Conceptions of the Self: Implications for Cognitive Science'.
45. 'I wager that I shall have a better understanding of man and of the bond between the being of man and the being of all beings if I follow the indication of symbolic thought. This wager then becomes the task of verifying my wager and saturating it, so to speak, with intelligibility. In return, the task transforms my wager: in betting *on* the significance of the symbolic world, I bet the same time *that* my wager will be restored to me in power of reflection, in the element of coherent discourse' (*SE* 5).
46. 'attestation . . . retains something specific with respect to the sole fact the being-true it expresses has to do with the self' (*OA* 302)
47. Ricœur's 'cogito brisée' (broken cogito) moves on from Merleau-Ponty's characterisation of the cogito as irreducibly corporeal to highlight its necessarily dialogic detour: 'On ne peut même pas dire qu'il [the cogito: CW] monologue, dans la mesure où le monologue marque un retrait par rapport à un dialogue qu'il présuppose en l'interrompant' (SCA 16 n4); 'We cannot even say that it is a monologue, in the sense that a monologue presupposes an interruption of a dialogue' (*OA* 6 n8). Nancy will take these insights further in his *Ego sum* (see Chapter 5).
48. 'recognition-attestation' (*COR* 134).
49. 'I believe in order to understand'. See Aurelius Augustinus, *De Libero Arbitrio*, Book I, ch. 2, § 4; II, ch. 2, § 5.
50. 'We must understand in order to believe, but we must believe in order to understand . . . The circle is not a vicious circle, still less a mortal one; it is a living and stimulating circle' (*SE* 351).
51. Jervolino, *The Cogito and Hermeneutics* 96.
52. Anderson, 'Agnosticism and Attestation: An Aporia Concerning the Other in Ricœur's Oneself as Another' 76. See also Venema, *Identifying Selfhood* 162.
53. Derrida, '« Il faut bien manger »' 290; 'Something of this call of the other must remain nonreappropriable, nonsubjectivable, and in a certain way non-identifiable, a sheer supposition, so as to remain other' ('Eating well' 176).

54. Derrida, '« Il faut bien manger »' 301; 'this surplus of responsibility that summons or is summoned by the deconstructive gesture' ('Eating well' 286; translation altered).
55. Derrida, *Parages* 74; 'the risk: that the other of language happens in the step (not) beyond language' (author's translation).
56. Caputo, *The Prayers and Tears of Jacques Derrida* 204. It is this double bind of the necessity and unjustifiability of sacrifice that Daniel Punday fails to appreciate in his elaboration of *Narrative After Deconstruction*. Punday misunderstands what 'deconstruction' is, and his 'after deconstruction' is more deconstructive than his 'deconstruction': 'Major's novel [Clarence Major, *Reflex and Bone Structure*: CW]' claims Punday, 'embodies the complex textuality that I have associated throughout this study with writing after deconstruction. It is an understanding of writing that accepts practically everything we associate with deconstruction – the loss of subjectivity, the inadequacy of representation, and the slippage of meaning within language. At the same time, Major's novel struggles constantly not to allow these negatives to become the whole story' (Punday, *Narrative After Deconstruction* 171). This characterisation of deconstruction and narrative 'after deconstruction' is problematic on a number of levels. The openness engendered by the 'inadequacy of representation' etc. can *by definition* never become the whole story; deconstruction is nothing if not a disruption of closure. Furthermore, they are not 'negatives', for we have seen how the affirmative moment in deconstruction is precisely a function of the openness of incompletion. Most of all, however, the 'struggle' of the double bind of the decision *is* deconstruction, if anything is. We might indicate (following Nicholas Royle's *After Derrida*) that 'after', in the title of Punday's book, can also mean 'in pursuit of'. It appears that Punday labours to arrive, in the name of superseding Derrida, at the thought of the Derrida he is seeking to leave behind.
57. Cornell, *Philosophies of the Limit* 93.
58. Derrida, '« Il faut bien manger »' 297; 'there is duty in deconstruction' ('Eating well' 272; translation altered).
59. Bourgeois, *Philosophy at the Boundary of Reason* 79.
60. Bourgeois, *Philosophy at the Boundary of Reason* 112.
61. Critchley, *The Ethics of Deconstruction* 42.
62. Derrida and Dufourmantelle, *De l'Hospitalité* 29; 'requires that I open up my home and that I give not only to the foreigner (provided with a family name, with the social status of being a foreigner, etc.), but to the absolute, unknown, anonymous other, and that I give place to him, that I let him come, that I let him arrive . . . The law of absolute hospitality commands a break with the hospitality of right' (*On Hospitality* 25; translation altered).
63. Catherine Malabou et al., 'Questions à Jacques Derrida' 197; 'a multiplicity of places which are not under the authority of the *ipse*, of the oneself' (author's translation).

64. See Ricœur, 'La promesse d'avant la promesse' 31.
65. Ricœur, *Autrement*; 'Otherwise'.
66. Cohen, *Ethics, Exegesis and Philosophy* 291.
67. Kearney, 'Desire of God' 127.
68. Kearney, *Strangers, Gods and Monsters* 69.
69. Derrida, *Voyous* 205; 'The incalculable unconditionality of hospitality, of the gift or of forgiveness, exceeds the calculation of conditions, just as justice exceeds law, the juridical, and the political. Justice can never be reduced to law, to calculative reason, to lawful distribution, to the norms and rules that condition law' (*Rogues* 149).
70. Derrida, *Voyous* 215; *Rogues* 128.
71. Bourgeois, *Philosophy at the Boundary of Reason* 79.
72. 'Nobody witnesses for the witnesses'. 'Aschenglorie' is found in Celan's *Atemwende*.
73. Suspicion is a pulling off of the mask (DI 40) whose protagonists dispense with the horizon in order to attain a more authentic word (DI 43). Sceptical doubt, by contrast, offers no question beyond its destructiveness (DI 43).
74. 'in every contestation of the real, which is the way in which a value surges forth into the world, an affirmation of being is contained' (*HT* 322).
75. Derrida, *Force de loi* 44; 'to hear, read, interpret it, to try to understand where it comes from', 'Force of Law' 20.
76. Derrida, *Force de Loi* 52; 'with the initiative of learning, reading, understanding, interpreting the rule, and even in calculating' ('Force of law' 24).
77. Derrida, *Spectres de Marx* 94; 'the being of what we are is first of all inheritance, whether we like it or know it or not' (*Spectres of Marx* 54).
78. See Derrida, *Spectres de Marx* 94; *Spectres of Marx* 54.
79. Derrida, *Force de loi* 45; 'the good conscience that dogmatically stops before any inherited determination of justice' ('Force of law' 20).
80. Derrida, *Spectres de Marx* 94; 'This inheritance must be reaffirmed by transforming it as radically as will be necessary' (*Spectres of Marx* 54). But how do we decide (and who is the deciding 'we'?) how much transformation 'is necessary', unable as we are to fore-guess the other to come?
81. Under the constraints of time and speaking extempore in a foreign tongue, Derrida comes more acutely to the point at the Villanova Roundtable: 'There is no responsibility, no decision, without this inauguration, this absolute break. That is what deconstruction is made of: not the mixture but the *tension* between memory, fidelity, the preservation of something that has been given to us, and, at the same time, heterogeneity, something absolutely new, and a break' (Caputo (ed.), *Deconstruction in a Nutshell* 6). Though it would be unwise to extrapolate too much from Derrida's anglophone extemporising, his use of the word 'tension' to describe this relation is tantalising, given the importance of the motif for Ricœur.
82. Ricœur takes special care to develop a notion of responsibility open to the future as well as to the past: 'Jusqu'à présent, on considérait quelqu'un comme responsable seulement d'actes passés dont il était

reconnu être l'auteur et qu'on pouvait dès lors lui imputer. Hans Jonas, dans *Le Principe responsabilité*, conçoit au contraire une responsabilité tournée vers le futur lointain. Quelque chose nous est confié qui est essentiellement fragile. L'objet de la responsabilité, affirme Jonas, c'est le périssable en tant que tel . . . Une tradition n'est vivante que si elle donne l'occasion d'innover' (CFP); 'Up until now, we considered someone to be responsible only for past actions of which he was the recognised author and that we could from then on impute to him. But Hans Jonas, in *The Imperative of Responsibility*, conceives of a responsibility oriented to the distant future. Something which is essentially fragile is entrusted to us. The object of responsibility, Jonas affirms, is the perishable as such . . . A tradition is only living if it allows for innovation' (author's translation).

83. In *Force de loi* Derrida insists that a moment of madness is necessary for the decision in order to break with predictable, mechanical calculability (*Force de loi* 56; 'Force of law' 26). In *The Politiques de l'amitié* Derrida expands, insisting that '*une décision est inconsciente en somme*, si insensé que cela paraisse, elle comporte l'inconscient et reste pourtant responsable' (Derrida, *Politiques de l'amitié* 68); 'In sum, a decision is unconscious – insane as that may seem, it involves the unconscious and nevertheless remains responsible' (*Politics of Friendship* 69). But surely this returns us to the 'strangers, gods and monsters' problem. What does the unconscious guarantee that consciousness does not? Why is the unconscious a benevolent, not a malevolent intrusion? It seems not only that Derrida cannot respond to these questions, but that he *must* not respond, for so to do would recuperate precisely the madness he is introducing into the decision. This is a serious problem for Derridean ethics, and it goes beyond the simple point that Derrida makes in *Force de loi* that I can never say of myself in the present that 'I am just'.

84. The following argument, along with the Lévinasian and Derridean references upon which it relies, is greatly indebted to De Greef, 'Skepticism and Reason'.

85. Derrida, 'Le discours d'assistance' in *La Dissémination* 361; 'But who is it that is addressing you? Since it is not an "author," a "narrator," or a "deus ex machina," it is an "I" that is both part of the spectacle and part of the audience; an "I" that, a bit like "you," attends (undergoes) its own incessant, violent reinscription within the arithmetical machinery; an "I" that, functioning as a pure passageway for operations of substitution, is no longer some singular and irreplaceable existence, some subject or "life," but only, moving between life and death, reality and fiction, etc., a mere function or phantom' (*Dissemination* 357; translation altered).

86. Bourgeois, *Philosophy at the Boundary of Reason* 219.

87. Bourgeois, 'Hermeneutics and Deconstruction: Paul Ricœur in Postmodern Dialogue' 348.

88. It is certainly more appropriate than any ill-advised attempt to refute deconstruction for, as Leonard Lawlor rightly points out, 'Derrida is an

incredibly powerful philosopher insofar as he is a philosopher *du tout* . . . like Hegel, Derrida can absorb any other position that is opposed to his. In other words, one cannot find a position outside his system' (Lawlor, Thinking Through French Philosophy 151).
89. Nor can it be answered with an appeal to merely pragmatic arguments. Patrick Bourgeois makes this mistake when he argues that 'Ricœur's view of reading a text, reconfiguring and reappropriating its world, thus expanding and fusing one's own horizons, provides a healthy and compelling alternative to clotural reading, and is far more rewarding and insightful, leading to richer Being-in-the-world' (Bourgeois, Philosophy at the Boundary of Reason 81–2; author's emphasis). Elsewhere in this compelling study Bourgeois does argue more carefully, but to suggest here that health, reward and richness are the criteria by which to judge a reading is to assume precisely what is up for grabs in the relation between phenomenology and deconstruction. If such riches were a phantasm, would not the best reading be one that acknowledged the fact, and only then thought what to do about it? Daniel Punday similarly misfires when he claims that 'in the language of location, I will show, is the striving toward a post-deconstructive style of writing, a kind of narrative that will reinvision textual construction in a much more productive and satisfying way' (Punday, Narrative After Deconstruction 25; author's emphasis), and Richard Kearney makes a similar move when he claims that 'the attempt to build hermeneutic bridges between us and "others" (human, divine or whatever) should not, I will argue, be denounced as ontology, ontotheology or logocentrism – that is to say, as some form of totalising reduction bordering on violence.' Why ever not, we might ask? 'For such a denunciation ultimately denies any form of dialogical interbeing between self and other' (Kearney, Strangers, Gods and Monsters 9; author's emphasis). It would seem odd to bar a given denunciation because it might have uncomfortable consequences. The truth or otherwise of the denunciation and the consequences to which it may or may not lead ought to be dealt with separately.
90. What follows is not intended to imply that Derrida is a sceptic, any more than the discussion above about his undeconstructible commitment to alterity was to suggest that he is straightforwardly a philosopher of commitment. Nevertheless, to the extent that deconstruction can be characterised – though not exhaustively understood – in terms of an *epoché* of judgement, a consideration of interrogative scepticism (the questioning of affirmation as opposed to the affirmation of denial) is helpful in understanding how Derrida's thought might relate to Ricœur's.
91. Critchley, 'Deconstruction and Pragmatism – Is Derrida a Private Ironist or a Public Liberal?' 32. Quoted in Cary Wolfe, Zoontologies 50.
92. See de Greef, 'Skepticism and Reason' 171.
93. See de Greef, 'Skepticism and Reason' 166.
94. Kearney, *On Paul Ricoeur* 167.

4. *Paul Ricœur: Justice*

In the previous chapter we explored the relationship between Ricœur's hermeneutic phenomenology and Derrida's deconstruction by moving the ontological question from a focus on 'what?' to 'who?' While allowing us to make progress in understanding how the question of alterity in Derrida must be reconsidered when we are coming to grips with Ricœur's hermeneutics of the self and narrative identity, the investigation also opened, without satisfactorily resolving, the issue of coherence and multiplicity. In stating *that* the various discourses of Ricœur's hermeneutics of the self cohere, we left hanging the question as to *how* they cohere, which is precisely what is at stake between deconstruction and phenomenology at this point. In order to address Ricœur's response to the question of coherence, we turn now to one sphere of interpretation which, in the last decade of his life, he explored at length: the sphere of justice. In this chapter we shall argue that the way Ricœur develops his notion of justice (through readings of John Rawls, Michael Walzer, Luc Boltanski and Laurent Thévenot) is through a meditation on the coherence of diverse discourses, navigating between the Scylla of reductive violence and the Charybdis of paralysing incommensurability, between recuperated unity and disseminated multiplicity. This will complete our Ricœurean response to the searching ontological questions posed to his philosophy by deconstruction.

To anyone studying the progression of Ricœur's thought, it is surprising that it was only in his later years that he gave himself to a sustained consideration of the question of the just and the area of legal interpretation, though in truth they were never completely absent from his earlier work, though often only obliquely apparent. Although the problem of justice came increasingly to feature in Ricœur's philosophy from the 1990s onwards, he grapples with questions of law as early as 'Le paradoxe politique' (May 1957). The 1967 article 'L'interprétation du mythe de la peine' (CI 348–69; 'Interpretation of the myth of punishment', CI 351–75) and the seminal 'Le juste entre le légal et le bon' ('The Just Between the Legal and the Good') (L1 176–95) are but two more salient points in a philosophical journey that repeatedly tarries with the question of justice. *Soi-même comme un autre* is peppered with legal terms – 'attestation', 'arbitration', 'attribution', 'ascription', 'testimony', 'objection', 'doubt' – and the title of the final Gifford lecture not published with the other ten, 'le sujet convoqué' ('the summoned subject'), testifies to a similar influence.[1] The central importance of the question of justice in *Soi-même comme un autre* is clear in Ricœur's summary statement of the good life in his 'little ethics' (studies seven to nine): 'la visée de la vie bonne avec et pour autrui *dans des institutions justes*' (SCA 202; author's emphasis).[2] The question of justice is also to the fore in Ricœur's theological reflections, not least in his work on the Golden Rule and the greatest commandment in *Amour et justice*, to which we shall have occasion to return at the end of this chapter. In addition to these important interventions, Ricœur has published two volumes of collected articles dealing directly with the question of justice: *Le Juste 1* (1995) and *Le Juste 2* (2001).

Gadamer argues for the 'exemplary significance of legal hermeneutics' in 'the recovery of the fundamental hermeneutic problem',[3] and in addition a consideration of legal decision-making harbours distinct advantages from the point of view of bringing into focus what is at stake in the decision more widely. First of all, the decision-making procedures in a court of law are formalised, regulated and even ritualised, making evident what in other hermeneutic spheres would remain assumed or veiled (the weighing of the reliability of witnesses, making explicit the justifications for arriving at a given decision and so on). Secondly, the stakes of the decision are more immediately accessible than in, say, literary interpretation. The immediate future of the accused rests, to a large extent, on the verdict arrived at (not to mention the professional reputation of any advocates or judge involved, and to say nothing of public confidence in the legal system itself).[4]

Secondly, the dynamics of court procedure also dramatise the ethical responsibility of hermeneutics, for the legitimate exertion of violence is integral to the rule of law. Peter Brooks writes in *Law's Stories*:

> Law fascinates the literary critic in part because people go to jail, even to execution, because of the well-formedness and force of the winning story. Conviction in the legal sense results from the conviction created in those who judge the story.[5]

While the stakes in legal interpretation are perhaps no greater than in the arguments surrounding other hermeneutic spheres, they are undoubtedly more immediately apprehensible. Thirdly, the court procedure imposes upon the decision-making process a certain urgency. The responsibility to arrive at a verdict presses in upon the court with an intensity not necessarily felt in less ritualised hermeneutic contexts.

In addition to these reasons, it is also a happy coincidence that both Derrida and Ricœur concerned themselves with jurisprudential questions in the 1990s, and so their respective approaches can be compared. Asked about Derrida's intellectual trajectory, Ricœur comments that 'I like his first works on Husserl very much, *Speech and Phenomena* and then *Of Grammatology*. After that I followed his work rather less closely, especially all the parts on deconstruction, and I joined him once again in his recent work on the politics of friendship and the texts on justice, which places him again in the vicinity of Lévinas.'[6] Indeed, 'in this way we [Derrida, Ricœur and Lyotard: CW] meet, in a sort of "gang," with the idea of justice, in the neighbourhood of Lévinas.'[7] For these reasons, a consideration of Ricœur's hermeneutics through a legal prism promises a fruitful engagement with the issues we have raised but as yet not resolved.

What, though, is 'justice' for Ricœur? In conversation with François Azouvi and Marc de Launay he defines the term in terms of a dialectic of the political and the moral. On the one hand justice addresses the question of legitimacy, which is never entirely exhausted by the political and its meditation on power; on the other hand it is irreducible to the moral, because it assumes the legitimacy of coercion (CC 177/CC 116). In 'Le juste entre le légal et le bon', the just is located in a similar tension between a Kantian deontological conformity to law and an Aristotelian teleological ethics of the 'good life'. Justice is that which looks both ways (SCA 265/OA 228). In a dialectic of (sanctionable) legality and (moral) goodness, or of power and legitimacy, justice is situated between private vengeance and public impotence (CC 178/CC 117).

We shall examine Ricœur's response to the problem of justice – and through it the questions raised by deconstruction – in terms of four relations. First, the relation of justice and space, and how Ricœur understands interpretation to be animated by distributive and cosmological concerns. This will return us in the second section to the question of faith and commitment in relation to justice. The way in which commitment helps us to advance an understanding of the decision as neither arbitrary nor absolute will be demonstrated by drawing on Ricœur's work on the 'fiction' of the social contract and the desire, at the root of social cohesion, to live together. This desire is complicated, however, in a society in which conceptions of the just are fragmented, and so our third section will ask how 'justice' can meaningfully be evoked when, in a given society, there is an incommensurable multiplicity of 'justices'. We will see that, although Ricœur comes very close to a Derridean understanding in his treatment of fragmented justice, an abyss still separates the two. This difference is most acutely evident in Ricœur's treatment of the relation of justice and love, which we explore in the fourth and final section of this chapter. Drawing on our considerations of space and commitment we will mark as precisely as possible the ways in which Ricœur and Derrida differ on the ethics and mechanics of the decision in relation to love and the gift, and begin to engage the question of how we might arbitrate between the Derridean and Ricœurean positions.

4.1 JUSTICE AND SPACE

Following Merleau-Ponty's 'cosmology of the visible' and the idea of an intersection point of different discourses we encountered in the previous chapter, the question of justice for Ricœur is posed in terms of space, distributions and distances in two main ways. First, the theatre of justice, the court, is analysed in terms of the constellation of distances that structure it and that it sets in place, and secondly, the larger community is understood as a just (or unjust) distribution of distances with similarities to the microcosmic courtroom. We will take each of these dimensions in turn. Ricœur defines the space of the court in contradistinction to the abolition of the space between bodies in the reign of unrestrained violence and vengeance (J1 10/J xi), which is to say that, while the court replays the conflicts which lacerate civil society, it does so in a codified and distanced way (L1 193) which mitigates and controls their violence. The law, with its procedures, rituals and structures, interposes itself as a third party, a mediating institution in bilateral conflicts (J2 272/ROJ 236) which serves to separate the two parties in disagreement and forces each to 'make room' ('faire une place') for his or her adversary (JM 15). This distancing maintains the court as the privileged place in society for ordered and ritualised decision-making (CC 180/CC 118).

As well as being defined by its web of ritualised relationships, the space of the law-court is at bottom a narrative space. The matrix of distances that characterises it is defined in terms of a web of narratives, which may sometimes be consensual and sometimes conflictual. First, the suspension of unrestrained personal vengeance within the space of the court is achieved by the victory language gains over violence (J2 89/ROJ 76), where unrestrained conflict is transmuted within a legal discourse, which takes the form of the assault of words and the competition of arguments (CC 180/CC 118). Secondly, in the institutionalised space of the court competing narratives are in ritual tension and the due process of the courts – those public agencies that have authority to construct the new coherence required by new cases (SCA 323/OA 278) – is a way of handling a conflict of interpretations. Taken as a process for dealing with narrative disagreements, the entire court procedure, from the citation of particular laws to the handing down of the verdict and sentence and everything that comes between the two, is nothing but a prolonged discourse (L1 193). Thirdly, in addition to the stories circulating within the court – differing accounts of events, interpretations of law, summing up and verdict – the unfolding ritual of the court itself structures the proceedings as narrative. The form which courtroom procedure lends to a trial, with a definite beginning, a structured and procedurally constrained deliberation and the outcome (in most cases) of a verdict, itself reflects the coherence of the Aristotelian 'well-wrought story'. The verdict and sentence grasp together the conflicting stories the court has considered, and they produce a new narrative, the point of which is not in the first instance to arrive at agreement among all the parties involved, but rather to divide and separate them, establishing a 'just distance' between them: before its constraining function, the sentence aims to speak the law, to put the parties in their just places (L1 194).

This restoration of a 'just distance' (L1 193) is fundamental to the Ricœurean conception of justice. Found at the chiasm of shared comprehension and the capacity for impartiality, just distance is brought about by the pronouncement of the law within the continuity of a public space for the condemned person who is also thereby excluded from it (J2 104/ROJ 89). Its distributing function is to separate parties 'trop près dans le conflit et trop éloignés l'un de l'autre dans l'ignorance, la haine ou le mépris' (J1 192),[8] avoiding both the confusion of collision and the disdain that makes discussion impossible (L1 139), and thereby keeping open a space of language and deliberation which would be closed down by either insufficient or excessive distance.

If the space of the court is structured by the narratives that circulate within it, then the space of circulation is itself temporally bounded by two judgements. Like any other narratives, the stories circulating within the court require interpretation, and in 'Justice et vengeance' (J2 257–66; 'Justice and vengeance', ROJ 223–31) Ricœur identifies two distinct interpretative moments which open and close the space of the court. The first is the choice of the particular law in relation to which to try the case, the 'jugement de droit' ('judgement of law'), and the second is a judgement as to whether the 'facts' constitute an infraction of the particular law in play ('mise en jeu') in the case (J2 262/ROJ 227): the 'jugement de fait' ('judgement of fact'). We will follow this chronological and logical progression from the 'judgement of law' to the 'judgement of fact' as we explore the space of the court, for the way in which power and legitimacy are brought together in the courtroom (and therefore part of Ricœur's response to deconstruction's questions) is a function of the interaction of these two moments of interpretation.

The question of how to find the law in terms of which it is appropriate to bring a given case (the 'judgement of law') is the *sine qua non* of the ritualised space of the court. It is a pre-judgement (in relation to the trial), yet still involves on its own an enormous work of interpretation (CC 179/CC 117). Furthermore, once this first, preliminary judgement has been made, the chosen law not only makes possible the space of the court as a web of relations, but also regulates what can and cannot be recognised within that space. Only those elements of the case which have a bearing on deciding if the chosen law 'fits' in the case in question are permitted to enter the courtroom deliberation. Without the 'judgement of law' the narratives circulating in the court can have no legal meaning and the 'judgement of fact' would be impossible.

The two judgements which open and close the narrative space of the court find their counterparts in Ricœur's understanding of community in general. Much of his consideration of issues concerning the notion of community is born out of an engagement with the historical development of social contract theory, primarily mediated by two seminal anglophone works: John Rawls' *A Theory of Justice* and Michael Walzer's *Spheres of Justice*.[9] Nevertheless Ricœur distances himself, as we shall see, from both Rawls and Walzer. On Ricœur's reading, Rawls sees a given community as a space of distribution, the common space unfolded by the will to live together (J2 284/ROJ 247; cf. L1 41), whose rules delimit a domain of what is permitted (J2 272/ROJ 236). Within this public space are distributed social goods of various sorts (rights, duties, revenue and property, responsibilities and powers), giving the members of the community the identity neither of isolated individuals brought together *a posteriori* into an uneasy coexistence, nor of a homogenous collective with no meaningful individuality. In a distributive framework the members of a community are partners, each receiving a share ('une part') in society, and the community is characterised neither by the Lévinasian interpellation of the face of the Other, nor the average, normal nobody of Heidegger's 'das Man', but rather by the 'chacun' ('each one') of a congregationalist, mutualist society (L1 218). While 'they' is anonymous, 'chacun' is distributive, insists Ricœur in an interview with Yvanka Raynova: 'I believe that this is very important, because we often say: after "you" there is "they." No, there is not "they," there is "each one." And the relation of justice is: "To each his or her right." '[10] The 'chacun' is neither singular nor multiple, or rather it is both of these. This is one aspect of a wider insistence, in Ricœur's work, on the validity of mutuality as opposed to reciprocity, of sharing as opposed to giving, receiving and keeping accounts.

In the centripetal and centrifugal forces at play in the community each one (*chacun*) has a share (*part*), yet each one's share is his or her own. It is this tension within the sharing of goods that structures in turn the act of judging:

> L'acte de juger a pour horizon un équilibre fragile entre les deux composantes du partage: ce qui départage ma part de la vôtre et ce qui, d'autre part, fait que chacun de nous prend part à la société. (J1 189–90)[11]

Both court judgement and societal distribution exist in a tension between deficient and excessive distance. Both the distribution of goods and the court verdict aim to establish a 'just distance'.

The inaugurating function of the 'judgement of law' is also reflected in Ricœur's account of the origin of a society of distribution. In an attempt to understand the contract that draws a community together (Latin *contrahere*, to draw together), John Rawls elaborates what he holds to be a purely procedural theory of justice. Like Hobbes and Rousseau before him, he imagines the origin of community in terms of a social contract struck in a fictional 'original situation', a hypothetical state of affairs in which the principles of justice that are to govern the putative society are chosen by its members.[12] The choice proceeds under three strict 'conditions of fairness', namely that each participant should (1) have a general knowledge of the psychology of human nature, (2) know what every reasonable being would wish to possess, and (3) have suitable knowledge of the different principles of justice in competition (SCA 269–70; OA 231–2). For his part, Rawls puts forward two such principles: first, the assurance of equal freedoms of citizenship (expression, assembly, vote, speech) for all; and secondly a 'principle of difference' which, assuming certain unavoidable inequalities, selects, according to the rule of 'maximin' (the maximisation of the minimum share in any distribution), the most equitable situation compatible with the rule of unanimity (SCA 270–4/OA 232–6). This brief sketch of Rawls' conditions of fairness and principles of justice allows us to see that the 'original situation' reflects the conventions of the law court (a space of just distances inaugurated by a judgement as to the measure of justice), and it is looking at these relations that will allow us to begin to appreciate how the question of legitimacy is recast by Ricœur in (a)topographical terms.

The spaces of court and community have five points of similarity. First, it is necessary in the original situation, as in the court, to have rules which govern discussion and guarantee fairness (at least in principle). The separation ensured by ritual and procedure is as indispensable to the court as are the principles of justice and procedural protocols to the Rawlsian original situation. Secondly, the only way to bestow the necessary authority on the deliberation that takes place in the original situation is to search for a dialectic between procedure and certain 'convictions bien pesées'/'considered convictions', for example that none in a society should be disadvantaged. Considered convictions serve as provisional fixed points that any conception of justice whatsoever has to respect (L1 223). Without them, and without the back and forth between conviction and procedure – a movement Rawls calls 'reflective equilibrium' (L1 225) – the proto-community of the original situation has no basis on which to be drawn together in a contract. This original, pre-judicial conviction mirrors the court's meaning-giving condition of possibility set in place by the 'judgement of law'. Thirdly, principles of justice issuing from the movement of reflective equilibrium within the original situation themselves relate to the practice of the community founded by the contract in the same way that the 'judgement of law' provides a yardstick by which to measure the facts of the case.

The fourth similarity between court and community is that both the law court and the original situation constitute not so much spaces of tension between two or more competing narratives as a struggle between narrative coherence and disintegration, attestation and suspicion, cosmos and chaos. Conviction is obtained by virtue of the court arriving at an account of the case which displays a sufficient level of Aristotelian coherence – a beginning, middle and end – such that to doubt the account would be unreasonable. The defence counsel is not bound to present an equally elaborate and rival story, but needs only to sow sufficient doubt that the events related by the prosecution may, in fact, lack coherence. It asks the suspicious question 'How do you know?' Similarly, the original situation is an attempt to fashion narrative cosmos – the ordered space of distribution cohering a community – out of the contingent chaos of its prehistory. Finally, and following on from this tension of coherence and incoherence, even the denial of any narrative coherence *is* an alternative narrative: it coherently, and perhaps also persuasively, explains why the coherence of the prosecution narrative can after all be reasonably doubted. The assertion of incoherence must be encased in a persuasive discursive form which guarantees its communicability. If this is true of the law court it also obtains for the Rawlsian theory of justice more widely, for the tension between integration and disintegration in the hypothetical original situation is always already part of the coherent narrative of the original situation, itself recounted within the community.

Specifically, the original situation is always a story only ever told from within the community whose existence it is supposed to explain and legitimate. It is a retroactive fiction that stages an encounter of cosmos and chaos within a relatively stable narrative frame.

Our final reflection on the relation of justice and space in Ricœur modifies this model of coherence and disintegration, for social space is not simply a tension between centrifugal and centripetal forces; it is expressed by Ricœur as the relation between space and non-space – the *atopos*. Discussing the relation of ideology and utopia, Ricœur asserts that 'imaginer le non-lieu, c'est maintenir ouvert le champ du possible' (TA 390), continuing 'l'utopie est ce qui empêche l'horizon d'attente de fusionner avec le champ de l'expérience. C'est ce qui maintient l'écart entre l'espérance et la tradition' (TA 430).[13] This is important because it disrupts the stability of the horizon. The tension of coherence and incoherence does not take place within a totalisable domain or within a single spatial horizon; the *écart* (gap) between justice and the social space, society and utopia, is a strange interval indeed, separating and therefore spanning the topographical and the a-topographical which, by definition, cannot be mapped in relation to each other. It is, to borrow a Derridean motif, an impossible measurement. Here we cross for the first time a problem to which we will have occasion to return below: what purchase can fiction have on reality? What relation can there be between somewhere and nowhere? The coherence of space (understood as a web of relations) needs, and is sustained by, its relation non-space, and this problematic relation provides for the process of deliberation, decision and appeal necessary to Ricœur's notion of the just 'between the legal and the good'.

Mapping the question of justice in terms of space and distribution, both within the court and in the wider community, begins to show how we might understand the legitimate exercise of violence in the execution of justice and, by extension, the possibility of engaging meaningfully with a Derridean suspicion of such claims. This violence does not rest on a totalitarian foundation and does not exist as an absolute right of the court, but derives what legitimacy it has from the utopia (non-place) of narrative, the avowedly fictional account of the original situation in which the principles of fairness were 'agreed'. It is precisely because this fictional justification is uncertain – an uncertainty which prevents the court arrogating to itself the absolute right to inflict coercive violence upon a given malefactor – that it requires an ongoing commitment on the part of the society in which it circulates as a founding fiction. But what sort of legitimation can such commitment provide? It is to an examination of this question that we now turn.

4.2 JUSTICE AND COMMITMENT

The justice exercised in both court and community seeks its legitimation in the non-space of a text: the law chosen in the 'judgement of law' and the fiction of the 'original situation' respectively. That it can be no other way, at least on a Rawlsian model of justice, Ricœur seeks to establish by evoking the fairness ('équité') necessary in the choice among the principles of justice in the original situation:

> Les principes de la justice peuvent devenir le propos d'un choix commun si, et seulement si, la position originelle est équitable, c'est-à-dire égale. Or, elle ne peut être égale que dans une situation hypothétique. (L1 203)[14]

Why can the fairness of the original situation only be assured hypothetically? The essay 'John Rawls: de l'autonomie morale à la fiction sociale' (L1 196–215) provides a response, using Kantian terminology to link autonomy and justice and their respective validations. Autonomy is self-validating, a Kantian 'fact of reason' (L1 212) that imposes itself on consciousness without presupposition and 'proclaims itself as originating law'.[15] Justice, however, is not a fact of reason; a country's laws are not attested by conscience in the presuppositionless, immediate way that characterises the Kantian *factum rationis*. The fairness of the original situation does not supplement this lack – along with the vacuum of legitimacy it engenders – with an *a priori* ground in conscience, but instead with a retrojected fictional moment of 'foundation' that is also a 'justification' (both terms being used by Ricœur as translations of Kant's *Begründung*) which legitimises *a posteriori*, and never absolutely, the coercive exercise of justice within the community.

Although no claim is made that the original situation was an actual state of affairs at a given moment in an unbroken historical sequence leading to the present, this is not the main reason that it has to be fictional. The primary philosophical justification for its fictionality is that, as the inauguration of the community, it cannot be unproblematically thought from within the bounds of the community it thus founds. The created cannot stage its own creation. *Oubli* (forgetting), which is inherent in the constitution of the consent that legitimises power (L1 29), separates the community from its foundation, which can only exist in relation to the community as a fictional trace. The constitution of legitimate power, just like the rule of law in a court of law, is pre-judicial par excellence, but not for that reason subjective or unjust. Ricœur explains:

> Le pacte n'a pas eu lieu? Précisément, il est de la nature du consentement politique, qui fait l'unité de la communauté humaine organisée et orientée par l'État, de ne pouvoir être récupérée que dans un acte qui n'a pas eu lieu, dans

un contrat qui n'a pas été contracté, dans un pacte implicite et tacite qui n'apparaît que dans la prise de conscience politique, dans la rétrospection, dans la réflexion. (HV 265)[16]

So there is no community without contract, but also no contract outside community, for the original situation exists only ever as a fictional retrojection from within the community. Between community and contract is an irreducible aporia of time. Moreover, like any 'fact' which 'has not taken place', the founding fiction cannot be mapped in relation to the space of the community.[17]

It would be wrong to equate talk of 'foundation' here with a violent and unimpeachable assertion of unchangeable laws that invest the machinery of justice with an unerring accuracy. Because the community has no fact of reason to attest its legitimacy in conscience, its nature is not that of an incontrovertible imperative. It must constantly engage in the to and fro of continual challenges to its 'just distances'. It is, in a formulation which evokes the cosmological tension of proximity and distance discussed in the previous section, 'conflictual-consensual' (L1 219). The tension of these centripetal and centrifugal forces allows the community to continue as a conflictual-consensual (not primarily conflictual-coercive) partnership.[18]

The tension between consensus and conflict in the community and the resultant danger of fracture are not only a threat to its survival, however, but also furnish its very condition of possibility. The community does not endure by virtue of its partners uncontroversially telling the same story of its origin any more than the space of the court is characterised by consensus from the outset. Indeed, if the latter were the case, the court could not exist as a court; as a mechanism for resolving conflict it would be redundant. The community is not threatened by, but relies on, the conflict engendered by claims of unjust distribution that would seem on one level to threaten it with disintegration. It is precisely because the community has mechanisms for dealing with different narratives and challenges to accepted narratives that it can persist as a community at all.

Given this impossibility of securely founding the community, something other than the acknowledgement of a fact of reason is required to maintain its fragile coherence, and that something is an irreducible but rigorously unjustifiable commitment. This is the thrust of Ricœur's critique of Rawls' social contract theory. In positing the condition of fairness and the principles of justice, Rawls seeks to rid his original situation of any teleological conviction about the nature of the good, but as Ricœur argues in 'Le cercle de la démonstration' (L1 216–230) (to take but one instance of his oft-repeated critique of Rawls), this supposedly procedural approach is in fact – though Rawls will not acknowledge it – a dialectic of procedure and conviction. Rawls does indeed introduce a prejudice into his reasoning, in the form of 'preliminary convictions' which are progressively validated in the process of choosing the principles of justice in the original situation. The procedural aspect of the theory provides an *a posteriori* justification for its preliminary convictions. Indeed, Ricœur holds that the same is true of all great moral theories, for moral philosophy founds nothing *ex nihilo*, but justifies the most widespread moral convictions only after the fact (L1 230). In thus maintaining that teleology can never be completely eradicated from a procedural account of justice, Ricœur stands not only against Rawls but also against Rousseau and Kant, both of whom speak of an original situation before all notions of the just (L1 203).

Ricœur's tensional theory of justice, relying on an original fiction and ineliminable convictions, provides a way to negotiate the opposition of demonstrability and arbitrariness (L1 168), the dichotomy of the absolute and totalitarian embodiment of Justice in a judgement, and a judgement made arbitrarily, according to no criteria of the just. This position is important, because, as we are about to see, it challenges the Derridean claim that this sort of mediation between the arbitrary and the absolute is impossible. It also means that Ricœur has a response (not an absolute response, but still a response) to the question 'why *this* judgement?', the question of what legitimises one particular dispensation of justice over another. Let us now look at Ricœur's mediation more closely, first considering his avoidance of a judgement which would claim to be absolute.

Ricœur forestalls any absolute, violent incarnation of justice by making the just contingent on the very denial of absolute justice. In the same way that, in his theory of metaphor, the literal reference of descriptive discourse must be suspended before the more primordial second-order metaphorical reference can emerge (MV 279/RM 300), so also a community must renounce inscribing justice absolutely (or 'literally') in any exercise of coercive violence before its dispensation of justice can be considered legitimate. Such a renunciation of the incarnation of justice (though not the aspiration to justice) in any given judgement is pre-eminently ethical and opens a space – in a manner again reminiscent of the metaphor which can bring new meanings into language – for a justice adjusted to the specificity of the case. This opened space is that of a 'specific plurivocity' (TA 227/*TA* 160), a multiplicity of interpretations which are neither endless nor all equally valid.

The trial does not issue in univocal dogmatism, but in a decision that, while not claiming to be the Last Word on justice, nevertheless establishes a just distance between the parties while remaining open to appeal. The space of the court in Ricœur's thinking is a space of interpretation *between* scientific proof and sophistry. This space of opinion between *doxa* and *epistēmē*, the place in which Ricœur in 'Éthique et politique' (TA 433–08; 'Ethics and Politics', *TA* 325–37) situates the 'opinion droite' ('honest opinion' – TA 445/*TA* 335), has three characteristics: it is rhetorical, hermeneutical and poetical (L2 479–94). First, it is a place of rhetoric because the arguments circulating within it are not susceptible of apodictic proof but must be judged according to the 'logic of the probable' which inclines without necessitating. Secondly, it is a hermeneutic space, and cannot be reduced to conviction alone. If a judgement is to be reached, the law court must be, and must continue to be, a space of deliberation. Thirdly, the nature of the judgement exercised in such a space is poetic, creating a decision beyond the predictability of mere calculability, and taking account of the singularity of the case.

The problem of negotiating the extremes of demonstrability and arbitrariness is addressed by Derrida in *Force de loi*. For Derrida, the impossibility of justice being present hangs on the aporia between, on the one hand, the Other of *la Justice*, singular and radically unknowable, and, on the other hand, universalising and determined *le droit* (law). Derrida is careful to distinguish the decision from mere rule-following, an act of administrative calculation without reference to incalculable and heterogeneous justice, and as such only capable of attaining a level of *justesse* (precision), a measure of correspondence, 'l'adéquation entre ce qui est et ce qui est dit ou pensé, entre ce qui est et ce qui est compris'.[19] The just decision, where 'just' is understood in terms of *justice* (not *justesse*), however, is the decision which, *per impossibile*, 'passes through' the aporia, calculates the incalculable in an 'impossible experience'. Such a judgement can never be identified; one can never say 'I am just'.[20] The second of the three related moments that Derrida identifies in *Force de loi* as aporetic, '*la hantise de l'indécidable*'[21] states the aporia of law in the following terms: a decision which does not pass by the undecidable (that which cannot, but must, be calculated) is not just (according to *justice*), for it is not free and responsible but mere pre-programmed rule following. The undecidable itself, however, is unjust, for justice demands to be enshrined in a law which can be enforced, and only a decision can be just. On the one hand, justice is that which must not wait,[22] which demands a decision right now, but if this demand is heeded, any decision which interrupts the undecidable is illegitimate, premature and unjust.[23] The urgent pressure to decide, to enforce the law, culminates in a moment of arbitrariness and madness, as an action 'sans calcul et sans règle, sans raison ou sans rationnalité théorique'.[24] A just and responsible judgement must be a repetition (it must not *only* follow a rule of law, but this it must nonetheless do), but also a fresh pleading of the justice of the law, a re-petition: 'à la fois réglée et sans règle'.[25] In Derrida's concern not to inscribe justice within the horizon of the same, to allow for a genuine surprise, the moment of madness in which justice is 'calculated' is radically indeterminate, a-rational, and therefore there is no way to discern whether one judgement is more or less just than another. The radical impossibility of arbitration is the price paid for the radical unpredictability of the form which the radical Other of Justice will take. The just cannot be predicted, but neither by that same token can it be judged.

Nevertheless, these considerations do go some way to addressing Richard Kearney's concerns that deconstruction cannot distinguish between 'strangers, gods and monsters'.[26] Justice for Derrida is irreducibly incalculable, but that does not mean it has nothing to do with calculation or that it is (to coin a term too often and hastily employed in these arguments) 'arbitrary'. What Derrida is attempting to achieve in his careful negotiation of *droit* and *justice* (and also what Ricœur is attempting when he conjures with original fiction and commitment) is a position which capitulates neither to the calculable nor to the arbitrary. What Derrida ends up with is (1) more of a compromise than a radical solution, for in the judgement which is 'both regulated and without regulation' the possibilities for the radically unexpected are, whatever the rhetoric, circumscribed, and (2) inasmuch as this is the case, Derrida's solution is vanishingly close in its outcome to Ricœur's specific plurivocity or Merleau-Ponty's empirical pregnancy, with the difference (massive in procedural terms, but not so great when viewed in relation to the 'verdicts' which each position is capable of producing) that Derrida passes through aporia and madness where Merleau-Ponty and Ricœur draw on creativity and imagination. The great difference between them at this point is not the negotiation of precedent and singularity but the possibility of arbitrating between competing versions of justice, and it is in turning our attention to this crucial difference that our investigation leads us to a consideration of the fragmentation and eventual incommensurability of different measures of justice.

4.3 JUSTICE AND FRAGMENTATION

If the space of justice is conflictual-consensual because of its fictional foundation and the ineliminable commitment of those who desire to live together, then the notions of justice circulating within this space are plural, even incommensurable. A critical reading of Rawls through Michael Walzer's *Spheres of Justice* and Luc Boltanski and Laurent Thévenot's *De la Justification*[27] leads Ricœur to affirm that there is no such thing as one unified measure of justice, but a host of different justices which society must find a way to negotiate fairly.

In contrast to Rawls' understanding of the just as a single measure in *A Theory of Justice*, a position he manages to maintain by not evaluating the nature of the goods to be distributed in the original situation, Walzer identifies a multiplicity of goods (revenue, land, services, education, health, security, public jobs, citizenship and so on), each with its *own* measure of justice. The key to Walzer's approach is the dual role played by the good of political power. The last chapter of *Spheres of Justice* deals with political power in part as a good distributed like any other, yet political power also entertains a unique relationship with the act of distribution itself, a relationship which Ricœur terms 'the political paradox', according to which politics seems both to constitute one sphere of justice among others and to envelop all the other spheres (J1 127/J 81). Ricœur situates the idea of 'spheres of justice' at the all-important middle ground between dogmatism and arbitrariness that we have been elaborating as a means of responding to Derrida's questioning; 'between the procedural unity of justice and the fragmentation of legal formations all over the world, there is some kind of intermediate level, that of the spheres of justice.'[28] Ricœur relates these concerns directly to the wider question of coherence and fragmentation as he continues with the following observation:

> You can see, therefore, that I am much interested in that which was called *metaxu*, 'intermediary' by the Greeks, which is between the infinitely scattered variety and the too formal, too empty, too abstract unity.[29]

The idea of spheres of justice by no means suggests that the goods are easily measured against each other, or that the distribution is a matter of mathematical proportionality alone.[30] 'Entre ces biens, aucune priorité ne s'impose d'elle-même comme une évidence absolue ou comme un ordre des choses',[31] and the difficulty inherent in measuring the goods is clear in Ricœur's succinct question in *Parcours de la reconnaissance*: what is the standing of a great industrialist in the eyes of a great orchestral conductor? (PR 305/COR 209). Nevertheless, as he was dissatisfied with the Rawlsian presumption of the commensurability of goods, so too Ricœur expresses doubts concerning Walzer's understanding of justice, for the distributing function of political power still assumes that conflicts are arbitrated by shared values. In order to move away from this assumption Ricœur turns to the work of Luc Boltanski and Laurent

Thévenot, for whom arbitration proceeds in terms of a number of strategies of justification each belonging to a city (*cité*) or world (*monde*) (PR 301/COR 205). Ricœur explains:

> Il s'agit en effet de régimes d'actions justifiées, qui méritent d'être appelés des « cités » dans la mesure où ils donnent une cohérence suffisante à un ordre de transactions humaines; des « mondes », dans la mesure où des choses, des objets, des dispositifs servent de référents stables, à la façon d'un « monde commun » dont les épreuves se déroulent dans une « cité » donnée.[32]

Boltanski and Thévenot's theory of plural cities avoids both a Rawlsian formal universalism and the opposite extreme (from which it is hard to distinguish the Derridean understanding of the decision) of an in principle limitless pluralism, proposing instead a regulated pluralism ('pluralisme réglé')[33] according to which the inhabitants of one world can be woken up to the values of another without having to share them:

> Une nouvelle dimension de la personne est ainsi révélée, celle de comprendre un autre monde que le sien, capacité que l'on peut comparer à celle d'apprendre une langue étrangère au point d'apercevoir sa propre langue comme autre parmi les autres. (PR 306)[34]

Recognition here is not adoption and does not suppose an aporia of decision in the case of someone who is woken to new values. It is compatible with ongoing commitment and conviction. In order better to understand what Ricœur, elaborating further on recognition, means by an individual's 'competency to live in several worlds',[35] a comparison with the paradigm of translation is instructive. Translation is a way of making what is incomparable comparable (PR 306/COR 209) and provides 'le remède à la pluralité en régime de dispersion et de confusion' (J2 37).[36] Translation does not produce an identical copy, nor a copy which is indistinguishable from the source text, yet there is some equivalence with what it translates, an 'équivalence sans identité'/'equivalence without identity' (J2 38/ROJ 29) (note again the cosmological tension of proximity and distance) as a compromise marrying singularity and communicability and remaining at a just distance from the translated text (J2 40/ROJ 31). The translation is a recognition both of the irreducible difference of languages and also of the possibility of communication despite such differences, and neither of these two points is sacrificed to the other.

In terms of the paradigm of translation (J2 125–40/ROJ 106–20), the relation of the elements of a community is not one of identity, nor one of absolute incommensurability; it is once more an equivalence without identity (J2 134/ROJ 114), neither subsumption nor untranslatability, but conflictual-consensual tension. In the terms of *De la Justification*, the mediation of singularity and communicability is found in the motif of compromise:

> Dans un compromis, on se met d'accord pour composer, c'est-à-dire pour suspendre le différend, sans qu'il ait été réglé par le recours à une épreuve dans un seul monde.[37]

As a result, compromises are 'fragile and ill-founded'[38] and just as judgements are always open to appeal, so also compromise is always threatened with being denounced by pamphleteers from all sides as a surrender of principle (PR 306/COR 210). The theory of compromise is neither a Rawlsian unitary, procedural solution nor an affirmation of incommensurable individualities, for 'la thèse de la pluralité des régimes d'actions justifiées reste celle d'un rationalisme pluriel selon lequel chaque ordre ouvre des possibilités et impose des exigences. La contingence et l'arbitraire trouvent ici leur limite.'[39] Compromise does not seek to eliminate difference but finds a way to mediate in a situation of différend, providing the capacity to pass from one regime of greatness to another without becoming locked into an oscillation between disillusioned relativism and the accusation of the pamphleteer.[40] The stakes here are clear: Ricœur is claiming to chart a course between dogmatism and undecidability, and therefore, for our purposes, to avoid the disconcerting inability of deconstruction to arbitrate between different 'others' and different measures of justice.

This way of mediating between univocity and equivocity in arbitration allows Ricœur to go further than Alistair MacIntyre, who gloomily asserts that, faced with the different normative or evaluative concepts of rival arguments (rights versus universalisability), arbitration is reduced to a game of assertion and counter-assertion, there being 'no other way to engage in the formulation, elaboration, rational justification and criticism of accounts of practical rationality and justice except from within one particular tradition in conversation, cooperation and conflict with those who inhabit the same tradition.'[41] For Ricœur, by contrast, while there is no scientific way to decide the public good (SCA 300/OA 258) and no obvious candidates for the role of a universal to act as common ground between different regimes of greatness, there are 'universels potentiels ou inchoatifs' still to be discussed and worked out between cultures (SCA 336).[42] Universals themselves become a matter of interpretation:[43] universals 'in context' (L1 226). In matters of practical wisdom the universal cannot be constitutive but only regulative (CC 103/CC 65), and it seeks to go beyond the debate between the universalists and the communitarians (CC 106/CC 67). This is not unlike the 'principles' that Drucilla Cornell adduces at the end of *Philosophies of the Limit* to defend Derrida against charges of 'nihilism'.[44]

The genius of Ricœur's move here, one of a series of such moves that he makes, is to recognise and exploit the difference between an economy of reciprocity and an economy of mutuality.[45] Understanding the relation to the other in terms of reciprocity leaves one trapped in an interminable and impossible calculation of debt and credit according to which, as Derrida rightly notes, the only possible gift or promise is the impossible gift or promise, that which is not understood or recognised as such either by the donor or the recipient.[46] For Derrida, a gift is something that can never be recognised as such.[47] This leads in Derrida's thought to a double bind of gift-giving (or hospitality, or justice) and a reiteration of the problem of deciding between different 'others'. If, however, relations are understood in terms of mutuality then they are not subject to the paralysing calculation of debt and credit which necessitates any pure promise or pure gift being the impossible gift or promise. The emphasis moves from the changing balance of debt and credit and the impossible but unavoidable injunction to do justice to all others to the shared interest of the part-takers, while the overlapping spheres of the social space also allow for the independent development of different cities with their varying, even incommensurable economies of greatness.

Ricœur's appropriation of Boltanski and Thévenot's theory of compromise and his own argument for moving from a reciprocal to a mutual understanding of social relations allow him to retain the ubiquity of conflict without it paralysing communication and the desire to live together. More than that, the attempt to rid a democracy of conflicts is not desirable (SCA 300/OA 258), for what marks out a democracy is its recognised rules for the arbitration of disagreement. Democracy is the regime that accepts contradictions to the point where it institutionalises conflict (L1 174). Democracy, notes Ricœur, approvingly echoing Claude Lefort, acknowledges a fundamental indeterminacy (SCA 303/OA 260–1) and, as in the law court, the conflict and the convictions which lie at its heart are neither violently resolved nor violently suppressed, but rather institutionalised, the violence of their potential confrontation sublimated into ritual procedures of establishing a 'just distance'. It is simply not good enough any more to seek a Rawlsian solution to social cohesion, insists Ricœur in an interview with Richard Kearney, for 'in modern republics, the origin of sovereignty is in the people, but now we recognise that we have *many* peoples. And, many peoples means many centres of sovereignty – we have to deal with that.'[48]

Nevertheless, Ricœur does still introduce an overarching good of sorts, the desire to live a fulfilled life ('une vie achevée') (PR 126/COR 81). Is this a return to a Rawlsian universalism? Not quite, for whereas Rawls argues tenaciously for a strictly procedural theory of justice, Ricœur is quick to admit, as we have seen, that the procedural alone cannot account for his own understanding of arbitration, resting as it does on a presumption that, 'en dépit de la pluralité et de la violence, il existe un recoupement fondamental entre les différentes cultures, les différentes religions, etc. Il y a donc un acte de foi fondamental, que j'exprimerais par l'expression « en dépit de »' (DDH 81).[49] But what sort of relation can there be between the procedural and the pistic? Is Ricœur mediating the fragmentation of different measures of justice with a blithe shrug of the shoulders, leaping effortlessly over the interminable but necessary calculations which Derrida faces and takes seriously? Is his navigation of arbitrariness and absolutism at bottom a refusal to engage with the threat of either? In order to respond to this question we shall now focus on one of the most thoroughly developed instances of such navigation in Ricœur's thought: the relation of justice and love.

4.4 JUSTICE AND LOVE

The imperative to live together which drives Boltanski and Thévenot's theory of compromise finds philosophical expression in Emmanuel Lévinas' injunction that 'il faut une justice entre les incomparables' (PR 237).[50] This is the fundamental problem of justice, and whether we begin from the (Husserlian) pole of the *ego* or the (Lévinasian) pole of the *alter*, each time it is a case of comparing the incomparable and somehow making the incommensurable equal before the law (PR 238/COR 209). The way that Ricœur approaches the Lévinasian impasse is by attempting to understand the relation of love and justice, compassion and rigour. His aim is to move beyond a simple opposition according to which, to take an example from Boltanski, a clash of different principles of justification fuels conflict, whereas *agapē* ignores calculation and makes references to equivalence redundant.[51] Between a blindness to equivalence and an uncompromising demand for equivalence – or, better, *beyond* the opposition of the two – Ricœur searches for mediation. But what measure can there be between agapic love, which 'keeps no record of wrongs'[52] and a justice which is precisely about keeping records and ensuring equitable distributions? Is Ricœur painfully and belatedly coming to appreciate the impasse in which Derrida has been struggling all along?

Sensitive to the difference between the rule of justice and the singularity of *agapē*, Ricœur's hermeneutic phenomenology does not – and here he is markedly unlike Lévinas and Derrida – consider an aporetic disjunction of love and justice the price to pay for maintaining an ethicity beyond the merely calculable. We will briefly consider Ricœur's mediation of love and justice through two texts, *Amour et justice*[53] and the third study of *Parcours de la reconnaissance*, entitled 'La reconnaissance mutuelle' (PR 227–355),[54] showing how Ricœur cautiously feels his way towards a just love, moving beyond an aporetic disjunction of justice and *agapē*.

In Ricœur's intertwining of ethics and ontology, love emerges as the lodestar of his investigation. In *Amour et justice*, love is not merely the other of justice; it is otherwise than justice, of an incommensurable order. Ricœur glosses this incommensurability in terms of the difference between two economies: justice and the economy of equivalence, and *agapē* and the economy of superabundance. The question Ricœur poses in *Amour et justice* is: 'si nous donnons d'abord le pas à la disproportion, comment ne pas retomber dans . . . l'exaltation ou la platitude?' (AJ 10).[55] Precisely, Ricœur will argue (in a motif evoking the pull of centrifugal and centripetal forces with the like of which we are now familiar) with a 'living tension'. Without the ethics of love, justice would become the utilitarian 'do ut des': I give so that you will give (AJ 58/*LJ*, 200). Conversely love, the hypermoral, is for its own part dependent on the structures of justice for its expression:

> Si le supra-moral ne doit pas virer au non-moral, voire à l'immoral – par exemple à la couardise – , il lui faut passer par le principe de la moralité, résumé dans la Règle d'Or et formalisé par la règle de justice. (AJ 56)[56]

The relation of love and justice is one of entanglement and overlapping, not an irrecoverable dichotomy. Ricœur is both close to and far removed from Derridean patterns of thought at this point, recognising both the need for, and the inadequacy of, the rule of justice. Indeed, as Derrida comments, the difference between them is the slender but profound difference between the difficult and the impossible.[57] Far from seeking radically to dislocate superabundant love and calculating justice, Ricœur seeks to accomplish the difficult task of seeing their intertwining as a condition of ethics. He explores the relation of love and justice through a meditation on the biblical text of Luke 6: 27–31, with its 'strange contiguity' of the command to love one's enemies and the Golden Rule.[58] Neither the rule nor the commandment cancels the other, and '*l'éthique commune dans une perspective religieuse* consiste, selon moi, dans la tension entre l'amour unilatéral et la justice bilatérale et dans l'interprétation de l'une dans les termes de l'autre.'[59] Love speaks well enough, but it speaks otherwise than in the language of justice. Its pre-judicial imperative comes before the intervention of *Dikē's* scales. Here Ricœur resists the equation of discourse per se with reductive violence, challenging the dichotomy of an impossible escape from, or collapse into, ontologically totalising language.

Ricœur's understanding of the relation of love and justice as a 'living tension' is possible because both participate in the economy of the gift, not for Ricœur an economy of gift exchange on the model of Marcel Mauss' influential study,[60] but according to an understanding which foregrounds the mutuality of the relation between the giver and receiver of the gift, not the reciprocity of giving and receiving. In addition to the two poles of donor and recipient Ricœur identifies a third term, the relation that the shared practice of gift-giving and gift-receiving establishes between the parties, as the basis of thinking gift-giving in terms of mutuality.

In *Amour et justice* Ricœur moves back from the specifically theological concern of the association of the commandment to love one's enemies and the Golden Rule to consider love and justice per se, arguing that 'il est donc légitime d'étendre à la pratique sociale de la justice et aux principes de justice eux-mêmes le soupçon qui vient de frapper la Règle d'Or au nom de la logique de surabondance sous-jacente au commandement supra-éthique d'aimer ses ennemis' (AJ 52–4).[61] Nevertheless, the central question remains: does (the new commandment of) love annul justice (in the Golden Rule)? Do love and the logic of superabundance suspend justice and the logic of equivalence? Can love be commanded? Ricœur comments that another interpretation is possible, in which the commandment to love does not abolish the Golden Rule but instead reinterprets it in terms of generosity (AJ 54/*LJ* 200). In this other interpretation, the logic of equivalence is transformed, receiving from its confrontation with the logic of superabundance what Ricœur calls the capacity of raising itself above its perverse interpretations (AJ 58/*LJ* 200). What is undermined by the 'harsh words' of the logic of superabundance is not so much the logic of equivalence of the Golden Rule as its perverse interpretation (AJ 58/*LJ* 200). On Ricœur's reading, justice is understood through a hermeneutics of love.

This approach contrasts with a Derridean reading of the gift as 'totally foreign to the horizon of economy, ontology, knowledge, constative statements, and theoretical determination and judgement.'[62] Derrida is bound – because he understands the gift in terms of debt and reciprocity, not in terms of relationship and mutuality – rigorously to separate the gift from any economy of exchange:

> A gift is something that is beyond the circle of re-appropriation, beyond the circle of gratitude. A gift should not even be acknowledged as such. As soon as I know I give something . . . I just cancelled the gift. I congratulate myself or thank myself for giving something and then the circle has already started to cancel the gift . . . If the gift is given, then it should not even appear to the one who gives it or to the one who receives it, not appear as such . . . That is the condition the gift shares with justice . . . Justice and gift should go beyond calculation.[63]

Though it is clear why Derrida would want – and need – to maintain such a strict separation between the economy of equivalence and the economy of superabundance, it is also clear that the need is not shared by Ricœur, for whom there is no insuperable incommensurability of love and justice, if such an incommensurability is to be understood to mean that love is radically incomprehensible and aporetically removed from the hopelessly ontologising discourse of justice. The extravagance of the parabolic, the hyperbole of the eschatological and the logic of superabundance in ethics to which Ricœur appeals are not ranged against discourse and calculation. More than being simply intertwined with justice, however, love issues an insatiable demand for justice:

> L'amour ne nous dispense pas de justice, l'amour exige toujours plus de justice. C'est en cela que je retrouve l'universalité: il faut que la justice soit de moins en moins particulière, qu'elle soit de moins en moins inégalitaire, et donc qu'elle soit à la hauteur de l'exigence d'amour. (DDH 87)[64]

Concomitantly, justice is the necessary medium of love (AJ 62/LJ 201). But does this attempt to think love and justice as somehow intertwined not inevitably compromise each for the sake of the other in precisely the way that Derrida seeks to avoid? Not at all, and Ricœur argues that love deforms rules of justice towards an ever more lively singularity *and* towards an ever greater universality (AJ 66). This seemingly utopian construal can be appreciated only once we disengage from an understanding of justice as ossified and totalising rules and love as the radically unknowable and unspeakable. Both these characterisations belong to an economy of reciprocity, not to the sharing of mutuality. As Ricœur remarks, the tenacious incorporation, step by step, of a supplementary degree of compassion and generosity in all our codes (he is referring specifically to penal codes and codes of social justice) constitutes a perfectly reasonable, yet difficult and interminable task (AJ 66/LJ 202).

Ricœur is far from unaware of the threat, inherent in the idea of any intertwining of love and justice, that agapic discourse will become annexed as a mute legitimation of calculating justice. How can Ricœur's economy of the gift avoid an inevitable return to utilitarian reciprocity? For a response to this question we turn now to our second text, the third study of *Parcours de la reconnaissance*, and to its examination of gift exchange. Does not giving a gift in return for a gift received reduce the gesture to a logic of equivalence, imprisoning it in a stultifying *quid pro quo* of calculating reciprocity? It is surely this suspicion that prompts Derrida's posture in 'En ce moment même dans cet ouvrage me voici',[65] where he agonises over how to give to his friend Emmanuel Lévinas that which is not immediately inscribed in a circle of economy, while still offering him something: 'Si je restitue, si je restitue sans faute, je suis fautif. Et si je ne restitue pas, en *donnant* au-delà de la reconnaissance, je risque la faute.'[66]

What breaks the circle of symmetry for Derrida here is to make his offering to Lévinas beyond all restitution, in radical ingratitude,[67] which he does by exploring the relation in the thought of Emmanuel Lévinas (E.L., elle) between sexual difference and alterity as the 'tout autre' ('wholly other') beyond, or before, sexual difference.[68]

Ricœur for his part maintains a clear and crucial distinction between two different understandings of the gift: reciprocal, ceremonial gift exchange, and market exchange (PR 341/COR 235), unlike Marcel Mauss who places them in the same category, understanding the ceremonial gift as the archaic form of market exchange (PR 328/COR 225). What Ricœur calls the problematic of return in gift exchange is dealt with in *Parcours de la reconnaissance* by splitting the analysis of the gift into two levels: the level of the rule of exchange and the level of the discrete gestures of individuals. The 'circle of the gift,' belonging as it does to the first of these two levels, is a theory for a modern description of archaic societies, but practitioners of the gift avoid the problematic of return by reorienting the question governing reciprocity from 'why return?' to 'why give?': 'Au lieu d'obligation à rendre, il faut parler, sous le signe de l'*agapè*, de réponse à un appel issu de la générosité du don initial' (PR 351).[69] We must think the second gift as the second first gift (PR 350/COR 242), for instead of the obligation to reciprocate, any subsequent gift does not annul the first gift but reinforces the relation which it inaugurates: to give a gift in return is to recognise the generosity of the first giver through a corresponding gesture of reciprocity, to recognise the relation for which the initial gift is only a vehicle (PR 336/COR 232). Furthermore, *Parcours de la reconnaissance* situates the logics of equivalence *and* superabundance in terms of the regulated exchange of the market economy. The gift is still present in such an economy, where it is both embedded in and separate from the market laws of exchange, and between gift and transaction there is neither radical disjunction nor confusion.

This juxtaposition can be clarified with reference to a passage in *La Critique et la conviction* where Ricœur draws attention to the juxtaposition of a thriving philanthropic civil society and a market economy in the United States as a salient model of this paradoxical coexistence (we might say 'living tension') of the economy of justice and the gift which cuts across it, a coexistence of non-market relations to money and the most implacable system of profitability (CC 78/CC 48). Though Ricœur may find this juxtaposition ultimately 'inscrutable', an important principle has been established: gift exchange need not threaten the society of distribution and market exchange, just as exchange and charitable excess can, while not being reduced one to the other, inhabit the same social space, intertwined as they are in everyday practice (PR 343/COR 236). In a gesture which Ricœur calls the festive gift (PR 354/COR 245), justice is exceeded without being denied. Love does not stop short of justice, but intensifies it in a festive mode. This approach, though it does provide an alternative to reciprocity and debt, cannot silence the Derridean objection that thinking reciprocity as mutuality does not abolish the dissymmetry of self and other (PR 373/COR 260). Ricœur gives no definitive reply to Derrida's question further to his distinction between ceremonial gift and market exchange, acknowledging rather that mutual recognition is always fragile and never secured.

A detour via Ricœur's theory of justice has allowed us to identify with greater clarity what is at stake in the difference between Ricœur and Derrida. By thinking justice in terms of space, with its just distances and conflictual-consensual relations, and particularly the non-space of the 'original situation', Ricœur provides himself with an understanding of legitimacy that is neither absolute nor arbitrary. He develops this refusal of both extremes through arguing for the legitimacy of coercion in terms of the fragile and tensional commitment of the desire to live together and the role of a fictional narrative in the appeal to justice. But this raises the question succinctly stated by Alistair MacIntyre as 'whose justice?',[70] and Ricœur must supplement his study of Rawls with further detours via Walzer, and Boltanski and Thévenot, to account for a situation in which competing conceptions of justice exist alongside each other. In seeking neither to suppress difference nor to escalate it to the point where all differences become incommensurable, and building on Boltanski and Thévenot's notion of compromise and his own work on translation, Ricœur holds out a 'limited' or 'specific' plurivocity in contrast to deconstructive madness and undecidability. The move which this entails, from reciprocity and account-keeping to mutuality, sharing and relation, not only builds on Ricœur's own understanding of social relations in terms of part-taking and distribution but also adumbrates the intertwining of love and justice that he develops first in a theological register but then expands beyond purely theological concerns.

In terms of our investigation into the question of ontology in the relation of deconstruction and phenomenology this is a considerable advance. Ricœur almost splits the horns of the dilemma of incommensurability (deciding between different witnesses) and regress (who will witness for the witness?) that has emerged as the deconstructive-phenomenological impasse. He fails to solve the second question, however, for an ineliminable commitment does remain at the core of his attempts to overcome commensurability with compromise and translation. Indeed, is it possible to take account of each problem and give an adequate answer to both at once? In other words: is there such a thing as a deconstructive phenomenology? Ricœur has taken us as far as he can down this road, and now we must seek another companion, one whose philosophy displays many features both of Derrida's radical disjunction of economy and gift and Ricœur's community based on the mutuality of sharing. Our final companion, then, is Jean-Luc Nancy, and in the following two chapters we explore how far he can take us towards a deconstructive phenomenology.

NOTES

1. See Paul Ricœur, 'Le sujet convoqué'; 'The Summoned Subject', which was not published with the other ten studies but in a Catholic journal because of its overtly religious tenor.
2. 'aiming at the "good life" with and for others, *in just institutions*' (*OA* 172).
3. Hans-Georg Gadamer, *Truth and Method* 320–35.
4. Ricœur's treatment of jurisprudence is sufficiently generic not to be tied to any one legal system. It is therefore not necessary for him to discuss the major differences between Anglo-Saxon case law and the 'code civil' of the Cinquième République.
5. Brooks and Gewirtz (eds), *Law's Stories* 18.
6. Ricœur and Raynova, 'All That Gives Us to Think' 691.
7. Ricœur and Raynova, 'All That Gives Us to Think' 391.
8. 'too close in cases of conflict and too distant in those of ignorance, hate, and scorn' (*J* 132; translation altered).
9. Walzer's, *Spheres of Justice*, subtitled *A Defence of Pluralism and Equality*, is in part a critique and revision of Rawls' theory.
10. Ricœur and Raynova, 'All That Gives Us to Think' 674.
11. 'the act of judging has as its horizon a fragile equilibrium between these two elements of sharing: that which separates my share or part from yours and that which, on the other hand, means that each of us shares in, takes part in society' (*J* 132).
12. The 'original situation' is not original, nor is it a situation. It is not, nor ever was, a situation because it is entirely hypothetical, and it is not original

because it is a story told only retrospectively from within a community that retrojects it.
13. 'to imagine the non-judgement is to keep open the field of the possible . . . utopia is what prevents the horizon of expectation from fusing with the field of experience. It is what maintains the gap between hope and tradition' (author's translation).
14. 'The principles of justice can become the object of a communal choice if, and only if, the original position is equitable, or equal. But it cannot be equal other than in a hypothetical situation' (author's translation).
15. Kant, *Critique of Practical Reason* 31.
16. 'The pact has not taken place? Precisely, it is of the nature of political consent, which gives rise to the unity of the human community organised and orientated by the state, to be able to be recovered only in an act which has not taken place, in a contract which has not been contracted, in an implicit and tacit pact which appears as such only in political awareness, in retrospection, and in reflection' (*HT* 252).
17. Although Jean-Luc Nancy in *La Communauté désœuvrée* is suspicious of the closed nature of a community founded on myth, and although he will seek to think the world without myth, or more precisely with myth interrupted (CD 107–74/IC 43–70), he nevertheless provides a helpfully succinct characterisation of the fragility of Ricœur's reading of the original fiction in the gnomic sententia 'myth is a myth', by which he means both that the foundation is a fiction, and that fiction is a foundation (CD 140–1/IC 55).
18. It will be noted that the 'conflictual-consensual' structure of community echoes Ricœur's 'tensive' theory of metaphor, according to which the metaphorical 'is' signifies at the same time both 'is not' and 'is like' (MV 11; *RM* 18). Indeed, the tension of cosmos and chaos is a recurring idea that structures Ricœur's thought on a wide variety of subjects.
19. Derrida, *Force de loi* 16; 'an adequation between what is and what is said or thought, between what is said and what is understood' ('Force of Law' 4).
20. Derrida, *Force de Loi* 39; 'Force of Law' 10. It is this impossibility of recognition that Lawlor is forgetting when he boldly claims that 'in Derrida, the impossible can happen' (Lawlor, *Thinking Through French Philosophy* 48).
21. *Force de loi* 52 (JD's emphasis); '*the ghost of the undecidable*' ('Force of Law' 24).
22. Derrida, *Force de loi* 57; 'Force of Law' 26.
23. Ricœur acknowledges the same problem when he notes that the justification of penal sanction is the blind spot of the judicial system: 'selon moi, toute tentative de justification rationnelle de la peine et de la pénibilité de la peine paraît bien avoir échouée' (Ricœur, 'Le Juste, la justice et son échec' 294); 'in my opinion, every attempt rationally to justify punishment and the hardness of punishment seems rather to have failed' (author's translation). The difference between Ricœur and Derrida on this point will be explored below when we evoke the 'difficult' and the 'impossible'.

24. *Force de loi* 56; 'without calculation and without rules, without reason and without theoretical rationality' ('Force of Law' 25; translation altered).
25. *Force de loi* 51; 'both regulated and without regulation' ('Force of Law' 53).
26. See Kearney, *Strangers, Gods and Monsters*.
27. Boltanski and Thévenaut, *De la Justification*; *On Justification*.
28. Ricœur and Tóth, 'The Graft, the Residue, and Memory' 650.
29. Ricœur and Tóth, 'The Graft, the Residue, and Memory' 650.
30. Ricœur explains: 'C'est ici qu'une théorie pluraliste de la justice appelle plus que toute autre une réflexion spécifique sur la consistance du pouvoir politique en tant qu'arbitrage de distributions inégales. Un calcul d'optimum ne suffit pas à rendre légitime une distribution inégale' (Ricœur, 'La place du politique dans une conception pluraliste des principes de justice' 83); 'It is here that a pluralist theory of justice calls more than any other for a particular reflection on the consistency of political power as arbiter of unequal distributions. A calculation of the optimum is not enough to make an unequal distribution legitimate' (author's translation).
31. Droit, 'Un entretien avec Paul Ricœur. "La cité est fondamentalement périssable. Sa survie dépend de nous" '; 'Between these goods, no priority imposes itself as absolutely clear or as the very order of things' (author's translation).
32. Ricœur, 'Droit de cités'; 'So it is a case of justified regimes of action, that merit the name "cities" insofar as they give a sufficient degree of coherence to an order of human transactions, and "worlds" insofar as things, objects and systems serve the function of stable referents, like a "common world" whose tasks take place in a given "city" ' (author's translation).
33. Ricœur, 'Droit de cités'.
34. 'A new dimension of personhood is thereby revealed, that of understanding a world other than one's own, a capacity we can compare to that of learning a foreign language to the point of being able to appreciate one's own language as one among many' (*COR* 209).
35. Ricœur, 'Droit de cités'.
36. 'the remedy for plurality in a world of disperson and confusion' (*ROJ* 28).
37. PR, 306. Quoting Boltasnki and Thévenot, *De la Justification* 337; 'In a compromise one agrees in order to work things out – that is, in order to suspend the difference of opinion – without its having been governed by recourse to a test in just one world' (*On Justification* 337).
38. Ricœur, 'Droit de cités'.
39. Ricœur, 'Droit de cités'; 'the thesis of the plurality of justified regimes of action remains that of a plural rationalism according to which each order opens possibilities and imposes demands. Contingency and arbitrariness find their limit here' (author's translation).
40. PR, 307; *COR*, 210. Quoting Boltanski and Thévenot, *De la Justification* 421 (*On Justification* 346).
41. Alistair MacIntyre, *Whose Justice? Which Rationality?* 350.
42. 'potential or inchoate universals' (*OA* 289).

43. This refusal of both arbitrariness and absolutism bears marked resemblances to Jean-Luc Nancy's negotiation of universals, in which 'si l'universel n'est pas donné, ce n'est pas qu'il est à mimer ou à rêver ... c'est qu'il est à faire' (CMM 69); 'if the universal is not given, this does not mean that it needs to be dreamt or "mimicked" ... it means that it is to be invented' (CWG 60), and 'je ne juge pas d'après un universel que j'aurais vu, mais je ne juge pas non plus à l'aveuglette, je juge *de* l'universel, autrement dit, j'en décide. Je décide de l'*universum*' (DI 25) – 'I do not judge according to a universal that I have seen, but nor do I judge blindly, I *assess* the universal, in other words, I decide upon it. I decide upon the *universum*' (author's translation).
44. Cornell's 'principles' attempt to negotiate precisely the dichotomy of demonstrability and arbitrariness that we have seen Ricœur navigating. 'We can think of a principle', she explains, 'as the light that comes from the lighthouse, a light that guides us and prevents us from going in the wrong direction', and 'as for which principles we ultimately adopt within the *nomos*, we are left with the process of pragmatic justification based on the ability to *synchronise* the competing universals embodied in the *nomos*' (Cornell, *Philosophies of the Limit* 106). This seems rather a conservative construal that, once more, constrains the possibility of the truly unheard-of: more of a compromise than a radical solution.
45. Ricœur explains his use of the two terms: 'Par convention de langage, je réserve le terme de « mutualité » pour les échanges *entre* individus et celui de « réciprocité » pour les rapports systématiques dont les liens de mutualité ne constitueraient qu'une des « figures élémentaires » de la réciprocité' (PR 338); 'In accord with linguistic convention, I shall reserve the term *mutuality* for exchanges between individuals, and use *reciprocity* for those systematic relations for which such ties of mutuality constitute only one of the "elementary forms" of such reciprocity' (COR 223; translation altered).
46. It is instructive, in the light of the importance of the gift and related motifs in Derrida's ethics to note that Ricœur places gift giving, along with vengeance, in the category of reciprocation (Ricœur, 'Le Juste, la justice et son échec' 296).
47. 'un don destiné à la reconnaissance s'annulerait aussitôt' (Derrida, 'Donner la mort' 36); 'a gift given in order to elicit gratitude would annul itself immediately' (author's translation).
48. Ricœur and Richard Kearney, 'Universality and the Power of Difference' 147.
49. 'In spite of plurality and violence, there is a fundamental correspondence between different cultures, different religions etc. There is therefore a fundamental act of faith, that I would express with the words "in spite of"' (author's translation).
50. 'there must be justice among incomparable ones' (COR 161).
51. See Boltanski, *L'Amour et la justice comme compétences*.

52. 1 Corinthians 13: 5.
53. Paul Ricœur, *Liebe Und Gerechtigkeit = Amour et justice*.
54. 'Mutual recognition' (*COR* 150–246).
55. 'if we begin by acknowledging the disproportionality [of love and justice], how can we avoid falling into . . . exaltation or platitudes?' (*LJ* 189).
56. 'If the hypermoral is not in turn towards the nonmoral – not to say the immoral – for example, cowardice – it has to pass through the principle of morality, summed up in the Golden Rule and formalised by the rule of justice' (*LJ* 200; translation altered).
57. See Derrida, 'La parole. Donner, nommer, appeler'. A similar difference obtains between Merleau-Ponty and Derrida, for 'unlike Merleau-Ponty, for whom everything turns on the notion of possibility, for Derrida everything turns on the notion of impossibility' (Lawlor, *Thinking Through French Philosophy* 59).
58. 'But I say unto you which hear, Love your enemies, do good to them which hate you, Bless them that curse you, and pray for them which despitefully use you. And unto him that smiteth thee on the one cheek offer also the other; and him that taketh away thy cloak forbid not to take thy coat also. Give to every man that asketh of thee; and of him that taketh away thy goods ask them not again. And as ye would that men should do to you, do ye also to them likewise' (Luke 6: 27–31, KJV. See AJ 54–6/*LJ* 197).
59. Ricœur, 'Entre philosophie et théologie: la règle d'or en question' 8, PR's emphasis; 'communal ethics in a religious perspective consists, I think, in the tension between unilateral love and bilateral justice, and in the interpretation of the one in terms of the other' (author's translation).
60. Marcel Mauss, 'Essai sur le don. Forme et raison de l'échange dans les sociétés archaïques'; *The Gift: Forms and Functions of Exchange in Archaic Societies*.
61. 'it is legitimate for us to extend to the social practice of justice and to the principles of justice themselves the suspicion that strikes the golden rule through the logic of superabundance underlying the hyper-ethical commandment to love one's enemies' (*LJ* 199).
62. Derrida, in Kearney, 'On the Gift: A Discussion between Jacques Derrida and Jean-Luc Marion' 59.
63. Caputo, *Deconstruction in a Nutshell* 18–19.
64. 'Love does not excuse us from justice; love demands ever more justice. It is there that I rediscover universality: justice must be less and less particular, less and less unequal, and so it must be up to the demand of love' (author's translation).
65. Translated as 'At This Very Moment in this Work Here I Am', in *Re-Reading Levinas* 11–48.
66. Derrida, 'En ce moment même' 24; 'If I restitute, if I restitute without fault, I am at fault. And if I do not restitute, by giving beyond acknowledgment, I risk the fault' ('At this very moment' 14).
67. Derrida, 'En ce moment même' 25; 'At This Very Moment' 15.

68. Derrida, 'En ce moment même' 52; 'At This Very Moment' 40.
69. 'Instead of the obligation to give in return, it would be better, under the sign of agape, to speak of a response to a call coming from the generosity of the first gift' (COR 243).
70. See MacIntyre, *Whose Justice? Which Rationality?*

5. Jean-Luc Nancy: Sense

A consideration of Paul Ricœur's hermeneutic phenomenology has allowed us to trace points of (more usually) proximity and (occasionally) divergence between Derrida and Ricœur on questions of alterity and coherence. In terms of alterity, 'life' and 'narrative' for Ricœur are inextricably intertwined, and the meaning of prefigured action is not posited but attested in the context of a hermeneutic wager: it is a 'broken attestation'. Similarly, Derrida cannot justify the 'good' of alterity, but assumes it. As regards the question of coherence, Ricœur's thought deals with a constant tension between chaos and cosmos: narrative is a 'discordant concordance' and justice is 'conflictual-consensual'. Furthermore, the relation of incommensurable terms in the notion of justice is a matter not of correspondence but of translation and compromise, and coherence is achieved on the basis not of reciprocity but of mutuality. Derrida, elaborating a notion of gift-giving and receiving which privileges reciprocity, cannot avail himself of the coherence that mutuality, compromise and translation afford Ricœur. We found it possible to address these two problems more adequately, however, by moving away from considering the *what* to the *that* and the *who* of the problem, from *what* is asked in the question 'How do you know?' to the event of the question and its provocation to 'justify yourself!'

This raised a further question. Is there any way of mediating between the positions we have called 'Ricœur' and 'Derrida' and, more broadly, between 'phenomenology' and 'deconstruction', the 'difficult' and the 'impossible'? This tantalising prospect brings with it a host of further questions. Can we, after all, talk of 'presence', 'contact' and ontology 'after' deconstruction? What might Ricœur's spacing and fictionalising of justice look like in a deconstructive mode? Is the impossibility of distinguishing and arbitrating between different others an ineliminable trait of the deconstructive aporetics of decision? In order to press these questions further, we turn now to the work of Jean-Luc Nancy. Nancy is a strategic interlocutor for our purposes because he is (as Ian James has persuasively demonstrated)[1] indebted to Merleau-Ponty[2] and also (as I am the first to argue) draws substantially on the work of his former thesis director Paul Ricœur. Not only this, but his warm friendship and intellectual admiration for Derrida place him, relationally at least, at precisely the crossover it is our purpose to interrogate. But how are we to name Nancy's work? James remarks that his thought 'develops into what one might call a postphenomenological philosophy of existence',[3] and Derrida in *Le Toucher* talks about 'une sorte de réalisme absolu et post-déconstructif',[4] while B. C. Hutchens warns that Nancy merits the appellation 'Derridean' 'only in a very general, and ultimately unhelpful, way'.[5] While all these attempts to situate Nancy are heuristically helpful as we begin to look at his work, we shall refrain from arbitrating between them at the outset, letting his relation to existence, deconstruction and the post-deconstructive emerge in the course of our interrogation. In this chapter we shall examine Derrida's uneasiness with Nancy's ontological claims and elaborate a Nancean response, focusing primarily on Nancy's understanding of ontology as opening and exposure, presence as passage and contact as interruption. Bringing to light the importance in his work of the motif of the *sans pourtant* ('yet without') we shall mount a careful but robust reply to the Derridean questioning, which will not leave Nancy's thought without problems of its own.

Until now, Nancy has been predominantly interpreted in terms of 'the political' and the question of community,[6] but while this reflects the concerns of his earlier work (principally *La Communauté désœuvrée*) it neglects the growing importance in his more recent writings of a broadening set of concerns. It is time to move the reception of Nancy's work on, and this is best served by situating his thought on the broadest canvas possible, which we will choose to summarise here under the motif of *kosmos*.

Kosmos and meaning are intimately related in Nancy's thought, as is most clearly seen in the way in which he divides the historical relation of sense and world into three broad epochs. In ancient times, signification was accessed 'en tant que la disposition du monde' (OP 39),[7] where the world is understood as:

> *mundus*, pur, propre, bien disposé, bien arrangé, monde. C'est ce que, selon Plutarque, Pythagore a voulu dire avec le mot *kosmos*: le monde est un bel arrangement, bien net, pur et propre. Le monde, c'est ce qui n'est pas immonde. (ES 98)[8]

In the modern age, however, Kant's disjunction of noumenal law and phenomenal nature, along with the withdrawal of meaningfulness witnessed by Pascal in his anxiety at the 'silence éternel des espaces infinis'[9] indicate for Nancy a Blanchotian 'désastre du sens' (SM 70):[10] There is no longer any 'consideration' or 'constellation' of the world, which is now understood in terms of mathematical precision and calculation, and accessed by way of the will to produce signification (OP 39), a will driven in matter of fact by the loss of signification. There is no longer a *mundus* or *cosmos*, in which we have a place and orientate ourselves (SM 13/SW 4), and the world is no longer the *monde* whose signification is guaranteed by the relation of the 'ici-bas' ('here below') and the 'au-delà' ('beyond') of the ancient cosmology (OP 40). The world can now only be understood according to the infinite expansion – the dissemination – of *univers*. What has come to an end is the ability to give the world a determinable sense (SM 15/SW 5). But this modern understanding of sense has in turn passed, and Nancy's main preoccupation is to explore what its passing opens onto.

5.1 OPENING

The third epoch of sense is described by Nancy variously in terms of opening, dis-closure ('déclosion') and exhaustion. What is exhausted is *signification* or *verité*, and what is opened is *sens*. *Signification* consists in establishing or assigning presence. From Plato to Saussure, *signification* is the conjunction of the sensible and the intelligible (OP 31). As such it is *'le modèle même de la structure ou du système fermé sur soi, ou mieux encore en tant que fermeture sur soi'* (OP 32; J-LN's emphasis).[11] *Sens*, on the other hand, is anterior to all *signification*, making all significations possible (SM 21/SW 9), and it precedes, succeeds and exceeds every appropriation of signification (SM 24/SW 11).

Sens opens a space that *signification* punctuates, a spatiality before all space and time, the archi-spatiality of the matricial or transcendental form of the *world* (SM 29/SW 14). *Sens* itself is not *what* is communicated, but *that* it is communicated (SM 178/SW 114); it is 'que soit possible quelque chose comme la transmission d'un « message ». Il est rapport comme tel, et rien d'autre' (SM 184).[12] In short, 'la signification, c'est le sens repéré – tandis que le sens ne réside peut-être que dans la venue d'une signification possible' (OP 14).[13] Now, space is no longer understood as extensible volume (EsEP 12), and when we think space today 'cette pensée qui se dit elle-même *de l'espace*, c'est la nécessaire réouverture de l'espace et des places après le temps de leur conquête et de leur implosion' (EsEP 13).[14] What is opened is sense.

The relation of signification to sense is one of exhaustion and limit. Commenting on the production of sense in Modernity, Nancy argues that we cannot grasp the signification of the West, but only 'rencontrer, sur une limite insignifiable de la signification, quelque chose qui se présente comme la réalité et comme la nécessité de cet accomplissement' (OP 70–1).[15] It arrives and communicates to us in a shock, not as a signification but a quantity of movement, as the momentum, departure or sending of a destination (OP 71). This destination proposes itself in the following form: the West, as it comes to an end, requires neither that we resusscitate significations, nor that we resign ourselves to their annulment, but that we understand that the demand of sense now comes via the exhaustion of significations (OP 70–1). Meaning here no longer carries determinate content, but is rather exposure to/at the limit, a characterisation that refers back to the *thaumazein* of the pre-Socratics (and resonates, for that same reason, with Merleau-Ponty's interrogative), for astonishment is nothing other than that which arrives at the limit (OP 104). At the limit, truth is simple presentation ('la *simple* presentation', J-LN's emphasis), presence before signification.

Elsewhere, Nancy elaborates on this 'simple presentation' in terms of the 'patency' of sense:

> ... la présentation de la présentation n'est pas une représentation ... la patence est rapportée à elle-même – comme si l'on énonçait simplement: *patet*, « il est manifeste », « il est évident » ... pour faire paraître ... le *il* « sujet » de l'évidence. (M 62)[16]

With the motif of patency, Nancy is expressing the phenomenological 'given' – that of which sense is made – in a postphenomenological register,[17] with the difference that for Nancy there can be no eidetic reduction and no givenness of meaning, for the world is not given, but simply *is*. Once more, what is 'patent' is not the *what* (*quid sit*) but the *that* (*an sit*) of sense.

Sense, affirms Nancy, can take no other 'form' today (if indeed it is a form) than that of the opening, the form through which that which belongs to sense can arrive (OP 13). This brings about a shift in the meaning of 'the real': no longer the conjunction of the sensible and the intelligible, it is 'ce qui heurte ou ce qui viole la signification – l'ouverture du sens, ou encore sa mise à nu' (OP 106).[18] Nancy characterises this openness as a gaping (*béance*) of sense (CA 12), echoing the possibility-laden 'empirical pregnancy' so central to Merleau-Ponty's account of intramundane meaning. In *L'Évidence du film* Nancy appropriates the Merleau-Pontean vocabulary more directly:

> Il s'est ainsi constitué une nouvelle configuration de l'expérience: bien plus que l'invention d'un art surnuméraire, il nous est apporté ce qu'on pourrait nommer une nouvelle *prégnance*, si l'on veut bien entendre par là, et fidèlement à ce terme, *une forme et une force qui précède et qui fait mûrir une mise au monde, la pousée d'un schème de l'expérience en train de prendre ses contours*. (EF 21; author's emphasis)[19]

Pregnancy here is not experience itself, with its contours and meanings, but the possibility of such experience, astonished exposure at the limit of meaningfulness rather than the presentation of meanings.

The demand is not merely for a new thought, but for a new thinking, a new style of thought, and philosophy needs a new style because it can no longer signify truth in terms of signification. This new style is one that can think openness without myth or morals, think the *sens* of *signification*, and not just the *signification* of *sens*. It is what Nancy identifies as the demand of reason in Derrida and Deleuze. This demand casts light on its own obscurity, not by bathing it in light, but by acquiring the art (strength, discipline) to let the obscure emit its own clarity (*DDC* 6). The challenge to which Nancy's thought is responding is the need to think sense not as *what* but *that*, or rather as 'that *as* what':

> Désormais, il nous revient d'approcher à nouveau cela, qui n'est ni science, ni religion, ni philosophie – ce qui ne donne pas un sens à échanger, mais qui est le sens de l'échange, ou encore l'échange lui-même en tant que sens: de notre existence en commun. (PD 43)[20]

The determination not to reduce *sens* to *signification* but to let its own obscurity shine forth means that the question of the presence of meaning in the world is recast along lines that are by now familiar from our investigations of Merleau-Ponty and Ricœur. For Nancy, the relation of language and world is not collapsed, but problematised. With echoes of Merleau-Ponty's promiscuity and Ricœur's account of the relation of 'life' and 'narrative', Nancy insists that we must interrogate the truth in terms of something of the thing in language, and something of language in the thing (OP 84). This issues in a different notion of 'presentation', not simply the communication of a meaning but, once more in a register with Merleau-Pontean resonances, 'aussi bien celle de l'exposition d'une chose, et celle d'un *appel*, ou celle d'un clin d'œil' (OP 85; author's emphasis).[21] So presentation is not the representation of signification, but a call, a wink and an invitation. The 'call' of sense is a call not to foreclose sense in signification, but a call to 'résister à l'installation, au calcul, à la domination etc. C'est donc asymptotiquement un appel à se régler sur l'impossible, sur l'incalculable.'[22]

In a meditation on reading, Nancy combines a Merleau-Pontean sensitivity to the call with the Lévinasian distinction between *Dire* (Saying) and *le dit* (the said):

> Le livre ne parle pas *de*, il parle *à*, ou bien il ne parle pas *de* sans aussi parler *à*, et de telle façon que cette adresse est indissociable, essentiellement indétachable de cela « adont » il est parlé ou écrit . . . (SCP 22)[23]

Crucially, Nancy goes on to situate the address in terms of *form*, and to make the crucial distinction between the affirmative call to understand, the *that* of a to-be-understood, and the *what* of understanding, however much the latter may try to frustrate the former:

> L'Idée, la Forme, désigne ici très exactement la forme de l'adresse, et, mieux encore, la forme *en tant qu'*adresse. Un livre est une adresse ou un appel. Sous la ligne mélodique de son chant court, sans interruption, la basse continue de son invitation, de sa demande, de son injonction ou de sa prière: « Lis-moi! lisez-moi! » (Et cette prière murmure toujours, même lorsque l'auteur déclare: « Ne me lisez pas! » ou: « Jette mon livre ! ») (SCP 22–3)[24]

The tension here has the same form as that between the question 'How do you know?' and 'How do you know?' *as* a question, and the evocation of the call here parallels the move from the 'what?' to the 'who?' in Ricœur: meaning is to be understood less as a particular signification and more as a call or interpellation, according to Heidegger's reading of *hermeneuein*, which Nancy glosses as the sense of the transmission of a message, or the announcement of a piece of news and of its carriage by a bearer (OP 89).

Consonant with the *sens* which opens *signification*, the call to which Nancy responds has no determinate content but is itself a spacing, the possibility of content. Nancy uses the motif of 'resonance' to shift the burden of the call from a significative intramundane interpellation to the rhythm of the world: 'derrière la réponse, il y a quelque chose que, pour l'occasion j'aimerais appeler la résonance'.[25] What Merleau-Ponty called 'style', Nancy seeks to render in more musical terms, evoking, in addition to 'resonance', 'rhythm' and 'melody'. Melody, according to Nancy, 'haunts' an animal, giving it a manner of existing:

> le déploiement d'un *Umwelt* c'est une mélodie, une mélodie qui se chante elle-même . . . Le thème de la mélodie animale n'est pas en dehors de sa réalisation manifeste, c'est un thématisme variable que l'animal ne cherche pas à réaliser par la copie d'un modèle, mais qui hante ses réalisations particulières sans que ces thèmes soient le but de l'organisme. (N 228, 233)[26]

This recalls from the *Phénoménologie de la perception* 'cette manière de vibrer et de remplir l'espace qu'est le bleu ou le rouge' (PP 245).[27] Nancy also picks up Merleau-Ponty's link between corporéalité and resonance, suggesting that in dance 'l'autre, là-bas, proche dans son éloignement, tendu, plié, deplié, retentit dans mes jointures. Je ne le perçois proprement ni par les yeux, ni par l'ouïe, ni par le toucher. Je ne perçois pas, je résonne' (All 139).[28] In addressing the question of where this resonance comes from, Nancy echoes Merleau-Ponty's rejection of transactional contact and Ricœur's critique of reciprocity. It comes 'forcément d'un autre encore, d'un encore plus autre au fond d'elle-même. *Autrement même*. Et pour cette raison, *encore moins reçu comme un message*. Mais plutôt surpris dans un saisissement, à la manière d'une crampe ou d'une crispation – à moins que ce n'ait été une détente, une relâche, un dessaisissement' (All 140).[29]

Nancy's evocation of call as a cosmological interpellation – a function of the spacing of the world and not a propositional content – still gives Derrida misgivings. The call beyond the calculable, Derrida suggests, may well be what Nancy means by *sens*, but he wonders if it is a call to carry oneself, precisely, beyond sense.[30] The call must not itself have a sense; it must exceed sense. For Derrida, 'tout autre est tout autre' means that there is a multiplicity of others and of calls, before each one of which I am equally responsible. Each is infinite, and I must measure myself against its incommensurability with all others. To respond to one I must sacrifice my responsibility for the others. The call, for Derrida, cannot have meaning. But is the pregnancy of *sens* – the communication *that*, not the communication *what* – not sufficiently removed from determinate content? We shall return to this question in our discussion of the decision at the close of this chapter.

For Nancy the world is patently and tautologically meaningful, for the disjunction of sense and world is always already false. At the heart of being and the world there is (as we have seen in Merleau-Ponty's pregnancy and Ricœur's prefiguration) an obscure sense to which we have an obligation (CA 20). Rather than being figured in the affirmative (and also distinct from Merleau-Ponty's interrogation or Ricœur's attestation), Nancy's sense is a 'but . . .' in the closure of signification. A 'not . . . but not . . .' pattern recurs in Nancy's thinking with the motif of the *sans pourtant* ('yet without').[31] Nancy expresses the task of philosophy as 'ne pas abandonner l'office de la vérité ni celui de la figure, *sans pourtant* combler de sens l'écart qui les sépare' (UJ 11; author's emphasis).[32] Similarly, he characterises the contemporary universe as 'sans providence *et pourtant non* privée de sens' (SM 62; author's emphasis).[33] We live not in a cosmos, nor in chaos, but in the 'not . . . but not . . .' of an acosmos, suspending the chaos/cosmos binary. To think meaning after the death of God we must 'discerner l'insensé *sans pourtant* disposer du sens' (PF 33; author's emphasis),[34] and in terms of being we are to conceive an 'être dépourvu de règles, *sans être dépourvu* de vérité' (PF

34; author's emphasis).³⁵ This is neither a reaffirmation of meaning nor a nihilistic scepticism, for we need to think reason and scepsis differently, have other constellations, other 'assemblages de sens' ('gatherings of sense') (SM 74/SW 45). This is certainly more circumspect than both Merleau-Ponty and Ricœur; whether it is a 'deconstructive phenomenology' (whatever we decide that means) remains to be seen.

The programme indicated by the motif of the *sans pourtant* itself attracts scepticism, however. Alexander García-Düttmann doubts that such a response to the nihilism of the Modern production of signification can resist resolving to the dogma it seeks, equally, to avoid:

> On ne pourra affronter le nihilisme qu'à partir d'une évidence qui, elle, réclame d'être établie, puisque, afin d'apparaître, elle requiert une décision essentiellement injustifiable, une violence.³⁶

García-Düttmann gives this decision a name, 'Jean-Luc Nancy', and brings us back once more to the problem we discussed in relation to Derrida on hospitality. For García-Düttmann, the only defeater for nihilism is foundationalism. But, as we have already seen in Derrida's vociferous response to the accusations clustering like barnacles to his unconditional hospitality, holding that calculation must be supplemented by the incalculable by no means suggests that calculation is dispensable. Can we defend Nancy here with a similar response? It is by no means clear that we can, for whereas Derrida's calculation and its excess happen within symbolic structures and their interruption, the patency and exposure of Nancy's *sens* are pre-symbolic.

But to suggest that Nancy cannot draw on the same response as Derrida is not to conclude that he has no response at all, for Nancy can marshall arguments similar to those we have put forward in defence of Merleau-Ponty and Ricœur against Derridean questioning, labouring under the assumption that nihilism can only be evaded with an abrupt and violent fiat, taking the 'short route', to adopt a Ricœurean term. It is cosmos *or* chaos, the accusation goes, and there is no middle ground. Anything purportedly in between either resolves to 'nihilism' or to 'foundationalism'. It will be the burden of this chapter and the next to show why this is an unduly hasty and misguided rebuttal of what Nancy is claiming, and to argue for Nancy's *sans pourtant* as a non-nihilistic alternative to foundationalism.

5.2 PRESENCE

In seeking to trace the contours of this *sans pourtant* in a way that can respond to the criticisms levelled at it, it is important to come to an understanding of how Nancy thinks about presence. If it is neither foundationalist nor nihilistic (and for Nancy foundationalism is nihilism, that is to say the extinction of *sens* in the reign of *signification* (DDC 181/DDC 86)), then for what sort of ontology do openness, the *sans pourtant* and the interruption of *signification* by *sens* make?

Unlike Derrida, Nancy does not dismiss presence as metaphysics, but seeks to think it differently, otherwise than as self-presence:

> La formation de l'Occident (ce que nous avons jadis nommé « le miracle grec ») procédait de et par la désinstallation du monde des présences (nommées « divines » ou « sacrées »). Ce qui, aujourd'hui, déferle sur nous comme un autre monde qui n'est plus l'autre du monde... ne s'y retrouvant plus et ne s'y reconnaissant plus ni *cosmos* ni « *terre des hommes* », c'est quelque chose qui n'est plus de l'ordre de la présence, et ce *n'est pourtant pas* [author's emphasis] non plus l'absence comme envers simple ou comme le négatif d'une présence. C'est *ce monde-ci* et rien d'autre, ce monde-*ci* sans *là-bas* au-delà, mais de telle façon que toute l'évidence et la prégnance d'un « *ci* », d'un *ici-et-maintenant* sont à gagner à nouveaux frais, selon une toute nouvelle disposition et un tout nouvel abord de la présence. (PD 16)[37]

A number of themes are to be noted here. First, presence is not the presence in the world of the other-worldly, the sacred or divine. The *patence* of the world is all there is to presence. Secondly, presence for Nancy follows the pattern of the *sans pourtant*, not presence, nor absence as the negative of presence. Thirdly, presence is not punctual but the pregnancy of a 'here'. In other words, presence is the act by which the thing is put forward ('mise devant'): *prae-est* (TP 6). Like Merleau-Ponty's evocation of the figure-ground relation in which figure and ground are never dichotomised,[38] presence is fluid and context-sensitive:

> La nature de la chose est dans sa naissance, comme l'indique le nom de « nature », et dans son déploiement au sein de ces relations. Elle n'a sa subsistance que dans ce mouvement, et sa permanence est dans ce passage. (TP 6)[39]

Nancy is challenging the dichotomy of presence and absence, elaborating a notion of presence inextricable from absence, of presence as passage, where 'celui qui passe n'est là qu'en passant. Il est là, il est présent, mais sa présence est toute dans l'écart de son pas, dans la distance donc, et dans la vitesse qui l'approchent et qui l'éloignent' (P 14).[40]

To think presence this way is a finite thought, but finitude is not to be understood, Nancy stresses, as a lack to be deplored and which, it is hoped, will be filled. Finitude must be understood wholly otherwise ('tout autrement'), as designating 'la fin de la présence comme être stable, permanent, disponible, impossible – comme chose donnée et comme figure dessinée, comme mythe constitué ou comme raison établie' (PD 19).[41] Nancy's 'good finitude' or 'absolute finitude' has nothing to do with 'bad finitude', the inevitable incompletion imposed on the human condition in a Hegelian dialectic. Good finitude is 'existence dont la *vérité* consiste à laisser son sens toujours plus au-delà ou en deçà de tout accomplissement' (PD 21).[42] One crucial move that Nancy makes in refiguring presence is to break the equation of presence and immediacy, which he does by understanding presence as *technē*. Nancy adopts from Heidegger the twin notions of *phusis* as a coming to presence or to being and *technē* as the mode that this coming takes today (M 49 n2/M 38). Presence is irreducibly technical (C 89) and *technē* itself is irreducibly plural (PF 44/FT 24). When Nancy describes *technē* as a 'supplement' of nature (SM 66/SW 41) this relation is to be understood in terms of what Derrida in *De la Grammatologie* calls the originary supplement, or originary *écriture*,[43] not coming after an original pure presence but that without which there could be no presence.[44] Technique only supplements a natural order, Nancy explains in *Une Pensée finie*, if nature is conceived as pure immanence (PF 45/FT 25). But in Greek thought, *phusis* is indissociable from *technē*, and technique should not be understood to transcend any prevenient immediate experience of the world (PF 45 n1/FT 324 n29). Nature is 'une extériorité des places' and technique is 'la mise en jeu de cette extériorité comme existence' (PF 45),[45] a relation which evokes neither immanence nor transcendence. There is no difference between the 'natural' and the 'technical' (C 69). The technical prosthesis at the 'heart' of presence is, for Derrida, the distinguishing mark of Nancy's thought, and it sets him apart from other philosophers of corporeality. Didier Franck and Jean-Louis Chrétien may pay attention to the irreducible other and the untouchable in the experience of touch, and they may think the spacing or interruption of contact, but on Derrida's reading their thought is deficient insofar as they fail to accord the same constituting role as Nancy to *technē*.[46] Derrida also notes that *technē* signals for Nancy – in what it must be acknowledged is a decidedly Ricœurean tone – 'aucune présence sans détour'.[47] To clarify the difference brought by thinking *technē* and *phusis* together, Nancy employs a distinction between (phenomenological) presence and the (technical) present, in which 'le présent est contraire à la présence: il la ruine, il l'enlève, du même mouvement par lequel il l'apporte' (TP 23).[48]

The present understood as *technē* has no foundation, for 'la technique est la déshérence de l'origine et de la fin: l'exposition à un manque de sol et de fondement . . . une dévastation du sol, du « naturel » et de « l'origine »' (M 50).[49] This by no means forces us to renounce metaphysics, however, but instead to refigure metaphysics as techno-logy, technique of the *logos* (CMM 133/CWG 89). *Technē* is understood by

Nancy in terms of openness and spacing, 'ce qui ne va pas de soi, ni à soi, disparité, contiguïté, essence inachevé et inachevable de l' « avec »' (ESP 93).[50] Once more, it moves the locus of existence from substance to coherence.

If we are to ask if meaning is in the world, the world must henceforth be understood in terms of the originary supplementarity of *phusis* and *technē*, and meaning must be understood as the technical disposition or spacing of the world: the world is structured *as* sense. This parallels Ricœur's intrication of life and narrative, though with a much more pronounced deconstructive tone. The question of meaning in the world becomes a tautology (SM 18/SW 8), for the world does not *have* sense, it *is* sense (SM, 19 SW 8); the sense of the world is the world of sense and the world that is sense. The difference between the sense of the world as *phusis-technē* and meaning as signification is that the world of technology, as Nancy explains in *Le Sens du monde*, is the world becoming world, that is neither 'nature' nor 'universe' nor 'earth', because 'nature', 'universe' and 'earth' (and 'sky') are names of givens, sets or totalities, significations that have been surveyed, tamed and appropriated. 'World', he continues, is the name of a gathering or being-together that arises from a *technē*, and the sense of which is identical with the very exercise of this art (SM 66/SW 41).

The link between *technē* and art, reinforced in Nancy's writing on the visual arts, also develops the idea that presence and existence are to be understood (a)cosmologically and as exposure. 'The present' for Nancy is a matter of arrangement and disposition, a cosmological feature, and not a question of immediacy or substance:

> Le mot *poiesis* provient d'une famille verbale qui désigne la mise en ordre, l'arrangement, la disposition. La poésie dispose. L'art est la disposition. Il dispose la chose selon l'ordonnance de la présence. Il est la technique de la présence. (TP 5)[51]

Nancy elaborates the link between the cosmological and technique in relation to the work of art insisting that:

> Il n'y a pas d'art qui ne soit cosmologique, parce que la technique productive de l'espacement produit chaque fois le monde, une ordonnance de monde, le monde en tout ou en partie, mais toujours le tout dans chaque partie chaque fois . . . ce qu'on appelle une œuvre d'art est chaque fois une concrétion singulière, monadique et nomade, du cosmos. (TP 12)[52]

So is this presence found or made? It is made, and it relies for its veracity on the dynamic of attestation:

> Il faut faire, fabriquer, composer, modeler, et donc feindre la présence du présent. . . . Sa véracité (d'être la date du jour de la peinture) n'a aucune autre

attestation qu'elle-même, qui pourrait néanmoins avoir été peinte un autre jour. (TP 26)⁵³

Such a present – made, composed, modelled – could only be considered in some way 'inferior' to a more 'immediate' presence if we were still clinging to the primacy of *phusis* over *technē*; in terms of Nancy's prosthetic ontology it is 'real presence', 'une intimité sacrée qu'un fragment de matière livre à l'absorption. Elle est présence réelle parce qu'elle est présence contagieuse, participante et participée, communicante et communiquée dans la distinction de son intimité' (AFI 27).⁵⁴ The importance of participation in thinking the present evokes the Merleau-Pontean work of expression, and Nancy makes the affinity more explicit by drawing on and appropriating Merleau-Ponty's 'invisible' which, Nancy insists, is not something hidden from view but the thing itself, its being (AFI 28/GOI 141).

Sense relates language and objects differently to signification. It searches for a presentation of the thing that is not the end of language, and a linguistic presentation that is not an instrument to signify things (OP 83), for a movement that would not mediate presence and distance one by the other, but carry away the whole system of this mediation, letting another function or figure of philosophy be traced out (OP 80). It seeks a relation of thing and language that is not presentation, because presentation keeps presence at a distance (OP 82). From these observations we can see the possible contours of a reading of the Nancean project in terms of a transposition of the Merleau-Pontean characterisation of the visible and the invisible as intertwined to a 'flattened' understanding of the relation between world and sense in which sense is patent and exposed in the spacing of the world.

5.3 CONTACT

What does this move from immediate presence to the technique of the present mean for the question of contact? Just as Ricœur took the long detour via narrative and the interrogative 'who?', Nancy explores enunciation and the fable, and elaborates contact in terms of the space of the body. The contact between sense and existence is discussed by Nancy in terms of the motif of the mouth, a space irreducible to mathematical extension. In evoking the mouth, Nancy distinguishes the 'bouche orale' or the mouth that speaks from the more primitive 'bouche buccale', the mouth that spits, rasps, eats and breathes, the mouth that fastens itself to the breast: 'bucca, c'est les joues gonflées, c'est le mouvement, la contraction, et/ou la distension du souffler' (ES 162);⁵⁵ it is a place of spacing: 'la bouche est l'ouverture de l'ego. Ce qui s'y passe, c'est qu'il s'y espace' (ES 162).[56] This is the mouth as bodily *différance*!

Nancy characterises the buccal mouth in terms of the 'common incommensurability' of thought and extension:[57] 'C'est l'incommensurable qui rend possible la quasi permixtio de l'union . . . Dans la quasi permixtio, la pensée s'étend' (ES 161).[58] This does not mean, however, that thought and extension are united in the mouth; the union is a '*quasi permixtio*'; it is a fiction (ES 133). But how can the buccal mouth bring together two incommensurabilities? For Merleau-Ponty, the incarnate sense of embodied existence encircles and penetrates matter (PP 374/*PP* 324), but matter is impenetrable to meaning (C 50/Cor 17). Where Merleau-Ponty has the reversibility of the toucher touched, Nancy has touch in distance: con-tact. That matter and sense are impenetrable does not mean, however, that no relation is possible between them – just as we saw that there was relation, even tautology, between sense and world – for though they do not penetrate, they touch: 'writing touches bodies according to the absolute limit which separates the sense of one from the skin and nerves of the other' (Cor 12–13). Just what Nancy means by this gnomic utterance can be discerned through a consideration of the way he relates thought (*pensée*) and weight (*pesée*). Weight for Nancy, glosses Derrida, is that which eludes and marks the limit of thought, 'ce qui, dans le toucher, se marque comme tangible par la résistance opposée . . . lieu de l'altérité ou de l'inappropriabilité absolue, limite, pesanteur, donc finitude'.[59] Thought and weight do not interpenetrate, and 'nous n'avons pas accès au poids du sens pas plus (par conséquent) qu'au sens du poids . . . Et c'est de ne pas avoir cet accès qui nous fait pensants, aussi bien que pesants' (Poids 33).[60]

In terms of the relation between thought and language, Nancy describes how 'la pensée, qui est langage, n'est pourtant pas langage: mais ce n'est pas parce qu'elle serait « autre chose » . . . c'est parce que le langage lui-même est par « essence » de ne pas être ce qu'il est' (PF 50).[61] Although *pensée* and *pesée* are impenetrable to each other, they are nevertheless related, in their incommensurability, by their mutual inter-reliance. Merleau-Ponty might call this their 'promiscuity', but Nancy prefers the more disjunctive 'excription': the inscription of the un-inscribable in inscription itself, inscription's constitutive excess which is the final truth of inscription (Poids 8) and an *écart* between writing and signification (C 63). The notion of excription is important in any understanding of how Nancy thinks the ontological. The Nancean notions of *corps*, *chair* and *style* are, warns Derrida, akin to the seductive but dangerous honeyed paper to which he saw flies fatally attracted in his Algerian youth. 'Moi, j'ai toujours eu les réflexes de fuir',[62] he adds, avowing that he is only willing to accept such notions strategically, and for a time. But are Derrida's 'reflexes' justified? As Ian James points out, and as we have seen in the relation of *sens* and *signification*, Nancy's figures (*sens, communauté, corpus, être*) do not signify a presence or a substance, but they excribe a certain excess of signification.[63] They follow, insists James, the paradoxical logic of presentation and withdrawal. As Nancy himself comments, 'l'ontologie dont il s'agit n'est pas l'ontologie de l'Être, ou de ce qui est: mais de l'être en tant qu'il n'est rien de ce qui est' (Com 65).[64] Nancy's is an ontology thought otherwise than in terms of discrete presence and immediate contact. A finite thinking thinks the inaccessibility of sense as the very means of accessing sense (PF 29/FT 14).

Thought is not intertwined with matter, as it is for Merleau-Ponty, but pressed up against it in their mutual impenetrability (C 54). The relation of meaning and existence is not one of representation or reference, but the interrupted touch of con-tact. This is not to suggest, however, that such pressing yields an immediacy in the relation of language and the body, for contact, once more, is not immediate but technical. It is a 'se toucher-s'écarter' ('touching-distancing') that never becomes a grasping: 'Toucher à soi, être touché à même soi, hors de soi, sans rien qui s'approprie, c'est l'écriture, et l'amour, et le sens. *Le sens est le toucher*' (PF 293; author's emphasis).[65]

Where Bataille is happy to write of an access to, or attainment of, the truth, for Nancy the truth is touched,[66] a term which conveys an ineliminable distance, even in 'contact'. Touch is no guarantee of immediacy, but rather the separation of a promised immanence (CD 96/IC 96). Furthermore, proximity and distance are accomplished in the same gesture. In his discussion of Pontormo's *Noli me tangere*, Nancy notes that Christ's hands both bless Mary Magdalene and keep her at a remove in a singular combination of distance and tenderness (NMT 57), for Christ, in the very gesture of distancing himself (*s'écarter*) from Mary, lightly touches her breast (VPC 32–1). A similarly bivalent gesture appears in *Le Sens du monde* in terms of the relation between world and sense. Here, tact (*le tact*) is in turning away from sense, not in order to protect oneself from sense, but – in an echo of a Ricœurean hermeneutics – 'parce que ce détour, ce détournement, est encore le sens' (SM 252).[67] The distant proximity of con-tact is not a disabling but an enabling condition of the apprehension of sense. It is to be desired, as Nancy stresses in translating 'noli me tangere' as 'ne *veuille* pas me toucher' ('do not wish to touch me') and 'aime ce qui t'échappe' ('love what escapes your grasp') (NMT 60). Like the necessity of *technē* for the presence of *phusis*, the interruption of the 'proper' at the moment of touch is not the failure of touch, but an interruption which *constitutes* touch; for Nancy 'Le toucher, ce n'est possible qu'à ne pas toucher. Expérience de l'impossible'.[68] So when Nancy writes of touch touching-distancing (C 54–8) he is, once more, not employing a paradox but a tautology. Contact is that which spaces touch, an irreducible spacing that requires technicity at the heart of the *corps propre* (one's own body). Though both Nancy and Ricœur employ the figure of the detour, Ricœur still entertains the notion of a horizon of sense from which the detour departs and to which it never returns, whereas for Nancy the detour *is* sense.

Derrida's agenda in *Le Toucher* is to dislocate the motif of touch from any ontology of presence: 'Aucune logique de sens, et pas même une logique du toucher . . . ne saurait alors, me semble-t-il, se plier à une ontologie de la présence, si on peut encore oser ce pléonasme.'[69] On Derrida's reading, touch for Nancy is an 'absolute realism', post-deconstructive and irreducible to any metaphysics of presence.[70] Nevertheless, Derrida wants to expose the theological underpinnings of touch: the haptocentric metaphysics of a tradition to which Nancy both belongs and does not belong.[71] The objection is nuanced by a triple qualification, but Derrida still accuses Nancy of having a '*quasi-hyper-transcendental ontologisation of tact*'.[72] The multiple caveats in this hypertrophied phrase suggest that Derrida is concerned that, despite Nancy's re figuring of ontology and presence in terms of sense and exposure respectively, there still remains a vestige of unreconstructed metaphysics in the technology of touch. But the question now needs to be: Does Nancy's 'quasi-hyper-transcendental ontologisation' succumb to the dangers that Derrida sees inherent in ontology traditionally understood, or has he succeeded in thinking ontology sufficiently *otherwise* to avoid the totalisation and violence that Derrida is so persistent in exposing?

For his part, Nancy is more willing to explore what Ricœur might call a 'just distance' of touch, between the equally undesirable 'not touch it enough' and 'touch it too much'. 'Do not touch me' also means 'caress me, do not touch me' (NMT 82), and at the origin of touch there is the law 'tu ne toucheras pas trop' (NMT 62).[73] In a juxtaposition of terms that Derrida elsewhere resists, in *Le Toucher* he confesses to being tempted to call the caress the only possible experience of the messianic.[74] It is not a gesture of appropriation or control, but it gives without return a unilateral 'reçois' ('receive') beyond any 'je te donne' ('I give to you') which would presume recognition and reciprocity.[75] The caress, along with the blow and the kiss, are furthermore, touches that address themselves to a 'who', not a 'what', and not 'the other' in general.[76] If the caress allows an 'experience' of the messianic, it also distinguishes between persons and things (*quis sit* and *quid sit*). It accomplishes for Derrida's reading of Nancy the two advances that Ricœur worked out in his hermeneutics of the self: the reorientation of the interrogative 'what?' to 'who?', and the gift that does not inaugurate a stultifying economy of credit and debt but rather affirms the relation of giver and receiver. From different starting points, Ricœur and Nancy (and Derrida's reading of Nancy) discern the same responses to the difficulties with which they each grapple.

In line with the incommensurability/ 'quasi permixtio' of thought and extension in the buccal mouth, Nancy's ontology is an ontology of enunciation, largely elaborated as a reading of Descartes' *Discours de le méthode*. Appealing to Descartes himself, for whom the certainty of the ego eventuates each time that it is pronounced, Nancy concludes that 'la bouche ou l'esprit c'est tout un: c'est toujours le corps.'[77] Not the body *of* the ego, but 'corpus ego'.[78] In *Technique du présent*, Nancy draws a link between this enunciation and presence as bare exposition, suggesting that in the 'ego sum, ego existo' the certainty of the 'ego sum' is coextensive with the time of its enunciation (or its thought) (TP 27). So enunciation is constitutive of the Cartesian subject, for the *Discours de la méthode* 's'instaure le droit métaphysique inouï de la vérité comme certitude – de la vérité comme énonciation par le sujet de sa propre substance et de cette substance *comme elle-même constituée par l'énonciation de l'ego*' (IC 47).[79] Ontology is a phonology (IC 151), and an interrupted phonology at that, interrupted by the mouth that closes between 'ego sum' and 'ego existo', interrupting the self-presence of the ego and requiring its repetition:

> Car « soi », ce n'est jamais qu'*à* soi, *en* soi ou *pour* soi: ce n'est jamais qu'un renvoi, un rappel, un rapport, un report, et au fond de toute cette réversion une répétition originaire, générative, par laquelle advient l'*à soi*. (Asc 8)[80]

The ego, the subject of being, exists as it is proffered. 'It resounds in order to be, and to resound it must have a hollow body' (MD). This 'enunciative ontology' reperforms a relentless proffering, hearing in its own echo a coincidence: *e(g)o ipso*; cogito in the tone of a toll (*glas*). In 'ego sum, ego existo', being immediately amounts to two, and is *ipso facto* dislocated. Enunciative ontology proffers a madness of identity – fragmented and unable to be brought to unity (MD). Reason itself, in doubling itself, interrupts itself. The enunciated 'ego' is each time different (in Augustine, Descartes, Rousseau, Nietzsche, Rimbaud . . .), a fractured polysemy of the self never returning to a stable and repeatable form.[81] Enunciative ontology is being as an address, being as addressing, 'to be' as a transitive verb, being as a response to the question 'who?' Furthermore, being, if there is such a thing, is personal.[82] Personal, yes, but not a personal*ism*,[83] and the question of the bivalent 'personne' is far from closed, as Nancy explores so poignantly in *l'Intrus*:

> J'ai (qui, « je » ? C'est précisément la question, la vieille question: quel est ce sujet de l'énonciation, toujours étranger au sujet énoncé, dont il est forcément l'intrus et pourtant forcément le moteur, l'embrayeur ou le cœur) (I 13)[84]

The 'je' is 'personne' ('no one'), both the enunciation and the interruption of the subject, and in this ambiguity, self-relation has become a problem, a difficulty or an opacity (I 39). This 'personne' is like Nancy's *sans pourtant*, a double negative which, while stopping short of being something (or someone), is not nothing. The subject of interrupted enunciation, the subject who hears the echo of enunciation, is the subject constituted by resonance and spacing, a 'sujet-écoute' ('subject-listening') like the subject listening to music, who 'n'est rien d'autre ou n'est personne d'autre que la musique elle-même, et plus précisément rien d'autre que l'œuvre musicale' (Asc 9).[85]

The implications of this non-self-identity are brought into sharp focus in *Corpus*, where Nancy evokes the gathering of the self in terms of a spasm: 'Un corps s'expulse: comme corpus, espace spasmé, distendu, rejet-de-sujet, « immonde » s'il faut garder le mot. Mais c'est ainsi que le monde a lieu' (C 94).[86] Understanding the subject in terms of spasmatic convulsion is, once more, a move from the *what* to the *that*, evacuating determinate content and thereby also circumventing the totalisation that would draw the accusation of ontological violence. For Nancy, it is the statement as such that is true; the truth consists in the enunciation, and not in its content or message (ES 121). This is not just a performative statement, Nancy insists, for in contrast to any other event accomplished by a performative, the event here is nothing other than the performance itself, or the being coextensive with this performance: 'je suis' (ES 122). In a series of distinctions reminiscent once more of the Lévinasian moves with which we complemented Ricœur's hermeneutics of the self at the end of the third chapter, true being ('l'être vrai') no longer hangs on a statement ('un énoncé'), nor on the substance of a speaker ('un énonciateur'), nor in an utterance ('une énonciation'), but in an announcing ('un énoncer') (ES 123). The cogito is not merely 'thought out' ('excogité': a term that Nancy reminds us was accepted French both before and after Descartes), but it is itself the 'excogitation': 'comble simultané de la pensée et de l'extravagance, du discours direct de la vérité et de la machination inouïe du récit fabuleux' (ES 115).[87] This reference to narrative and fiction, strongly evoking Ricœur's prolonged labours in the area of narrative identity, also highlights an important aspect of Nancy's appropriation of the Cartesian cogito.

In contrast to the minimal 'ego sum' coextensive with its own enunciation, the stable, enduring subject is not a fable that we must believe; it is not a 'true story' (ES 102). But like Ricœur's use of the Rawlsian 'original situation', the fictionality is intended to expose the truth of the world by accounting for its constitution. In Ricœurean terms, the *fabula* is a long (not to say interminable) detour, and for Nancy 'la structure et la fonction du *cogito* sont de part en part soumises à cette loi fabulatrice' (ES 97).[88] Finally, and of crucial importance, the possibility of saying 'ego sum, ego existo' also assumes, and is logically and chronologically preceded by, social existence, and so every *ego sum* is an *ego cum* (or *mecum*, or *nobiscum*) (PD 117). It is to this irreducibility of being-with that we shall turn in the next chapter, after having drawn together the threads of our current exploration of Nancy's ontology.

5.4 THE DECISION: BETWEEN GOOD AND EVIL

How, we are now in a position to ask, do Nancy's various rereadings and reappropriations – the move to *sens* as openness, exposition and call, the refiguring of presence as the bare exposition of finitude and the technique of the present, the con-tact of *pensée* and *pesée* (thought and weight) in the buccal mouth and the enunciative ontology of the storied ego – bear on our questions of meaning and alterity? At each point Nancy's concessions to the ontological have been bought at the price of a move from the *what* to the *that*, and this move would seem to indicate that, whatever 'contact' with a meaningful world may mean for Nancy, it does not mean that we can tell strangers from gods and gods from monsters. In moving closer to deconstruction, his work also begins to struggle with the problems that emerge for Derrida's thought from its engagement with Merleau-Ponty and Ricœur. We can see how Nancy attempts to navigate this difficulty by turning to his work on freedom and the decision.

Nancy is clear that there can be no assumption about the values in relation to which a decision is to be made. The only free decision is the decision free of criteria of decision, which therefore 'ne se mesure à rien d'autre qu'à la liberté. C'est-à-dire à la limite de ma capacité de juger, à la grandeur absolue inconcevable et imprésentable' (DI 31).[89] In *L'Expérience de la liberté* he is more specific:

> La liberté est liberté pour le bien *et* pour le mal. Sa décision, si c'est dans la décision que la liberté advient ou survient à elle-même, est donc décision du bien *et* du mal. (EL 174)[90]

As Peter Melville notes, Nancy follows Heidegger in allowing freedom 'to slip through every opposition, to escape or retreat into the abysmal "nothingness" of the "unground" between or "beneath" opposition itself.'[91] This is understandable as far as it goes, but it leaves a question unanswered: what do 'good' and 'evil' mean, here? How can freedom be freedom both for good and for evil unless we have a way of distinguishing what, even if provisionally, is to count as 'good' and what as 'evil'? It is a question that vexes Andrew Norris, who asks how Nancy's conception of the authentically free decision might act as a moral compass: 'Does it offer a standard of any sort with which we can distinguish between the wise and the foolish, or the virtuous and the wicked, or the decent and the depraved?'[92]

Nancy is aware of the problem of using the terms 'good' and 'evil' in the very phrase in which he denies their place in an understanding of freedom, and he is not in the least paralysed by the problem:

> Refuser que la liberté se présente comme un arbitre placé en face de valeurs ou de normes transcendantes à sa propre transcendance finie, cela ne revient pas à refuser que la liberté, en décidant, décide du bien *ou* du mal. (EL 174)[93]

The reason that Nancy argues he can have his cake of authentic liberty and eat its distinction of good and evil is that there *is* an imperative in Nancy's thought, but it is not the imperative to choose 'good' over 'evil', or any other imperative conjuring with the same two terms. It is the imperative to openness, the absolute duty to decide in favour of the question without a response (IC 122). An imperative, we might venture, to the *that* of the decision, not to its *what*. What makes us free is 'la liberté qui nous expose, et qui n'est ce qu'elle est que dans cette exposition. Ni arbitre, ni destin, mais le don de ce que Heidegger appelle « l'ouverture »' (EL 185).[94] Nancy's understanding of freedom parallels the distinction between *signification* and *sens*. Like *sens*, 'la liberté ne reçoit pas un espace qui lui serait donné, mais elle se donne l'espace, et elle se le donne comme espacement incalculable de singularités' (EL 187).[95] Indeed, 'sur le registre du sens comme sur celui du sujet, l'impératif n'est ou ne fait qu'espacement. L'impératif *espace*' (IC 134),[96] and this spacing procures for us neither determinate duties nor determinate rights (EL 185/*EF* 143). In fact, 'nous ne sommes pas seulement livrés à une errance, à une désorientation (si occidentale . . .) qui nous laisserait sans critères. Nous sommes exposés à un critère d'avant tout critère, qui dissout tout modèle de critère sans détruire le *fait* (transcendantal?) du *krinein*, de la séparation, du jugement' (Com 51).[97] The openness to which Nancy appeals is framed in 'Dies irae' in terms once more of calculability and excess, echoing the Nancean excribed ontology:

Il faut juger de telle façon que la loi même de la liberté soit toujours en reste ou en excès sur ce que mon jugement aura pu déterminer, et sur ce qui aura pu le déterminer. (DI 27)[98]

Elsewhere, the imperative to openness is framed as a responsibility to question. The duty of philosophising at and about the end of philosophy, insists Nancy, 'autrement dit l'éthique suprême, et pré ou post-éthique, serait celle de l'acte de la pensée, entendu en l'occurrence comme un « questionner » infini' (IC 122).[99] The duty is to preserve the freedom of the question as question (IC 123), and this imperative is not *an* ethical commandment but *the* commandment that precedes any ethics whatsoever (IC 123). The imperative to openness is the imperative of finite thought, where finitude is the dispropriation of any final end or goal, and as such duty becomes 'l'ouverture – et la question – de l'*ethos* propre du non-propre' (IC 124).[100]

The imperative, in being an imperative to openness, is also an imperative to interruption. As James Gilbert-Walsh explains, the imperative voice must interrupt itself, and '. . . the imperative is irreducible to the logicity of the present indicative, and to the present in general, for it does not even indicate something like a future present. Rather, it ruptures the present of its commandment in an originary manner.'[101] Gilbert-Walsh rightly emphasises that, although interruption is tied to withdrawal or retreat (*retrait*) for Nancy, it issues also in determinate ethical responsibility, being 'tied just as much to concrete presentation (i.e. interruption which has fallen, in an "adequately inadequate" manner, into its own *case*'.[102] Indeed, the imperative to openness by no means remains abstract for Nancy, but provides him with a number of ethical positions. Crimes against humanity, for instance, are understood to be the desire to force the infinite to have a sense.[103] Again, finite thought requires that we substitute the horizon of a multiplicity or diversity of measures of justice for the Kantian idea of a final totality or unity (DI 13), a justice (un)founded on the constitutive plurality of language and the absence of a universal language or general metalanguage (DI 13). But here we come up once more against the problem of competing measures of justice, the need to arbitrate between them and the question of how to judge.

The question '*comment juger?*' (how should we judge?) is precisely the problem Nancy poses at the beginning of 'Dies irae' (DI 10). Once more, it is with a move from the content to the act of judgement that he attempts to save his ontological position from becoming a determinate totalitarianism. Discussing Lyotard's reading of the Kantian Idea (the criterion in terms of which judgement is to be made), Nancy comments that:

> Dans l'usage pratique, nous *devons* poser l'Idée, parce que nous *devons* juger. Autrement dit, on ne juge pas sans Idée. Non pas au sens où il faut une idée – un critère – pour juger. Mais d'abord et fondamentalement au sens où c'est le devoir de juger qui est l'Idée. (DI 24)[104]

The imperative does not hang on *what* is to be the nature, or outcome, of the judgement, but *that* judgement is to be made. The indeterminacy of the judgement plays itself out less in terms of the content of the Idea than in the status or nature of the judgement itself, and as such it is less a response to the determination of the question of how to judge *well* than to the question of how to judge *at all* or, as Nancy puts it, 'comment cela se fait-il, juger?' (DI 16).[105] Again, the decision to be made, the Heideggerean *Ent-scheidung*, is the decision between a state of non-decision and the act of decision; it is the decision for the decision, and for decidability (EL 178/EF 43). As such, it is also a decision that can never be assured, much less guaranteed, without voiding its essence as decision: 'Toute décision se surprend. Toute décision se prend, par définition, dans l'indécidable' (EL 183).[106]

It is hard not to conclude, after all, that there is something circular and disquieting about this position. In Nancy's own words, 'cela ne nous munit pas d'une morale. Cela ne nous dicte pas ce que pourra vouloir dire, et quand, et comment, de « respecter autrui », de « se respecter soi-même », ou de « traiter l'homme comme une fin », ou de vouloir l'égalité, la fraternité et la justice de la communauté humaine' (EL 185).[107] So what *does* it do for us? It frees us for duty and right, and for the perversion of the one and the other (EL 185/EF 143). And if we choose perversion, then what? And how, furthermore, might we know whether perversion were such, and so be in a position to denounce – or at least to recognise – it as perversion? And what good is freedom for duty or perversion if, in the exercise of that freedom, duty and perversion themselves *are* sufficiently indiscernible that I am left in the glorious liberty of impotence, unable – and therefore not free – knowingly to decide for, or against, either? In extricating from his thought the problem of circularity that dogs Merleau-Ponty and Ricœur, Nancy is landed with the impossibility, as we have seen in the case of Derrida, of discerning good from evil.

The point here, that there is scant reason to bother judging in such a situation, is summed up well by David Ingram when he submits 'that without some global idea of the good to be attained, of the subject to be emancipated, or of justice pure and simple, there would probably be no reason for judging at all, let alone engaging in politics'.[108] Now, whether the idea of the good needs to be global is another question – and it is not at all clear that, for the point presently under discussion, it need be – but

Ingram's main point stands. Let us be clear, Nancy does not advocate refusing all judgement and remaining in undecidability, for that would be impossible and both Derrida and Nancy point it out frequently, vociferously and sometimes indignantly and wearily. The problem is the second (or third, or fourth . . .) order question of how to judge *between* two judgements. It is the problem of reaching a verdict in an adversarial system of justice or the problem, when the decision has been chosen over undecidability, of deciding for *this* over *that*, *her* over *him*, *them* over *us*. The imperative to openness and interruption cannot help us here; what, short of some determinate content, some idea of justice – however attenuated and circumscribed it be – can rescue us from a chilling impotence? Ingram thinks he has an answer when he notes that 'we have Nancy's own acknowledgment of a prescriptive content embedded in the ambiguous assertion that the community "must (*il faut que*) not be made an object of either a morality or a politics of community"',[109] but what we have here is not a prescriptive *content*, the *what* of a decision, but once more the imperative to openness, the *that* of freedom.

Norris joins the clamour of voices demanding a response from Nancy on this point:

> *The Experience of Freedom* concludes with two chapters on decision . . . Nancy's account of decision does not indicate on what grounds such a choice might be made . . . It seems fair to ask of Nancy, what should count as a reasonable or an unreasonable political judgement?[110]

Ian James responds to Norris, however, by noting that 'this call for a legislative framework would reintroduce a notion of identity or foundation, and Nancy would refuse this in the name of a fully rigorous thinking of finitude'.[111] Quite, and between them Norris and James nicely perform the bind that Nancy is in. But James goes on to mount a second defence of Nancy, arguing that Norris also ignores the centrality of praxis in *La Communauté désœuvrée*. For Nancy, 'the thinking of finite community leads not to a theory of judgement, but to a thinking of literature, and a specific notion of writing.'[112] This intervention is telling because it punctures the assumption that openness and determinacy are in a mutually exclusive dichotomy. The thinking of literature to which James refers is excription; openness describes the way that the determinate exceeds itself, not its opposite.

Nevertheless, there remains the problem of how to know *what* is good, and a fortiori to face the decision with anything more than a resigned insouciance. Although James draws attention to the fact that 'Nancy's understanding of judgement implies or rather necessitates a certain responsibility towards the singular plural' and 'articulates the need, in the act of judgement, to "Do justice to the multiplicity and the coexistence of singulars, to multiply therefore and to infinitely singularise ends" ',[113] this does nothing to help us decide between good and evil, as James himself concedes in noting that 'the struggle invoked can never be one for this or that particular world but must always be one for a world *affirmed* as shared finitude and for an affirmed sharing of that finitude.'[114] This is indeed the 're-inscription of a certain kind of universal within judgements',[115] but the universals that are reinscribed affirm the *that* of shared finitude and furnish no means to regulate or even discern what might be shared. All this shared notion of justice could achieve is a reductive ecumenism or, worse, a tyranny of the majority. Between radical openness and universals we must choose, and introducing openness itself *as* a universal at one remove, which is what James is helpfully drawing our attention to here, does not square the circle.

In circling once more round the problem we find that Nancy must, ultimately, like Derrida, rely on the same unwarranted commitment of which he is uneasy when he sees it in others, notably Ricœur.[116] There is in the Nancean decision a Ricœurean commitment 'beyond proofs', such that 'en jugeant je hasarde une « raison » (ou une déraison), qui se juge ainsi par ce qu'elle tente ou risque' (DI 20).[117] In the same way that we saw Derrida having, eventually, to fall back on the pistic, even though he is wary of it in Ricœur, so also here if we press Nancy's pirouette around the determinability of the decision far enough, we find the fragility of commitment.

Nancy prefers not to talk in terms of good or bad judgements, but of authentic judgements, where the authenticity of the judgement is its freedom (EL 180/EF 141). But this just brings us back round to the same question, this time phrased as 'la décision authentique, serait-ce donc le bien?' (EL 183).[118] Nancy does not reply directly to this question but, in a move which parallels Derrida's insistence in *Force de loi* that it can never be known whether or not a decision is just, he states that 'la décision ne peut pas s'apparaître à elle-même comme « bonne », pour autant qu'elle aura vraiment décidé. Elle ne peut pas s'apparaître, tout court' (EL 183).[119] It is not, therefore, that the judgement can be neither good nor bad, but rather that it cannot be *known* to be either good or bad. This is an important nuance, but it does not solve our problem.

Commenting on the 'il faut' of deconstruction, akin to his own imperative to openness, Nancy glosses:

> « Certes, jamais on ne *prouvera* (je souligne) *philosophiquement* qu'*il faut* (Derrida souligne) transformer une telle situation et procéder à une déconstruction effective pour laisser des traces irréversibles . . . Il y a un « Il faut »,

et il faut lui obéir, mais il est certain qu'il ne sera pas prouvé
(« philosophiquement »: mais n'est-ce pas là une redondance?) (IC 118–
19)[120]

Whether or not we can prove the duty to deconstruct (IC 120) (the *that*
of the decision) does not help us in deciding for the good (the *what* of
the decision). Is it not therefore Nancy's turn to miss the point here? The
point is not whether we can philosophically 'prove' the imperative, but
whether we may decide for anything over anything else on any grounds
other than convention or madness in any situation.

This question is not answered by Nancy's reworking of universality.
The universal for Nancy is neither given nor absent (which should give
pause to those ready to accuse him of arbitrariness), but to-be-made
(CMM 69/CWG 61), like Ricœur's potential or inchoate universals
(SCA 336/OA 289), still to be discussed and worked out between cultures.[121] Nancy rightly notes that Kant's reflective judgement must
invent the law, produce the universal itself (DI 18), and so I do not judge
according to a universal that I have seen, but nor do I judge blindly; I
assess the universal, I decide upon it (DI 33). But once more, this is fine
until there is a clash of universals. What is there to arbitrate between
them but some third party with a third universal, or one of the original
parties to the conflict who manages, by superior force or cunning, to
make her judgement prevail?

We have shown in this chapter that Nancy's sense as openness,
presence as passage and contact as interruption escape the problems
inherent in the determinability of judgement and sense in both
Merleau-Ponty and Ricœur, and as such he has a convincing reply to
the 'quis custodiet ipsos custodes?' question. In tracing this response it
has become clear, however, that he becomes unable to decide between
different witnesses, or between 'strangers, gods and monsters'. This
failure is not the final word though, for in the fourth chapter we saw
how what is ontologically at stake in the relation of deconstruction and
phenomenology is not substance but coherence and fragmentation,
and if anything like a deconstructive phenomenology is to emerge,
these are the questions with which it will primarily have to deal. They
are also prominent and constant questions in Nancy's own thought,
and so in one final turn we move now to a consideration of singularity, incommensurability and plurality in Nancy's work, under the twin
motifs of *corpus* and the 'singular plural'. With this we launch one final
attempt to find a satisfactory accommodation of the twin concerns of
who will witness for the witness and how to decide between different
witnesses.

NOTES

1. James, *The Fragmentary Demand*. See especially James' chapters on 'Space' (pp. 65–113) and 'Body' (pp. 114–51).
2. Derrida makes the same point in commenting on the relation between Merleau-Ponty and Nancy that the latter 'ne le cite pas souvent, mais bien qu'elles soient parfois difficiles à cerner ou à formaliser, les affinités implicites paraissent indéniables. Plus indéniables encore, certains gestes d'éloignement' (Derrida, *Le Toucher* 210); 'does not cite him often, but their implicit affinities seem undeniable although sometimes difficult to outline or formalise. Still less deniable are certain gestures of moving away' (*On Touching* 184).
3. James, *The Fragmentary Demand* 202.
4. Derrida, *Le Toucher* 60; 'a sort of absolute . . . post-deconstructive realism' (*On Touching* 46).
5. Hutchens, *Jean-Luc Nancy and the Future of Philosophy* 33.
6. See, for example, Robert Bernasconi, 'On Deconstructing Nostalgia for Community within the West: The Debate between Nancy and Blanchot'; Ingram, 'The Retreat of the Political in the Modern Age: Jean-Luc Nancy on Totalitarianism and Community'; Kaplan, 'Photography and the Exposure of Community: Sharing Nan Goldin and Jean-Luc Nancy'; Langsdorf, Watson and Bower, *Phenomenology, Interpretation, and Community*; Langsdorf, Watson and Smith, *Reinterpreting the Political: Continental Philosophy and Political Theory*; Hiddleston, *Reinventing Community: Identity and Difference in Late Twentieth-century Philosophy and Literature in French*.
7. 'qua the disposition of the world' (author's translation).
8. '*mundus*, pure, neat, precise, well-arranged, world. It is that which, according to Plutarch, Pythagoras meant by the word *kosmos*: the world is a beautiful composition, very clear-cut, pure and neat. The world is what is not unclean' (author's translation).
9. Pascal, *Pensées* 110; 'eternal silence of the infinite spaces' (author's translation).
10. 'disaster of sense' (*SW* 43). The term 'dés-astre' has obvious cosmological resonances, many of which are exploited by Blanchot in *L'Écriture du désastre*; *The Writing of Disaster*.
11. '*the very model of the structure or of the system closed in on itself*, or better still *as closure upon itself*' (author's translation).
12. 'that something like the transmission of a "message" should be possible. It is the relation as such, and nothing else' (author's translation).
13. 'signification is determinate sense – whereas sense resides perhaps only in the coming of a possible signification' (author's translation).
14. 'this thinking, which is called *of space*, is the necessary reopening of space and of places after the time of their conquest and implosion' (author's translation).

15. 'encounter, on an unsignifiable limit of signification, something that presents itself as reality and as the necessity of this achievement' (author's translation).
16. 'The presentation of presentation is not a representation: . . . Patency is related to itself – as if one were saying simply: *patet*, "it is manifest," "it is evident," . . . so as to make appear . . . the *it*, "subject" of the obviousness' (M 34).
17. Ian James makes a similar point in his discussion of *sens* in relation to art. See *The Fragmentary Demand* 219.
18. 'what runs up against or what violates signification – the opening of sense, or again its denuding' (author's translation).
19. 'In this way, a new configuration of experience is constituted: much more than the invention of a supernumerary art, we are brought what we could call a new *pregnancy*, if you understand by that, remaining faithful to this term, *a form and a force which precedes a coming into the world and matures it, the thrust of a schema of experience in the process of taking on its contours*' (author's translation).
20. 'from now on, we must approach once again that which is neither science nor religion nor philosophy – that gives no sense to exchange, but is rather the sense of the exchange, or again, the exchange itself *qua* sense: of our existence in common' (author's translation).
21. 'as well, [the communication] of the exposition of a thing, and that of a *call*, or that of a wink' (author's translation).
22. Derrida and Nancy, 'Responsabilité – du sens à venir', in Guibal and Martin (eds), *Sens en tout sens* 181; 'resist installation, calculation, domination etc. It is thus asymptotically a call to model oneself on the impossible, the incalculable' (author's translation).
23. 'The book does not speak *of*, it speaks *to*, or rather it does not speak *of* without also speaking *to*, and in such a way that this address is inseparable, essentially undetachable from that "to which" it is spoken or written' (author's translation).
24. 'Idea, Form, traces here very exactly the form of the address, and better still, the form *as* address. A book is an address or a call. Under the melodic line of its brief song, without interruption, the basso continuo of its invitation, its demand, its injunction or its prayer: "Read me! Read me!" And this prayer is still whispered, even when the author declares: "Don't read me!" or "Throw my book away!"' (author's translation).
25. Nancy and Derrida, 'Responsabilité – du sens à venir', in Guibal and Martin, *Sens en touts sens* 173; 'behind the response, there is something that, for our purposes, I would like to call resonance' (author's translation).
26. '. . . the unfurling of an *Umwelt* is a melody that is singing itself . . . The theme of the animal melody is not outside its manifest realisation; it is a variable thematics that the animal does not seek to realise by the copy of a model, but that haunts its particular realisations, without those themes being the goal of the organism' (N 173, 178).

27. 'this particular manner of vibrating and filling space known as blue or red' (*PP* 212).
28. 'The other, over here, near in his remoteness, tense, bent, unbent, resounds in my joints. I do not really perceive it with my eyes, nor hearing, nor touch. I do not perceive it, I resonate' (author's translation).
29. 'necessarily from yet another, from a still more other in the depths of itself. *Otherwise indeed*. And for this reason, *still less received as a message*. But rather surprised in a seizure, in the manner of a cramp or a tensing – unless it was a relaxation, a rest, a withdrawal' (author's translation).
30. Nancy and Derrida, 'Responsabilité – du sens à venir', in Guibal and Martin, *Sens en tous sens* 183–4.
31. Compare Ricœur's 'en dépit de' ('in spite of'): for icœur, the Rawlsian procedural approach to justice rests on a presumption that, in spite of plurality and violence, there is a fundamental correspondence between different cultures, different religions, etc. Ricœur calls this 'in spite of' a 'fundamental act of faith' (DDH 81).
32. 'not to abandon the office of truth, nor that of the figure, yet without filling the gap that separates them with sense' (author's translation).
33. 'devoid of providence and yet not deprived of sense' (SW 38).
34. 'discern senselessness without the help of Sense' (*FT* 16).
35. 'being deprived of rules, without being deprived of truth' (*FT* 16; translation altered).
36. Alexander García-Düttmann, 'L'évidence même', in Guibal and Martin (eds), *Sens en tous sens* 152. 'We will not be able to face nihilism other than by beginning with an obvious fact that demands to be established since, in order to appear, it requires an essentially unjustifiable decision, a violence' (author's translation).
37. 'The forming of the West (what we have formerly called "the Greek miracle") proceeded from and by getting rid of presences (called "divine" or "sacred") from the world. What opens upon us today as another world which is no longer the other of the world . . . no longer finding its home there and recognising there neither a cosmos nor a *land of men*, is something no longer of the order of presence, *nor is it* [author's emphasis] an absence which is the simple reverse or negative of presence. It is *this* world here and nothing else, this world *here* without an *over there* beyond it, but in such a way that all the obviousness and pregnancy of a "here", of a *here-and-now* are to be had with a new effort, according to a wholly new disposition and a new construal of presence' (author's translation).
38. The similarity of Merleau-Ponty's figure-ground relation to Nancy's bare presence is not to be taken too far, and there are many points of disagreement, as we shall explore in the next chapter.
39. 'The nature of the thing is in its birth, as the word "nature" indicates, and in its unfurling within these relations. It can subsist only in this movement, and its permanence is in the passing' (http://www.egs.edu/faculty/nancy/nancy-the-technique-of-the-present.html).

40. 'the one who passes by is there only in passing. He is there, he is present, but his presence is all in the interval between his paces, in distance, then, and in the speed of approach and withdrawal' (author's translation).
41. 'the end of presence as a stable, permanent, available, impossible being – as a given thing and a drawn figure, as a constituted myth or as established reason' (author's translation).
42. 'existence the *truth* of which consists in leaving its meaning always increasingly beyond or short of any fulfilment' (author's translation).
43. Nancy adopts the term écriture in *Une Pensée finie* and *Corpus*, where he maintains that 'l'ontologie s'avère comme écriture' (C 19); 'ontology turns out to be writing' (author's translation), and in similar terms to the description elsewhere of technē, écriture is described as 'cela qui s'écarte de la signification, s'excrit' (C 63); 'that which departs from signification, excribes itself' (author's translation).
44. The difference between Nancean *technē* and Ricœur's 'long détour' is the logic of supplementarity.
45. ' "nature" designates an exteriority of places', 'the putting into play of this exteriority as existence' (*FT* 25).
46. Derrida, *Le Toucher* 251; *On Touching* 223.
47. Derrida, *Le Toucher* 148; 'no presence whatsoever, without a detour' (*On Touching* 130).
48. 'The present opposes presence: it ruins it, abducts it, in the same movement by which it brings it' (http://www.egs.edu/faculty/nancy/nancy-the-technique-of-the-present.html).
49. 'Technique is the obsolescence of the origin and the end: the exposition to a lack of ground and foundation . . . a devastation of the ground, the "natural," and the "origin" ' (*M* 26).
50. 'what neither proceeds from nor to itself, with disparity, contiguity, and, thus, with an unachieved and unachievable essence of the "with" ' (*BSP* 202).
51. 'The word *poiesis* is derived from a word family that designates ordering, arrangement, or disposition. Poetry disposes. Art is disposition. It disposes the thing according to the order of presence. It is the technique of presence' (http://www.egs.edu/faculty/nancy/nancy-the-technique-of-the-present.html; translation altered).
52. 'There is no art that is not cosmological, because the productive technique of spacing produces the world each time, an ordering of the world, the world in whole or in part, but always the whole in each part each time . . . what is called a work of art is each time a singular, monadic and nomadic solidification of the cosmos' (http://www.egs.edu/faculty/nancy/nancy-the-technique-of-the-present.html).
53. 'The presence of the present must be made, fabricated, composed, modeled and thus feigned. . . . Its truth (being the date of the date of the painting) has no other attestation than itself, which could nonetheless

have been painted on another date' (http://www.egs.edu/faculty/nancy/nancy-the-technique-of-the-present.html).
54. 'sacred intimacy that a fragment of matter gives to be taken in and absorbed. It is a real presence because it is a contagious presence, participating and participated, communicating and communicated in the distinction of its intimacy' (*GOI* 11).
55. 'bucca is puffed-out cheeks, it is movement, the contraction and/or distension of the breath' (author's translation).
56. 'the mouth is the opening of the ego. What happens there is that there is spacing there' (author's translation).
57. The notion of a common incommensurability is prefigured in the Merleau-Pontean notion of selfhood glossed by Rudi Visker, which 'seems to emerge when, trying to translate the other's thoughts into my own without loss, I fail, or when I fail to become utterly absorbed in hers.' It is, notes Visker referring to a Merleau-Pontean motif at home in Nancy's buccal mouth, at that moment that I can become attentive to that 'inner diaphragm' (see PP 95/PP 92). Visker goes on to argue that the 'working notes' try to generate a new concept of subjectivity from attentiveness to the diaphragm, not an identity with oneself but non-difference with oneself, an identity that would be 'difference of difference' and a same that would be 'the other than the other' (Visker, 'Raw Being and Violent Discourse: Foucault, Merleau-Ponty and the (Dis-)Order of Things' 125). See VI 312/VI 264.
58. 'It is incommensurability that makes possible the quasi permixtio of the union ... In the quasi permixtio, thought is extended' (author's translation).
59. Derrida, *Le Toucher* 331; 'that which, in touch, is marked as tangible by the opposed resistance ... the place of alterity or absolute inappropriability (limit, weight, thus finitude, and so forth)' (*On Touching* 295).
60. 'we have no access to the weight of sense, no more (as a consequence) than we do to the sense of weight ... And it is this not having access that causes us to think, as well as to weigh' (author's translation).
61. 'thought, which is language, is, however, not language. Not because it might be "something else" ... but because language itself, in "essence", is not what it is' (*FT* 28; translation altered).
62. Derrida, in 'Responsabilité – du sens à venir', in Guibal and Martin (eds), *Sens en tous sens* 168; 'For my part, I always had the reflex to flee away' (author's translation).
63. James, *The Fragmentary Demand* 64.
64. 'the ontology in question is not the ontology of Being, or of what is: but of being inasmuch as it is nothing of what it is' (author's translation).
65. 'To touch oneself, to be touched right at oneself, outside oneself, without anything being appropriated. That is writing, love, and sense. *Sense is touching*' (*FT* 109–10).
66. The distinction is made by Derrida in *Le Toucher* 135; *On Touching* 117.

67. 'this detour, this turning away, is still sense' (*SW* 167).
68. Derrida, *Le Toucher* 334; 'To touch, to touch him/it, is possible only by not touching. Experience of the impossible' (*On Touching* 298).
69. Derrida, *Le Toucher* 148–9; 'No logic of sense, and not even a logic of touch, not even an ultratactile haptics, would then yield, it seems to me, to an ontology of presence (if one still dares use this pleonasm)' (*On Touching* 130).
70. Derrida, *Le Toucher* 60; *On Touching* 46.
71. See, for example, Derrida, *Le Toucher* 167–72; *On Touching* 145–9.
72. See Derrida, *Le Toucher* 328; *On Touching* 292. JD's emphasis.
73. 'thou shalt not touch too much' (author's translation).
74. Derrida, *Le Toucher* 94 n1; *On Touching* 330 n18.
75. Derrida, *Le Toucher* 94; *On Touching* 78–9.
76. Derrida, *Le Toucher* 84; *On Touching* 69.
77. 'the mouth or the mind, it is all the same: it is still the body' (author's translation). This meditation on the cogito can be seen in incipient form in Merleau-Ponty's acknowledgment that the certainty obtained in the cogito is itself a sort of perception, the apprehension of a meaning obtained through the sensible world – '« Je pense », mais à condition qu'on entende par là « je suis à moi » en étant au monde' (*PP* 466); ' "I think", but only provided that we understand thereby "I belong to myself" while belonging to the world' (*PP* 474) – and, as we noted in the previous chapter, it is further elaborated in Ricœur's dialogic detour of the 'cogito brisée' (broken cogito).
78. This characterisation resonates strongly with Merleau-Ponty's alliance of enunciation and self-presence in *Le Visible et l'invisible*: 'Comme le cristal, le métal et beaucoup d'autres substances, je suis un être sonore, mais ma vibration à moi je l'entends du dehors; comme a dit Malraux, je m'entends avec ma gorge' (*VI* 187); 'Like crystal, like metal and many other substances, I am a sonorous being, but I hear my own vibration from within; as Malraux said, I hear myself with my throat' (*VI* 144).
79. 'establishes the unheard-of metaphysical law of truth as certainty – of truth as the subject's enunciaion of his own substance and of this substance as itself constituted by the enunciaton of the ego' (author's translation).
80. 'because "self" is only ever *to* itself, *in* itself or *for* itself: it is only ever rejection, a reminder, a relation, a postponement, and at the bottom of all this reversion is an originary repetition, generative, by which the *to itself* comes' (author's translation).
81. Once more, Merleau-Ponty's reading of the Cartesian *cogito* foreshadows Nancy here. Merleau-Ponty notes in relation to the 'ego' of the 'ego cogito' that 'je, vraiment, c'est personne, c'est l'anonyme; il faut qu'il soit ainsi, antérieur à toute objectivation, dénomination, pour être l'Opérateur, ou celui à qui tout cela advient' (*VI* 294); 'The I, really, is nobody, is the anonymous; it must be so, prior to all objectification,

denomination, in order to be the Operator, or the one to whom all this occurs' (*VI* 246). Merleau-Ponty continues 'Mais est-ce là *celui qui pense*, raisonne, parle, argumente, souffre, jouit etc.? Non évidemment, puisque ce n'est *rien* – celui qui pense, perçoit etc., c'est *cette négativité comme ouverture, par le corps, au monde*' (VI 294); 'But is this he who thinks, reasons, speaks, argues, suffers, enjoys, etc.? Obviously not, since it is nothing – he who thinks, perceives, etc. is this negativity as openness, by the body, to the world' (*VI* 246). In this quotation from Merleau-Ponty we have the ego as opening and as corporeal, the two main axes of Nancy's reading of Descartes.

82. From a personal conversation with Nancy.
83. A similar point is made in Ricœur's 'Meurt le personnalisme, revient la personne' (L2 195–202).
84. 'I (who is this "I"? That is the whole question, the old question: what is this subject of enunciation, always different from the enunciated subjet, upon which it necessarily intrudes and yet is necessarily its driving force, the clutch, or the heart)' (author's translation).
85. 'is nothing other, or is no one other than the music itself, and more precisely nothing other than the musical work' (author's translation).
86. 'A body expels itself: as corpus, spasmatic space, distended, reject-of-a-subject, "unclean" if we must keep this word. But it is in this way that the world takes place' (author's translation).
87. ' "excogitation": simultaneous highpoint of thought and extravagance, of direct discourse of truth and of unheard-of plot of the fantastic story' (author's translation).
88. 'the structure and the function of the *cogito* submit completely to this law of storytelling' (author's translation).
89. 'is measured against nothing except freedom. That is, against the limit of my capacity of judgement, against unconceivable and unpresentable magnitude' (author's translation)
90. 'Freedom is freedom for good *and* evil. Its decision, if it is in the decision that freedom occurs or happens to itself, is therefore the decision for good *and* evil' (*EF* 135).
91. Melville, 'Spectres of Schelling: Jean-Luc Nancy and the Limits of Freedom' 162–3.
92. Norris, 'Jean-Luc Nancy and the Myth of the Common' 286.
93. 'Denying that freedom presents itself as an arbiter placed before values or norms transcendent to its own finite transcendence does not amount to denying that freedom, in deciding, decides for good *or* evil' (*EF* 153).
94. 'the freedom that exposes us and that is only what it is in this exposure. Neither will nor destiny, but the gift of what Heidegger calls "disclosedness" ' (*EF* 143–4).
95. 'freedom does not receive a space that would be given to it, but it gives itself space and gives space to itself as the incalculable spacing of singularities' (*EF* 145–6).

96. 'in the register of sense as well as of the subject, the imperative is only, or makes only, spacing. The imperative *spaces*' (author's translation).
97. 'we are not only delivered over to an erring, to a disorientation (so Western . . .) that would leave us without criteria. We are exposed to a criterion that precedes all criteria, that dissolves every model of criteria without destroying the *fact* (transcendental?) of the *krinein*, the separation, the judgement' (author's translation).
98. 'We must judge in such a way that the law of freedom itself is always short of or in excess of what my judgement could have determined, and of what could have determined it' (author's translation).
99. 'or the supreme ethics, as well as pre- and post-ethical, would be the thought-act, understood in this context to be an infinite "questioning"' (author's translation).
100. 'the opening – and the question – of the *ethos* itself of that which is not itself' (author's translation).
101. Gilbert-Walsh, 'Broken Imperatives' 41.
102. Gilbert-Walsh, 'Broken Imperatives' 42.
103. Nancy and Ferenczi, 'Un entretien avec Jean-Luc Nancy'.
104. 'In practical usage, we must posit the Idea, because we *have to* judge. In other words, we do not judge without an Idea. Not in the sense that an idea – a criterion – is necessary for judgement. But first and fundamentally in the sense that it is the duty to judge which is the Idea' (author's translation).
105. 'judging: how does that happen?' (author's translation).
106. 'every decision surprises itself. Every decision is made, by definition, in the undecidable' (*EF* 142).
107. 'this does not arm us with a morality. This does not dictate to us what it will mean, and when and how, "to respect others," "to respect oneself," "to treat humanity as an end," or to want equity, fraternity, and justice for the human community' (*EF* 143).
108. David Ingram, 'The Retreat of the Political' 116.
109. Ingram, 'The Retreat of the Political' 117. Quoting *IC* 182.
110. Norris, 'Jean-Luc Nancy and the Myth of the Common' 283.
111. James, *The Fragmentary Demand* 195.
112. James, *The Fragmentary Demand* 195.
113. James, 'On Interrupted Myth' 346. Quoting CMM 72/*CWG* 61.
114. James, 'On Interrupted Myth' 347.
115. James, 'On Interrupted Myth' 347.
116. See note 29 to Chapter 3 above.
117. 'in judging I venture a "reason" (or an unreason), that is so judged by what it attempts or risks' (author's translation).
118. 'would the authentic decision then be the good?' (*EF* 142).
119. 'decision cannot appear to itself as "good" insofar as it will have truly decided. It cannot, quite simply, appear to itself' (*EF* 142).

120. 'to be sure, we will never prove [author's emphasis] *philosophically* that *it is necessary* [Derrida's emphasis] to transform such a situation and move to an effective deconstruction in order to leave irreversible traces . . . There is an "it is necessary", and it is necessary to obey it, but it will certainly never be proved ("philosophically": but is that not redundant?)' (author's translation).
121. For a discussion of Ricœur's universals, see Dauenhauer, 'Response to Rawls' 214.

6. *Jean-Luc Nancy: Plurality*

> ... one and one and one and one doesn't equal four ... Just one and one and one and one ... they cannot be exchanged, one for the other. They cannot replace each other.
>
> Margaret Atwood, *The Handmaid's Tale*

The previous chapter dealt with the question of alterity in Nancy's work. Now we turn to the problem of commensurability. Chapter 5 considered the possibility of contact with a meaningful world, while this chapter pursues the issue of the conflict of meaning(s) in the world: what is to be done when a number of incommensurable values must be measured against each other or, in other words, how are we to calculate the incalculable? It is the problem we have been posing to Derrida's deconstruction; it is also the question at the heart of the cosmological motif we have been tracing through Merleau-Ponty, Ricœur and Nancy. Can Nancy deal successfully with both the 'quis custodiet ipsos custodes?' and the 'strangers, gods and monsters' objections? Once again, are we dealing in Nancy with what we might venture to call a 'deconstructive phenomenology'?

In order to address these questions we need to explore a theme touched on in Nancy's work by the motifs of community, *Mitsein*, globalisation, the 'singular plural' and *corpus*. What is at stake is how to translate between different scales of value or different measures, whether that be the senses, the arts or ideas of justice. Much of Nancy's work is an attempt to relate the fractured and the incommensurable. Thus for Ian James, Nancy's writing 'unfolds as a decision to respond to the demand imposed by the multiple and the fragmentary', and his philosophy 'needs to be seen as a response to a fragmentary demand.'[1] It is a philosophy of the multiple when unity is no longer that in relation to which the multiple can be said.[2] Faced with the realisation that 'il y a du « commun », de l' « ensemble », et du « nombreux », et que nous ne savions peut-être plus du tout comment penser cet ordre du réel' (CA 31–2),[3] Nancy sets out to understand the spacing of bodies and of sense in the world, as well as the spacing of the world itself.

The need for such an understanding stems from what Nancy calls the dispersal of the sacred, a historical crisis of meaning that can be understood, as we saw in the previous chapter, in terms of changing paradigms of the cosmological. Neither the Judeo-Christian cosmos (gathered in the Word) nor the mathematised world of modernity (distributed according to the infinite extension of Cartesian space) are left available to us, and 'ce qui nous arrive est un épuisement de la pensée de l'Un et d'une destination unique du monde' (CA 12).[4] Our predicament is a crisis of the cosmological, the dissemination of the meaning that Christian and Cartesian cosmoi gathered and distributed respectively. Nancy's response to this predicament is to develop a thinking that goes beyond the dichotomies of gathering and scattering, fragmentation and wholeness, themes we will explore in terms first of *corpus* and then of the world.

6.1 CORPUS

We begin this exploration by reviewing Nancy's reworking of the motifs of the figure-ground relation, organisation and distribution that we encountered in Merleau-Ponty and Ricœur. Nancy disengages from the notion of (mathematically, intentionally) organised or structured space. The ancient or Judeo-Christian cosmos was an organised universe, 'le monde des places distribuées, lieux donnés par les dieux et aux dieux' (C 36).[5] The world, thought after the death of God (though the death of God is an event that is still taking place, according to Nancy), is 'mundus corpus', 'le monde comme le peuplement proliférant des lieux (du) corps. Monde du départ mondial : espacement du partes extra partes, sans rien qui le surplombe ni le soutienne' (C 37).[6] This world is not organised but fragmented, lacking unity in its explosion, spacing and dislocation of being (*être*) in its birth (*naître*), the opposite of the sacrifice or 'eucharistie qui rassemble et qui incorpore les fragments de sa grâce' (SM 211).[7] It is not a world of the many as opposed to, and therefore still reliant on, the One. The dichotomies of the one and the many, the part and the whole, no longer hold good (to the extent that 'part' presupposes 'whole' and 'many' presupposes 'one'), and so Nancy searches for a new way of thinking space and relation that does not conform to this dichotomy.

In the lecture *Le Portrait (dans le décor)*, the relation that Nancy puts forward between portrait and decor bears striking affinities to the Merleau-Pontean understanding of figure and ground:

Jean-Luc Nancy: Plurality

> le décor pourrait être qualifié comme l'objet qui ne doit pas tirer à lui l'intentionnalité d'un sujet (un bon décor ne doit pas, comme on dit, « se faire remarquer »), mais qui doit porter ou proposer, qui doit ouvrir une possibilité de présence pour un sujet. (PDD 9)[8]

He even adopts a Ricœurean register in suggesting that 'toute peinture, . . . n'est-elle pas, non pas à la fois et indiscernablement décor et portrait, mais faite d'une *tension vive* entre ces deux pôles, ou bien encore, entre cet avers et ce revers d'une même présence?' (PDD 10; author's emphasis).[9] The difference which Nancy introduces into this relation, however, is a flattening of the relief of figure on ground to the spacing of exposure:

> Les images sont toujours la force de ce qui provient d'une profondeur insondable, de ce qui monte de l'abîme: mais voici qu'aujourd'hui elles ne configurent plus l'abîme d'où elles viennent, elles le font plutôt venir et elles exposent ceci, qu'elles sont sans fond. En ce sens, elles ne font plus, non plus, figure. (PDD 18)[10]

Nancy argues against the structure of figure and ground as adequate terms in which to describe the world. The figure-ground structure that Nancy rejects, however, is one closely (and curiously, given the analysis of foregoing chapters) allied with foundationalism, and his critique is situated in a wider disquiet with foundationalist assumptions. The following quotation from *La Déclosion* illustrates the sort of 'ground' that Nancy rejects:

> L'éclosion du monde doit être pensée dans sa radicalité: non plus une éclosion *sur fond de monde donné*, ni même de création donnée, mais l'éclosion elle-même et l'espacement de l'espace lui-même . . . Il ne s'agit pas de *racines*, mais de béance . . . Les lieux sont délocalisés et mis en fuite par un espacement qui les précède . . . Ni lieux ni cieux ni dieux: pour le moment, c'est la déclosion générale, plus encore que l'éclosion . . . Déconstruction de la *propriété*, celle de l'homme et celle du monde. (DDC 230; author's emphasis)[11]

Many important motifs in Nancy's thinking of space are here: *espacement*, *béance*, *déclosion*. But the ground from which he is distancing himself – this 'ground' spoken in the same breath as 'given', 'roots' and 'property' – is not the ground with which we are familiar from our engagement with Merleau-Ponty, for whom it is merely the case that the perceptual 'something' is always in the middle of something else, it always forms part of a 'field' (PP 10/*PP* xxviii). Merleau-Ponty's ground is not a foundation but introduces a gap (*écart*) in perception:

> Comprendre que le « avoir conscience » = avoir une figure sur un fond, et qu'il disparaît par désarticulation – la distinction figure-fond introduit un troisième terme entre le « sujet » et « l'objet ». C'est cet *écart-là* d'abord qui est le *sens* perceptif. (VI 247)[12]

Indeed, the relation of figure and ground in Merleau-Ponty resembles Nancy's excription of sense, in that 'voir, c'est voir plus qu'on ne voit' (VI 300).[13] For Merleau-Ponty there is no origin, the origin has 'broken up' and 'la philosophie doit accompagner cet éclatement, cette non-coïncidence, cette différenciation' (VI 163).[14] Being is not grounded on a foundation, but on a 'seul éclatement d'Être qui est à jamais' (VI 318),[15] for 'la source de sens n'est pas plus en arrière de nous, qu'en avant, pas plus un immédiat perdu, qu'un point oméga à atteindre ... elle est dans le voir, le parler, le penser' (NC 375).[16] Nancy rejects any ground (*fond*) that is a foundation (*fonds*) (M 51/M 26), but so did Merleau-Ponty. The move from cosmology to spacing and juxtaposition is summed up in *La Déclosion*, in the essay which gives the book its title. Noting that satellites have collapsed space in a similar way to the discovery of the 'New World', Nancy writes:

> L'espace des séparations cède sous la poussée d'un espacement qui sépare les séparations d'elles-mêmes, qui saisit la configuration générale pour, simultanément, l'étaler dans un continuum et la contorsionner dans un entrelacs de réseaux. Le *partes extra partes* devient, tout en gardant son extériorité, un *pars pro toto* en même temps qu'un *totum in partibus*. (DDC 229)[17]

This is close to Merleau-Ponty's position that 'le monde est cet ensemble où chaque partie quand on la prend pour elle-même ouvre soudain des dimensions illimitées, devient partie totale' (VI 271),[18] but Nancy goes further than Merleau-Ponty in flattening the relief of the figure on the ground. In *Au Fond des images* he comments on a canvas by Hans von Aachen[19] in which a man (von Aachen himself) embraces a young woman (von Aachen's wife) while holding a mirror at such an angle that the woman's face is reflected for the viewer to see. The passage is worth quoting *in extenso* for it demonstrates how Nancy collapses the depth of the figure-ground relation:

> Dans cette double opération, le fond disparaît. Il disparaît dans son essence de fond, qui est de ne pas apparaître. On peut donc dire qu'il apparaît pour ce qu'il est en disparaissant. Disparaissant comme fond, il passe intégralement dans l'image. Il n'apparaît pas pour autant, et l'image n'est pas sa manifestation, ni son phénomène. Il est la force de l'image, son ciel et son ombre. Cette force se passe « au fond » de l'image ou plutôt elle est la pression que le fond exerce sur la surface – c'est-à-dire sous elle, en cet impalpable non-lieu qui n'est pas simplement le « support », mais le *revers* de l'image. Celui-ci n'est pas un « revers de la médaille » (une autre face, et décevante), mais le sens insensible (intelligible) *comme tel senti* à même l'image. (AFI 22–3)[20]

The difference between the ground which disappears and the figure which appears in relief on the ground is suspended, and the impalpable 'non-lieu'[21] that is the force of the image is not the ground of the canvas, but – again following the logic of excription and the pressing up of thought (*pensée*) against weight (*pesée*) – the impalpable sense flush against the image. So 'ce n'est pas comme un filet ou comme un écran que l'image se tient devant le fond. Nous ne coulons pas, mais le fond monte à nous dans l'image' (AFI 31).[22]

Bearing in mind these important differences, we must also note that Nancy does employ the idea of ground in his own thinking, though it is always with qualifications. Although there is no substantial, foundational ground, Nancy uses the term *fond*, in a way that echoes Ricœur's resistance to the third person 'on' ('one') in favour of the 'chacun' ('each') and 'les autres « en général »' ('others "in general" ')', to designate a 'les-uns-les-autres' ('one another') and 'chaque un' ('each one') which is neither Same nor Other but rather 'une pluralité primordiale qui com-paraît' (ESP 89).[23] This, along with the flattening of figure and ground, will be important when we come to consider how Nancy understands plurality and commensurability. The figure does not detach itself from a ground, but (in a juxtaposition of proximity and distance familiar from the discussion of con-tact in the previous chapter) 'fait d'un seul coup écart et contact, coexistence dont l'entrelacs indéfini est le seul « fond » sur lequel s'enlève la « forme » de l'existence' (CMM 176).[24] Briefly to evoke a term with which we shall deal more fully below, there is no ground, only the *avec* ('with'), with the proximity of its spacing. If Nancy's singularity does have a ground, it is made up of the interlacing and sharing of the singularities themselves, a web (*réseau*) or *Ungrund*, but not *Abgrund* (CD 70/IC 27). There is nothing *behind* singularity, only 'l'espace immatériel et matériel qui la distribue *et* qui la partage comme singularité' (CD 70).[25] Ground is rethought in terms of exposition as the evidence or patency (*patence*) of being, with existence as the infinite multiplicity of the world.[26]

A form is a ground which draws away from itself. The figure is ground out of joint: 'Une forme est la force d'un fond qui s'écarte et qui se disloque, son rythme syncopé' (M 59).[27] Nancy's concern here is to avoid a dichotomy of figure and ground, with the concomitant relation of positivity and negativity. To this end, he quotes Gérard Lépinois' 'La vallée de la figuration':

> Une figure n'est jamais entièrement détachée du fond. C'est toujours, plus ou moins, le fond qui avance en tant que figure, et qui reculera bientôt pour redevenir simple espace. (M 59)[28]

Once more, we might wonder against whom Nancy is defining his position here, for it is certainly not Merleau-Ponty. In addition to this question of quite who Nancy is disagreeing with when he condemns ground as foundation, his flattening of the figure-ground relation raises a further problem. Nancy's rejection of a foundationalist reading of the motif can be traced to what Todd May identifies as a dichotomy in Nancy's thought: meaning must conform *either* to some common substance of signification, *or* to spacing, either to foundationalism or to difference.[29] This would indeed account for his identification of ground with foundation. But the Merleau-Pontean construal of figure and ground argued in Chapter 1 and briefly reprised above militates for a position between the two dichotomous poles that seem to exhaust the possibilities of Nancy's thought on the subject. This must be argued, however, in terms of a subtler intervention than May's own, for he makes the same mistake as does Andrew Norris's 'call for a legislative framework' discussed in the previous chapter which, though it is a short route to solving the problem, lands Nancy in precisely the territory he is labouring to avoid. May's argument is that 'we can appeal to something like common substances, but nonfoundationally, drop sharing, and get a good nontotalitarian conception of community.'[30] This is May's 'contingent holism' between foundationalism and spacing. It sounds impressive, but May does not explain how he proposes to escape the bind of avoiding both an ontology of substance and arbitrariness. The problem May identifies is that Nancy and others link foundationalism with giving an account: 'All of this suspicion of theoretical articulation banks on a view of language that holds the giving of accounts and philosophical foundationalism to be inseparable.'[31] May goes on to reject this identification, arguing that theoretical articulation does not always point to philosophical totalitarianism. Indeed it need not, and Nancy's excription is a good example of how it does not have to. In short, May tries too quickly to have the best of both worlds, without feeling the weight of the bind in which the decision finds itself. Feeling that weight all too keenly, Nancy develops his non-substantial response to the problem of coherence in terms of finitude, corpus and the spasm.

Nancy's 'finite thinking' is neither grounded nor groundless. 'Finite' as it is employed by Nancy means three things: that there is, for us, (1) a thinking that is finished; (2) a thinking equal to the significance of the end; (3) any attempt to think finitude must be a finite thinking that, without renouncing truth, universality or sense, thinks only insofar as it touches on its own limit and singularity (PF 12–13/FT 4). The *infondement* ('un-foundation') of thought is dependent not on a ground, but on the *il y a* of sense, an *il* 'qui n'est personne ni aucune chose, ni un principe, *ni un fond*, mais le singulier pluriel des occurrences d'existence, ou de présence, ou de passage' (M 62; author's emphasis).[32] This is no relativistic thought (which implies the absolute), but a thought of absolute finitude (PF 48/FT 27) or essential finitude (PF 13/FT 4). Once more, Nancy is stressing that there is nothing behind or underneath the web of singular plural spacing, which is its own (un)founding. Unfoundation is a foundation *without* foundation, the *sans pourtant* of a non-foundation.

Taking up the challenge that the 'death of God' necessitates a radical reassessment of our understanding of the body, meaning and the world, Nancy sustains over a number of texts[33] a meditation on what he calls *corpus,* a term which intentionally blurs the boundary of the corporeal and the literary and in terms of which he seeks to elaborate an (a)cosmological understanding of existence. *Corpus* cannot be thought using the Lockean dichotomy of unity and diversity, or in terms of Plato's understanding of the opposition of the one and the many. Starting from the position that, 'with the death of God we have lost this glorious body . . . this microcosm of his immense work, and finally this visibility of the invisible, this mimesis of the inimitable' (Cor 19), Nancy does not seek to un-make corporeal coherence, for again he searches for a position otherwise than the binary opposition of chaos and cosmos. He describes *corpus* as neither chaos nor organism, nor between the two, but elsewhere, the prose of an other space (C 48).

There *is* a unity in the corpus, and there is gathering, but rather than being in a living tension (as was the case with Ricœur), they are refigured as spacing:

> Le corps se sent sentir à la fois comme une unité (*je* vois, *je* me brûle) et comme une pluralité elle-même à la fois dispersée (toucher du clavier, vision de l'écran, audition de la radio) et rassemblée, mais aussi comme le « système » de ses différences (je ne touche pas ce que je vois, je n'entends pas ce que je touche). (M 171)[34]

Corpus is not a whole or a totality not least because of its technical prostheses. It is a resistance to the gathering of the microcosm in a surveyable form, reflecting Nancy's suspicion of man *defined* at all (CD 13/IC 9). Instead, 'tel est le monde des corps: il a en lui cette désarticulation, cette inarticulation du corpus . . . non plus la signification, mais . . . un « parler » – corps qui ne s'organise pas' (C 95).[35] *Corpus* is neither straightforwardly centripetal nor centrifugal, nor is it in a Ricœurean tension between the two. It refuses the opposition.

Instead of *corpus* being a function of spatial organisation, Nancy once more evokes the motif of the spasm which, unlike Ricœur's distribution, does not even-handedly apportion and divide space, but convulses it. It cannot be thought in terms of extension, but rather as spacing and distension.[36] 'Un corps s'expulse: comme corpus, espace spasmé, distendu, rejet-de-sujet, « immonde »' (C 93).[37] Such a spasmatic creation is 'impossibility itself', an ineluctable 'gaping' (*écartement*), an architectonic fractal catastrophe.[38] The preponderance of reflexive, instinctive tropes here is reminiscent of the Derridean description of the decision in terms of madness, out of a need to escape the horizon of the calculable and the possible. The body itself is a convulsion or a syncope: 'cette syncope que le corps est . . . d'une seule tenue, tendue entre un cri de naissance et un soupir de mort' (DDC 127).[39]

We must not assume that convulsion and distension are equal and opposite movements for Nancy. The diastole is not one element of a regular diastolic-systolic rhythm. Nevertheless, Nancy's convulsive, spasmatic self is not as unproblematically disseminated as it seems Derrida would like to have it when he characterises the diastole as a 'dilation sans retour'.[40] Convulsions of the self and knots (*nouages*) of the ego (SM 176/SW 113) are not figures on the ground of sense, but neither are they a ceaseless and unmitigated dissemination. In rejecting phenomenological coherence, Nancy still replies to Derridean deconstruction with a *sans pourtant*.

One expression of the dis-articulation of *corpus* is the disjointed contiguity of Nancy's lists of body parts.[41] *Corpus* is not a *logos* or a well-wrought story, but an asyndetic juxtaposition without articulation (C 48), not a cosmo-logy but cata-logue. Existence, then, is a question of relation,[42] the problem of the many, spatiality and spacing, (a)cosmology, and 'one must not consider the anatomy of dissection, but of configurations, of shapes' (Cor 24). In line with Nancy's flattening and spacing of the figure-ground relation, the *corpus* or catalogue is the recitation of an empirical *logos* (Cor 17), 'a simple nomenclature of bodies, of the places of the body. A recitation annunciated from nowhere' (Cor 18), a list whose members are '*without any order* or system, making neither sign nor sense, but exposing all the entries of sense' (Cor 31). *Corpus*, then, does not frustrate every notion of identity, but requires identity to be thought otherwise than in terms of substance: 'Le corps n'est ni substance, ni phénomène, ni chair, ni signification. Mais l'être-excrit' (C 20).[43] The 'identity' of *corpus* is not to be anchored to any particular feature, but emerges in the non-rigid distribution of an indefinite number of parts: '(la) propriété ne réside en rien dans « mon » corps. Elle n'est située nulle part, ni dans cet organe [the heart: CW] dont la réputation symbolique n'est plus à faire' (I 26).[44] Identity is an (a)cosmological notion, a function of the spacing of the catalogue of the body, a Merleau-Pontean *phénomène-enveloppe* with, so to speak, the envelope left open.

We must not read Nancy's lists as aleatory. Derrida rightly points out that, by virtue of being written down, they are, in one way at least, fixed, and 'tout reste très exactement calculé.'[45] An interesting and challenging issue is raised by Derrida when he asks if Nancy's lists are completable (*cloturable*).[46] Derrida is uneasy that the lists end with an aposiopesis,[47] and equally concerned that in *Corpus* Nancy appears to take one element from the list (*peser* – weigh) and make it a sort of transcendental for the others, claiming that 'tout finit par communiquer avec la pesée' (C 82).[48]

Perhaps the best response to Derrida's concern over the recurrent aposiopeses in Nancy's lists is the touching account of Nancy's own heart transplant in *L'Intrus*. As Nancy recounts his experience ten years after the fact (although the transplant itself is not part of the experience) he meditates on the fragile concept of the 'corps propre' (one's own body): 'c'est toute l'affaire du « proper », on l'a compris – ou bien ce n'est pas du tout ça, et il n'y a proprement rien à comprendre' (I 13).[49] Beyond revolt and acceptance, and beyond all metaphysics of *salut* (health/salvation) and 'le proper' (the clean/own), a notion of what is 'properly' the body becomes lost in the midst not only of a transplant but the avalanche of immuno-depressants, the incalculable contingencies of a health service which offers a range of interventions different to those of previous decades and no doubt soon to be superseded by still others. Like the figure for Merleau-Ponty, Nancy's corpus has 'ragged edges'. In this welter of contingency, 'toujours « je » se trouve étroitement serré dans un créneau de possibilités techniques' (I 14).[50]

How are we to mark the frontiers of the self, when absolutely nothing can distinguish the organic, the symbolic and the imaginary, nor distinguish continuity from interruption (I 15)? The frontier of what is proper to the self simply cannot be circumscribed, let alone policed, amid this general feeling of the impossibility of being dissociated from a web of measures, observations and chemical, institutional and symbolic connections. In short, 'I' become(s) a science fiction android, or a 'living-dead', as Nancy's youngest son is reported to have observed (I 35). What is there left to say, but 'Quel étrange moi!' ('what a strange me!') (I 35)?

6.2 THE SINGULAR PLURAL

The spacing of *corpus* is one aspect of a larger concern in Nancy's work to rethink space in terms of Heideggerean *Ent-scheidung* and *Mitsein*, in the service of which he employs a number of figures: *partage* (sharing), *le singulier pluriel* (the singular plural), *nous* (we), *avec* (with), *chaque un* (each one), and *être-en-commun* (being-in-common) to name but the most common. The major dissonance between Heideggerean *Mitsein* and Nancy's appropriation of it, according to Nancy, is that for

Heidegger the 'Mit-' supervenes upon the *Dasein* previously established whereas Nancy thinks the two as coextensive, commenting that 'aucun . . . n'a radicalement thématisé l'*avec* comme le trait essentiel de l'être et comme sa propre essence singulière plurielle' (ESP 54).[51]

Nancy characterises his own project in terms of the imperative that 'il faut refaire l'ontologie fondamentale . . . *à partir du singulier pluriel des origines,* c'est-à-dire à partir de l'*être-avec*' (ESP 45; J-LN's emphasis),[52] and 'que l'être, absolument, est être-avec, voilà ce qu'il nous faut penser' (ESP 83–4).[53] Nancy claims no major theoretical innovation here, insisting rather that being-with is always already implied in being-there:

> L'être modalisé *mit-da* – son unique modalisation, peut-être, mais en même temps indéfiniment plurielle – ce n'est rien d'autre que l'être partageant ou *se partageant* selon le *da*, qui s'efforce de désigner l'« ouvert » – l'« ouvert » de l'ex-posé. En sorte qu'être-avec est la même chose qu'être-ouvert . . . *Mitdasein* serait donc une sorte de bégaiement ou de tautologie de la pensée. (Con 10)[54]

A similar point is made in Nancy's reading of Descartes' 'ego sum, ego existo', where he insists that 'l'existence sociale de Descartes précède logiquement et chronologiquement la possibilité de l'énonciation d'*ego sum* . . . tout *ego sum* est un *ego cum* (ou *mecum*, ou *nobiscum*)' (PD 117).[55] It is only because we are together that we can say 'I' at all, he continues, for if I were alone there would be nothing from which I could distinguish myself. So there can be no absolute; the logic of the absolute is self-defeating, and 'ce qui existe, quoi que ce soit, parce qu'il existe, co-existe' (ESP 49).[56] Being-with cannot be added to being-there. In fact, Nancy is not supplementing Heidegger at all, for 'l'ontologie du « commun » et du « partage » ne serait pas autre chose que l'ontologie de l'« être » radicalement soustrait à une ontologie de la substance, de l'ordre et de l'origine' (Com 57).[57] Instead of an ontology of substance and the re-emergence of a thinking of subjectivity in the Heideggerean *Dasein*, for Nancy the essence of being is co-essence, and this co-, Nancy adds, is not made into an essence itself (ESP 50/BSP 30). It is a sharing (*partage*) of essentiality. Nancy's 'being-with' is not the secondary and random dispersion of a primordial essence (ESP 29/BSP 26). On the contrary, being-with singular plural is the only measure of existence (ESP 98/BSP 89). Nancy is unsettled by 'ownness' or 'propriety' in Heidegger; in this Ian James is undoubtedly correct. But it is less clear that we should continue, as does James, by asserting that Heidegger's centripetal gathering becomes centrifugal dispersal in Nancy.[58] It would seem more in line with Nancy's reworking of cosmological motifs to suggest that he does not oppose a chaotic, entropic, centrifugal dissemination to

Heideggerean gathering, but rather suspends their opposition. Nancy's being-in-common is a resistance to fusion (CD 52–3/IC 20), not an unfettered dissemination.

The ontology that Nancy is elaborating is an ontology of relations,[59] and singular beings appear (*paraissent*) only to the extent that they compear (*comparaissent*) (CD 146/IC 58). Furthermore, *comparution* (compearing) is not a 'paraître ensemble' (appearing together), because 'ensemble' here is extrinsic to the subjects it qualifies. It resolves neither to a juxtaposition *partes extra partes*,[60] nor to a gathering *totum intra totum*. The 'ensemble' as it is used here is not a predicate of being but the trait of being itself, an absolutely originary structure (ESP 83; BSP 61). Relation does not, however, occupy the place taken by individuality in the regime of signification. Individuality, in the precise sense of the term, and pure collective totality are equally impossible (CD 22/IC 6). From one singular to the next there is certainly contiguity, but not continuity (ESP 24/BSP 5). Similarly, a 'group' is not an identity of a superior order, but a stage, a place of identification (ESP 88/BSP 66).

In his reworking of *Mitsein*, Nancy refuses to posit either a Husserlian originary subject or a Lévinasian originary otherness, in addition to refusing either originary (centrifugal) chaos or originary gathered cosmos. Thus the *with* is not 'love', 'relation' or 'juxta-position', but rather '*le régime propre de la pluralité des origines en tant qu'elles s'originent, non pas les unes des autres, ni les unes pour les autres, mais les unes en vue des autres ou à l'égard des autres*' (ESP 106; J-LN's emphasis).[61] It must not be presumed that the *with* of *being-with* is merely the site at which being, or signification, happens. It entertains the same relation to being as *sens* to *signification*:

> l'« avec » . . . n'est pas un lieu, puisqu'il est bien plutôt le lieu lui-même . . . l'*avec* ou l'*entre* n'étant précisément pas autre chose que le lieu lui-même, le milieu ou le monde d'existence. (PD 120)[62]

Echoing strongly Ricœur's work on distributive justice in *Le Juste 1*, Nancy evokes the 'just measure of the *with*', which is the measure of the gap between one origin and another origin, neither self-present identity nor entropic dissemination. The *with* is 'sec et neutre: ni communion ni atomisation, seulement le partage d'un lieu, tout au plus un contact: un être-ensemble sans assemblage' (CA 43).[63] There is neither merely gathering nor simply dissemination, but rather a distance at the heart of proximity and intimacy.

The *with* is closer to Ricœur's 'concordant discordance' than Derrida and others would care to admit:

> Toujours il y a conjonction et disjonction, disconjonction, réunion *avec* division, proche *avec* lointain, *concordia discors* et insociable sociabilité . . . Cette disconjonction est notre problème depuis au moins Rousseau. (PD 118)⁶⁴

The con-tact or *concordia discors* of being requires Nancy to shift his thinking away from oppositions such as individuality and collectivity, the one and the multiple. In *Une Pensée finie*, first published in 1990, Nancy talks of 'singularités multiples' (multiple singularities), and in subsequent publications his attempt to rethink individuality and plurality employs the motif of the singular plural. The question of *l'être social* (social being), not plural as opposed to singular, but 'singular plural', should constitute *the* ontological question (ESP 78/BSP 57), and for this we need another Copernican Revolution after which *l'être social* would now revolve around itself, not the Subject, the Other or the Same (ESP 78–9/BSP 57).

The singular being is not, Nancy insists, the individual, which itself is nothing but the residue left from the ordeal of the dissolution of community (CD 16/IC 3). The individual is separate and indivisible, whereas the singular being 'ne s'enlève ni ne s'élève sur le fond d'une confuse identité chaotique des êtres, ni sur celui de leur assomption unitaire, ni sur le fond d'un devenir, ni sur celui d'une volonté. Un être singulier *apparaît*, en tant que la finitude même: à la fin (ou au début), au contact de la peau (ou du cœur) d'un autre être singulier, aux confins de la *même* singularité qui est, comme telle, toujours *autre*, toujours partagée, toujours exposée' (CD 70).⁶⁵ There is no insularity in singularity. But if *le singulier* is not the individual, then neither is it the subject which, as the relation of self to self, is always a supposition, and the supposition is always called God. The subject of philosophy is 'supposed' in two senses: 'posé lui-même de lui-même au fondement de soi', its own self-sufficient origin, and 'l'hypothèse de sa propre hypostase/fiction/illusion', a fictional proposition raised to, and disguised as, a supposition (SM 112).⁶⁶

The relation of singularity and plurality is expressed somewhat runically by Nancy in *Le Sens du monde* when he maintains that there is not merely one thing in the world, and only thus can there be something (SM 109/SW 67). The fact that there is more than one thing in the world does not mean, however, that there is many times one thing: 'Singulus' does not exist. Nancy explains:

> il ne peut y avoir une seule chose sans qu'il y ait aussi une séparation entre elle et autre chose. Il ne peut donc y avoir moins de deux choses. L'un-seul est sa propre immédiate négation, et l'espace-temps constitue la structure de cette négation. (DDC 228)⁶⁷

This does not amount, however, to a privileging of plurality over singularity. Plurality is not the ground of singularity, for singularity does have a 'ground'; it is made up of the interlacing and sharing of singularities. There is nothing behind singularity, only the immaterial and material space that distributes it and shares it out as singularity (CD 69/IC 27). Conversely, no originary unity underpins Nancy's singular plurality:

> Le commun, l'avoir en commun ou l'être en commun exclut de lui-même l'unité antérieure, la subsistance et la présence en soi et par soi. Être avec, être ensemble, et même être « unis », c'est tout justement ne pas être « un ». De communauté une, il n'y en a que morte, et encore, pas au cimetière, qui est un lieu d'espacement et de distinction. (ESP 179)[68]

Neither unity nor multiplicity is primary (ESP 59/BSP 39), and Nancy is not merely operating a reversal of individuality and collectivity, privileging the latter in the place of the former. He is suspending, not reordering, the hierarchy of the two, a move emphasised in his warning that fragmentation can, if we are not careful, become the reverse (and therefore the twin) of totalisation (SM 189/SM 123).

Nancy's (re)thinking of being-with draws fire from some quarters, for it is suspected of not paying sufficient respect to alterity. For Simon Critchley, 'Nancy's conception of being-with risks reducing intersubjectivity to a relation of reciprocity, equality and symmetry, where I rub shoulders or stand shoulder to shoulder with the other, but where I do not *face* him. The face-to-face risks effacing itself in the reciprocity of the "with"'.[69] Robert Bernasconi for his part suggests that Nancy refuses radical alterity and the Other. In a discussion of Nancy and Lévinas, Bernasconi suggests that Lévinas' priority of the Other becomes in Nancy a priority of the inoperative community.[70] For Nancy, the relation with the face is not primordial; I can grasp it only as secondary and constituted (PF 261/FT 270). From a Lévinasian point of view, Bernasconi argues, making the face to face secondary obliterates alterity and ties Nancy's account of alterity to the philosophy of immanence he sets out to avoid.

Bernasconi's intervention culminates in the charge: 'Does not deconstruction tend at a certain moment to be threatened by nostalgia for so-called Western metaphysics, securing Western philosophy's identity at the very moment that it questions it?'[71] One cannot help thinking that Derrida and Nancy would answer in chorus 'But of course!' The parasitic discourse of deconstruction inhabits a text exposing its metaphysics of presence, and its 'double reading' is nothing but a massive, excessive affirmation of the text – Nietzsche's 'yes, yes' – beyond its hitherto accepted meaning. In suggesting that Christianity, or metaphysics or phenomenology, self-deconstructs, Nancy is doing nothing if not affirming Western metaphysics *à l'outrance* and to the point of its opening (*ouverture*). It is, similarly, far from it being a damning indictment of deconstruction to suggest that it is 'threatened by nostalgia', for deconstruction reads the tradition with a hypertrophied faithfulness, an excessive nostalgia by means of which deconstruction analyses (that is: loosens, *ana-lusis*) the text, opening it to what may previously have been considered its 'outside'. Does this 'secure Western philosophy's identity'? Not a simple question. To borrow a Ricœurean distinction, it certainly does not affirm the *idem*-identity of Western philosophy, its unchanging self-sameness and self-sufficiency, but it does attest (if not secure) its *ipse*-identity, its development through time and through a series of ruptures, through the opening of its sense, rewriting its heritage with the promise of new readings. Western philosophy lives on, even if it is a borderline existence.

In reply to Simon Critchley's concern that 'the face-to-face risks effacing itself in the reciprocity of the "with" ', Ignaas Devisch suggests that 'Nancy's thinking of the "with" is doing just the opposite. The relative structure of our being-in-common is a sort of transcendence in immanence, which Nancy has called "transimmanence." '[72] Devisch is right to underscore the way in which Nancy is not supplanting the priority of alterity with the symmetry of reciprocity, but moving beyond, or withdrawing before, that opposition is established. Exposition is neither transcendent nor immanent, for both these terms rely on the cosmology of the *ici-bas* and the *au-delà*:

> Dès que l'apparence d'un dehors du monde est dissipée, le hors-lieu du sens s'ouvre *dans* le monde – pour autant qu'il y ait encore du sens à parler d'un « dedans » – , il appartient à sa structure, il y creuse ce qu'il faudra savoir nommer mieux que la « transcendance » de son « immanence » – sa *transimmanence*, ou plus simplement et plus fortement, son existence et son exposition. (SM 91)[73]

It is not that Nancy neglects the priority of the other, but rather that he is labouring to elaborate a thought more fundamental than the same/other dichotomy. Nancy characterises the singular plural not in terms of same and other, but *soi* (self), which is more originary than *moi* or *toi*. It is 'l'élément dans lequel "moi" et "toi" et "nous" . . . peuvent avoir lieu' (ESP 119).[74] Speaking of an element, rather than of individuals, is indicative of the way Nancy figures multiplicity. Selves, he insists, are not in relation (*en rapport*) but together (*ensemble*) (CD 258/FH 160). Everything passes *between* us, but this between is not a tissue, glue or cement. It is the stretching out and distance opened by the singular as such (ESP 3/BSP 5). The singular plural cannot be thought in terms of the same-other opposition, for it issues an injunction 'de ne plus penser ni à partir de l'un, ni à partir de l'autre, ni à partir de leur ensemble lui-même compris tantôt comme l'Un tantôt comme l'Autre' (ESP 54).[75] Instead, we must think from the *être-avec* (being-with), difficult as that may be. To the clamour that this opens the door to ethical violence and totalisation, Nancy replies that if *self* does not become *same* to begin with, there is no need for the *other* (ESP 101/BSP 53). Ian James is surely right when he argues that 'the ethical relation is not "passed over" in Nancy, it is simply thought of differently as a relation of being side-by-side rather than an "otherwise than being" of transcendence in the face-to-face.'[76]

It does not follow that Nancy has no place for alterity, of course. On the contrary, when he thinks singularities as 'other origins of the world' (ESP 27/BSP 9) he affirms that 'ce qui fait l'altérité de l'autre, c'est son être-origine' (ESP 29).[77] This alterity is not, however, the absolute Otherness of transcendence which belongs in the old cosmology. Rather, 'l'être-autre de l'origine n'est pas un Autre que le monde,' it is 'l'altérité du monde' (ESP 29),[78] not *aliud*, *alius* or *alienus*, but the distributive *alter*: 'l'un des deux' ('one of the two'). There is no Other (ESP 37/BSP 12–13), but a diaresis or dissection of the self (*soi*) that precedes any relation to the other:

> Dans cette diérèse, l'autre *est* déjà le même, mais cet « être » n'est pas une confusion, encore moins une fusion: il est l'être-autre du soi en tant que ni « soi », ni « autre », ni quelque rapport des deux (PF 17; J-LN's emphasis)[79]

In a manner that recalls Ricœur's chiasm of Husserl and Lévinas in the tenth study of *Soi-même comme un autre*, the self no more founds the other than the other founds the self for Nancy. Rather, the same-other distinction is disrupted by technicity, what Nancy calls the *technē* of the neighbour (C 79). The technical intrusion of the other can never be reduced,[80] and there is no interior core of selfhood which accretes technical supplements. Nancy's self is technological all the way down.

Nancy draws heavily on the major Ricœurean theme of 'oneself as another', though he refashions it for his own purposes, when he describes existence as '*ne pas* être en la présence immédiate ou dans l'immanence d'un étant', but rather 'exister consiste donc à considérer son « soi-même » comme une « altérité »', such that 'chaque moi-même . . . n'est « moi-même » qu'en tant qu'autre' (CD 257–8/FH 160).[81] As Merleau-Ponty would say, I borrow myself from the other; self-identity is routed through the 'oneself as another'. In a footnote, Nancy refers to Ricœur, commenting that 'on s'apparaît à soi en tant qu'on est déjà pour soi-même un autre' (ESP 89).[82] We must be careful here not to see the *soi* as the ground against which the figures of self and other appear. 'Les autres « en général »' (others "in general") or 'les-uns-les-autres' (one-another) is/are 'une pluralité primordiale qui com-paraît' (ESP 89),[83] an exposure at the limit of being, and not the substance of being. Once again, there is no return to the same in this relationality, for though 'nous sommes des semblables . . . le semblable n'est pas le pareil. Je ne me retrouve pas, ni ne me reconnais dans l'autre' (CD 83).[84]

In *Le Sens du monde* Nancy describes 'monde' itself as 'la configuration ou la constellation de l'être-à en son singulier pluriel' (SM 56).[85] Expanding on this cosmological theme, he insists that our *acosmos* is neither preceded nor followed by anything, nor is it gathered in the vision of the panoptic *kosmotheoros* (SM 62/SW 38). The spacing of sense resists gathering. It is fractal, a diffraction and spacing of linear and cumulative histories, as opposed to the 'classical' fragment, which is still a gathering (SM 191/SW 124).

The *nous* is not a given, but remains a task and a responsibility. Faced with the twin menaces of a self-sufficient ego and an anonymous, statistical mass, it avoids both simple gathering and scattering. Conjuring with pronouns, Nancy insists that there is:

> un travail commun, c'est-à-dire en rien collectif, mais travail imposé à *nous* tous *ensemble* . . . d'avoir à nous soucier de la possibilité d'être, précisément, ensemble et de dire « nous », au moment où cette possibilité paraît s'évanouir tantôt dans un « on », tantôt dans un « je » aussi anonymes et monstrueux l'un que l'autre, et en vérité complètement intriqués l'un dans l'autre. (PD 116)[86]

Elsewhere, Nancy characterises this tension as the problem of community:

> Comment dire « nous » autrement que comme un « on » (= tous et personne) et autrement que comme un « je » (= une seule personne, ce qui est encore personne)? Comment donc être en commun sans faire ce que toute la tradition (mais après tout récente, c'est-à-dire tributaire de l'Occident qui s'achève en se répandant) appelle une communauté (un corps d'identité, une intensité de propriété, une intimité de nature)? (Con 6)[87]

This tensional understanding of community and the *concordia discors* makes it clear that the spacing of sense does not mean that the notion of unity has been left behind. On the contrary, 'l'unité d'un monde n'est rien d'autre que sa diversité, et celle-ci est à son tour une diversité de mondes' (CMM 173).[88] The unity of a world is the mutual sharing and the exposition in this world of all worlds. In other words, the unity of a world is the singular difference of a touch (M 38/M 19). Similarly, the notion of a centre is not lost with spacing and the dispersal of the sacred. There is a centre, but never otherwise than as a relation.[89]

Indeed, there is a totality of the community, for the singular beings relate in their singularities to form a sort of totality which resembles an organism, without being an organic whole (CD 187/IC 76). The totality of community is of a different sort, a whole of articulated singularities (CD 184/IC 76), an opening of singularities in their articulations. This articulation is not an organisation, however, but a dialogic whole. It is the unity of the world conceived *as* its multiplicity, with sharing as its law. Sharing is never given, but constantly creates itself. It is not the production of a totality, but 'the co-existence creating itself as world'.[90] In *La Communauté désœuvrée*, Nancy uses the metaphor of train passengers to characterise this tensional relationality. The passengers are more than a mass (*foule*) but less than a group (CD 223/OBIC 7), a (non)relation, a juxtaposition of singularities one to the other, just as the coexistence of singular pluralities is equidistant from juxtaposition and integration (CMM 175/CWM 110).

6.3 ARBITRATION

We are now in a position to bring Nancy's *corpus*, being-with and singular plurality to bear on the problem of arbitration or commensurability. Some previous discussion of these issues is attested in the secondary literature on Nancy, but once again, it has been limited in the main to the notion of community. Andrew Norris[91] suggests that thinking community as shared finitude lacks an effective and properly rigorous theory of political judgement, allowing for no standards with which to differentiate alternatives. According to Norris, Nancy's affirmation of being-in-common as our fundamental state is a take-it-or-leave-it proposition.[92] We began to explore this problem in the previous chapter, but now we approach it with a different set of concerns. How can Nancy respond to the appeal 'justify yourself'? First, we are not to expect a full and exhaustive response. Not that a non-exhaustive response would be a failure to respond, but because only a non-exhaustive response would be faithful to the regime of finite sense. What marks out all great philosophies, Nancy notes (and this is what makes them great, he says), is that they do not simply offer an all-encompassing vision of the world, but they also show the limits of such a vision. Each has its aporias and enigmas: the Good or Love for Plato (and, we might venture in view of the discussion so far, for Derrida also), evidence for Descartes, joy for Spinoza, the Kantian schematism, logic for Hegel, praxis for Marx (OP 75). More than this, he continues, to misunderstand this essential incompleteness is to forget philosophy (OP 76). Whatever else we might conclude from this, we should certainly not expect Nancy to attempt an exhaustive account of his own philosophical position; any philosophy that claims a complete answer to the appeal 'justify yourself!' should be treated with suspicion: it has forgotten itself. Given this caveat, how does Nancy approach the problem of arbitration within his finite thinking? We shall answer this question in terms of three aspects of Nancean thinking where the problem of multiplicity and relationality are to the fore: the relation of the senses, the relation of the arts and the relation of spheres of social action.

First, the senses. We shall define Nancy's position in contradistinction to Derrida's. In *Le Toucher*, Derrida rejects any unproblematic commensurability between the senses, suggesting that 'il faut sauter de l'un à l'autre, aveuglément, comme un aveugle-né, par-dessus un abîme infini',[93] elaborating this position in contrast to, among others, Maine de Biran and Merleau-Ponty. Biran relates the senses to each other in what Derrida calls an 'analogism', and considers all the senses to be a form of touch, of which the hand is the privileged organ.[94] This amounts, for Derrida, to a 'humainisme'.[95] As for Merleau-Ponty, Derrida is unconvinced by the easy transition he allows between the senses. Quoting from *Phénoménologie de la perception*, where Merleau-Ponty himself quotes Descartes and concludes that the blind 'voient des mains',[96] Derrida questions Merleau-Ponty's faithfulness to Descartes' text: Descartes only offers a 'comparison' between sight and touch. Derrida also allies the Merleau-Pontean 'unité intersensorielle de la chose'[97] to his wider disquiet at his concept of world or being in the world, the 'être tout court qui organise cette phénoménologie de la perception.'[98] For his own part, Derrida upholds a strict incommensurability of the senses: 'Même si c'est la « même chose », ce que nous voyons est une chose, et ce que nous touchons en est une autre', he insists, adding that 'ces différents objets portent ensuite le même nom, c'est donc toute la question du langage . . . de sa théologie.'[99]

Although Nancy does seek to relate the senses in terms that Derrida would perhaps not himself choose, the Nancean position is not so far removed from Derrida's as semantic differences might suggest. First we note that, for Nancy, the difference between the senses is not totalisable: 'la différence des sens sensibles n'est rien d'autre que la différence en soi du sens sensé: la non-totalisation de l'expérience, sans laquelle il n'y aurait pas d'*expérience*' (M 174).[100] Secondly, touch for Nancy is both one of the senses and also that in terms of which the senses are thought to cohere. For Nancy, touch is not just one of the five senses but it is rather 'l'extension générale et l'extraposition particulière du sentir. Le toucher *fait corps* avec le sentir, ou il fait des sentirs un corps, il n'est que le *corpus* des sens' (M 35–6).[101] But here Nancy is not unifying the senses in the same way that Walzer's political power both participates in and distributes the goods in a society. It is a coherence not of inclusion but of spacing and separation, the list and the catalogue. For Nancy, then, the senses are spaced, but what sort of relation does that afford? The relation is figured in terms of the motifs of exposure and touch:

> le rire est la joie des sens et du sens sur leur limite. Dans cette joie, les sens se touchent entre eux, et ils touchent au langage, à la langue dans la bouche. Mais ce toucher lui-même les espace. Ils ne se pénètrent pas. (PF 321–2)[102]

The relation of the senses for Nancy is banal. There is no principle of plurality, but rather the plural itself as principle (M 12/M 2). The senses *are* plural, *are* spaced in a manner familiar to us from the discussion of singular plurality above, and we can understand this difference better by turning to the relation of the arts.

As in the case of the senses, Nancy is careful not to limit the number of the arts:

> il est devenu impossible de dénombrer les arts supplémentaires, vidéo, performance, body-art, installation, etc.: non parce que les espèces seraient trop nombreuses, mais parce que le décompte n'a pas de sens; si c'est l'art comme tel qui devient essentiellement multiple et même nombreux; autrement dit, l'« art » perd une unité présumée. (EF 23)[103]

The arts do not form a system, nor are they strictly incommensurable; their relation is by no means straightforward. Indeed, each 'art' is itself essentially diverse (PDD 9). In *Les Muses*, Nancy articulates an (a)cosmological relationality of the arts:

> On ne cherche pas ici une « définition » . . . de l'art. On cherche seulement une façon de ne pas quitter cette diversité, une façon, non pas de « dire », mais *d'articuler* quelque chose de l'« art », singulier pluriel, à même sa pluralité inorganique et sans synthèse ou sans système. (M 66)[104]

The relation again is liminal, a contact *sans* contact and the spacing that is beyond, or before, the distinction of the one and the many. The arts are in a relation of fragmentation, but not the fragmentation *of* a prior whole, communicating only by the impossibility of passing from one to another (SM 198/SW 130), and Nancy asserts elsewhere that 'c'est la caractéristique majeure de la pluralité constitutive des arts: chacun initie tous les autres et les tient à l'écart de soi' (All 113).[105] This subtly differs from Derrida's leap from one sense to the other; it is the difference of con-tact, of the *sans pourtant* or of the 'pressing up against' that characterises the relation of thought and weight. The incommensurability of art(s) is open to this fragmentation of sense that existence *is* (SM212/SW 139). The arts are exposed to each other, and 'au lieu de l'Art, les arts s'offrent à nous, en leur irréductible multiplicité, dans l'écart anarchique de leurs « techniques » diverses.'[106] There is no unifying principle, and no essence, guaranteeing the relation of the arts, and as in the case of singular plurality, the plural is not the plural *of* the singular which pre-exists it in isolation:

> les pratiques artistiques, dans leur disparité (de la poésie à la vidéo, de la performance à la musique, du « povera » au « body », etc.), ne surgissent pas d'un fond ni d'une identité commune qui serait « l'art », mais . . . cette identité – peut-être introuvable – n'est formée que par l'ensemble des pratiques dans leurs différences, sans que cet « ensemble » résorbe si peu que ce soit leur hétérogénéité. (M 163)[107]

Once more, the relation is tensional, a *concordia discors* of touch and distance in which the arts come into being through a mutual relation of proximity and exclusion, attraction and repulsion, and their respective works operate and communicate in this double relation (M, 163). The arts are not in a relation of reciprocity, but of mutual proximity.

To characterise this (non-)relation Nancy, like Ricœur, looks to the motif of translation, arguing that the arts, though not themselves languages, are related to each other as languages in that they are both translatable and untranslatable, where the thin thread of translatability is like the trace of 'art' in the singular, situated neither above nor beneath the arts, but between them (M 166). In a move which brings the incommensurability of the arts and the senses together, Nancy goes even further in *Allitérations*, suggesting that:

> le sens de la danse est le sens de la séparation dans un bond qui ouvre et qui franchit en même temps la division des corps: sens d'avant tous les sens et qui les ferme puis les rouvre un par un, se glissant entre tous, sursaut au fond de chacun et de l'un à l'autre, entre le même et la mêlée d'un corps singulier ou de corps pluriels, faisant de l'un plusieurs et de plusieurs une danserie'. (All 149)[108]

This use of dance to articulate the senses[109] is reminiscent of the motif of rhythm, important for both Merleau-Ponty and Nancy, and it is in dissonance with Derrida's 'leap' from one sense to another. Like Derrida, however, Nancy refuses any commensurability of the arts; like Ricœur's phenomenology he refuses to abandon thinking the translatability of the arts.

If the arts are related, the relation is not substantial but by virtue of their gaps (*écarts*). In the course of a discussion of presence as passage, Nancy notes that:

> il n'est pas impossible de s'essayer à dire que cet espace et ce temps vides du présent en son passage, c'est un autre art qui le remplit : l'art de la musique. (On tenterait ainsi d'amorcer un lien des arts par leurs écarts, qui serait le lien unique mais indéfectible de l'« art » en général. (P 27)[110]

A little further on, Nancy continues:

> il en irait ainsi du « système » entier des arts : tous hétérogènes entre eux, et chaque fois séparés par une crevasse infranchissable. Ce qui les sépare, et qui, de cette manière les rassemble en circulant d'entre eux, mais aussi à l'intérieur de chacun d'eux, c'est ce qui écarte la présence d'elle-même: ce qui la repousse et qui la désire, ce qui la repousse pour la désirer et pour la toucher au passage (P 31).[111]

It is their spacing, their incommensurability, which they share, and nothing more.

In the same way that the spacing of sense means that each inscription of sense excribes a constitutive excess, the relation of the arts is understood in terms of an excess of sense. Although art receives 'political' or 'ethical' legitimation today, Nancy argues that the only legitimation it can have is the sensuous attestation to and inscription of the overflowing of sense (DDC 13 n2/DDC 176 n3). This 'overspill' of sense is developed, via a quotation from Gilles Deleuze's *Logique de la sensation*,[112] into a manner of relating both the arts and the senses:

> Entre une couleur, un goût, un toucher, une odeur, un bruit, un poids, . . . il y aurait une communication existentielle qui constituerait le moment « pathique » (non représentatif) de la sensation . . . Il appartiendrait donc au peintre de faire voir une sorte d'unité originelle des sens, et de faire apparaître visuellement une Figure multisensible. Mais cette opération n'est possible que si la sensation de tel ou tel domaine . . . est directement en prise sur une puissance vitale qui déborde tous les domaines et les traverse. Cette puissance, c'est le Rythme, plus profond que la vision, l'audition etc. . . . C'est diastole-systole: le monde qui me prend moi-même en se fermant sur moi, le moi qui s'ouvre au monde, et l'ouvre lui-même. (M 45–6)[113]

The arts and the senses are related in that each excribes an excess which it cannot contain, and it is this excess, this incommensurability, that is shared. So the 'original unity' of the senses is not governed by any one sense, but figured in terms of a 'vital force' that overflows them all. This force, or rhythm, is not a linking but a distancing and estrangement, for it is the 'écart du battement qui le fait rythme' (M 46).[114] Rhythm for Nancy brings no synaesthesia of ordinary perception (contra Merleau-Ponty and Deleuze), but rather the beating of appearance ('le battement de l'apparaître') which does not itself appear.

Nancy glosses the meaning of *rhuthmos*, in the words of Emile Benveniste, as a characteristic arrangement of the parts into a whole (SM 216/SW 142). Rhythm is what makes a collection (*ensemble*) into a system (*système*), in a similar way to Ricœur's narrative *muthos* turning a succession into a configuration. But there is a fundamental difference between Ricœur and Nancy here. Whereas narrative configures in terms of of *quid sit*, Nancean rhythm carries no determinate sense. To reduce for a moment the complexity of Nancy's position for the sake of clarity, we might say that it is (once more) not in terms of the *what* of the senses or the arts that they are related, but in their *that*, in the structural excess they share.

Although there is no original synaesthesia or 'life' to gather the senses or the arts together, Nancy employs the familiar motifs of call, response and promise to develop the relation. The plurality of arts 'décompose l'unité vivante de la perception ou de l'action' (M 42),[115] and dislocates *sens commun* (common/shared sense) and ordinary synaesthesia. Nevertheless, 'l'art dégage le sens de la signification, ou plutôt, il dégage le monde de la signification' (M 43),[116] and 'la synesthésie dis-loquée . . . engage . . . un renvoi ou, selon le mot de Baudelaire, une réponse de touche à touche',[117] neither a relation of external homology nor of internal osmosis but rather (according to the etymology of *respondere*), a pledge or promise given in response to a demand (M 45). Similarly, in Nancy's incalculable *se-toucher-toi* (touch-oneself-you), the 'toi' is 'le pôle touchable. . . d'un vocatif ou d'une adresse apostrophante'.[118] Though the signification of the arts is incommensurable, their sense is commensurable *in its incommensurability*: a structural, not a substantial commensurability.

For the third facet of our investigation into incommensurable commensurability, we turn now to the question of arbitration between the spheres of political life in the essay 'Tout est-il politique?'[119] In *Être singulier pluriel*, Nancy addresses the demand to invent, in the absence of any given measure, something that would facilitate the articulation of inter-human relations in the an-archy of our space (ESP 208/BSP 180).[120] Alterity (capital A) cannot fulfil this task – it can only oppose to dispersion a sovereign identity of unification, for 'the Other is the place of community as communion' (ESP 102/BSP 79). To think *justice* (justice) and *justesse* (precision) together, an account of the Same and the Other just will not do. We need an 'ontologie de l'être-les-uns-avec-les-autres' (ESP 75),[121] with both proximity and distance. Just how Nancy argues for a certain 'justice between incomparables' can be seen in 'Tout est-il politique?', where the political plays not a distributive function, as it did in Walzer's spheres, but is characterised in the less centralising and deliberative term 'diffusion', according to which 'les moments ou morceaux divers de l'existence commune relèvent tous à quelque titre du moment ou morceau nommé « politique », auquel revient donc un privilège de diffusion ou de transversalité' (TEP 77).[122] Indeed 'c'est la sphère « politique » qui détermine ou qui commande l'activité des autres sphères' (TEP 77).[123] Very Walzerian. However, the political only becomes totalising when it is determined as the global nature of the *oikos*: or, more precisely, as an *oikological* globality (TEP

78/*IEP* 17), in which context 'everything is political' amounts to asserting that 'man' is self-sufficient in the sense that he produces his own nature and, therein, nature as a whole (TEP 79/*IEP* 18).

Nancy resists such an 'oikological globality', however – and this is where his reading diverges dramatically from the Walzerian account – arguing that the exercise of justice (the power of coercion) is incompatible with identification on the basis of an *oiko-nomie* (natural self-sufficiency): 'il est devenu patent qu'il n'y a pas d'oikonomie: il n'y a, à tous égards, qu'une *écotechnie*, c'est-à-dire un lieu commun ou une habitation dans la production, l'invention et la transformation incessante de fins qui ne sont jamais données' (TEP 81).[124] Any arbitration between the different spheres cannot take place on the basis of the 'oikonomical', but must follow the 'ecotechnical' route, according to which 'la politique se retrace comme lieu d'exercice du pouvoir en vue d'une *justice incommensurable* – soit comme lieu de revendication d'une in-finité de l'être-homme et de l'être-monde' (TEP 81; author's emphasis).[125] So politics no longer absorbs into itself all the other spaces of existence. In these other spaces, – 'art', 'religion', 'thought', 'science', 'ethics', 'conduct', 'exchange', 'production', 'love', 'war', 'kinship', 'intoxication', though an infinite number of names could be used – 'leurs distinctions et leurs circonscriptions mutuelles (qui n'empêchent ni contiguïtés, ni compénétrations) définissent chaque fois l'occurrence d'une configuration selon laquelle a lieu une certaine présentation' (TEP 81).[126] These configurations are incommensurable with each other, stresses Nancy, but (employing the characteristic double negative we encountered in the *sans pourtant* in the previous chapter) without excluding ('sans exclure') their contacts and contagions (TEP 81/*IEP* 20). So incommensurability is figured in cosmological terms ('configuration'), and 'la politique se redessine à cette place: comme le lieu d'où il s'agit de maintenir cette incommensurabilité ouverte, et ouverte en général l'incommensurabilité de la justice comme celle de la valeur' (TEP 81).[127] The political is no longer an overarching sphere that integrates the distributed goods of a society, but instead it ensures mutual exposure; the measure of its coherence of the other spheres is that it ensures precisely the maintenance of incommensurability. We see here a similar move to the universal of openness 'in the second degree' that we explored at the end of the previous chapter. Politics is in charge of space or spacing (of space-time), but not in charge of figures (TEP 82/*IEP* 20).

This brings us to a wider consideration of what we could call an 'incommensurability in common'. We arrive at a notion of arbitration *without* arbitration as an 'incommensurability in-common' between the incommensurable spheres, and 'la politique est le lieu d'un « en-commun » en tant que tel – mais seulement sur le mode de l'incommensurabilité maintenue ouverte' (TEP 82).[128] This 'in-common' is not subsumed under any type of union, subject or epiphany (TEP 82/*IEP* 21), and rather than being the locus of integration and arbitration, politics becomes, precisely, a site of detotalisation (TEP 82/*IEP* 21).

The incommensurability which Nancy evokes here is a division which unites. There is a common measure that is not an 'étalon unique appliqué à tous et à toutes choses', namely 'la commensurabilité des singularités incommensurables: l'égalité de toutes les origines-de-monde' (ESP 98).[129] Unique and incommensurable, singularities are unsubstitutable, are all 'également les uns avec les autres' or in other words 'substituable à tout autre *en tant qu'insubstituable*' (C 80–1).[130] As Nancy states in *La Communauté désœuvrée*, 'ce qui est partagé n'est pas cette annulation du partage, mais le partage lui-même, et par conséquent la non-identité de tous, de chacun avec lui-même et avec autrui' (CD 164).[131] Again, it is not meanings that are shared, but the absence of meaning itself that insists on being shared (Com 57).

In addition to singularities being commensurable in their incommensurability, Nancy also explores the limits of arbitration in terms of calculating the incalculable, a motif familiar to readers of Derrida.[132] Even the most calculating financial logic knows the immeasure of responsibility, and even in insurance, what is calculated is a segment taken from a whole which is not strictly infinite, but incommensurable (PD 174). Ignaas Devisch is therefore quite right to question Todd May's characterisation of *partage* as 'communal nature', for Nancy means quite the opposite: there is no measurable commonality at the root of his community. 'May claims to be correcting Nancy's thoughts with an anthropological and sociological filling-in of community. That is not Nancy's question.'[133] Quite so, and it is precisely what Nancy's understanding of community sets out to avoid. On a similar note, May is also mistaken in his assertion that Nancy's concept of community 'presumes a prior commitment to a type of community bond that the conception itself excludes as totalitarian.'[134] Avoiding totalitarianism, May argues, cannot be given as a reason for espousing Nancy's community. 'The only reason a community could adopt Nancy's model is for no reason whatsoever. Why? Because any reason for adopting it would appeal to a value or principle, and the conception precludes this. Nancy's conception of community can give us no reason for adopting it'.[135] May has arrived at this conclusion as a result of failing to make a number of distinctions along the way. First, Nancy does not have a concept of community or, put another way, the community in Nancy's thought, as the spacing of sense, is pre-conceptual and pre-symbolic. Secondly, Nancy's community does not 'presume a prior commitment to a type of community bond', both because the *partage* (sharing) of the community is not a bond (which would be an *ensemble* (togetherness) supervening on pre-existent individuals) but a singular plural spacing, and then a fortiori because this spacing is not a presumption. So Nancy's community does not stand or fall on there being a 'reason' to 'adopt' it. May is quite right in suggesting that 'any reason for adopting it would appeal to a value or principle', and would relocate Nancy's thought in the determinacy of arbitration to which it has been the burden of this and the previous chapter to argue it does not conform. A reason is precisely, quite precisely, what Nancy cannot and must not give. His finite thought does not offer an all-encompassing understanding of the world, but shows the limits of any such understanding. To what sort of reason, value or principle, do we expect a finite thought to appeal for its ultimate justification?

With this question, we reach the end of our investigation. We asked at the beginning of this chapter if Nancy could avoid both the problems to which deconstruction draws attention in phenomenology and the difficulties that are highlighted in deconstructive thought by an engagement with the phenomenological. The answer is that he cannot. If a finite thinking appeals to a principle or value for its justification, then the 'quis custodiet ipsos custodes?' objection is swift in coming. If it does not, then it cannot, for all its care and agonising, ultimately, ethically, differentiate between strangers, gods and monsters. Nancy's notions of *corpus* and *le singulier pluriel* take up Ricœur's struggle to think a tensive coherence but reject the motif of tension in favour of spacing and the spasm, but using the test cases of the senses, the arts and incommensurable social spheres we have seen how Nancy's ontological thought is brought to bear on the question of coherence in a way which struggles ethically to arbitrate between incommensurable claims. Nancy cannot calculate the incalculable. Overall, we have been forced to acknowledge that any single position, however nuanced, will encounter at its limit a problem to which it cannot respond in its own terms, whether it is the problem of the Good in Derrida and Nancy or the problem of attestation in Merleau-Ponty and Ricœur. But this is not, and must not be, the final word in this exploration of the relation of phenomenology and deconstruction for, as we shall argue now in conclusion, it is in the ever-changing relation of such positions to each other, in the impasse of their encounter, that the most decisive observations are to be made.

NOTES

1. James, *The Fragmentary Demand* 2.
2. See James, *The Fragmentary Demand* 3. James is referring to Blanchot's *L'Entretien infini* 234.
3. 'there is that which is "common", "together", and "many", and that perhaps we no longer had any idea how to think this order of the real' (author's translation).
4. 'what comes to us is an exhaustion of the thought of the One and of a single destiny for the world' (author's translation).
5. 'the world of distributed spaces, places given by the gods and to the gods' (author's translation).
6. 'the world as the proliferating peopling of the places (of the) body. World of worldwide departure: spacing of the *partes extra partes*, without anything that overhangs or underpins it' (author's translation).
7. 'a eucharist that gathers and incorporates the fragments of its grace' (*SW* 138).
8. 'the decor could be qualified as the object that must not draw the intentionality of the subject on itself (a good decor must not, as we say, "draw attention to itself"), but should carry or propose, should open up a possibility of presence for a subject' (author's translation).
9. 'every painting . . . is it not, is not at the same time and indiscernably décor and portrait, but rather is made of a *lively tension* between the two poles, or better, between the front and the back of a same presence' (author's translation).
10. 'Images are always the force of what comes from an unfathomable depth, what comes up from the abyss: but today they do not configure the abyss from whence they come, they rather make it come and they expose precisely this: that they are without ground. In this sense, they are neither, any longer, a figure' (author's translation).
11. 'The eclosure of the world must be thought in its radicalness: no longer an eclosure *against the background of a given world*, or even against that of a given creation, but the eclosure of eclosure itself and the spacing of space itself. . . . it is not a question of *roots*, but of wide-openness . . . Locations are delocalised and put to flight by a spacing that precedes them . . . Neither places, nor heavens, nor gods: for the moment it is a general dis-enclosing, more so than a burgeoning . . . Deconstruction of *property* – that of man and that of the world' (*DCD* 160–1).
12. 'Understand that the "to be conscious" = to have a figure on a ground, and that it disappears by disarticulation – the figure-ground distinction introduces a third term between the "subject" and the "object." It is that separation first of all that is the perceptual meaning' (*VI* 197).
13. 'to see is always to see more than one sees' (*VI* 247).
14. 'philosophy must accompany this break-up, this non-coincidence, this differentiation' (*VI* 124).

15. 'one sole explosion of Being which is forever' (*VI* 265).
16. 'the source of meaning is not so much behind us, but in front, not so much a lost immediacy but an omega point to reach . . . it is in sight, speech, thought' (author's translation).
17. 'The space of separations is yielded beneath the thrust of a spatiality that separates the separations from themselves, that seizes the general configuration, in order simultaneously to spread it out in a continuum and to contort it into an interlacing of networks. The *partes extra partes* is becoming, while retaining its exteriority, a *pars pro toto* at the same time as a *totum in partibus*' (*DDC* 160; translation altered).
18. 'The "World" is this whole where each "part," when one takes it for itself, suddenly opens unlimited dimensions – becomes a total part' (*VI* 218).
19. Hans von Aachen, *Young Couple*, Vienna, Kunsthistorisches Museum.
20. 'In this double operation, the ground disappears. It disappears in its essence as ground, which consists in its not appearing. One can thus say that it appears as what it is by disappearing. Disappearing as ground, it passes integrally into the image. But it does not appear for all that, and the image is not its manifestation, nor its phenomenon. It is the force of the image, its sky and its shadow. This force exerts its pressure "in the ground" of the image, or, rather, it is the pressure that the ground exerts on the surface – that is, under this force, in this impalpable non-place that is not merely the "support" but the *back* or the *underside* of the image. The latter is not an "other side of the coin" (another surface, and a disappointing one), but the insensible (intelligible) sense that *is sensed as such*, self-same with the image' (*GOI* 7–8; translation altered).
21. 'Non-lieu', literally 'non-place', also carries the meaning, in a legal register, of the suspension of a trial before it has reached a verdict: a non-judgement.
22. 'the image stands in front of the ground not as a net or a screen. We do not sink into it, but the ground rises up to us in the image' (author's translation).
23. 'a primordial plurality that co-appears' (*BSP* 67).
24. 'in one stroke separates and makes contact, a coexistence whose indefinite intertwining is the sole ground on which the "form" of existence rises' (*CWM* 111).
25. 'the immaterial *and* material space that distributes and shares the confines of other singularities' (*IC* 27).
26. M 51; M 27. Quoting Badiou and Wahl, *Conditions* 361.
27. 'A form is the force of a ground that sets apart and dislocates itself, its syncopated rhythm' (*M* 32).
28. 'A figure is never entirely detached from the ground. It is always, more or less, the ground that comes forward as figure and that will soon move back to become again simple space' (*M* 32).
29. May, *Reconsidering Difference* 47.
30. May, *Reconsidering Difference* 49 n36.

31. May, *Reconsidering Difference* 12.
32. 'being neither a person nor a thing, nor a principle, nor a ground, but the singular plural of occurrences of existence, or presence, or passage' (*M* 34).
33. See especially C, Cor, I, M and NMT.
34. 'The body feels itself feeling at one and the same time like a unity (*I see, I burn myself*) and like a plurality which is at the same time dispersed (touching the keyboard, looking at the screen, hearing the radio) and gathered, but also as the "system" of these differences (I do not touch what I see, I do not hear what I touch' (author's translation).
35. 'such is the world of bodies: it has in itself this disarticulation, this inarticulation of the corpus . . . no longer signification, but . . . a "speaking" – a disorganised body' (author's translation).
36. Derrida, *Le Toucher* 70; *On Touching* 56–7.
37. 'A body expels itself: like corpus, spasmatic space, distended, reject-of-subject, "unclean"' (author's translation).
38. Derrida, *Le Toucher* 70; *On Touching* 56–7.
39. 'this syncope that the body is . . . in one uninterrupted block, sustained from the cry of birth to the last breath' (*DDC* 83).
40. Derrida, *Le Toucher* 282; 'dilation without return' (*On Touching* 282).
41. See C 82, 105.
42. We are reminded of the concluding sentence of Merleau-Ponty's *Phénoménologie de la perception*: 'L'homme n'est qu'un nœud de relations, les relations comptent seules pour l'homme' (PP 520; quoting A. de Saint-Exupéry, *Pilote de guerre* 174); 'Man is but a network of relationships, and these alone matter to him' (*PP* 530).
43. 'The body is neither substance nor phenomenon nor flesh nor signification. But being-excribed' (author's translation).
44. 'the property in no way resides in "my" body. It is situated nowhere, not even in this organ whose symbolic reputation has already been made' (author's translation).
45. Derrida, *Le Toucher* 325; 'everything remains exactly calculated' (*On Touching* 289).
46. Derrida, *Le Toucher* 86; *On Touching* 71.
47. Derrida, *Le Toucher* 86; *On Touching* 71.
48. 'everything finally communicates with weight' (author's translation).
49. 'it is the whole business of "own" [*propre*], as you will have understood – or rather it is not that at all, and there is really [*proprement*] nothing to understand' (author's translation).
50. '"I" aways finds itself tightly gripped in a niche of technical possibilities' (author's translation).
51. 'no one . . . has radically thematised the "with" as the essential trait of Being and as its proper singular plural essence' (*BSP* 34).
52. 'it is necessary to refigure fundamental ontology . . . *from the singular plural of origins*, from *being-with*' (*BSP* 26).

53. 'that Being is being-with, absolutely, this is what we must think' (*BSP* 26).
54. 'The modalised being *mit-da* – its unique modalisation, perhaps, but at the same time indefinitely plural – it is nothing other than being sharing or sharing *itself* according to the *da*, that strives to name the "open" – the "open" of the ex-posed. Such that being-with is the same thing as being-open . . . *Mitdasein* would thus be a sort of gaping or tautology of thought' (author's translation).
55. 'the social existence of Descartes logically and chronologically precedes the possibility of the enunciation of the *ego sum* . . . every *ego sum* is an *ego cum* (or *mecum*, or *nobiscum*)' (author's translation).
56. 'That which exists, whatever this may be, coexists because it exists' (*BSP* 29; translation altered).
57. 'the ontology of the "common" and of "sharing" would be nothing other than the ontology of "being" radically subtracted from an ontology of substance, from order and origin' (Author's translation).
58. James, *The Fragmentary Demand* 102.
59. Indeed, he refers in passing to Étienne Balibar's ontology of relations, without treating it at any length (see ESP 95 n1/*BSP* 202 n62).
60. *Partes extra partes*, notes James (*The Fragmentary Demand* 143), is central to fractured thinking, reminding his reader that Merleau-Ponty defines *partes extra partes* in his *Phénoménologie de la perception* as an object which admits between its parts or between itself and other objects only exterior or mechanical relations (PP 90/PP 87). Derrida observes that *partes extra partes* traverses Nancy's œuvre from around 1979, especially in relation to *psyche* and Freud (see Derrida, *Le Toucher* 71 n1; *On Touching* 325 n37. Cf Poids, 14).
61. 'the proper realm of the the plurality of origins insofar as they originate, not from one another or for one another, but in view of one another or with regard to one another' (*BSP* 82).
62. 'the "with" . . . is not a place, because it is rather the place itself . . . the *with* or the *between* being precisely nothing other than the place itself, the milieu or the world of existence' (author's translation).
63. 'dry and neutral: neither communion nor atomisation, only the sharing of a place, at the most a contact: a being-together without assembly' (author's translation).
64. 'There is always a conjunction and disjunction, disconjunction, joining *with* division, close *with* remote, *concordia discors* and unsociable sociability . . . This disconjunction has been our problem since at least Rousseau' (author's translation).
65. 'A singular being does not emerge or rise up against the background of a chaotic, undifferentiated identity of beings, or against the background of their unitary assumption, or of a becoming, or of a will. A singular being *appears*, as finitude itself: at the end (or at the beginning), with the contact of the skin (or the heart) of another singular being, at the confines of the

same singularity that is, as such, always *other*, always shared, always exposed' (*IC* 28).
66. 'it will have posited itself on its own as its own foundation, and it will have been the hypothesis of its own hypostasis, fiction or illusion' (*SW* 69).
67. 'There cannot be one sole thing without there being a separation between itself and something else. Therefore there cannot be fewer than two things. The one-sole is its immediate negation, and space-time constitutes the structure of that negation' (*DDC* 159; translation altered).
68. 'The common, having-in-common or being-in-common, excludes interior unity, subsistence, and presence in and for itself. Being with, being together and even being "united" are precisely not a matter of being "one". Within unitary community there is nothing but death, and not the sort of death found in the cemetery, which is a place of spacing or distinction' (*BSP* 154).
69. Critchley, *Ethics, Politics, Subjectivity* 251–2.
70. Bernasconi, 'On Deconstructing Nostalgia . . .' 12.
71. Bernasconi, 'On Deconstructing Nostalgia . . .' 18.
72. Devisch, 'A Trembling Voice in the Desert: Jean-Luc Nancy's Rethinking of the Space of the Political' 245. See also SM 91; M 63.
73. 'As soon as the appearance of a beyond of the world is dissipated, the out-of-place instance of sense opens itself up *within* the world (to the extent that it would still make sense to speak of a "within"). Sense belongs to the structure of the world, hollows out therein what it would be necessary to name better than by calling it the "transcendence" of its "immanence" – its *transimmanence*, or more simply and forcefully, its existence and exposition' (*SW* 55).
74. 'the element in which "me" and "you," and "we," . . . can take place' (*BSP* 154). We are reminded of Ricœur's move whereby 'j'échange le moi, maître de lui même, contre le soi, disciple du texte' (TA 60); 'I exchange the me, master of itself, for the self, disciple of the text' (*TA* 37).
75. 'no longer thinking: – beginning from the one, or from the other, – beginning from their togetherness, understood now as the One, now as the Other' (*BSP* 34).
76. James, 'On Interrupted Myth' 343.
77. 'The alterity of the other is its being-origin' (*BSP* 53).
78. 'the being-other of the origin is not the alterity of an "other-than-the-world" . . . it is a question of the alterity or alteration *of* the world' (*BSP* 11).
79. 'In this diaresis, the other is already the same, but this "being" isn't confusion, still less a fusion; no, it is the being-other of the self as neither "self" nor "other," nor as some founding or original relation between them' (*FT* 7).
80. Derrida, *Le Toucher* 131; *On Touching* 113.

81. 'not to be in the immediate presence or in the immanency of a "being-thing"... to exist, therefore, is to hold one's "selfness" as an "otherness" [such that] each "myself" is "myself" only as an other' (*FH* 160).
82. 'one appears to oneself insofar as one is already an other for oneself' (*BSP* 67).
83. 'a primordial plurality that co-appears' (*BSP* 67).
84. 'we are alike... The like is not the same. I do not rediscover myself, nor do I recognise myself in the other' (*IC* 33).
85. 'the configuration or constellation of being-toward in its plural singularity' (*SW* 33).
86. 'a common task, that is to say not at all collective, but a task imposed on *us* all *together* . . . to care about the possibility of being, precisely, together and saying "us" at the moment when this possibility seems to vanish sometimes into a "one", sometimes into an "I" just as anonymous and monstrous as each other, and in truth completely entangled in each other' (author's translation).
87. 'How can we say "us" otherwise than as a "one" (= everyone and no one) and otherwise than as an "I" (= a lone person, which is still a person)? How then can we be in common without making what the whole tradition (but after all a recent one, that is to say tributary of the West that is coming to an end as it spreads out) calls a community (a corporeal identity, an intensity of ownness, a natural intimacy)?' (author's translation).
88. 'The unity of a world is nothing other than its diversity, and its diversity is, in turn, a diversity of worlds' (*CWM* 109).
89. See Jean-Clet Martin, 'Le murmure des pierres', in Guibal and Martin (eds), *Sens en tous* sens 105.
90. Ziarek, 'Is all technological?' 154.
91. In 'Jean-Luc Nancy and the Myth of the Common'.
92. Norris, 'Jean-Luc Nancy and the Myth of the Common' 286.
93. Derrida, *Le Toucher* 116; 'one needs to leap from one to the other blindly, like someone born blind, across an infinite abyss' (*On Touching* 98).
94. Derrida, *Le Toucher* 164; *On Touching* 142.
95. Derrida, *Le Toucher* 176; 'humanualism' (*On Touching* 153).
96. Derrida, *Le Toucher* 162n2; 'see with their hands' (*On Touching* 341 n6).
97. Derrida, *Le Toucher* 166; 'intersensory unity of the thing' (*On Touching* 144).
98. Derrida, *Le Toucher* 166; 'mere being – a concept organising this phenomenology of perception' (*On Touching* 144; translation altered).
99. Derrida, *Le Toucher* 116; 'Even if it is the "same thing," what we see is one thing, what we touch is another . . . Later on, these different objects will go by the same name . . . this is the whole question of language . . . and the question of theology' (*On Touching* 98–9).
100. 'the difference between the physical senses is nothing other than the difference in itself of sense as meaning: the non-totalisation of experience, without which there would be no *experience*' (author's translation).

101. 'the general extension and particular extraposition of sensing. Touch *forms one body* with sensing, or it makes a body of the sensing faculties; it is but the *corpus* of the senses' (M 17).
102. 'laughter is the joy of the senses and of sense at their limit. In this joy the senses touch each other, and they touch on language, on the tongue in the mouth. But this very touching spaces them. They do not penetrate each other' (author's translation).
103. 'it has become impossible to number the supplementary arts, video, performance art, body art, installation art, etc.: not because there are too many types, but because counting them has no sense; if it is art as such that becomes essentially multiple and even numerous; in other words, "art" loses an asumed unity' (author's translation).
104. 'we are not seeking a "definition" [of art]. We are seeking merely a fashion of not leaving this diversity behind, a fashion not of "saying" but of articulating something of "art", singular plural, right at its inorganic plurality and without synthesis or without system' (*M* 36–7).
105. 'it is the major characteristic of the constitutive plurality of the arts: each one initiates all the others and holds them at a distance from itself' (author's translation). The quotation comes from a section of *Allitérations* composed of a number of fragments from the correspondence between Nancy and Claire Denis which the editor takes care to stress are attributed explicitly to neither correspondent. The ambiguity in this case is an apt *mise en abyme* of the problematic to which the quotation draws our attention.
106. Guibal, 'Venue, passage, partage' 368; 'rather than Art, the arts offer themselves to us, in their irreducible multiplicity, in the an-archic gap of their diverse techniques' (author's translation).
107. 'Artistic practices in their disparity (from poetry to video, from performance art to music, from "povera" to "body", etc.), do not arise from a ground, nor from a common identity called "art", but . . . this identity – perhaps it can never be found – is only formed by the totality of the practices themselves, with all their differences, without this "totality" even in the smallest way reabsorbing any of their heterogeneity' (author's translation).
108. 'the sense of dance is the sense of separation in a bound that at once both opens and crosses the division of bodies: sense before all the senses, which closes them and then reopens them one by one, sliding between them all, a jolt to the bottom of each one and from one to the other, between the same and the tangle of a singular body or plural bodies, making one into several and several into a dance' (author's translation).
109. Dance has recently become a motif of increasing importance for Nancy, linked to the notion of rhythm and to the figure of the (a)cosmos that has become the guiding thread in his recent writing: 'Le cosmologique, le social, le rituel, à un pôle – le physique, l'animal, le séparé à l'autre. Dans la danse populaire telle que le rock l'a mondialement transformée, jusqu'à

la *break dance* ou à la techno, on se donne un cosmos en mouvement brownien, une scintillation de particules sur fond de vide intense et dense' (All 113); 'The cosmological, the social, the ritual, at one pole – the physical, the animal, the separate at the other. In popular dance after its worldwide transformation by rock, through to break dance or techno, we are given a cosmos in a Brownian movement, particles twinkling on a ground of deep and intense void' (author's translation).

110. 'It is not impossible to attempt to say that it is another art that fills this empty space and time of the present in its passing: the art of music. (One would attempt here to initiate a link between the arts via their gaps, which would be the unique but unfailing link of "art" in general)' (author's translation).

111. 'The same would be the case for the entire "system" of the arts: each heterogeneous from the other, and each time separated by an uncrossable crevasse. What separates them, and what, in this way, gathers them together by circulating between them, but also inside each one of them, is what creates a gap between presence and itself: what repels it and what desires it, what repels it in order to desire it and to touch it in passing' (author's translation).

112. Deleuze, *Francis Bacon: logique de la sensation*; *Francis Bacon: The Logic of Sensation*.

113. 'Between a color, a taste, a touch, a smell, a sound, a weight . . . there would be an existential communication that constitutes the "pathic" (nonrepresentative) moment of sensation . . . It is therefore the painter's task to *make one see* a kind of original unity of the senses and to cause a multi-sensible Figure to appear visually. But this operation is possible only if the sensation of any particular domain . . . is directly plugged into a vital power that exceeds all domains and traverses them. This power is Rhythm, which is more profound than vision, hearing, etc. . . . It is diastolic-systolic: the world that makes me by closing itself down on me, the self that opens itself to the world, and opens up the world' (M 23).

114. 'it is the gap of the beat that makes it into rhythm' (M 24).

115. 'breaks down the living unity of perception or action' (M 21).

116. 'art disengages the senses from signification, or rather, it disengages the world from signification' (M 22).

117. 'the dislocated synesthesia . . . sets off . . . a reference or, in Baudelaire's terms, a response from one touch to the other' (M 23).

118. Derrida, *Le Toucher* 317–18; 'the touchable . . . pole of a vocative or an apostrophising address' (*On Touching* 282).

119. Translated as 'Is Everything Political? (A Brief Remark)'.

120. Derrida is careful to distinguish the Nancean *démarche* here from Merleau-Ponty's 'confused' attempt to think the relation of self and alterity: Nancy 'dit le « *partage* sentant/senti » et non la confusion ou la réflexion sentant-senti ou touchant-touché . . . Partage sans fusion. Communauté sans communauté, langage sans communication. Etre-avec sans confusion' (Derrida,

Le Toucher 221); 'Nancy says "the sensing/sensed *apportioning*", and not the confusion or the reflection sensed-sensing or touched-touching . . . It is a sharing without fusion, a community without community, language without communication, a being-with without confusion' (*On Touching* 195). However, as we have seen it is by no means clear that what Derrida approves in Nancy, namely 'partage comme participation *et* comme partition, comme continuité et interruption' (*Le Toucher* 225) ('sharing out as participation *and* partition, as continuity and interruption' (*On Touching* 199)), is absent from Merleau-Ponty's thought.

121. 'ontology of being-with-one-another' (*BSP* 53).
122. 'the moments or diverse elements of shared existence all in some ways belong to the moment or element called the "political", to which falls a privilege of diffusion or transversality' (*IEP* 15).
123. 'the "political" sphere is that which determines or controls the activity of the other spheres' (*IEP* 15).
124. 'it has become patent that there is no oikonomy: there is, in every respect, only an *ecotechny*: that is to say, a common ground or habitation in the production, invention, and incessant transformation of ends that are never given' (*IEP* 19).
125. 'politics is retraced as a place where power is exercised with a view towards an incommensurable justice – that is, as a place where one asserts an in-finity of human-being or of world-being' (*IEP* 20).
126. 'their mutual distinctions and circumscriptions (that prevent neither contingencies nor co-penetrations) define in each case the occurrence of a configuration according to which a certain presentation takes place' (*IEP* 20; translation altered).
127. 'Politics is redrawn at the place where one must keep open this incommensurability, whether that means, generally, the incommensurability of justice, like that of value' (*IEP* 20).
128. 'politics is the site of an "in-common" as such – but only in the manner of an incommensurability that is kept open' (*IEP* 20).
129. 'There is a common measure, which is not some one unique standard applied to everyone and everything . . . the commensurability of incommensurable singularities, the equality of all the origins-of-the-world' (*BSP* 75).
130. 'equally one with the other . . . substitutable for every other *as unsubstitutable*' (author's translation).
131. 'what is shared therefore is not this annulment of sharing, but sharing itself, and consequently everyone's nonidentity, each one's nonidentity to himself and to others' (*IC* 66).
132. See, for instance, *Force de loi* 61 ('Force of Law' 7) and '« Il faut bien manger »' 287 ('Eating well' 273).
133. Devisch, 'A Trembling Voice in the Desert' 254 n6.
134. May, *Reconsidering Difference* 41.
135. May, *Reconsidering Difference* 42.

Concluding Remarks

We began this book by opening three sets of questions: (1) What is the relation 'between' phenomenology and deconstruction? (2) How can contemporary French thought develop responses to the problems of alterity and coherence? (3) In the light of these concerns, what resources are there in the thought of Maurice Merleau-Ponty, Paul Ricœur and Jean-Luc Nancy for thinking ontology *otherwise*? We have, of course, not been able exhaustively to investigate each of these questions, but that has not been our aim. Rather we have sought to show that the three sets of questions are each enhanced by treatment in relation to each other. It is the aim of this conclusion to argue for the success, and irreducibility, of this approach.

It became clear from the early encounters we staged between Merleau-Ponty and Derrida that a recurring question posed to the phenomenologist, whether existential or hermeneutic, is 'how do you know?' How does Merleau-Ponty know that the world is 'pregnant with meaning'? How does Ricœur know that narrative and life are 'intertwined'? It also became clear that there would be no quick or simple response to these questions, for any putatively speedy answer would have to perform an impossibility: it would have to ground knowledge on something radically other to itself which it could articulate in its own terms. It would, literally, have to think the unthinkable. Nevertheless, it has gradually emerged that there are resources in the phenomenological tradition for responding persuasively to deconstructive questioning, provided that we take an indirect, oblique approach.

In Chapter 1 we saw how Merleau-Ponty argues for worldly meaningfulness not in terms of essence and substance but as form and structure, and in the context of a diplopic or indirect ontology. Meaning emerges in the tensions and relations of the 'cosmology of the visible'. With the help of cosmological motifs, Merleau-Ponty moves the discussion of meaning from (roughly speaking) the content of the world to its form, and in so doing he problematises the subject/object dichotomy upon which the 'how do you know?' question relies. He also thinks presence otherwise than the Derridean 'plein de présence immédiate requis par toute ontologie ou par toute métaphysique,'[1] for the motif of pregnancy, the to-be-interpreted and the relation of call and response are more complicated than such a pleromatic account of presence can allow. Presence and the ontological are not punctual but irreducibly distended. These insights allowed us to offer a response to a problem which Derrida identifies but which he cannot resolve, given his assumptions about the nature of phenomenology: the reconciliation of two seemingly incommensurable readings of Merleau-Ponty's philosophy.

In the discussion of Merleau-Ponty's understanding of language in Chapter 2, 'contact' with the world was shown to be unverifiable when philosophical discourse is assumed to be the paradigm of all language, but Merleau-Ponty's priority of language use over contemplation allowed a different, oblique notion of contact to emerge. Merleau-Ponty's ontology is indirect on three counts. It thinks being (1) in the mode of the interrogative, (2) in a dialogue of call and response, the origin of which can be traced neither to self nor to world, and (3) according to what Merleau-Ponty calls 'the work of expression'. This ontological obliqueness opened up the possibility of responding to Derrida's concerns *otherwise* than with an indicative assertion, and we began to see how a response might be heard in the call itself. In the two chapters on Merleau-Ponty we twice moved from considering *what* is said to *that* it is said, first in relation to the problem of 'two Merleau-Pontys' that Derrida discerns in *Le Toucher*, and secondly moving from the substance of deconstruction's question or provocation to the question *as* question.

These motifs of interrogative, call and expression foreground the question 'who?', which we then moved to consider more directly in the thought of Paul Ricœur. In Chapter 3 we saw how Ricœur thinks narrative as a fragile tension of cosmos and chaos in a 'discordant concordance', and how his understanding of the relation of life and narrative borrows from the inextricability of self and world in Merleau-Ponty. Extending the oblique ontology sketched by Merleau-Ponty, Ricœur develops an ontology of attestation, drawing on the motifs of wager and testimony. The relation of attestation and suspicion, we found, does not paralyse phenomenology's response to the deconstructive question; it *becomes* the response to the question. Once more, the investigation moved from content to form, from what is said to that it is being said, this time with the additional question 'who?' The risk entailed in such attestation, we observed, bears similarities to the Derridean *parti pris* for alterity, which is similarly and necessarily beyond explanation or calculation. It became increasingly clear that both the positions labelled 'phenomenology' and 'deconstruction' have their problems. Phenomenology struggles with the question of who will witness for the witness, and deconstruction with the necessity of arbitrating between different witnesses.

The need to work through these respective problems more directly drove us then to consider Ricœur's work on justice in Chapter 4, in the context of which we made two important advances. First, we saw how a tensional understanding of justice as 'conflictual-consensual' allows Ricœur to arbitrate between incommensurable measures in the sphere of jurisprudence, and how compromise and translation provide him with a model for calculating the incalculable. Building on the relation between life and narrative from the previous chapter, we explored how a utopian fictional (non)space can nevertheless serve to legitimate the exercise of judicial coercion, albeit in a way always vulnerable to challenge. Secondly, we explored the difference between Derrida's calculation of relations on the basis of reciprocity, debt and credit and Ricœur's preference for mutuality. This came into sharper focus as we considered Ricœur's understanding of the gift, differing from the Derridean model in its affirmation of the mutual relation of giving and receiving, rather than focusing exclusively on reciprocally transacted gifts. This difference means that, where the just decision for Derrida is impossible, for Ricœur it is difficult.

Turning in Chapter 5 to Nancy's thought we pursued the question of how far it is possible to go in mediating deconstructive and phenomenological approaches, with a final aim of avoiding both the problems identified in the previous discussion. Nancy continues the Merleau-Pontean and Ricœurean rethinking of presence, developing the notions of exposure, patency and the a-punctual presence-as-passage. In contrast to Derrida's insistence on absolute alterity, Nancy develops the motif of the *sans pourtant*, which disrupts the chaos/cosmos binary without privileging either gathering or dissemination, articulating this a-cosmological spacing with the figure of the spasm. The intervention that we first introduced in relation to Ricœur with help from Lévinas at the end of the second chapter was reprised with a greater sophistication by Nancy's enunciative ontology, and the move from content to form, from *what* to *that*, became more pronounced in Nancy in terms of the decision which obeys an imperative of openness. Nancy's thought does not share the problem of the infinite regress of attestation which dogs Ricœur and Merleau-Ponty, but it remained to be seen whether Nancy could avoid the difficulties that Derrida's thought encounters. This was to be the substance of the final chapter.

We began Chapter 6 by discussing the similarities between Merleau-Ponty and Nancy in the way they understand the figure-ground relation, despite Nancy's attempts to define his position in contradistinction to Merleau-Ponty's. There is an important difference between them, however, for Nancy flattens Merleau-Pontean depth and replaces 'ground' with singular plural spacing. He also dissents from the Merleau-Pontean idea of the body in his elaboration of the technico-prosthetic *corpus*: a catalogue of parts neither gathered nor scattered which Nancy describes using the (unacknowledged) Ricœurean motif of *concordia discors*. He rejects the dichotomy of the many and the one, thinking instead in terms of the singular plural in which, to use Heideggerean terms, the *Mit-* is equiprimordial with the *Da-* in *Mitdasein*. Considering the relation of deconstruction to Western philosophy, we observed (to use the Ricœurean opposition in a way of which Derrida would disapprove) that deconstruction affirms the *ipse* identity of what it deconstructs by undermining its *idem* identity. We also saw that it would be unreasonable to ask a finite thinking to 'justify itself'. Moreover, to misunderstand this essential incompletion is to forget philosophy.

So is Nancy's thought phenomenological? Any direct answer is likely to tell us more about how we choose to define the term 'phenomenology' than it is to reveal anything significant about Nancy's thought. Such philosophical housekeeping is not our business here.[2] What is significant is how we have seen a similar move in all four of our philosophers (including Derrida), from thinking being and meaning in terms of *what* questions, questions of content, to thinking being and meaningfulness in terms of *that* questions, questions of form. We have of course seen that this *that/what* opposition is is itself radically problematised, but it would be just as hasty to reject it absolutely as it would be to assume it absolutely. Merleau-Ponty's cosmology of the visible, Ricœur's concordant discordance and his spatial understanding of justice with its 'just distances', Nancy's elaboration of the decision in terms of openness, Derrida's disjunction of absolute, incalculable justice and calculable law, all perform this move. Phenomenological vestiges of *what* raise the Derridean hackles and the question of who will testify for the witness; a deconstructive premium on the *that* elicits the question as to the basis on which to arbitrate between different witnesses. Though he develops a sophisticated interreading of phenomenological and deconstructive motifs, Nancy does not in the end escape the problems facing Derrida and, in this sense, his thought is not deconstructively phenomenological.

Thus the ontological question as it is played out between Merleau-Ponty, Ricœur, Nancy and Derrida remains in the interrogative and is haunted by an ineliminable suspicion, but we now understand what is at stake in the question. As one recent treatment of twentieth-century French thought has put it, 'a genuine question has two characteristics. On the one hand, a genuine question demands to be left open, even left without a response . . . On the other hand, a genuine question demands to be closed off, even answered once and for all.'[3] It is in the tension between these two irreducible demands that 'deconstruction' and 'phenomenology' move.

So what is the relation of 'phenomenology' to 'deconstruction'? Much of the time they are doing the same thing – moving the question of meaning from *what* to *that* – but to different ends. Is it perhaps the case, then, that the difference is not between two procedures, but two sets of assumptions, two ideas of the Good or two ontological predispositions? Both deconstruction and phenomenology have their assumptions, and both sets of assumptions bring their own problems, tagged above as 'strangers, gods and monsters' and 'quis custodiet ipsos custodes?' respectively. There appears to be no satisfactory way of mediating the two positions such that neither of the sets of problems arises, for to be able to decide between different 'others' is precisely already to have decided who will witness for the witness, and to leave that latter question open is precisely to foreclose the possibility of deciding between different 'others'.

Nevertheless, this is not a counsel of despair. What our investigation has discounted is not ontology *tout court* but the position that argues that full and immediate presence is required by every ontology and by every metaphysics. The mistake would be to think that this were the end of the matter. In and through the very exposure of the inability of phenomenology to think punctual presence we have seen emerge an ontology *otherwise* than the ontological self-presence of which deconstruction exposes the self-refuting assumptions. There is a presence as passage, an ontology resituated in the relational and the pistic, in the mode of the interrogative and vulnerable attestation, an indirect ontology thought in terms of a mutual implication of 'subject(s)' and 'world' in a play of call and response, and this ontology destabilises the dichotomy (*justice* and *justesse*; hospitality of justice and hospitality of law; the pure gift and the economy of reciprocal gift-giving) which deconstruction requires in order to ask its questions.

Is this a 'deconstructive phenomenology', a 'phenomenological deconstruction', 'phenomenology after deconstruction' or one of any number of other possible appellations? Those who write the history of philosophy will no doubt tell us in time, but what we choose to call the position that, in this book, we are labelling for convenience 'ontology otherwise' is a matter of little import in understanding the twists and turns in the relation of deconstruction and phenomenology. This is what David Wood understands when, stopping wisely short of saying what contours a putative 'deconstructive phenomenology' would take, he is content to indicate what, if there is such a thing, it might achieve. Faced with 'being exposed to the pressures and exigencies of the world,' Wood ventures that 'it is something like a deconstructive phenomenology that will best allow us to formulate and appropriate the risks and opportunities of that recursive possibility of exposure. And in this way, phenomenology will live on.'[4] In the studies presented here we have begun to show what Wood names, but does not describe, and the difficulties with which any such 'deconstructive phenomenology' will have to deal.

These 'risks and opportunities' are precisely those highlighted in responding to the questions we have been posing to phenomenology and deconstruction, and they come down to the possibility of a way of being in the world that can cope with the demand to arbitrate between different 'strangers' – a need all too painfully evident in the shrill but confused tones in which today's debates about immigration, asylum and terrorism are conducted – without leaving itself open to the charge of pre(-)judicial fiat or the inability to question its own judgements. Such a negotiation is as urgent as it is hitherto lacking, and the impossibility of 'deconstructive phenomenology' is a timely way of considering our contemporary being in the world in a way that holds complexity and aporia with incisiveness and attestation in a concordant discordance.

This is not to say, however, that the relation will have ever been thought through once and for all, or that we are to expect a simple 'answer'. The possibilities of being in the world that this book opens do not allow us to settle on a definitive description of the relation of deconstruction and phenomenology, but they do allow us to learn from the difficulties that characterise this relation. Instead of trying to conflate or separate phenomenology and deconstruction, we should appreciate the moves and counter-moves in their complex and intricate *pas de deux*. Neither is about to administer a knockout blow to the other; neither is impregnable to questions posed by the other. Rather, their turns and twists perform, together, the agony of the ethical decision.

No doubt phenomenology has had to respond to the steps that deconstruction has danced for it, and this project has been a small contribution to that responsive phenomenological choreography, but there is no indication that the piece is soon to be over. Other dancers have joined in along the way – existentialism, hermeneutics – but the dance has continued, and the movement of these encounters has itself become the locus of investigation. In the relation of phenomenology and deconstruction we can see that 'rien n'est arrivé, et pourtant quelque chose arrive déjà, depuis tout le temps que ce corps est corps plié, face sur la surface élémentaire à l'altitude nulle' (All 143),[5] as we look on at the spectacle of phenomenology dancing with its own shadow. The dance does not tell us how to calculate the incalculable or maintain an ontological toe-hold in the face of deconstructive questioning; it does show us, however, how to keep on thinking ontologically – with an ontology both humbled and therefore, paradoxically, more robust – not despite but *because of* that very questioning.

If this is the case, then the attempt to separate 'phenomenology' and 'deconstruction' would be committing the same error as we have been labouring through six chapters to avoid, through Merleau-Ponty's ontological diplopia, Ricœur's long detour and Nancy's *sans pourtant*. 'Phenomenology' and 'deconstruction' are reifications, commodifications of fluid movements in philosophical thought, not monolithic moments in some chronicle of world thinking. Worse than this, such an attempt would destroy, for the sake of preserving some notion of a pure phenomenology, the very difficulties that yield phenomenology's most circumspect, but for that reason most supple and nuanced, ontological moves. How can we tell the dancers from the dance? We need not. We must not. Any such distinction would murder to dissect. Is that not the lesson that has emerged from our investigation of Merleau-Ponty, Ricœur and Nancy?

In a section of *Allitérations* which (perhaps fittingly) reproduces fragments of the correspondence between Nancy and Claire Denis that remain without ascription to either correspondent, we read the answer to an absent question:

> Si la danse raconte quelque chose: oui, nécessairement. S'il y a déroulement, il y a récit, succession enchaînée. Elle déroule chaque fois une histoire précise, qui reste à découvrir – pas une narration, une portée, une tenue, une venue, un suspens . . . (All 116)[6]

NOTES

1. Derrida, *Le Toucher* 138; 'the fullness of immediate presence required by every ontology or metaphysics' (*On Touching* 120).
2. In this I fully concur with Jean Greisch in his assessment of the relation of deconstruction and hermeneutics: 'Refusant de faire de l'herméneutique une paroisse de la pensée, je m'interdis par le fait même d'assimiler les pensées dites de la « déconstruction » à une paroisse adverse. Tant que nous nous

laisserons obnubiler par ces querelles de chapelles, la confrontation entre la philosophie herméneutique et les pensées de la déconstruction ne peut que dégénérer en guerre de tranchées idéologique' (Greisch, *Paul Ricœur* 223); 'refusing to make hermeneutics a local parish of thought, I will not allow myself, by that token, to assimilate the thinking of so-called "deconstruction" into an opposing parish. As long as we remain obsessed by petty parish rivalries, the confrontation between hermeneutic philosophy and the thinking of deconstruction can only degenerate into ideological trench warfare' (author's translation).
3. Lawlor, *Thinking Through French Philosophy* 1.
4. Wood, *The Step Back* 137.
5. 'nothing has happened, and yet something is happening already, ever since the body has been bent, face down on the elementary surface at zero altitude' (author's translation).
6. 'Does dance recount something? Yes, necessarily so. If there is a sequence, there is a story, linked succession. Each time, it unfolds a particular story, which remains to be discovered – not a narration, a span, a behaviour, a coming, a suspense . . .' (author's translation).

Bibliography and Further Reading

Abel, Olivier. *Paul Ricœur: la promesse et la règle*, Bien commun. Paris: Michalon, 1996.
Aeschlimann, Jean-Christophe, ed. *Éthique et responsabilité: Paul Ricœur*, Langages. Neuchâtel: À la Braconnière, 1994.
Alcoff, Linda Martin. 'Merleau-Ponty and Feminist Theory on Experience'. In *Chiasms: Merleau-Ponty's Notion of Flesh*, ed. Fred Evans. Albany: State University of New York Press, 2000.
Altieri, Lorenzo. 'Moses at the Threshold of Canaan: The Incomplete Ontology of Paul Ricœur'. In *Between Suspicion and Sympathy: Paul Ricoeur's Unstable Equilibrium*, ed. Andrzej Wierciński, pp. 22–43. Toronto: Hermeneutic Press, 2003.
Amsterdam, Anthony G. and Jerome S. Bruner. *Minding the Law*. Cambridge, MA: Harvard University Press, 2000.
Anderson, Pamela Sue. 'Ricoeur's Reclamation of Autonomy: Unity, Plurality, and Totality.' In *Paul Ricoeur and Contemporary Moral Thought*, eds J. Wall, W. Schweiker and W. D. Hall, pp. 15–31. London: Routledge, 1999.
Anderson, Pamela Sue. 'Agnosticism and Attestation: An Aporia Concerning the Other in Ricoeur's *Oneself as Another*'. *Journal of Religion* 74, no. 1 (1994): 65–76.
Andrew, D. 'François Dosse, *Paul Ricœur: les sens d'une vie*. Tracing Ricoeur'. *Diacritics* 30, no. 2 (2000): 43–69.
Ansell-Pearson, Keith. *Deleuze and Philosophy: The Difference Engineer*, Warwick Studies in European Philosophy. London: Routledge, 1997.
Ansell-Pearson, Keith. *Viroid Life: Perspectives on Nietzsche and the Transhuman Condition*. London: Taylor & Francis, 1997.
Atkins, K. 'Ricoeur on Objectivity: Between Phenomenology and the Natural Sciences'. *Philosophy Today* 46, no. 4 (2002): 384–95.
Audard, C. 'Rawls in France'. *European Journal of Political Theory* 1, no. 2 (2002): 215–28.
Augustinus, Aurelius. *De Libero Arbitrio*. Turnholti: Brepols, 1970.
Augustinus, Aurelius. *The Confessions of Saint Augustine*. London: Signet Classic, 2001.

Auxentios, Hieromonk, Bishop Chrysostomos of Oreoi and James Thornton. 'Notions of Reality and the Resolution of Dualism in the Phenomenological Precepts of Merleau-Ponty and the Orthodox Responses to Iconoclasm'. *American Benedictine Review* 41, no. 1 (1990): 80–98.

Azouvi, François. 'L'essentielle fragilité du politique'. *Le Monde*, 1 November 1991.

Badiou, Alain. *Deleuze: la clameur de l'être*, Coup double. Paris: Hachette, 1997.

Badiou, Alain and François Wahl. *Conditions*, L'Ordre philosophique. Paris: Éditions du Seuil, 1992.

Bannan, J. F. 'The Later Thought of Merleau-Ponty'. *Dialogue* 5 (1966): 383–403.

Barash, Jeffrey Andrew and Mireille Delbraccio. *La Sagesse pratique: autour de l'œuvre de Paul Ricœur. Colloque international, université de Picardie Jules Verne, Amiens, 5–7 mars 1997*. Paris: Centre National de Documentation Pédagogique, 1999.

Barbaras, Renaud. 'A Phenomenology of Life'. In *The Cambridge Companion to Merleau-Ponty*, eds Taylor Carman and Mark B. N. Hansen, pp. 206–30. Cambridge: Cambridge University Press, 2005.

Barbaras, Renaud. *De l'Être du phénomène: sur l'ontologie de Merleau-Ponty*. Paris: Éditions Jerôme Millon, 2001.

Barbaras, Renaud. 'De la parole à l'être: le problème de l'expression comme voie d'accès à l'ontologie'. In *Maurice Merleau-Ponty: le philosophe et son langage*, ed. François Heidsieck, pp. 61–81. Grenoble: Groupe de recherches sur la philosophie et le langage, 1993.

Barbaras, Renaud. *Le Tournant de l'expérience: recherches sur la philosophie de Merleau-Ponty*. Paris: Vrin, 1998.

Barbaras, Renaud. *Merleau-Ponty: de la nature à l'ontologie*, Chiasmi international 2. Paris: Vrin, 2000.

Barbaras, Renaud. 'Perception and Movement: The End of the Metaphysical Approach'. In *Chiasms: Merleau-Ponty's Notion of Flesh*, ed. Fred Evans, pp. 77–89. Albany: State University of New York Press, 2000.

Barbaras, Renaud. *The Being of the Phenomenon: Merleau-Ponty's Ontology*, trans. Ted Toadvine and Leonard Lawlor. Bloomington: Indiana University Press, 2004.

Barbaras, Renaud and Patrick Burke. 'Présentation'. In *Merleau-Ponty: De la nature à l'ontologie*, eds Renaud Barbaras and Patrick Burke, pp. 11–16. Paris: Vrin, 2000.

Barker, Stephen. *Signs of Change: Premodern, Modern, Postmodern*, Contemporary Studies in Philosophy and Literature 4. Albany: State University of New York Press, 1996.

Barresi, J. 'On Becoming a Person'. *Philosophical Psychology* 12, no. 1 (1999): 79–98.

Bate, Michele. 'The Phenomenologist as Art Critic: Merleau-Ponty and Cézanne'. *British Journal of Aesthetics* 14 (1974): 344–50.

Baugh, Bruce. *French Hegel: From Surrealism to Postmodernism*. London: Routledge, 2003.

Beistegui, Miguel de. *Thinking with Heidegger: Displacements*, Studies in Continental Thought. Bloomington: Indiana University Press, 2003.

Belin, Emmanuel. *Une Sociologie des espaces potentiels*. Brussels: De Boeck University Press, 2001.

Bergeron, André. 'La Conscience engagée dans le régime des significations selon Merleau-Ponty'. *Dialogue* 5 (1966): 373–82.

Berman, Art. *From the New Criticism to Deconstruction: The Reception of Structuralism and Post-structuralism*. Urbana: University of Illinois Press, 1988.

Bernasconi, Robert. 'On Deconstructing Nostalgia for Community Within the West: The Debate between Nancy and Blanchot'. *Research in Phenomenology* 23 (1993): 3–21.

Bertram, Maryanne. 'The Different Paradigms of Merleau-Ponty and Whitehead'. *Philosophy Today* 24 (1980): 121–32.

Bezeczky, G. 'Paul Ricoeur and the Assumption of Linguistic Uniformity'. *Neophilologus* 81, no. 3 (1997): 325–39.

Bigger, Charles. *Between Chora and the Good: Metaphor's Metaphysical Neighborhood*, Perspectives in Continental Philosophy. Ashland, OH: Fordham University Press, 2005.

Bimbenet, Etienne. '« L'être interrogatif de la vie »: l'historicité de la vie dans les cours du Collège de France (1957–8)'. In *Merleau-Ponty: De la nature à l'ontologie*, eds Renaud Barbaras and Patrick Burke, pp. 143–64. Paris: Vrin, 2000.

Binder, Guyora, and Robert Weisberg. *Literary Criticisms of Law*. Princeton, NJ: Princeton University Press, 2000.

Blanchot, Maurice. *L'Écriture du désastre*. Paris: Gallimard, 1981.

Blanchot, Maurice. *L'Entretien infini*. Paris: Gallimard, 1969.

Blanchot, Maurice. 'Le « discours philosophique ».' *L'ARC* 46 (1971): 1–4.

Blanchot, Maurice. *The Writing of Disaster*, trans. Ann Smock. Lincoln: University of Nebraska Press, 1995.

Block, Ned, Jerry Fodor and Hilary Putnam. 'Anti-Reductionism Slaps Back'. In *Mind, Causation, and World*, ed. James E. Tomberlin. Boston: Blackwell, 1997.

Boeder, Heribert and Marcus Brainard. *Seditions: Heidegger and the Limit of Modernity*, SUNY Series in Contemporary Continental Philosophy. Albany: State University of New York Press, 1997.

Boella, Laura. 'Phenomenology and Ontology: Hannah Arendt and Maurice Merleau-Ponty'. In *Merleau-Ponty in Contemporary Perspectives*, eds Patrick Burke and Jan Van der Veken, pp. 171–82. London: Kluwer Academic, 1993.

Boer, Karin de. *Thinking in the Light of Time: Heidegger's Encounter with Hegel*, SUNY Series in Contemporary Continental Philosophy. Albany: State University of New York Press, 2000.

Bogue, Ronald. *Deleuze on Music, Painting, and the Arts*. London: Routledge, 2003.
Boltanski, Luc. *L'Amour et la justice comme compétences: trois essais de sociologie de l'action*. Paris: Éditions Métailié, 1990.
Boltanski, Luc and Laurent Thévenot. *De la Justification: les économies de grandeur*. Paris: Gallimard, 1991.
Boltanski, Luc and Laurent Thévenot. *On Justification: Economies of Worth*, trans. Catherine Porter. Princeton, NJ and Oxford: Princeton University Press, 2006.
Bonzon, Sylvie. 'De l'attestation, une nuée de témoins'. *Études de Lettres* 3–4 (1996): 125–39.
Bopry, Jeanette, ed. *Francesco J. Varela 1946–2001*, Cybernetics and Human Knowing 9. Exeter: Imprint Academic, 2004.
Bordo, Susan and Mario Moussa. 'Rehabilitating the "I".' In *Questioning Foundations*, ed. Hugh J. Silverman, pp. 110–33. London: Routledge, 1993.
Bourgeois, Patrick L. 'Ethics at the Limit of Reason: Ricoeur and Deconstruction'. *Philosophy Today* 41 Supp. (1997): 142–52.
Bourgeois, Patrick L. 'Hermeneutics and Deconstuction: Paul Ricoeur in Postmodern Dialogue'. In *Between Suspicion and Sympathy: Paul Ricoeur's Unstable Equilibrium*, ed. Andrzej Wierciński, pp. 333–50. Toronto: Hermeneutic Press, 2003.
Bourgeois, Patrick L. *Philosophy at the Boundary of Reason: Ethics and Postmodernity*. Albany: State University of New York Press, 2001.
Bourgeois, Patrick L. 'Ricoeur and Levinas: Solicitude, Reciprocity and Solitude in Existence'. In *Ricoeur as Another: The Ethics of Subjectivity*, eds Richard A. Cohen and James L. Marsh, pp. 109–26. Albany: State University of New York Press, 2002.
Bourgeois, Patrick L. 'Ricoeur in Postmodern Dialogue: Kantian Reflective Judgment and Darstellung'. *International Philosophical Quarterly* 41, no. 164 (2001): 421–38.
Bourretz, Pierre. 'L'Écriture entre la lettre et l'Être'. In *Paul Ricœur*, pp. 156–67. Paris: Éditions de l'Herne, 2004.
Breeur, Roland. 'Merleau-Ponty, un sujet désingularisé'. *Revue Philosophique de Louvain*: 96 (1998): 232–53.
Brennan, Teresa and Martin Jay. *Vision in Context: Historical and Contemporary Perspectives on Sight*. London: Routledge, 1996.
Brisson, Luc and F. Walter Meyerstein. *Inventing the Universe: Plato's Timaeus, the Big Bang, and the Problem of Scientific Knowledge*, SUNY Series in Ancient Greek Philosophy. Albany: State University of New York Press, 1995.
Brodsky, Joyce. 'Cezanne paints: "whole body" practices and the genre of self-portrayal'. *Visual Studies* 20 (2005): 37–55.
Brooke, Roger. *Pathways Into the Jungian World: Phenomenology and Analytical Psychology*. London: Routledge, 2000.
Brooks, Peter and Paul Gewirtz. *Law's Stories: Narrative and Rhetoric in the Law*. New Haven, CT: Yale University Press, 1996.

Brubaker, D. 'Merleau-Ponty's Three Intertwinings'. *Journal of Value Inquiry* 34, no. 1 (2000): 89–101.
Bryden, Mary. *Deleuze and Religion*. London: Routledge, 2000.
Burke, Patrick. 'Listening at the Abyss'. In *Ontology and Alterity in Merleau-Ponty*, eds Galen A. Johnson and Michael B. Smith, pp. 81–97. Evanston, IL: Northwestern University Press, 1990.
Burke, Patrick and Jan Van der Veken, eds *Merleau-Ponty in Contemporary Perspectives*, Phaenomenologica 129. London: Kluwer Academic, 1993.
Busch, Thomas W. *Circulating Being: From Embodiment to Incorporation: Essays on Late Existentialism*, Perspectives in Continental Philosophy 7. New York: Fordham University Press, 1999.
Busch, Thomas W. 'Merleau-Ponty's Circulating Being'. *Philosophy Today* (2001): 187–92.
Busch, Thomas W. 'The Flesh as *Urpräsentierbarkeit* in the Interrogative: The Absence of a Question in Derrida'. In *Écart and Différance: Merleau-Ponty and Derrida on Seeing and Writing*, ed. M. C. Dillon, pp. 60–70. Atlantic Highlands, NJ: Humanities Press, 1997.
Busch, Thomas W. and Shaun Gallagher. *Merleau-Ponty, Hermeneutics, and Postmodernism*. Albany: State University of New York Press, 1992.
Butler, Judith. 'Critical Exchanges: The Symbolic and Questions of Gender'. In *Questioning Foundations*. New York: Routledge, 1993.
Butler, Judith. 'Merleau-Ponty and the Touch of Malebranche'. In *The Cambridge Companion to Merleau-Ponty*, eds Taylor Carman and Mark B. N. Hansen, pp. 181–205. Cambridge: Cambridge University Press, 2005.
Caputo, John D., ed. *Deconstruction in a Nutshell: A Conversation with Jacques Derrida*. New York: Fordham University Press, 1997.
Caputo, John D. *More Radical Hermeneutics: On Not Knowing Who We Are*, Studies in Continental Thought. Bloomington: Indiana University Press, 2000.
Caputo, John D. *Radical Hermeneutics: Repetition, Deconstruction, and the Hermeneutic Project*. Bloomington: Indiana University Press, 1987.
Caputo, John D. 'The Experience of God and the Axiology of the Impossible'. In *The Experience of God: A Postmodern Response*, eds Kevin Hart and Barbara E. Wall, pp. 20–41. New York: Fordham University Press, 2005.
Caputo, John D. *The Prayers and Tears of Jacques Derrida: Religion Without Religion*, The Indiana Series in the Philosophy of Religion. Bloomington: Indiana University Press, 1997.
Carbone, Mauro. 'Le Sensible et l'excédant. Merleau-Ponty et Kant'. In Maurice Merleau-Ponty and Renaud Barbaras, *Notes de cours sur L'Origine de la géométrie de Husserl; suivi de Recherches sur la phénomènologie de Merleau-Ponty*, pp. 163–91. Paris: Presses Universitaires de France, 1998.
Carbone, Mauro. 'Nature et logos: "pourquoi y a-t-il plusieurs exemplaires de chaque chose?"' In *Merleau-Ponty: De la nature à l'ontologie*, eds Renaud Barbaras and Patrick Burke, pp. 261–79. Paris: Vrin, 2000.

Carbone, Mauro. 'The Thinking of the Sensible'. In *Chiasms: Merleau-Ponty's Notion of Flesh*, ed. Fred Evans. Albany: State University of New York Press, 2000.

Carman, Taylor. 'Sensation, Judgment, and the Phenomenal Field'. In *The Cambridge Companion to Merleau-Ponty*, eds Taylor Carman and Mark B. N. Hansen, pp. 50–73. Cambridge: Cambridge University Press, 2005.

Carman, Taylor and Mark B. N. Hansen. *The Cambridge Companion to Merleau-Ponty*, Cambridge Companions to Philosophy. Cambridge: Cambridge University Press, 2004.

Carman, Taylor and Mark B. N. Hansen. 'Introduction'. In *The Cambridge Companion to Merleau-Ponty*, eds Taylor Carman and Mark B. N. Hansen, pp. 1–25. Cambridge: Cambridge University Press, 2005.

Carr, David. 'Review of Temps et récit. Tome I'. *History and Theory* 23, no. 3 (1984): 357–70.

Carr, David. *Time, Narrative, and History*, Studies in Phenomenology and Existential Philosophy. Bloomington: Indiana University Press, 1986.

Carrithers, Michael, Steven Collins and Steven Lukes. *The Category of the Person: Anthropology, Philosophy, History*. Cambridge: Cambridge University Press, 1985.

Carroll, Noel. 'Time, Narrative and History'. *History and Theory* 27, no. 3 (1988): 297–306.

Carter, J. A. 'Telling Times: History, Emplotment, and Truth'. *History and Theory* 42, no. 1 (2003): 1–27.

Carter Mullen, Deborah. *Beyond Subjectivity and Representation: Perception, Expression and Creation in Nietzsche, Heidegger and Merleau-Ponty*. Oxford: University Press of America, 2000.

Cascardi Anthony, J. *The Subject of Modernity, Literature, Culture, Theory*. Cambridge: Cambridge University Press, 1992.

Casey, Edward S. *The Fate of Place: A Philosophical History*. Berkeley: University of California Press, 1997.

Casey, Edward S. 'The World at a Glance'. In *Chiasms: Merleau-Ponty's Notion of Flesh*, ed. Fred Evans. Albany: State University of New York Press, 2000.

Cassam, Q. 'Representing Bodies'. *Ratio* 15 (2002): 315–34.

Cataldi, Sue L. 'Embodying Perceptions of Death: Emotional Apprehension and Reversibilities of Flesh'. In *Chiasms: Merleau-Ponty's Notion of Flesh*, ed. Fred Evans. Albany: State University of New York Press, 2000.

Cazeaux, Clive. *The Continental Aesthetics Reader*. London: Routledge, 2000.

Cecilia, M. A. 'Imagination and Practical Creativity in Paul Ricoeur'. In *The Outburst of Life in the Human Sphere*, ed. Anna Teresa Tymieniecka, pp. 241–64. Norwell, MA: Kluwer Academic, 1999.

Cecilia, M. A. 'Symbol and Metaphor: The Search for the "Hidden Side" of Reality in Contemporary Philosophy'. In *The Visible and The Invisible in the Interplay between Philosophy, Literature and Reality*, ed. Anna Teresa Tymieniecka, pp. 11–26. London: Kluwer Academic, 2002.

Celan, Paul, *Atemwende*. Frankfurt am Main: Suhrkamp, 1990.

Cepl, Marc. 'La Narrativité comme moralité: pour une lecture "poétique" de l'éthique dans *Soi-même comme un autre*'. *Études de Lettres* 3–4 (1996): 141–58.

Chang Briankle, G. *Deconstructing Communication: Representation, Subject, and Economies of Exchange*. Minneapolis: University of Minnesota Press, 1996.

Changeux, Jean-Pierre. *L'Homme neuronal*. Paris: Fayard, 1983.

Changeux, Jean-Pierre. *Neuronal Man*, trans. Laurence Garey. New York: Pantheon Books, 1985.

Changeux, Jean-Pierre. *The Physiology of Truth*. London: Harvard University Press, 2004.

Changeux, Jean-Pierre and Alain Connes. *Conversations on Mind, Matter and Mathematics*. Princeton, NJ: Princeton University Press, 1995.

Changeux, Jean-Pierre and Paul Ricœur. *Ce qui nous fait penser: la nature et la règle*. Paris: Odile Jacob, 1998.

Chanter, Tina. 'Wild Meaning: Luce Irigaray's Reading of Merleau-Ponty'. In *Chiasms: Merleau-Ponty's Notion of Flesh*, ed. Fred Evans. Albany: State University of New York Press, 2000.

Chapelle, Daniel. *Nietzsche and Psychoanalysis*. Albany: State University of New York Press, 1993.

Chapman, Siobhan. *Philosophy for Linguists: An Introduction*. London: Routledge, 2000.

Charcosset, Jean-Pierre. 'La Tentation du silence'. *Esprit* 6 (1982): 53–63.

Chrétien, Jean-Louis. 'Dans la lumière de la promesse. Vœu et liberté'. In *La Philosophie au risque de la promesse*, eds Marc Crépon and Marc de Launay, pp. 35–58. Paris: Bayard, 2004.

Chrétien, Jean-Louis. *L'Appel et la réponse*. Philosophie. Paris: Éditions de Minuit, 1992.

Chrétien, Jean-Louis. *La Voix nue: phénoménologie de la promesse*, Philosophie. Paris: Éditions de Minuit, 1990.

Chrétien, Jean-Louis. *The Call and the Response*, trans. Anne A. Davenport. New York: Fordham University Press, 2004.

Clark, Timothy. *Martin Heidegger*, Routledge Critical Thinkers. London: Routledge, 2002.

Clarke, Melissa. 'Ontology, Ethics, and Sentir: Properly Situating Merleau-Ponty'. *Environmental Values* 11, no. 2 (2002): 211–25.

Cohen, Jeffrey Jerome and Gail Weiss. *Thinking the Limits of the Body*, SUNY Series in Aesthetics and the Philosophy of Art. Albany, NY: State University of New York Press, 2003.

Cohen, Richard A. *Ethics, Exegesis and Philosophy: Interpretation After Levinas*. Cambridge: Cambridge University Press, 2001.

Cohen, Richard A. 'Moral Selfhood: A Levinasian Response to Ricoeur on Levinas'. In *Ricoeur as Another: The Ethics of Subjectivity*, eds Richard A. Cohen and James L. Marsh, pp. 127–60. Albany: State University of New York Press, 2002.

Cohen, Richard A. and James L. Marsh. *Ricoeur as Another: The Ethics of Subjectivity*. Albany: State University of New York Press, 2002.

Colli, Francesco. 'Nell'imminenza della riposta: la responsabilità dell'interrogazione filosofica nell'ultimo Merleau-Ponty'. In *Merleau-Ponty: De la nature à l'ontologie*, eds Renaud Barbaras and Patrick Burke, pp. 433-49. Paris: Vrin, 2000.

Collins, H. M. *Changing Order: Replication and Induction in Scientific Practice*. London: University of Chicago Press, 1985.

Connor, Steven. *The Book of Skin*. London: Reaktion, 2004.

Contat, Michel. 'Le Philosophe dans la cité. Paul Ricœur, *Du Texte à l'action*'. *Le Monde*, 27 June 1987.

Coole, Diana H. *Negativity and Politics: Dionysus and Dialectics from Kant to Poststructuralism*. London: Routledge, 2000.

Cooper David, E. *Existentialism: A Reconstruction*. Oxford: Blackwell, 1990.

Cornell, Drucilla. *Philosophies of the Limit*. London: Routledge, 1992.

Cowley, Fraser. 'L'Expression et la parole d'après Merleau-Ponty'. *Dialogue* (1966): 360-72.

Cox, Christoph. *Nietzsche: Naturalism and Interpretation*. Berkeley: University of California Press, 1999.

Crang, Mike and N. J. Thrift. *Thinking Space*, Critical Geographies. London: Routledge, 2000.

Crépon, Marc. 'Du "Paradoxe politique" à la question des appartenances'. In *Paul Ricœur*, pp. 307-14. Paris: Éditions de l'Herne, 2004.

Cresswell, Tim. *Place: A Short Introduction*, Short Introductions to Geography. Oxford: Blackwell, 2004.

Critchley, Simon. 'Deconstruction and Pragmatism – Is Derrida a Private Ironist or a Public Liberal?' In *Deconstruction and Pragmatism*, ed. Chantal Mouffe, pp. 19-42. London: Routledge, 1996.

Critchley, Simon. *Ethics, Politics, Subjectivity: Essays on Derrida, Levinas and Contemporary French Thought*. London: Verso, 1999.

Critchley, Simon. 'Prolegomena to Any Post-Deconstructive Subjectivity'. In *Deconstructive Subjectivities*, ed. Simon Critchley, pp. 13-46. Albany: State University of New York Press, 1996.

Critchley, Simon. *The Ethics of Deconstruction: Derrida and Levinas*. Edinburgh: Edinburgh University Press, 1999.

Critchley, Simon and Robert Bernasconi. *The Cambridge Companion to Levinas*, Cambridge Companions. Cambridge: Cambridge University Press, 2002.

Critchley, Simon and Chantal Mouffe. *Deconstruction and Pragmatism*. London and New York: Routledge, 1996.

Critchley, Simon and William Ralph Schroeder. *A Companion to Continental Philosophy*, Blackwell Companions to Philosophy 12. Oxford: Blackwell, 1998.

Crossley, Nick. *The Politics of Subjectivity: Between Foucault and Merleau-Ponty*, Avebury Series in Philosophy. Aldershot: Avebury, 1994.

Crowther, Paul. 'Merleau-Ponty: Perception into Art'. *British Journal of Aesthetics* 22 (1982): 138–49.
Crump, Eric. 'Between Conviction and Critique: Reflexive Philosophy, Testimony, and Pneumatology'. In *Ricoeur as Another: The Ethics of Subjectivity*, eds Richard A. Cohen and James L. Marsh, pp. 161–86. Albany: State University of New York Press, 2002.
Crystal, David. *A Dictionary of Linguistics and Phonetics*, The Language Library. Oxford: Blackwell, 1997.
Csordas, Thomas J. *The Sacred Self: A Cultural Phenomenology of Charismatic Healing*. Berkeley: University of California Press, 1994.
Cumming, Robert Denoon. *Phenomenology and Deconstruction. Vol. 1: The Dream is Over*. Chicago: University of Chicago Press, 1991.
Cumming, Robert Denoon. *Phenomenology and Deconstruction. Vol. 2: Method and Imagination*. Chicago: University of Chicago Press, 1992.
Cumming, Robert Denoon. *Phenomenology and Deconstruction. Vol. 3: Breakdown in Communication*. Chicago: University of Chicago Press, 2001.
Cumming, Robert Denoon. *Phenomenology and Deconstruction. Vol. 4: Solitude*. Chicago: University of Chicago Press, 2001.
Daigler, Matthew A. 'Being as Act and Potency in the Philosophy of Paul Ricoeur'. *Philosophy Today* 42, no. 4 (1998): 375–85.
Daigler, Matthew A. 'Paul Ricoeur's Hermeneutic Ontology: Between Aristotle and Kant'. PhD thesis, Boston College, 1998.
Dallery, Arleen B., Charles E. Scott and P. Holley Roberts. *Ethics and Danger: Essays on Heidegger and Continental Thought*, Selected Studies in Phenomenology and Existential Philosophy 17. Albany: State University of New York Press, 1992.
Dallmayr, Fred R. 'Ethics and Public Life: A Critical Tribute To Paul Ricoeur'. In *Paul Ricoeur and Contemporary Moral Thought*, eds J. Wall, W. Schweiker and W. D. Hall, pp. 213–32. London: Routledge, 1999.
Dallmayr, Fred R. *Margins of Political Discourse*, SUNY Series in Contemporary Continental Philosophy. Albany: State University of New York Press, 1989.
Danto, Arthur Coleman. *The Body/body Problem: Selected Essays*. Berkeley: University of California Press, 1999.
Dastur, Françoise. *Chair et langage*. La Versanne: Encre marine, 2001.
Dastur, Françoise. 'Critique of Anthropologism in Heidegger's Thought'. In *Appropriating Heidegger*, eds James E. Faulconer and Mark A. Wrathall, pp. 119–36. Cambridge: Cambridge University Press, 2000.
Dastur, Françoise. 'Monde, chair, vision'. In *Maurice Merleau-Ponty, le psychique et le corporel*, ed. Anna-Teresa Tymienecka, pp. 136–7. Paris: Aubier, 1988.
Dastur, Françoise. 'World, Flesh, Vision'. In *Chiasms: Merleau-Ponty's Notion of Flesh*, ed. Fred Evans, pp. 23–49. Albany: State University of New York Press, 2000.

Dauenhauer, Bernard P. 'Response to Rawls'. In *Ricoeur as Another: The Ethics of Subjectivity*, eds Richard A. Cohen and James L. Marsh, pp. 203–21. Albany: State University of New York Press, 2002.

Dauenhauer, Bernard P. 'Ricoeur and the Tasks of Citizenship'. In *Paul Ricoeur and Contemporary Moral Thought*, eds J. Wall, W. Schweiker and W. D. Hall, pp. 233–50. London: Routledge, 1999.

Dauliach, Catherine. 'Expression et onto-anthropologie chez Merleau-Ponty'. In Maurice Merleau-Ponty and Renaud Barbaras, *Notes de cours sur L'Origine de la géométrie de Husserl; suivi de Recherches sur la phénoménologie de Merleau-Ponty*, pp. 305–30. Paris: Presses Universitaires de France, 1998.

Davies, Oliver. *A Theology of Compassion: Metaphysics of Difference and the Renewal of Tradition*. London: SCM Press, 2001.

Davies, Oliver. *The Creativity of God: World, Eucharist, Reason*, Cambridge Studies in Christian Doctrine 12. Cambridge: Cambridge University Press, 2004.

Davis, Colin. *Ethical Issues in Twentieth-Century French Fiction: Killing the Other*. Basingstoke: Macmillan, 1999.

De Certeau, Michel. 'La Folie de la vision'. *Esprit* 6 (1982): 89–99.

De Greef, J. A. N. 'Skepticism and Reason'. In *Face To Face With Levinas*, ed. Richard A Cohen, pp. 159–79. Albany: State University of New York Press, 1986.

De Vries, Hent. 'Anti-Babel: The "Mystical Postulate" in Benjamin, de Certeau and Derrida'. *Modern Language Notes* 107, no. 3 (1992): 441–77.

De Vries, Hent and Samuel M. Weber. *Religion and Media*, Cultural Memory in the Present. Stanford, CA: Stanford University Press, 2001.

Deguy, Michel. 'Un corps de pensée'. *Le Monde*, 10 July 2005.

Delacampagne, Christian. 'Jean-Luc Nancy touché au cœur'. *Le Monde*, 24 March 2000.

Delacampagne, Christian. 'Paul Ricœur, philosophe de tous les dialogues'. *Le Monde*, 22 May 2005.

Delacampagne, Christian. 'Peut-on oublier de penser?' *Le Monde*, 16 Janvary 1987.

Delacampagne, Christian. 'Ricœur, le métier de douter'. *Le Monde*, 15 March 1996.

Delacampagne, Christian. 'Un philosophe du sujet. Paul Ricœur explore dans ses multiples dimensions l'univers du soi'. *Le Monde*, 27 April. 1990.

Deleuze, Gilles. *Empiricism and Subjectivity: An Essay on Hume's Theory of Human Nature*, trans. Constantin V. Boundas, European Perspectives. New York: Columbia University Press, 1991.

Deleuze, Gilles. *Francis Bacon: logique de la sensation*, La vue, le texte. Paris: Éditions de la Différence, 1981.

Deleuze, Gilles. *Francis Bacon: The Logic of Sensation*, trans. Daniel W. Smith. London: Continuum, 2004.

Deleuze, Gilles. *La Philosophie critique de Kant*. Paris: Presses Universitaires de France, 1963.

Deleuze, Gilles. *Nietzsche et la philosophie*. Paris: Presses Universitaires de France, 1998.
Dennett, Daniel. 'The Origins of Selves'. *Cogito* 3 (1989): 163–73.
Deppman, J. 'Jean-Luc Nancy, Myth, and Literature.' *Qui Parle* 10, no. 2 (1997): 11–32.
DePryck, Koen. *Knowledge, Evolution, and Paradox: The Ontology of Language*, SUNY Series: The Margins of Literature. Albany: State University of New York Press, 1993.
Derczansky, Alexandre. 'L'unité de l'œuvre de Paul Ricœur'. In *Éthique et responsabilité: Paul Ricœur*, ed. Jean-Christophe Aeschlimann, pp. 103–31. Neuchâtel: À la Braconnière, 1994.
Derrida, Jacques. *Adieu à Emmanuel Lévinas*, Incises. Paris: Galilée, 1997.
Derrida, Jacques. 'At This Very Moment in This Work Here I Am'. In *Re-Reading Levinas*, eds Robert Bernasconi and Simon Critchley, pp. 11–48. Bloomington: Indiana University Press, 1991.
Derrida, Jacques. *De la Grammatologie*, Critique. Paris: Éditions de Minuit, 1967.
Derrida, Jacques. 'Donner la mort'. In *Jacques Derrida et la pensée du don: colloque de Royaumont, décembre 1990*, eds Jean-Michel Rabaté and Michael Wetzel, pp. 11–108. Paris: Métailié-Transition, 1992.
Derrida, Jacques. *Du Droit à la philosophie*, La philosophie en effet. Paris: Galilée, 1990.
Derrida, Jacques. ' "Eating Well" or the Calculation of the Subject', trans. Peggy Kamuf. In *Points . . . Interviews*, pp. 255–87. Stanford, CA: Stanford University Press, 1995.
Derrida, Jacques. *Edmund Husserl's Origin of Geometry: An Introduction*, trans. John P. Leavey Jr. Stony Brook, NY: Nicholas Hays, 1978.
Derrida, Jacques. 'En ce moment même dans cet ouvrage me voici'. In *Textes pour Emmanuel Lévinas*, ed. Peter Hoy, pp. 21–60. Paris: Jean-Michel Place, 1980.
Derrida, Jacques. *Force de loi. Le 'Fondement mystique de l'autorité'*. Paris: Galilée, 1994.
Derrida, Jacques. 'Force of Law: The Mystical Foundation of Authority'. In *Deconstruction and the Possibility of Justice*, eds Drucilla Cornell, Michel Rosenfeld and David Gray Carlson, pp. 3–67. New York: Routledge, 1992.
Derrida, Jacques. 'Forcener le subjectile'. In *Antonin Artaud: dessins et portraits*, ed. Paule Thevenin, pp. 55–108. Paris: Gallimard, 1986.
Derrida, Jacques. 'I Have a Taste for the Secret', trans. Giacomo Donis. In Jacques Derrida and Maurizio Ferraris, *A Taste For The Secret*. Cambridge: Polity Press, 2001.
Derrida, Jacques. '« Il faut bien manger » ou le calcul du sujet'. In *Points de suspension: entretiens*, eds Jacques Derrida and Elisabeth Weber, pp. 269–302. Paris: Galilée, 1992.
Derrida, Jacques. *Introduction à L'Origine de la géométrie de E. Husserl*. Paris: Presses Universitaires de France, 1962.

Derrida, Jacques. *Khôra*, Incises. Paris: Galilée, 1993.
Derrida, Jacques. *L'autre Cap; suivi de La Démocratie ajournée*. Paris: Éditions de Minuit, 1991.
Derrida, Jacques. *L'Écriture et la différence*. Paris: Éditions du Seuil, 1979.
Derrida, Jacques. *La Dissémination*. Paris: Éditions du Seuil, 1972.
Derrida, Jacques. 'La parole. Donner, nommer, appeler'. *Le Monde*, 22 May. 2005.
Derrida, Jacques. *La Vérité en peinture*. Champ philosophique. Paris: Flammarion, 1978.
Derrida, Jacques. *La Voix et le phénomène, introduction au problème du signe dans la phénoménologie de Husserl*, Epiméthée. Paris: Presses Universitaires de France, 1967.
Derrida, Jacques. *Le Touches, Jean-Luc Nancy*, Incices. Paris: Galilée, 2000.
Derrida, Jacques. *Limited Inc*. Paris: Galilée, 1990.
Derrida, Jacques. 'Maddening the subjectile'. *Yale French Studies* 84 (1994) 154–171.
Derrida, Jacques. *Marges de la philosophie*. Paris: Éditions de Minuit, 1975.
Derrida, Jacques. *Margins of Philosophy*, trans. Alan Bass. Chicago: University of Chicago Press, 1982.
Derrida, Jacques. *Mémoires d'aveugle: l'autoportrait et autres ruines*, Parti pris. Paris: Ministère de la Culture, de la Communication, des Grands Travaux, et du Bicentenaire, 1990.
Derrida, Jacques. *Of Grammatology*, trans. Gayatri Chakravorty Spivak. Baltimore, MD: Johns Hopkins University Press, 1998.
Derrida, Jacques. *On Hospitality*. Stanford, CA: Stanford University Press, 2000.
Derrida, Jacques. *On Touching*, trans. Christine Irizarry. Stanford, CA: Stanford University Press, 2005.
Derrida, Jacques. *Parages*, La philosophie en effet. Paris: Galilée, 1986.
Derrida, Jacques. *Politics of Friendship*, trans. George Collins. London: Verso, 1997.
Derrida, Jacques. *Politiques de l'amitié: suivi de L'Oreille de Heidegger*, La philosophie en effet. Paris: Galilée, 1994.
Derrida, Jacques. *Positions*. London: Athlone, 1981.
Derrida, Jacques. 'Reste, viens'. *Le Monde*, 12 October 2004.
Derrida, Jacques. *Sauf le nom*, Incises. Paris: Galilée, 1993.
Derrida, Jacques. *Spectres de Marx: l'état de la dette, le travail du deuil et la nouvelle Internationale*. La philosophie en effet. Paris: Galilée, 1993.
Derrida, Jacques. *Spectres of Marx*, trans. Peggy Kamuf. New York and London: Routledge, 2006.
Derrida, Jacques. 'The Ends of Man'. *Philosophy and Phenomenological Research* 30 (1969): 31–57.
Derrida, Jacques. *The Other Heading: Reflections on Today's Europe*, trans. Pascale-Anne Brault and Michael B. Naas. Bloomington: Indiana University Press, 1992.

Derrida, Jacques. 'The Time of a Thesis: Punctuations', trans. Kathleen McLaughlin. In *Philosophy in France Today*, ed. Alan Montefiore. Cambridge: Cambridge University Press, 1983.

Derrida, Jacques. *Voyous. La philosophie en effet*. Paris: Galilée, 2003.

Derrida, Jacques. *Writing and Difference*. trans. Alan Bass. London: Routledge, 2001.

Derrida, Jacques and Anne Dufourmantelle. *De l'Hospitalité*, Petite bibliothèque des idées. Paris: Calmann-Levy, 1997.

Derrida, Jacques and Henri Ronse. *Positions: entretiens avec Henri Ronse, Julia Kristeva, Jean-Louis Houdebine, Guy Scarpetta*, Critique. Paris: Éditions de Minuit, 1979.

Descombes, Vincent. *Le Même et l'autre: quarante-cinq ans de philosophie française, 1933–1978*. Paris: Éditions de Minuit, 1979.

Descomber, Vincent. *Modern French Philosophy*, trans. L. Scott-Fox and J. M. Harding. Cambridge: Cambridge University press, 1980.

Descombes, Vincent. *Objects of All Sorts: A Philosophical Grammar*. Oxford: Blackwell, 1986.

Descombes, Vincent. 'Une Philosophie de la première personne'. In *Paul Ricœur*, pp. 219–28. Paris: Éditions de l'Herne, 2004.

Devisch, Ignaas. 'A Trembling Voice in the Desert: Jean-Luc Nancy's Rethinking of the Space of the Political'. *Cultural Values* 4, no. 2 (2000): 239–52.

Devisch, Ignaas. 'La "négativité sans emploi"'. *Symposium* 4, no. 2 (2000): 167–87.

Dews, Peter. *The Limits of Disenchantment: Essays on Contemporary European Philosophy*. London: Verso, 1995.

DiCenso, James. *Hermeneutics and the Disclosure of Truth: A Study in the Work of Heidegger, Gadamer, and Ricœur*, Studies in Religion and Culture. Charlottesville, VA: University Press of Virginia, 1990.

Dillon, M. C. 'Écart: Reply to Lefort's "Flesh and Otherness"'. In *Ontology and Alterity in Merleau-Ponty*, eds Galen A. Johnson and Michael B. Smith, pp. 14–26. Evanston, IL: Northwestern University Press, 1990.

Dillon, M. C., ed. *Écart and Différance: Merleau-Ponty and Derrida on Seeing and Writing*. Atlantic Highlands, NJ: Humanities Press, 1997.

Dillon, M. C. 'Introduction: Écart and Différance'. In *Écart and Différance: Merleau-Ponty and Derrida on Seeing and Writing*, ed. M. C. Dillon, pp. 1–19. Atlantic Highlands, NJ: Humanities Press, 1997.

Dillon, M. C. *Merleau-Ponty's Ontology*, Northwestern University Studies in Phenomenology and Existential Philosophy. Evanston, IL: Northwestern University Press, 1997.

Dillon, M. C. *Merleau-Ponty vivant*, SUNY Series in Contemporary Continental Philosophy. Albany: State University of New York Press, 1991.

Dillon, M. C. *Semiological Reductionism: A Critique of the Deconstructionist Movement in Postmodern Thought*. Albany: State University of New York Press, 1995.

Direk, Zeynep and Leonard Lawlor. *Jacques Derrida*, 3 vols, Routledge Critical Assessments of Leading Philosophers. London: Routledge, 2002.
Dornisch, Loretta. *Faith and Philosophy in the Writings of Paul Ricoeur*, Problems in Contemporary Philosophy 29. Lampeter: Edwin Mellen Press, 1990.
Dosse, François. *Empire of Meaning: The Humanization of the Social Sciences*. Minneapolis: University of Minnesota Press, 1999.
Dosse, François. *Paul Ricoeur: les sens d'une vie*. Paris: Éditions la Découverte, 1997.
Dostal, Robert J. 'The World Never Lost: The Hermeneutics of Trust'. *Philosophy and Phenomenological Research* (1987): 413–34.
Dreyfus, Hubert L. 'Merleau-Ponty and Recent Cognitive Science'. In *The Cambridge Companion to Merleau-Ponty*, eds Taylor Carman and Mark B. N. Hansen, pp. 129–50. Cambridge: Cambridge University Press, 2005.
Dreyfus, Hubert L. and Stuart E. Dreyfus. 'The Challenge of Merleau-Ponty's Phenomenology of Embodiment for Cognitive Science'. In *Perspectives on Embodiment: The Intersections of Nature and Culture*, eds Gail Weiss and Honi Fern Haber, pp. 103–20. London: Routledge, 1999.
Dreyfus, Hubert L. and Mark A. Wrathall. *A Companion to Phenomenology and Existentialism*, Blackwell Companions to Philosophy 35. Malden, MA: Blackwell, 2006.
Droit, Roger-Pol. 'La face cachée du corps'. *Le Monde*, 7 April 1995.
Droit, Roger-Pol. 'La rationalité dans tous ses états'. *Le Monde*, 15 April 2005.
Droit, Roger-Pol. 'Paul Ricœur s'interroge sur la reconnaissance'. *Le Monde*, 30 January 2004.
Droit, Roger-Pol. '. . . suivant la disposition de leur cerveau'. *Le Monde*, 27 February 1998.
Droit, Roger-Pol. 'Un entretien avec Paul Ricœur. "La cité est fondamentalement périssable. Sa survie dépend de nous" '. *Le Monde*, 29 October 1991.
Dunne, Joseph. 'Beyond Sovereignty and Deconstruction: The Storied Self'. In *Paul Ricoeur: The Hermeneutics of Action*, ed. Richard Kearney, pp. 137–57. London: Sage, 1996.
Dworkin, Ronald. 'The Plurality of Sources of Law: Reply to Paul Ricoeur'. *Ratio Juris* 7, no. 3 (1994): 287.
Eaglestone, Robert. *Ethical Criticism: Reading After Levinas*. Edinburgh: Edinburgh University Press, 1997.
Edie, James M. *Merleau-Ponty's Philosophy of Language: Structuralism and Dialectics*, Current Continental Research 206. Lanham, MD: University Press of America, 1987.
Edie, James M. *Speaking and Meaning: The Phenomenology of Language*, Studies in Phenomenology and Existential Philosophy. Bloomington: Indiana University Press, 1976.
Edmundson, Mark. *Literature Against Philosophy, Plato to Derrida: A Defence of Poetry*. Cambridge: Cambridge University Press, 1995.

Etienne, J. 'La question de l'intersubjectivité: une lecture de *Soi-même comme un autre* de Paul Ricœur'. *Revue Théologique de Louvain* 28, no. 2 (1997): 189–215.

Evans, Fred. 'Chaosmos and Merleau-Ponty's View of Nature'. *Chiasmi International* 2 (2000): 63–82.

Evans, Fred. *Psychology and Nihilism: A Genealogical Critique of the Computational Model of Mind*. Albany: State University of New York Press, 1993.

Evans, Fred and Leonard Lawlor, eds *Chiasms: Merleau-Ponty's Notion of Flesh*. Albany: State University of New York Press, 2000.

Evans, Fred and Leonard Lawlor. 'The Value of Flesh: Merleau-Ponty's Philosophy and the Modernism/Postmodernism Debate'. In *Chiasms: Merleau-Ponty's Notion of Flesh*, eds Fred Evans and Leonard Lawlor. Albany: State University of New York Press, 2000.

Evans, J. Claude. 'Phenomenological Deconstruction: Husserl's Method of *Abbau*'. *Journal of the British Society for Phenomenology* 21, no. 1 (1990): 14–25.

Evans, Jeanne. *Paul Ricoeur's Hermeneutics of the Imagination*. New York: Peter Lang, 1995.

Faessler, Marc. 'Attestation et élection'. In *Éthique et responsabilité: Paul Ricœur*, ed. Jean-Christophe Aeschlimann, pp. 133–53. Neuchâtel: À la Braconnière, 1994.

Fairlamb, Horace L. *Critical Conditions: Postmodernity and the Question of Foundations*, Literature, Culture, Theory 8. Cambridge: Cambridge University Press, 1994.

Faulconer, James E. *Transcendence in Philosophy and Religion*, Indiana Series in the Philosophy of Religion. Bloomington: Indiana University Press, 2003.

Fenves, Peter. 'From Empiricism to the Experience of Freedom'. Foreword, in Jean-Luc Nancy, *The Experience of Freedom*, pp. xiii–xxxi. Stanford, CA: Stanford University Press, 1996.

Ferrari, Frederico and Jean-Luc Nancy. *Nus sommes: la peau des images*. Brussels: Yves Gevaert, 2002.

Fiddes, Paul S. *The Promised End: Eschatology in Theology and Literature*, Challenges in Contemporary Theology. Malden, MA: Blackwell, 2000.

Finlay, Linda. 'The Body's Disclosure in Phenomenological Research'. *Qualitative Research in Psychology* 3 (2006) 19–30.

Flood, G. 'Mimesis, Narrative and Subjectivity in the Work of Girard and Ricoeur'. *Cultural Values* 4, no. 2 (2000): 205–15.

Flood, Gavin D. *The Ascetic Self: Subjectivity, Memory, and Tradition*. Cambridge: Cambridge University Press, 2004.

Flynn, Bernard. 'Merleau-Ponty and Derrida: Difference/Identity'. In *Écart and Différance: Merleau-Ponty and Derrida on Seeing and Writing*, ed. M. C. Dillon, pp. 220–33. Atlantic Highlands, NJ: Humanities Press, 1997.

Flynn, Bernard. 'Merleau-Ponty and Nietzsche on the Visible and the Invisible'. In *Merleau-Ponty: Difference, Materiality, Painting*, ed. Véronique M. Fóti. Atlantic Highlands, NJ: Humanities Press, 1996.

Flynn, Bernard. 'Merleau-Ponty et la position philosophique du scepticisme'. In Maurice Merleau-Ponty and Renaud Barbaras, *Notes de cours sur L'Origine de la géométrie de Husserl; suivi de Recherches sur la phénoménologie de Merleau-Ponty*, pp. 147–61. Paris: Presses Universitaires de France, 1998.

Fodor, James. *Christian Hermeneutics: Paul Ricoeur and the Refiguring of Theology*. Oxford: Clarendon Press, 1995.

Foessel, Michaël. 'La lisibilité du monde: la véhémence phénoménologique de Paul Ricœur'. In *Paul Ricœur*, pp. 168–80. Paris: Éditions de l'Herne, 2004.

Ford, David. *Self and Salvation: Being Transformed*, Cambridge studies in Christian Doctrine. Cambridge: Cambridge University Press, 1999.

Fóti, Véronique M. 'The Evidences of Paintings: Merleau-Ponty and Contemporary Abstraction'. In *Merleau-Ponty: Difference, Materiality, Painting*, ed. Véronique M. Fóti. Atlantic Highlands, NJ: Humanities Press, 1996.

Fóti, Véronique M. *Merleau-Ponty: Difference, Materiality, Painting*. Atlantic Highlands, NJ: Humanities Press, 1996.

Fóti, Véronique M. 'Painting and The Re-orientation of Philosophical Thought in Merleau-Ponty'. *Philosophy Today* 24 (1980): 114–20.

Foucault, Michel. *Language, Counter-memory, Practice: Selected Essays and Interviews*. Ithaca, NY: Cornell University Press, 1977.

Foucault, Michel. *Les Mots et les choses: une archéologie des sciences humaines*, Bibliothèque des sciences humaines. Paris: Gallimard, 1993.

Foucault, Michel. 'Nietzsche, généalogie, histoire'. In *Hommage à Jean Hyppolite*, pp. 145–72. Paris: Presses Universitaires de France, 1971.

Foucault, Michel. 'Theatricum philosophicum'. *Critique* 282 (1970): 885–908.

Foucault, Michel. 'Theatricum Philosophicum'. In *Michel Foucault: Aesthetics, Method, Epistemology*, ed. Paul Rabinow, pp. 343–68. New York: New Press, 1998.

Friend, James A. 'Nature, Man and God: A Temple Revisited'. *Reformed Theological Review* 41, no. 2 (1982): 34–41.

Froman, Wayne J. 'Alterity and the Paradox of Being'. In *Ontology and Alterity in Merleau-Ponty*, eds Galen A. Johnson and Michael B. Smith, pp. 98–110. Evanston, IL: Northwestern University Press, 1990.

Froman, Wayne J. 'At the Limits of Phenomenology: Merleau-Ponty and Derrida'. In *Merleau-Ponty: Difference, Materiality, Painting*, ed. Véronique M. Fóti. Atlantic Highlands, NJ: Humanities Press, 1996.

Fuller, Andrew Reid. *Insight into Value: An Exploration of the Premises of a Phenomenological Psychology*. Albany: State University of New York Press, 1990.

Gablik, Suzi. *The Reenchantment of Art*. London: Thames & Hudson, 1991.

Gadamer, Hans Georg. *Truth and Method*. London: Continuum, 2003.

Gagnon, Martin. 'Étonnement et interrogation.' *Revue Philosophique de Louvain* 93 no. 3 (1995): 370–91.

Gallagher, Shaun. 'Philosophical Conceptions of the Self: Implications for Cognitive Science'. *Trends in Cognitive Science* 4. no. 1 (2000): 14–21.

Gallagher, Shaun and J. Shear. *Models of the Self*. Thorverton: Imprint Academic, 1999.
Gardner, Sebastian. *Routledge Philosophy Guidebook to Kant and the Critique of Pure Reason*. London: Routledge, 1999.
Garelli, Jacques. 'Il y a le monde'. *Esprit* 6 (1982): 113–23.
Gasché, Rodolphe. *Inventions of Difference: On Jacques Derrida*. Cambridge, MA: Harvard University Press, 1994.
Gatens, Moira. *Imaginary Bodies: Ethics, Power and Corporeality*. London: Routledge, 1996.
Gauchet, Marcel. 'Le lieu de la pensée'. *L'ARC* 46 (1971): 19–30.
Gehl, Paul F. 'An Answering Silence: Claims For The Unity Of Truth Beyond Language'. *Philosophy Today* 30 (1986): 224–33.
Genosko, Gary. *Deleuze and Guattari*, Critical Assessments of Leading Philosophers. London: Routledge, 2001.
Gerhart, Mary. *The Question of Belief in Literary Criticism: An Introduction to the Hermeneutical Theory of Paul Ricoeur*. Stuttgart: Akademischer Verlag Hans-Dieter Heinz, 1979.
Gesché, Adolphe. *L'Homme*, Dieu pour penser 2. Paris: Éditions du Cerf, 1993.
Gibbs, Robert. *Why Ethics? Signs of Responsibilities*. Princeton, NJ: Princeton University Press, 2000.
Gibson, Andrew. *Postmodernity, Ethics, and the Novel: From Leavis to Levinas*. London: Routledge, 1999.
Giddens, Anthony. 'Modernity and Self-Identity: Tribulations of the Self'. In *The Discourse Reader*, eds Adam Jaworski and Nikolas Coupland, pp. 415–27. London: Routledge, 1999.
Gifford, Paul. 'The Resonance of Ricoeur: Soi-même comme un autre'. In *Subject Matters. Subject and Self in French Literature from Descartes to the Present*. Amsterdam: Rodopi, 2000.
Gifford, Paul and Johnnie Gratton. *Subject Matters: Subject and Self in French Literature From Descartes to the Present*. Amsterdam: Rodopi, 2000.
Gilbert, P. 'Paul Ricœur: réflexion, ontologie et action'. *Nouvelle Revue Théologique* 117, no. 3 (1995): 339–63.
Gilbert, P. 'Un tournant métaphysique de la phénoménologie française? M. Henry, J.-L. Marion et P. Ricoeur'. *Nouvelle Revue Théologique* 124, no. 4 (2002): 597–618.
Gilbert-Walsh, James. 'Broken Imperatives: The Ethical Dimension of Nancy's Thought'. *Philosophy and Social Criticism* 26, no. 2 (2000): 29–50.
Giles, James. *French Existentialism: Consciousness, Ethics, and Relations with Others*, Value inquiry book series 87. Amsterdam: Rodopi, 1999.
Gill, Jerry H. 'Merleau-Ponty, Metaphor, and Philosophy'. *Philosophy Today* 34, no. 1 (1990): 48–66.
Gilmore, Jonathan. 'Between Philosophy and Art'. In *The Cambridge Companion to Merleau-Ponty*, eds Taylor Carman and Mark B. N. Hansen, pp. 291–317. Cambridge: Cambridge University Press, 2005.

Glendinning, Simon. *In the Name of Phenomenology*. Oxford: Routledge, 2007.
Godway, Eleanor. 'Towards a Phenomenology of Politics: Expression and Praxis'. In *Merleau-Ponty, Hermeneutics, and Postmodernism*, eds Thomas W. Busch and Shaun Gallagher, pp. 161–70. Albany: State University of New York Press, 1992.
Goetz, Stewart C. 'Questions about Emergent Dualism'. *Philosophia Christi* 2, no. 2 (2000): 175–81.
Goldie, Charles M. and Richard G. E. Pinch. *Communication Theory*, London Mathematical Society Student Texts 22. Cambridge: Cambridge University Press, 1991.
Good, James and Irving Velody. *The Politics of Postmodernity*. Cambridge: Cambridge University Press, 1998.
Goodchild, Philip. *Rethinking Philosophy of Religion: Approaches From Continental Philosophy*, Perspectives in Continental Philosophy 29. New York: Fordham University Press, 2002.
Gordon, Haim. *The Heidegger-Buber Controversy: The Status of the I-Thou*, Contributions in Philosophy 81. London: Greenwood Press, 2001.
Greisch, Jean. 'In Praise of Philosophy: A Hermeneutical Rereading'. In *Chiasms: Merleau-Ponty's Notion of Flesh*, ed. Fred Evans. Albany: State University of New York Press, 2000.
Greisch, Jean. *Paul Ricœur: l'itinérance du sens*, Krisis. Grenoble: J. Millon, 2001.
Greisch, Jean. 'Testimony and Attestation'. In *Paul Ricoeur: The Hermeneutics of Action*, ed. Richard Kearney, pp. 81–98. London: Sage, 1996.
Greisch, Jean. 'Vers une herméneutique du soi'. In *Éthique et Responsabilité: Paul Ricœur*, ed. Jean-Christophe Aeschlimann, pp. 155–73. Neuchâtel: À la Braconnière, 1994.
Griffiths, A. Phillips. *Contemporary French Philosophy*, Royal Institute of Philosophy Lectures 21. Cambridge: Cambridge University Press, 1987.
Gualandi, Alberto. *Le Problème de la vérité scientifique dans la philosophie française contemporaine: la rupture et l'événement*, La Philosophie en commun. Paris: Harmattan, 1998.
Guibal, Francis. 'Venue, passage, partage: la voix singulière de Jean-Luc Nancy'. *Études* 393, no. 4 (2000): 357–71.
Guibal, Francis and Jean-Clet Martin. *Sens en tous sens: autour des travaux de Jean-Luc Nancy*, La philosophie en effet. Paris: Galilée, 2004.
Gutting, Gary. *French Philosophy in the Twentieth Century*. Cambridge: Cambridge University Press, 2001.
Gyllenhammer, Paul. 'From the Limits of Knowledge to the Hermeneutics of Action (From Derrida to Ricoeur)'. *American Catholic Philosophical Quarterly* 72, no. 4 (1998): 559–80.
Haar, Michel. 'Painting, Perception, Affectivity'. In *Merleau-Ponty: Difference, Materiality, Painting*, ed. Véronique M. Fóti. Atlantic Highlands, NJ: Humanities Press, 1996.

Hachamovitch, Yfat. 'Ploughing the Delirium'. In *Merleau-Ponty: Difference, Materiality, Painting*, ed. Véronique M. Fóti. Atlantic Highlands, NJ: Humanities Press, 1996.

Haight, David. 'The Source of Linguistic Meaning'. *Philosophy and Phenomenological Research* 37 (1976): 239–47.

Hall, W. D. 'The Site of Christian Ethics: Love and Justice in the Work of Paul Ricoeur'. In *Paul Ricoeur and Contemporary Moral Thought*, eds J. Wall, W. Schweiker and W. D. Hall, pp. 143–63. London: Routledge, 1999.

Hallward, Peter. *Badiou: A Subject to Truth*. Minneapolis: University of Minnesota Press, 2003.

Hamrick, William S. 'A Process View of the Flesh: Whitehead and Merleau-Ponty'. *Process Studies* 28, nos. 1–2 (1999): 117–29.

Hansen, Mark B. N. 'The Embryology of the (In)visible'. In *The Cambridge Companion to Merleau-Ponty*, eds Taylor Carman and Mark B. N. Hansen, pp. 231–64. Cambridge: Cambridge University Press, 2005.

Hantaï, Simon, Jean-Luc Nancy and Jacques Derrida. *La Connaissance des textes: lecture d'un manuscrit illisible*. Paris: Galilée, 2001.

Harrison, Bernard. 'Deconstructing Derrida'. In *Comparative Criticism*, ed. E. S. Schaeffer, pp. 3–24. Cambridge: Cambridge University Press, 1987.

Hart, Kevin. *The Trespass of the Sign: Deconstruction, Theology and Philosophy*. Cambridge: Cambridge University Press, 1989.

Hartog, François. 'L'historien et la conjoncture historiographique'. *Débat* 102 (1998): 4–10.

Hartog, François. 'Le témoin et l'historien'. *Gradhiva* 27 (2000): 1–14.

Hartshorne, Charles. *Insights and Oversights of Great Thinkers: An Evaluation of Western Philosophy*, SUNY Series in Systematic Philosophy. Albany: State University of New York Press, 1983.

Hass, Marjorie and Lawrence Hass. 'Merleau-Ponty and the Origin of Geometry'. In *Chiasms: Merleau-Ponty's Notion of Flesh*, ed. Fred Evans. Albany: State University of New York Press, 2000.

Hatley, James. 'Recursive Incarnation and Chiasmic Flesh: Two Readings of Paul Celan's "Chymisch" '. In *Chiasms: Merleau-Ponty's Notion of Flesh*, ed. Fred Evans. Albany: State University of New York Press, 2000.

Hauerwas, Stanley and Alasdair Macintyre. *Revisions: Changing Perspectives in Moral Philosophy*. Notre Dame, IN: University of Notre Dame Press, 1983.

Heidegger, Martin. *Four Seminars*, Studies in Continental Thought. Bloomington: Indiana University Press, 2003.

Heidegger, Martin. *Kant and the Problem of Metaphysics*. Bloomington: Indiana University Press, 1962.

Heidegger, Martin. *Pathmarks*, trans. William McNeill. Cambridge: Cambridge University Press, 1999.

Heidegger, Martin. *Phenomenological Interpretation of Kant's Critique of Pure Reason*, Studies in Continental Thought. Bloomington: Indiana University Press, 1997.

Heidegger, Martin. *The Phenomenology of Religious Life*, Studies in Continental Thought. Bloomington: Indiana University Press, 2004.

Heidegger, Martin and Eugen Fink. *Heraclitus Seminar, 1966/67*. Tuscaloosa: University of Alabama Press, 1979.

Heidegger, Martin and John Van Buren. *Supplements: From the Earliest Essays to Being and Time and Beyond*, SUNY Series in Contemporary Continental Philosophy. Albany: State University of New York Press, 2002.

Heidsieck, François. *L'Ontologie de Merleau-Ponty*, Bibliothèque de philosophie contemporaine. Paris: Presses Universitaires de France, 1971.

Heidsieck, François. *Maurice Merleau-Ponty: le philosophe et son langage*, Recherches sur la philosophie et le langage 15. Grenoble: Groupe de Recherches sur la Philosophie et le Langage, 1993.

Henry, Michel. *Incarnation: une philosophie de la chair*. Paris: Éditions du Seuil, 2000.

Hiddleston, Jane. *Reinventing Community: Identity and Difference in Late Twentieth-century Philosophy and Literature in French*. Oxford: Legenda, 2005.

Hofstadter, Douglas R. *Gödel, Escher, Bach: An Eternal Golden Braid*. London: Penguin, 2000.

Hohler, Thomas P. 'The Limits of Language and the Threshold of Speech: Saussure and Merleau-Ponty'. *Philosophy Today* (1982): 287–300.

Holbrook, David. *What Is It to Be Human? New Perspectives in Philosophy*, Avebury Series in Philosophy. Aldershot: Avebury, 1990.

Holl, Steven. *Intertwining: Selected Projects 1989–1995*. New York: Princeton Architectural Press, 1996.

Horner, Robyn. *Rethinking God as Gift: Marion, Derrida, and the Limits of Phenomenology*, Perspectives in Continental Philosophy 19. New York: Fordham University Press, 2001.

Howells, Christina. *Derrida: Deconstruction from Phenomenology to Ethics*, Key Contemporary Thinkers. Cambridge: Polity Press, 1998.

Hughes, Cheryl L. 'Reconstructing the Subject of Human Rights'. *Philosophy and Social Criticism* 25, no. 3 (1999): 47–60.

Hunefeldt, T. 'Semantic Dualism and Narrative Identity-Paul Ricoeur on the Cognitive Sciences'. *Cognitive Processing* 6, no. 3 (2005): 153–6.

Husserl, Edmund. *L'Origine de la géométrie*, Épiméthée. Paris: Presses Universitaires de France, 1974.

Hutchens, B. C. *Jean-Luc Nancy and the Future of Philosophy*. Chesham: Acumen, 2005.

Hyde, Michael J. *The Call of Conscience: Heidegger and Levinas*. Columbia: University of South Carolina Press, 2000.

Hyppolite, Jean. *Études sur Marx et Hegel*. Paris: M. Rivière, 1955.

Ihde, Don. *Bodies in Technology*, Electronic Mediations 5. Minneapolis: University of Minnesota Press, 2002.

Ihde, Don. *Consequences of Phenomenology*. Albany: State University of New York Press, 1986.
Ihde, Don. *Experimental Phenomenology: An Introduction*. New York: Putnam, 1977.
Ihde, Don. *Hermeneutic Phenomenology: The Philosophy of Paul Ricœur*, Northwestern University Studies in Phenomenology and Existential Philosophy. Evanston, IL: Northwestern University Press, 1971.
Ihde, Don. 'Literary and Science Fictions: Philosophers and Technomyths'. In *Ricoeur as Another: The Ethics of Subjectivity*, eds Richard A. Cohen and James L. Marsh, pp. 93–105. Albany: State University of New York Press, 2002.
Ihde, Don and Hugh J. Silverman. *Hermeneutics and Deconstruction*, Selected Studies in Phenomenology and Existential Philosophy 10. Albany: State University of New York Press, 1985.
Ingram, David. 'The Retreat of the Political in the Modern Age: Jean-Luc Nancy on Totalitarianism and Community'. *Research in Phenomenology* 18 (1988): 93–124.
Irigaray, Luce. *Éthique de la différence sexuelle*. Critique. Paris: Éditions de Minuit, 1984.
Irigaray, Luce. *An Ethics of Sexual Difference*, trans. Carolyn Burke and Gillian C. Gill. Ithaca, NY: Cornell University Press, 1993.
Jackson, Michael. *At Home in the World*. Durham, NC and London: Duke University Press, 1995.
James, Ian. 'On Interrupted Myth'. *Journal for Cultural Research* 9, no. 4 (2005): 331–49.
James, Ian. 'Pierre Klossowski: The Suspended Self'. In *Theoretical Interpretations of the Holocaust*, ed. Dan Stone, pp. 55–77. Atlanta, GA: Rodopi, 2001.
James, Ian. *The Fragmentary Demand: An Introduction to the Philosophy of Jean-Luc Nancy*. Stanford, CA Stanford University Press, 2006.
Jay, Martin. 'The Lifeworld and Lived Experience'. In *A Companion to Phenomenology and Existentialism*, eds Hubert L. Dreyfus and Mark A. Wrathall, pp. 91–105. Malden, MA: Blackwell, 2006.
Jegstrup, Elsebet. *The New Kierkegaard*, Studies in Continental Thought. Bloomington: Indiana University Press, 2004.
Jervolino, Domenico. *The Cogito and Hermeneutics: The Question of the Subject in Ricoeur*, Contributions to Phenomenology 6. London: Kluwer Academic, 1990.
Johnson, Christopher. *System and Writing in the Philosophy of Jacques Derrida*, Cambridge Studies in French 40. Cambridge: Cambridge University Press, 1993.
Johnson, Galen A. 'Alterity as a Reversibility'. In *Ontology and Alterity in Merleau-Ponty*, eds Galen A. Johnson and Michael B. Smith, pp. xvii–xxxiv. Evanston, IL: Northwestern University Press, 1990.

Johnson, Galen A. 'The Problem of Origins: In the Timber Yard, Under the Sea'. In *Merleau-Ponty: de la nature à l'ontologie*, eds Renaud Barbaras and Patrick Burke, pp. 249–59. Paris: Vrin, 2000.

Johnson, Galen A. 'Thinking Color: Merleau-Ponty and Paul Klee'. In *Merleau-Ponty: Difference, Materiality, Painting*, ed. Véronique M. Fóti. Atlantic Highlands, NJ: Humanities Press, 1996.

Johnson, Michael G. and B. Henley Tracy. *Reflections on The Principles of Psychology: William James After a Century*. Hillsdale, NJ: L. Erlbaum Associates, 1990.

Johnston, Devin. *Precipitations: Contemporary American Poetry as Occult Practice*. Middletown, CT: Wesleyan University Press, 2002.

Joy, Morny. 'Recognition in the Work of Paul Ricœur'. In *Between Suspicion and Sympathy: Paul Ricoeur's Unstable Equilibrium*, ed. Andrzej Wierciński, pp. 518–30. Toronto: Hermeneutic Press, 2003.

Kant, Immanuel. 'Critique of Practical Reason'. In *Immanuel Kant: Practical Philosophy*, pp. 133–272. Cambridge: Cambridge University Press, 1996.

Kant, Immanuel. *Critique of Pure Reason*, eds Paul Guyer and Allen W. Wood, The Cambridge Edition of the Works of Immanuel Kant. Cambridge: Cambridge University Press, 1997.

Kant, Immanuel. *Critique of the Power of Judgement*, ed. Paul Guyer, The Cambridge Edition of the Works of Immanuel Kant. Cambridge: Cambridge University Press, 2000.

Kant, Immanuel. *Metaphysical Foundations of Natural Science*. Indianapolis, IN: Bobbs-Merrill, 1970.

Kant, Immanuel. *Political Writings*, eds Hugh Barr Nisbet and Hans Reiss, Cambridge Texts in the History of Political Thought. Cambridge: Cambridge University Press, 1991.

Kant, Immanuel. *Theoretical Philosophy after 1781*, eds Henry E. Allison and Peter Heath. Cambridge: Cambridge University Press, 2002.

Kaplan, David M. *Ricoeur's Critical Theory*, SUNY Series in the Philosophy of the Social Sciences. Albany: State University of New York Press, 2003.

Kaplan, Louis. 'Photography and the Exposure of Community: Sharing Nan Goldin and Jean-Luc Nancy'. *Angelaki* 6, no. 3 (December 2001): 7–30.

Kapust, Antje. 'The So-called "Barbarian Basis of Nature" and Its Secret Logos'. In *Merleau-Ponty: De la nature à l'ontologie*, eds Renaud Barbaras and Patrick Burke, pp. 167–83. Paris: Vrin, 2000.

Kearney, Richard. 'Desire of God'. In *God, the Gift and Postmodernism*, eds John D. Caputo and Michael Scanlon, pp. 112–45. Bloomington: Indiana University Press, 1999.

Kearney, Richard. *Dialogues with Contemporary Continental Thinkers: The Phenomenological Heritage*. Manchester: Manchester University Press, 1984.

Kearney, Richard. *Modern Movements in European Philosophy*. Manchester: Manchester University Press, 1995.

Kearney, Richard. *On Paul Ricoeur: The Owl of Minerva*, Transcending Boundaries in Philosophy and Theology. Aldershot: Ashgate, 2004.

Kearney, Richard. 'On the Gift: A Discussion between Jacques Derrida and Jean-Luc Marion'. In *God, the Gift and Postmodernism*, eds John D. Caputo and M. D. Scanlon, pp. 54–78. Bloomington: Indiana University Press, 1999.

Kearney, Richard. 'Paul Ricoeur and the Hermeneutic Imagination'. In *The Narrative Path: The Later Works of Paul Ricoeur*, eds T. Peter Kemp and David Rasmussen, pp. 1–31. Cambridge, MA: MIT Press, 1989.

Kearney, Richard. *Poetics of Imagining: Modern to Post-modern*. Edinburgh: Edinburgh University Press, 1998.

Kearney, Richard. *Strangers, Gods and Monsters: Interpreting Otherness*. London: Routledge, 2002.

Kearney, Richard. 'The Crisis of Narrative in Contemporary Culture'. *Metaphilosophy* 28, no. 3 (1997): 183–95.

Kearney, Richard. *The Wake of Imagination: Ideas of Creativity in Western Culture*. London: Hutchinson, 1988.

Kearney, Richard. *Twentieth-century Continental Philosophy*, Routledge History of Philosophy 8. London: Routledge, 2003.

Kearney, Richard and Mark Dooley. *Questioning Ethics: Contemporary Debates in Philosophy*. London: Routledge, 1999.

Keller, Catherine and Anne Daniell. *Process and Difference: Between Cosmological and Poststructuralist Postmodernisms*, SUNY Series in Constructive Postmodern Thought. Albany: State University of New York Press, 2002.

Kelly, Sean Dorrance. 'Merleau-Ponty on the Body'. *Ratio* 15 (2002): 376–91.

Kelly, Sean Dorrance. 'Seeing Things in Merleau-Ponty'. In *The Cambridge Companion to Merleau-Ponty*, eds Taylor Carman and Mark B. N. Hansen, pp. 74–110. Cambridge: Cambridge University Press, 2005.

Kemp, P. 'Narrative Ethics and Moral Law in Ricoeur'. In *Paul Ricoeur and Contemporary Moral Thought*, eds J. Wall, W. Schweiker and W. D. Hall, pp. 32–46. London: Routledge, 1999.

Kemp, Peter T. and David M. Rasmussen. *The Narrative Path: The Later Works of Paul Ricoeur*. Cambridge, MA: MIT Press, 1989.

Kerszberg, Pierre. 'Misunderstanding the Other'. In *Merleau-Ponty: Difference, Materiality, Painting*, ed. Véronique M. Fóti. Atlantic Highlands, NJ: Humanities Press, 1996.

Kim, Jaegwon and Ernest Sosa. *A Companion to Metaphysics*, Blackwell Companions to Philosophy. Oxford: Blackwell, 1995.

Kochler, Hans. 'The Problem of Reality as Seen from the Viewpoint of Existential Phenomenology'. In *Foundations of Morality, Human Rights, and the Human Sciences*, pp. 175–87. Dordrecht: D. Reidel, 1983.

Kopf, Gereon. *Beyond Personal Identity: Dogen, Nishida, and a Phenomenology of No-self*, Curzon Studies in Asian Religion. Richmond: Curzon, 2001.

Krasner, James. 'Doubtful Arms and Phantom Limbs: Literary Portrayals of Embodied Grief'. *PMLA* 119 (2004): 218–32.

Krell, David Farrell. 'Engorged Philosophy II'. In *Postmodernism and Continental Philosophy*, eds Hugh J. Silverman and Donn Welton, pp. 49–66. Albany: State University of New York Press, 1986.

Krell, David Farrell. *The Purest of Bastards: Works of Mourning, Art, and Affirmation in the Thought of Jacques Derrida*, American and European Philosophy. University Park, PA: Pennsylvania State University Press, 2000.

Kule, Maija. 'The Ontological Pre-conditions of Understanding and the Formation of Meaning'. In *The Turning Points of the New Phenomenological Era*, ed. Anna-Teresa Tymieniecka. Dordrecht: Kluwer Academic, 1992.

Labelle, G. 'Merleau-Ponty et le christianisme'. *Laval Théologique et Philosophique* 58, no. 2 (2002): 317–40.

LaCapra, Dominick. 'Who Rules Metaphor?' *Diacritics* 10 (1980): 26.

Lacoue-Labarthe, Philippe and Jean-Luc Nancy. *Les Fins de l'homme: à partir du travail de Jacques Derrida*. Paris: Galilée, 1981.

Langan, Thomas. *Merleau-Ponty's Critique of Reason*. New Haven, CT: Yale University Press, 1966.

Langer, Monika M. *Merleau-Ponty's Phenomenology of Perception: A Guide and Commentary*. Basingstoke: Macmillan, 1989.

Langsdorf, Lenore. 'The Doubleness of Subjectivity: Regenerating the Phenomenology of Intentionality'. In *Ricoeur as Another: The Ethics of Subjectivity*, eds Richard A. Cohen and James L. Marsh, pp. 33–55. Albany: State University of New York Press, 2002.

Langsdorf, Lenore, Stephen H. Watson and E. Marya Bower. *Phenomenology, Interpretation, and Community*, Selected Studies in Phenomenology and Existential Philosophy 19. Albany: State University of New York Press, 1996.

Langsdorf, Lenore, Stephen H. Watson and Karen A. Smith. *Reinterpreting the Political: Continental Philosophy and Political Theory*, Selected Studies in Phenomenology and Existential Philosophy 20. Albany: State University of New York Press, 1998.

Lash, Scott. *Another Modernity, a Different Rationality*. Oxford: Blackwell, 1999.

Latona, Max J. 'Selfhood and Agency in Ricoeur and Aristotle'. *Philosophy Today* 45, no. 2 (2001): 107–20.

Laus, Thierry. 'La fin du christianisme: désenchantement, déconstruction et démocratie'. *Revue de Théologie et de Philosophie* 133 (2001): 475–85.

Lawlor, Leonard. *Derrida and Husserl: The Basic Problem of Phenomenology*, Studies in Continental Thought. Bloomington: Indiana University Press, 2002.

Lawlor, Leonard. 'Eliminating Some Confusion: The Relation of Being and Writing in Merleau-Ponty and Derrida'. In *Écart and Différance: Merleau-Ponty and Derrida on Seeing and Writing*, ed. M. C. Dillon, pp. 71–93. Atlantic Highlands, NJ: Humanities Press, 1997.

Lawlor, Leonard. *Imagination and Chance: The Difference Between the Thought of Ricoeur and Derrida*, Intersections. Albany: State University of New York Press, 1992.

Lawlor, Leonard. 'Metaphors and Traces: A Note on Radical Alterity in Paul Ricœur and Jacques Derrida'. In *Between Suspicion and Sympathy: Paul Ricoeur's Unstable Equilibrium*, ed. Andrzej Wierciński, pp. 351–6. Toronto: Hermeneutic Press, 2003.

Lawlor, Leonard. 'Phenomenology and Metaphysics: Deconstruction in *La Voix et le phénomène*'. In *Jacques Derrida: Critical Assessments of Leading Philosophers*, eds Zeynep Direk and Leonard Lawlor, pp. 17–37. London: Routledge, 2002.

Lawlor, Leonard. 'The Need for Survival: The Logic of Writing in Merleau-Ponty and Derrida'. *Tympanum*, no. 4 (2000) [cited 30 August 2005]. Available from http://www.usc.edu/dept/comp-lit/tympanum/4/lawlor.html.

Lawlor, Leonard. *Thinking Through French Philosophy: The Being of the Question*. Studies in Continental Thought. Bloomington: Indiana University Press, 2003.

Lawlor, Leonard. '*Verflechtung*: The Triple Significance of Merleau-Ponty's Course Notes on Husserl's *The Origin of Geometry*.' In *Husserl at the Limits of Phenomenology*, eds Leonard Lawlor and Bettina Bergo, pp. ix–xxxvii. Evanston, IL: Northwestern University Press, 2003.

Lawlor, Leonard and Bettina Bergo, eds *Husserl at the Limits of Phenomenology*. Evanston, IL: Northwestern University Press, 2002.

Lefebvre, Henri. *La Production de l'espace, société et urbanisme*. Paris: Éditions Anthropos, 1974.

Lefebvre, Henri. *Writings on Cities*. Oxford: Blackwell, 1996.

Lefort, Claude. 'D'un doute à l'autre (Merleau-Ponty)'. *Esprit*, no. 6 (1982): 23–30.

Lefort, Claude. 'Flesh and Otherness'. In *Ontology and Alterity in Merleau-Ponty*, eds Galen A. Johnson and Michael B. Smith, pp. 3–13. Evanston, IL: Northwestern University Press, 1990.

Lefort, Claude. 'Philosophie et non-philosophie'. *Esprit* 66, June (1982): 101–12.

Lefort, Claude. 'Préface'. In Maurice Merleau-Ponty, *L'Institution dans l'histoire personnelle et publique. Le problème de la passivité, le sommeil, l'inconscient, la mémoire. Notes de cours au collège de France 1954–1955*, pp. 5–28. Paris: Belin, 2003.

Lefort, Claude. *Sur une colonne absente: écrits autour de Merleau-Ponty*. Paris: Gallimard, 1978.

Leiter, Brian. *Routledge Philosophy Guidebook to Nietzsche on Morality*, Routledge Philosophy Guidebooks. London: Routledge, 2002.

Lelièvre, F. '« L'Origine de la vérité » selon Maurice Merleau-Ponty dans *Le Visible et l'invisible*'. *Enseignement Philosophique* 51, no. 6 (2001): 3–16.

Lesaar, Henrik Richard. 'Judging Action: Paul Ricœur's Contribution to the Legal Interpretation of Facts'. In *Between Suspicion and Sympathy: Paul*

Ricoeur's Unstable Equilibrium, ed. Andrzej Wierciński, pp. 551–62. Toronto: Hermeneutic Press, 2003.

Levin, David Michael. 'Justice in the Flesh'. In *Ontology and Alterity in Merleau-Ponty*, eds Galen A. Johnson and Michael B. Smith, pp. 35–44. Evanston, IL: Northwestern University Press, 1990.

Levin, David Michael. 'Singing the World: Merleau-Ponty's Phenomenology of Language'. *Philosophy Today* 42, no. 3 (1998): 319–36.

Levin, David Michael. *The Opening of Vision: Nihilism and the Postmodern Situation*. London: Routledge, 1988.

Levin, David Michael. *The Philosopher's Gaze: Modernity in the Shadows of Enlightenment*. London: University of California Press, 1999.

Lévinas, Emmanuel. *Autrement qu'être, ou, au-delà de l'essence*, Phaenomenologica 54. The Hague: M. Nijhoff, 1974.

Lévinas, Emmanuel. *Entre nous: essais sur le penser-à-l'autre*. Paris: Grasset, 1991.

Lévinas, Emmanuel. *Hors sujet*. Saint-Clement-la-Riviere: Fata Morgana, 1987.

Lévinas, Emmanuel. *L'Au-delà du verset: lectures et discours talmudiques*. Critique. Paris: Éditions de Minuit, 1982.

Lévinas, Emmanuel. *Totalité et infini: essai sur l'extériorité*. The Hague: M. Nijhoff, 1961.

Lévinas, Emmanuel and Paul Ricœur. 'L'Unicité humaine du pronom *je*'. In *Langages*, ed. Jean-Christophe Aeschlimann, pp. 35–7. Neuchâtel: À la Braconnière, 1994.

Librach, Ronald S. 'Narration and The Life-World'. *Journal of Aesthetics and Art Criticism* 41 (1982): 77–86.

Librett, Jeffrey S. 'Between Nihilism and Myth: Value, Aesthetics and Politics in *The Sense of the World*', Translator's Foreword. In Jean-Luc Nancy, *The Sense of the World*, pp. vii–xxvi. Minneapolis: University of Minnesota Press, 1997.

Librett, Jeffrey S. 'The Practice of the World: Jean-Luc Nancy's Liminal Cosmology'. *International Studies in Philosophy* 28, no. 1 (1996): 29–44.

Liebsch, Burkhard. 'Archaeological Questioning: Merleau-Ponty and Ricoeur'. In *Merleau-Ponty in Contemporary Perspectives*, eds Patrick Burke and Jan Van der Veken, pp. 13–24. London: Kluwer Academic, 1993.

Lincoln, Andrew T. *Truth on Trial: The Lawsuit Motif in the Fourth Gospel*. Peabody, MA: Hendrickson, 2000.

Lingis, Alphonso. *Deathbound Subjectivity*, Studies in Phenomenology and Existential Philosophy. Bloomington: Indiana University Press, 1989.

Lingis, Alphonso. *Foreign Bodies*. London: Routledge, 1994.

Lingis, Alphonso. 'The Body Postured and Dissolute'. In *Merleau-Ponty: Difference, Materiality, Painting*, ed. Véronique M. Fóti. Atlantic Highlands, NJ: Humanities Press, 1996.

Lingis, Alphonso. *The Community of Those Who Have Nothing in Common*, Studies in Continental Thought. Bloomington: Indiana University Press, 1994.

Lippit, Akira Mizuta. *Electric Animal: Toward a Rhetoric of Wildlife*. Minneapolis: University of Minnesota Press, 2000.

Llewelyn, John. *Appositions of Jacques Derrida and Emmanuel Levinas*, Studies in Continental Thought. Bloomington: Indiana University Press, 2002.

Llewelyn, John. *The Hypocritical Imagination: Kant and Levinas*. London: Routledge, 1999.

Low, Douglas Beck. *Merleau-Ponty's Last Vision: A Proposal for the Completion of The Visible and the Invisible*, Northwestern University Studies in Phenomenology and Existential Philosophy. Evanston, IL: Northwestern University Press, 2000.

Lowe, Walter James. 'The Coherence of Paul Ricœur'. *Journal of Religion* 61 (1981): 384–402.

Lucaites, John Louis, Celeste Michelle Condit and Sally Caudill. *Contemporary Rhetorical Theory: A Reader*, Revisioning Rhetoric. London: Guilford Press, 1999.

Lucy, Niall. *Debating Derrida*. Carlton South: Melbourne University Press, 1999.

Lundin, Roger. *Disciplining Hermeneutics: Interpretation in Christian Perspective*. Leicester: Apollos, 1997.

Lundin, Roger, Clarence Walhout and Anthony C. Thiselton. *The Promise of Hermeneutics*. Grand Rapids, MI: Eerdmans, 1999.

Lyotard, Jean-François. *Le Différend*, Critique. Paris: Éditions de Minuit, 1983.

Macann, Christopher E. *Four Phenomenological Philosophers: Husserl, Heidegger, Sartre, Merleau-Ponty*. London: Routledge, 1993.

McBride, William Leon and Calvin O. Schrag. *Phenomenology in a Pluralistic Context*, Selected Studies in Phenomenology and Existential Philosophy 9. Albany: State University of New York Press, 1983.

MacCammon, L. M. 'Jacques Derrida, Paul Ricoeur, and the Marginalization of Christianity: Can the God of Presence be Saved?' In *Paul Ricoeur and Contemporary Moral Thought*, eds J. Wall, W. Schweiker and W. D. Hall, 187–212. London: Routledge, 1999.

MacIntyre, Alasdair. *After Virtue: A Study in Moral Theory*. London: Duckworth, 1985.

MacIntyre, Alasdair. *Whose Justice? Which Rationality?* London: Duckworth, 1988.

MacIntyre, Alasdair and Paul Ricœur. *The Religious Significance of Atheism*, Bampton Lectures in America 18. New York: Columbia University Press, 1969.

MacKay, David J. C. *Information Theory, Inference, and Learning Algorithms*. Cambridge: Cambridge University Press, 2003.

MacKay, Donald M. *Information, Mechanism and Meaning*. London: MIT Press, 1969.

McKenna William, R. and Claude Evans Joseph, eds. *Derrida and Phenomenology: Symposium on Phenomenology and Deconstruction:*

Selected Papers, Contributions to Phenomenology 20. Dordrecht; London: Kluwer Academic, 1995.

McQuillan, Martin. *The Narrative Reader*. London: Routledge, 2000.

Madison, Gary Brent. 'Being and Speaking'. In *Beyond the Symbol Model: Reflections on the Representational Nature of Language*, ed. John Stewart, pp. 69–98. Albany: State University of New York Press, 1996.

Madison, Gary Brent. 'Flesh as Otherness'. In *Ontology and Alterity in Merleau-Ponty*, eds Galen A. Johnson and Michael B. Smith, pp. 27–34. Evanston, IL: Northwestern University Press, 1990.

Madison, Gary Brent. 'Merleau-Ponty and Derrida: *La différEnce*'. In *Écart and Différance: Merleau-Ponty and Derrida on Seeing and Writing*, ed. M. C. Dillon, pp. 94–111. Atlantic Highlands, NJ: Humanities Press, 1997.

Madison, Gary Brent. 'Merleau-Ponty in Retrospect'. In *Merleau-Ponty in Contemporary Perspectives*, eds Patrick Burke and Jan Van der Veken, pp. 183–96. London: Kluwer Academic, 1993.

Madison, Gary Brent. 'Paul Ricœur: Philosopher of Being-human (Zuoren)'. In *Between Suspicion and Sympathy: Paul Ricoeur's Unstable Equilibrium*, ed. Andrzej Wierciński, pp. 481–501. Toronto: Hermeneutic Press, 2003.

Madison, Gary Brent. *The Phenomenology of Merleau-Ponty: A Search for the Limits of Consciousness*. Columbus: Ohio University Press, 1981.

Madison, Gary Brent and Ingrid Harris. *The Politics of Postmodernity: Essays in Applied Hermeneutics*, Contributions to Phenomenology 42. Dordrecht: Kluwer Academic, 2001.

Malabou, Catherine, Marc Crépon, Marc De Launay and Jacques Derrida. 'Questions à Jacques Derrida'. In *La Philosophie au risque de la promesse*, eds Marc Crépon and Marc de Launay, pp. 183–209. Paris: Bayard, 2004.

Maldiney, Henri. 'Flesh and Verb in the Philosophy of Merleau-Ponty'. In *Chiasms: Merleau-Ponty's Notion of Flesh*, ed. Fred Evans. Albany: State University of New York Press, 2000.

Mancini, Sandro. 'Merleau-Ponty's Phenomenology as a Dialectical Philosophy of Expression'. *International Philosophical Quarterly* 36, no. 4 (1996): 389–98.

Marcel, Gabriel, Paul Ricœur, Stephen Jolin and Peter McCormick. *Tragic Wisdom and Beyond; Including, Conversations between Paul Ricoeur and Gabriel Marcel*. Northwestern University Studies in Phenomenology and Existential Philosophy. Evanston, IL: Northwestern University Press, 1973.

Mardas, Nancy. 'Following the Golden Thread: A Journey through the Labyrinth of Tymieniecka's Logos and Life'. *Phenomenological Inquiry* vol. 27 (2003): 34–62.

Margolis, Joseph. 'Merleau-Ponty and Postmodernism'. In *Merleau-Ponty, Hermeneutics, and Postmodernism*, eds Thomas W. Busch and Shaun Gallagher, pp. 241–56. Albany: State University of New York Press, 1992.

Margolis, Joseph. 'Philosophical Extravagance in Merleau-Ponty and Derrida'. In *Écart and Différance: Merleau-Ponty and Derrida on Seeing and Writing*, ed. M. C. Dillon, pp. 112–32. Atlantic Highlands, NJ: Humanities Press, 1997.

Marion, Jean-Luc. 'La fin de la métaphysique ouvre une nouvelle carrière à la philosophie'. *Le Monde*, 22 September 1998.
Marsh, James L. 'The Right and the Good: A Solution to the Communicative Ethics Controversy'. In *Ricoeur as Another: The Ethics of Subjectivity*, eds Richard A. Cohen and James L. Marsh, pp. 223–34. Albany: State University of New York Press, 2002.
Matthews, Eric H. 'Merleau-Ponty's body-subject and psychiatry'. *International Review of Psychiatry* 16 (2004): 190–8.
Mauss, Marcel. 'Essai sur le don: forme et raison de l'échange dans les sociétés archaïques'. In *M. Mauss, Sociologie et anthropologie*, pp. 145–279. Paris: Presses Universitaires de France, 1997.
Mauss, Marcel. *The Gift: Forms and Functions of Exchange in Archaic Societies*. London: Routledge, 1988.
May, Todd. *Reconsidering Difference: Nancy, Derrida, Levinas, and Deleuze*. University Park, PA: Pennsylvania State University Press, 1997.
Mazis, Glen. 'Matter, Dream, and the Murmurs among Things'. In *Merleau-Ponty: Difference, Materiality, Painting*, ed. Véronique M. Fóti. Atlantic Highlands, NJ: Humanities Press, 1996.
Mazis, Glen A. 'Merleau-Ponty's Concept of Nature: Passage, the Oneiric, and Interanimality'. In *Merleau-Ponty: De la nature à l'ontologie*, eds Renaud Barbaras and Patrick Burke, pp. 223–47. Paris: Vrin, 2000.
Melville, Peter. 'Spectres of Schelling: Jean-Luc Nancy and the Limits of Freedom'. *Arachne* 7, nos. 1–2 (2000): 62–75.
Mensch, James R. *Knowing and Being: A Postmodern Reversal*. University Park, PA: Pennsylvania State University Press, 1996.
Mercury, Jean-Yves. *L'Expressivité chez Merleau-Ponty: du corps à la peinture*, L'Ouverture philosophique. Paris: L'Harmattan, 2000.
Merleau-Ponty, Maurice. *Éloge de la philosophie et autres essays*, Idées. Paris: Gallimard, 1960.
Merleau-Ponty, Maurice. 'Eye and Mind'. In *The Primacy of Perception, and Other Essays on Phenomenological Psychology, the Philosophy of Art, History and Politics*, pp. 159–190, ed. James M. Edie, trans. Carleton Dallery. Evanston, IL: Northwestern University Press, 1964.
Merleau-Ponty, Maurice. *Husserl at the Limits of Phenomenology*, eds Leonard Lawlor and Bettina Bergo. Evanston, IL: Northwestern University Press, 2002.
Merleau-Ponty, Maurice. 'Husserl aux limites de la phénoménologie'. In *Notes de cours sur L'Origine de la géométrie de Husserl*, ed. Renaud Barbaras, pp. 11–92. Paris: Presses Universitaires de France, 1998.
Merleau-Ponty, Maurice. *In Praise of Philosophy*, trans. John Wild and James M. Edie. Evanston, IL: Northwestern University Press, 1963.
Merleau-Ponty, Maurice. *L'Institution dans l'histoire personnelle et publique. Le problème de la passivité, le sommeil, l'inconscient, la mémoire. Notes de cours au collège de France 1954–1955*. Paris: Belin, 2003.
Merleau-Ponty, Maurice. *L'Œil et l'esprit*. Paris: Gallimard, 1964.

Merleau-Ponty, Maurice. *La Nature: notes de cours du Collège de France*, Traces écrites. Paris: Éditions du Seuil, 1994.
Merleau-Ponty, Maurice. *La Prose du monde*. Paris: Gallimard, 1969.
Merleau-Ponty, Maurice. *La Structure du comportement*, Bibliothèque de philosophie contemporaine. Paris: Presses Universitaires de France, 1942.
Merleau-Ponty, Maurice. *Le Primat de la perception et ses conséquences philosophiques; précédé de, Projet de travail sur la nature de la perception (1933); La nature de la perception (1934)*. Lagrasse: Verdier, 1996.
Merleau-Ponty, Maurice. *Le Visible et l'invisible. Suivi de notes de travail.* Paris: Gallimard, 1964.
Merleau-Ponty, Maurice. *Les Aventures de la dialectique*. Paris: Gallimard, 1955.
Merleau-Ponty, Maurice. *Nature: Course Notes form the Collège de France*, trans. Robert Vallier. Evanston, IL: Northwestern University Press, 2003.
Merleau-Ponty, Maurice. *Notes de cours sur L'Origine de la géométrie de Husserl; suivi de Recherches sur la phénoménologie de Merleau-Ponty*. Paris: Presses Universitaires de France, 1998.
Merleau-Ponty, Maurice. *Notes des cours au Collège de France, 1958–1959 et 1960–1961*, Bibliothèque de philosophie. Paris: Gallimard, 1996.
Merleau-Ponty, Maurice. *Parcours, 1935–1951, Philosophie*. Lagrasse: Verdier, 1997.
Merleau-Ponty, Maurice. *Parcours deux, 1951–1961, Philosophie*. Lagrasse: Verdier, 2001.
Merleau-Ponty, Maurice. *Phénoménologie de la perception*, Bibliothèque des idées. Paris: Gallimard, 1945.
Merleau-Ponty, Maurice. *Phenomenology of Perception*, trans. Colin Smith. London: Routledge, 2002.
Merleau-Ponty, Maurice. 'Préface'. In *L'Œuvre de Freud et son importance pour le monde moderne*, ed. A. Hesnard, pp. 5–10. Paris: Payot, 1960.
Merleau-Ponty, Maurice. *Psychologie et pédagogie de l'enfant: Cours de Sorbonne 1949–1952*. Paris: Verdier, 2001.
Merleau-Ponty, Maurice. *Résumés de cours. Collège de France 1952–1960*. Paris: Gallimard, 1968.
Merleau-Ponty, Maurice. *Sens et non-sens*, Bibliothèque de philosophie. Paris: Gallimard, 1996.
Merleau-Ponty, Maurice. *Sense and Non-Sense*, trans. Hubert L. Dreyfus and Patricia Allen Dreyfus. Evanston, IL: Northwestern University Press, 1968.
Merleau-Ponty, Maurice. *Signes*. Paris: Gallimard, 1960.
Merleau-Ponty, Maurice. *Signs*, trans. Richard C. McLeary. Evanston, IL: Northwestern University Press, 1964.
Merleau-Ponty, Maurice. 'The Primacy of Perception and its Philosophical Consequences', trans. James M. Edie. In *The Primacy of Perception*, pp. 12–42. Evanston, IL: Northwestern University Press, 1964.
Merleau-Ponty, Maurice. *The Prose of the World*, trans. John O'Neill, ed. Claude Lefort. London: Heinemann, 1974.

Merleau-Ponty, Maurice. *The Structure of Behaviour*, trans. Alden L. Fisher. London: Methuen, 1963.
Merleau-Ponty, Maurice. *The Visible and the Invisible*, trans. Alphonso Lingis, ed. Claude Lefort. Evanston, IL: Northwestern University Press, 1968.
Merleau-Ponty, Maurice. *Themes from the Lectures at the Collège de France 1952–1960*, trans. John O'Neill. Evanston, IL: Northwestern University Press, 1970.
Merleau-Ponty, Maurice. 'Un inédit de Maurice Merleau-Ponty'. *Revue de Métaphysique et de Morale* 4, December (1962): 401–9.
Merrell, Floyd. *Simplicity and Complexity: Pondering Literature, Science, and Painting*, Studies in Literature and Science. Ann Arbor: University of Michigan Press, 1998.
Mies, Francoise. 'L'Herméneutique du témoignage en philosophie: littérature, mythe et Bible'. *Revue des Sciences Philosophiques et Théologiques* 81, January (1997): 3–20.
Milbank, John. 'The Soul of Reciprocity. Part One, Reciprocity Refused'. *Modern Theology* 17, no. 3 (2001): 335–91.
Milburn, Colin Nazhone. 'Monsters in Eden: Darwin and Derrida'. *Modern Language Notes* 118, no. 3 (2003): 603–21.
Mitchell, W. J. Thomas. *Against Theory: Literary Studies and the New Pragmatism*. Chicago and London: University of Chicago Press, 1985.
Mongin, Olivier. 'De la justice à la conviction'. In *Éthique et responsabilité: Paul Ricœur*, ed. Jean-Christophe Aeschlimann, pp. 51–85. Neuchâtel: À la Braconnière, 1994.
Mongin, Olivier. 'Depuis Lascaux'. *Esprit* 6 (1982): 67–76.
Mongin, Olivier. 'La représentation du passé'. *Magazine Littéraire*, no. 390 (2000): 27–8.
Mongin, Olivier. *Paul Ricœur*. Paris: Éditions du Seuil, 1994.
Mongin, Olivier. 'Paul Ricoeur: renouer avec la tradition métaphysique'. *Magazine Littéraire*, no. 380 (1999): 61–2.
Monnier, Mathilde and Jean-Luc Nancy. *Allitérations: conversations sur la danse*. Incises. Paris: Galilée, 2005.
Montefiore, Alan, ed. *Philosophy in France Today*. Cambridge: Cambridge University Press, 1983.
Moran, Dermot. *Introduction to Phenomenology*. London: Routledge, 2000.
Morris, David. *The Sense of Space*, SUNY Series in Contemporary Continental Philosophy. Albany: State University of New York Press, 2004.
Morrison, Robert J. 'Merleau-Ponty and Literary Language'. *International Studies in Philosophy* 26, no. 4 (1994): 69–83.
Moya, Paula M. L. and Michael Roy Hames-Garcia, eds *Reclaiming Identity: Realist Theory and the Predicament of Postmodernism*. Berkeley: University of California Press, 2000.
Mulhall, Stephen. *Heidegger and Being and Time*, Routledge Philosophy Guidebook. London: Routledge, 1996.

Mullen, Deborah Carter. *Beyond Subjectivity and Representation: Perception, Expression, and Creation in Nietzsche, Heidegger, and Merleau-Ponty*. Oxford: University Press of America, 1999.

Muller, D. 'Les sources religieuses du soi et l'éthique de l'action juste'. *Laval Théologique et Philosophique* 58, no. 2 (2002): 341–56.

Naas, M. 'In and Out of Touch: Derrida's *Le Toucher*. Review of *Le Toucher, Jean-Luc Nancy* by Jacques Derrida'. *Research in Phenomenology* 31 (2001): 258–65.

Naas, Michael. 'Lyotard, Nancy, and the Myth of Interruption'. In *Lyotard: Philosophy, Politics, and the Sublime*, ed. Hugh J. Silverman, pp. 100–12. London: Routledge, 2002.

Nagel, Thomas. 'What is it like to be a bat?' *Philosophical Review* 83, no. 4 (1974): 435–50.

Nancy, Jean-Luc. *A Finite Thinking*, trans. Simon Sparks. Stanford, CA: Stanford University Press, 2003.

Nancy, Jean-Luc. *A l'Écoute*. Paris: Galilée, 2002.

Nancy, Jean-Luc. 'Ascoltando'. In *Écoute: une histoire de nos oreilles*, ed. Peter Szendy, pp. 7–12. Paris: Éditions de Minuit, 2001.

Nancy, Jean-Luc. *Au Fond des images*. Paris: Galilée, 2003.

Nancy, Jean-Luc. *Being Singular Plural*, trans. Robert D. Richardson and Anne E. O'Byrne. Stanford, CA: Stanford University Press, 2000.

Nancy, Jean-Luc. 'Conloquium'. In Roberto Esposito, *Communitas: origine et destin de la communauté*, pp. 3–10. Paris: Presses Universitaires de France, 2000.

Nancy, Jean-Luc. *Corpus*. Paris: Éditions du Seuil, 1992.

Nancy, Jean-Luc. 'Corpus'. In *Thinking Bodies*, eds J. F. MacCannell and L. Zakarin, pp. 17–31. Irvine, CA: Stanford University Press, 1990.

Nancy, Jean-Luc. 'Dies irae'. In *La Faculté de juger*, eds Jacques Derrida et al., pp. 9–54. Paris: Éditions de Minuit, 1985.

Nancy, Jean-Luc. *Dis-enclosure: The Deconstruction of Christianity*, trans. Bettina Bergo, Gabriel Malenfant and Michael B. Smith. New York: Fordham University Press, 2008.

Nancy, Jean-Luc. *Ego sum*, La philosophie en effet. Paris: Flammarion, 1979.

Nancy, Jean-Luc. *Être singulier pluriel*, La philosophie en effet. Paris: Galilée, 1996.

Nancy, Jean-Luc. 'Finite History'. In *The States of 'Theory': History, Art, and Critical Discourse*, ed. David Carroll, pp. 149–72. New York: Columbia University Press, 1990.

Nancy, Jean-Luc. *Hegel: l'inquiétude du négatif*. Paris: Hachette, 1997.

Nancy, Jean-Luc. 'Identité et tremblement'. In *Hypnoses*, pp. 14–47. Paris: Galilée, 1984.

Nancy, Jean-Luc. *L'Expérience de la liberté*. Paris: Galilée, 1988.

Nancy, Jean-Luc. *L'Impératif catégorique*, La philosophie en effet. Paris: Flammarion, 1983.

Nancy, Jean-Luc. 'L'espèce d'espace pensée'. Preface, in *La Dislocation: architecture et philosophie*, ed. Benoît Goetz, pp. 11–13. Paris: Éditions de la Passion, 2002.
Nancy, Jean-Luc. *L' "il y a" du rapport sexuel*, Incises. Paris: Galilée, 2001.
Nancy, Jean-Luc. *L'Intrus*, Lignes fictives. Paris: Galilée, 2000.
Nancy, Jean-Luc. *L'Oubli de la philosophie*, La philosophie en effet. Paris: Galilée, 1986.
Nancy, Jean-Luc. *La Communauté affrontée*, La philosophie en effet. Paris: Galilée, 2001.
Nancy, Jean-Luc. *La Communauté désœuvrée*, Détroits. Paris: Christian Bourgois, 1999.
Nancy, Jean-Luc. *La Comparution (politique à venir)*, Détroits. Paris: Christian Bourgeois, 1991.
Nancy, Jean-Luc. *La Création du monde, ou, la mondialisation*, La philosophie en effet. Paris: Galilée, 2002.
Nancy, Jean-Luc. *La Déclosion: déconstruction du christianisme, 1*. Paris: Galilée, 2005.
Nancy, Jean-Luc. *La Pensée dérobée*. Paris: Galilée, 2001.
Nancy, Jean-Luc. *La Remarque speculative*, La philosophie en effet. Paris: Galilée, 1973.
Nancy, Jean-Luc. 'Laïcité monothéiste'. *Le Monde*, 2 January 2004.
Nancy, Jean-Luc. *Le Partage des voix*, Débats. Paris: Galilée, 1982.
Nancy, Jean-Luc. *Le Poids d'une pensée*, Trait d'union. Sainte-Foy, Quebec: Éditions Le Griffon d'argile, 1991.
Nancy, Jean-Luc. 'Le Portrait (dans le décor)'. *Cahiers Philosophie de l'art*. Paris: Institut d'art contemporain, 1999.
Nancy, Jean-Luc. *Le Regard du portrait*. Paris: Galilée, 2000.
Nancy, Jean-Luc. *Le Sens du monde*, La philosophie en effet. Paris: Galilée, 1993.
Nancy, Jean-Luc. *Les Muses*, La philosophie en effet. Paris: Galilée, 1994.
Nancy, Jean-Luc. 'Mad Derrida'. In *Adieu, Derrida: A Series of Lectures held in Commemoration of Jacques Derrida, Marking the Launch of the Birkbeck Institute for the Humanities*. Birkbeck, University of London, 6 May 2005.
Nancy, Jean-Luc. 'Of Being-in-Common', trans. James Creech. In *Community at Loose Ends*, ed. Miami Theory Collective. Minneapolis: University of Minnesota Press, 1991.
Nancy, Jean-Luc. 'Sharing Voices'. In *Transforming the Hermeneutic Context: from Nietzsche to Nancy*, ed. Gayle L. Ormiston and Alan D. Schrift, pp. 211–59. Albany: State University of New York Press, 1990.
Nancy, Jean-Luc. *Sur le Commerce des pensées*, ed. Michel Delorme, Écritures/Figures. Paris: Galilée, 2005.
Nancy, Jean-Luc. 'Technique du présent: essai sur On Kawara'. *Cahiers Philosophie de l'art*. Paris: Institut d'art contemporain, 1999.
Nancy, Jean-Luc. *The Creation of the World, or, Globalization*, trans. François Raffoul and David Pettigrew. Albany: State University of New York Press, 2007.

Nancy, Jean-Luc. *The Experience of Freedom*, trans. Bridget McDonald. Stanford, CA: Stanford University Press, 1993.
Nancy, Jean-Luc. *The Ground of the Image*, trans. Jeff Fort. New York: Fordham University Press, 2005.
Nancy, Jean-Luc. *The Inoperative Community*, trans. Peter Connor. Minneapolis: University of Minnesota Press, 1991.
Nancy, Jean-Luc. *The Muses*, trans. Peggy Kamuf. Stanford, CA: Stanford University Press, 1996.
Nancy, Jean-Luc. *The Self-Deconstruction of Christianity: An Open Discussion with Jean-Luc Nancy*. European Graduate School EGS, 11/07/2005 2005 [cited 30 August 2005]. Available from http://www.egs.edu/faculty/nancy/nancy-self-deconstruction-of-christianity-2000.html.
Nancy, Jean-Luc. *The Sense of the World*, trans. Jeffrey S. Librett. Minneapolis: University of Minnesota Press, 1997.
Nancy, Jean-Luc. 'The Technique of the Present.' [cited 7 April 2008]. Available from http://www.egs.edu/faculty/nancy/nancy-the-technique-of-the-present.html.
Nancy, Jean-Luc. 'Tout est-il politique?' *Actuel Marx* 28 (2000): 77–82.
Nancy, Jean-Luc. *Un Jour, les dieux se retirent . . .*, Pharmacie de Platon. Bordeaux: William Blake, 2001.
Nancy, Jean-Luc. 'Une Pensée au partage des eaux'. *Le Monde*, 11 March 2005.
Nancy, Jean-Luc. *Une Pensée finie*. Paris: Galilée, 1990.
Nancy, Jean-Luc. *Visitation (de la peinture chrétienne)*, Lignes fictives. Paris: Galilée, 2001.
Nancy, Jean-Luc and Jean-Claude Conésa. *Être, c'est être perçu*. Paris: Éditions des Cahiers Intempestifs, 2000.
Nancy, Jean-Luc and Thomas Ferenczi. 'Un entretien avec Jean-Luc Nancy'. *Le Monde*, 29 March 2005.
Nancy, Jean-Luc and B. C. Hutchens. 'Interview: The Future of Philosophy'. In *Jean-Luc Nancy and the Future of Philosophy*, pp. 161–6. Chesham: Acumen, 2005.
Nancy, Jean-Luc and Abbas Kiarostami. *L'Évidence du film*. Brussels: Yves Gevaert, 2001.
Nancy, Jean-Luc and François Martin. *NIUM*. Valence: Ecole Régionale des Beaux Arts, 1998.
Natoli, Joseph P. *Mots d'ordre: Disorder in Literary Worlds*, SUNY series, The Margins of Literature. Albany: State University of New York Press, 1992.
Newman, L. and A. Nelson. 'Circumventing Cartesian Circles'. *Nous* 33, no. 3 (1999): 370–404.
Newton, N. 'Privileged Access and Merleau-Ponty'. *Analecta Husserliana* 75 (2002): 71–80.
Niebuhr, H. Richard. *The Responsible Self: An Essay in Christian Moral Philosophy*. New York: Harper & Row, 1963.
Nikolopoulou, Kalliopi. ' "L'art et les gens" 1: Jean-Luc Nancy's Genealogical Aesthetics'. *College Literature* 30, no. 2 (2003): 174–93.

Norris, A. 'Jean-Luc Nancy and the Myth of the Common'. *Constellations* 7, no. 2 (2000): 272–95.
Nuallain, Sean O. *The Search for Mind: A New Foundation for Cognitive Science*. Norwood, NJ: Ablex, 1995.
Nussbaum, M. C. 'Ricoeur on Tragedy: Teleology, Deontology, and Phronesis.' In *Paul Ricoeur and Contemporary Moral Thought*, eds J. Wall, W. Schweiker and W. D. Hall, pp. 264–78. London: Routledge, 1999.
O'Connor, Tony. 'Intentionality, Ontology, and Empirical Thought'. In *Questioning Foundations*, ed. Hugh J. Silverman. New York: Routledge, 1993.
O'Hear, Anthony. *Karl Popper*. The Arguments of the Philosophers. London: Routledge, 1980.
Olkowski, Dorothea. 'Merleau-Ponty and Bergson: The Character of the Phenomenal Field'. In *Merleau-Ponty: Difference, Materiality, Painting*, ed. Véronique M. Fóti. Atlantic Highlands, NJ: Humanities Press, 1996.
Olkowski, Dorothea and James Morley. *Merleau-Ponty, Interiority and Exteriority, Psychic Life, and the World*. Albany: State University of New York Press, 1999.
Olkowski-Laetz, Dorothea. 'Merleau-Ponty: The Demand for Mystery In Language'. *Philosophy Today* 31 (1987): 352–8.
Olson, Gary A. and Lynn Worsham. *Postmodern Sophistry: Stanley Fish and the Critical Enterprise*. Albany: State University of New York Press, 2004.
Pascal, Blaise. *De l'Esprit géométrique: entretien avec M. de Sacy; Écrits sur la Grâce et autres textes*. Paris: Flammarion, 1985.
Pascal, Blaise. *Pensées*. Paris: Gallimard, 1976.
Pellauer, David. 'At the Limit of Practical Wisdom: Moral Blindness'. In *Ricoeur as Another: The Ethics of Subjectivity*, eds Richard A. Cohen and James L. Marsh, pp. 187–201. Albany: State University of New York Press, 2002.
Perez, Josue. 'The Priority of Affirmation in the Philosophy of Paul Ricoeur'. *Philosophy Today* 46 no. 4 (2002): 396–405.
Peters, Michael and Peter Pericles Trifonas. *Derrida, Deconstruction and Education: Ethics of Pedagogy and Research*. Oxford: Blackwell, 2004.
Petitot, Jean. *Naturalizing Phenomenology: Issues in Contemporary Phenomenology and Cognitive Science*, Writing Science. Stanford, CA: Stanford University Press, 1999.
Pettigrew, David, and François Raffoul. *Disseminating Lacan*, SUNY Series in Contemporary Continental Philosophy. Albany: State University of New York, 1996.
Piercey, R. 'The Role of Greek Tragedy in the Philosophy of Paul Ricoeur'. *Philosophy Today* 49 (2005): 3–13.
Pietersma, Henry. *Phenomenological Epistemology*. New York: Oxford University Press, 2000.
Pile, Steve, and N. J. Thrift. *Mapping the Subject: Geographies of Cultural Transformation*. London: Routledge, 1995.

Pinar, William. *The Passionate Mind of Maxine Greene: 'I am – not yet'*. London: Falmer Press, 1998.
Polanyi, Michael. *Knowing and Being: Essays*. London: Routledge, 1969.
Polkinghorne, Donald E. *Narrative Knowing and the Human Sciences*, SUNY Series in the Philosophy of the Social Sciences. Albany: State University of New York Press, 1988.
Pollio, Howard R., Tracy B. Henley and Craig Thompson. *The Phenomenology of Everyday Life: Empirical Investigations of Human Experience*. Cambridge: Cambridge University Press, 1997.
Ponton, L. 'L'Anti-hégélianisme politique de Paul Ricoeur dans *Soi-même comme un autre*'. *Laval Théologique et Philosophique* 52, no. 2 (1996): 473–88.
Pontremoli, Edouard. 'Description fragmentaire d'un désastre; sur Merleau-Ponty et Claude Simon'. In *Merleau-Ponty, phénoménologie et expériences*, eds Marc Richir and Étienne Tassin, pp. 138–59. Grenoble: Millon, 1992.
Popper, Carl. *Conjectures and Refutations: The Growth of Scientific Knowledge*. London: Routledge, 2002.
Potworowski, C. F. 'The Question of Truth in the Hermeneutics of Origen and Paul Ricoeur'. *Liturgica, Second Century, Alexandria Before Nicaea, Athanasius and the Arian Controversy*, ed. E. A. Livingstone, pp. 308–12. Oxford: Peeters Press, 1991.
Prickett, Stephen. *Narrative, Religion, and Science: Fundamentalism Versus Irony, 1700–1999*. Cambridge: Cambridge University Press, 2002.
Priest, Graham. *Beyond the Limits of Thought*. Cambridge: Cambridge University Press, 1995.
Priest, Stephen. *Merleau-Ponty*, The Arguments of the Philosophers. London: Routledge, 1998.
Prosser, Diane L. *Transgressive Corporeality: The Body, Poststructuralism, and the Theological Imagination*. Albany: State University of New York Press, 1995.
Proust, Marcel. *À la recherche du temps perdu I*. Paris: Gallimard, 1987.
Proust, Marcel. *Swann's Way*, trans. C. K. Scott Moncrieff and Terence Kilmartin. London: Random House, 1998.
Pucci, E. 'History and the Question of Identity: Kant, Arendt, Ricoeur'. In *Ricoeur at 80 – Festschrift: Special issue of Philosophy and Social Criticism* 21, nos. 5–6 (1995): 125–36.
Punday, Daniel. *Narrative After Deconstruction*. Albany: State University of New York Press, 2003.
Putt, B. K. 'Indignation Toward Evil: Ricoeur and Caputo on a Protest'. *Philosophy Today* 41, no. 3 (1997): 460–71.
Raffoul, François. 'The Logic of the With: On Nancy's *Être singulier pluriel*'. *Studies in Practical Philosophy* 1, no. 1 (1999): 36–52.
Raffoul, François and David Pettigrew. *Heidegger and Practical Philosophy*, SUNY series in Contemporary Continental Philosophy. Albany: State University of New York Press, 2002.

Rainsford, Dominic and Tim Woods, eds *Critical Ethics: Text, Theory and Responsibility*. Basingstoke: Macmillan, 1999.

Rapaport, Herman. *Later Derrida: Reading the Recent Work*. London: Routledge, 2002.

Rasmussen, David M. 'Justice and Interpretation'. In *Between Suspicion and Sympathy: Paul Ricoeur's Unstable Equilibrium*, ed. Andrzej Wierciński, pp. 531–8. Toronto: Hermeneutic Press, 2003.

Rasmussen, David M. 'Rethinking Subjectivity: Narrative Identity and the Self.' In *Ricoeur as Another: The Ethics of Subjectivity*, eds Richard A. Cohen and James L. Marsh, pp. 57–69. Albany: State University of New York Press, 2002.

Rawls, John. *A Theory of Justice*. Oxford: Oxford University Press, 1999.

Raynova, Yvanka B. 'Vers une phénoménologie présente et vivante. Le tournant de Maurice Merleau-Ponty'. In *Essays in Celebration of the Founding of the Organization of Phenomenological Organizations*, eds Chan-Fai Cheung, Ivan Chvatik, Ion Copoeru, Lester Embree, Julia Iribarne and Hans Rainer Sepp [cited 30 August 2005]. Available from http://www.o-p-o.net.

Reagan, Charles E. *Paul Ricoeur: His Life and His Work*. Chicago: University of Chicago Press, 1996.

Reagan, Charles E. 'Personal Identity'. In *Ricoeur as Another: The Ethics of Subjectivity*, eds Richard A. Cohen and James L. Marsh, pp. 3–31. Albany: State University of New York Press, 2002.

Reynolds, Jack. *Merleau-Ponty and Derrida: Intertwining, Embodiment and Alterity*. Athens, OH: Ohio University Press, 2004.

Rezende, Antonio Muniz de. 'Le point de départ dans la philosophie de Merleau-Ponty'. *Revue Philosophique de Louvain*: 451–80.

Richir, Marc. 'Le sens de la phénoménologie dans *Le Visible et l'invisible*'. *Esprit* 6 (1982): 124–45.

Richir, Marc. 'Merleau-Ponty and the Question of Phenomenological Architectonics'. In *Merleau-Ponty in Contemporary Perspectives*, eds Patrick Burke and Jan Van der Veken, pp. 37–52. Dordrecht and London: Kluwer Academic, 1993.

Richir, Marc. *Phénomènes, temps et êtres: ontologie et phenomenology*, Krisis. Montbonnot St Martin: Jerôme Millon, 1987.

Ricœur, Paul. *Autrement: lecture d'Autrement qu'être ou au-delà de l'essence d'Emmanuel Lévinas*, Les essais du Collège international de philosophie. Paris: Presses Universitaires de France, 1997.

Ricœur, Paul. 'Commémoration du centenaire de la mort de Jules Lagneau: "Le jugement et la méthode réflexive selon Jules Lagneau" '. *Bulletin de la Société Française de Philosophie* 88, no. 4 (1994): 120–38.

Ricœur, Paul. 'Contingence et rationalité dans le récit'. In *Le Roman, le récit et le savoir: colloque Franco-Neerlandais sur les relations du roman, du récit et du savoir*, eds Evert van der Starre and Henk Hillenaar, pp. 131–46. Groningen: Département de Français, Université de Groningue, 1986.

Ricœur, Paul. *Critique and Conviction*, trans. Kathleen Blamey. New York: Columbia University Press, 1998.

Ricœur, Paul. *De l'Interprétation: essai sur Freud*. Paris: Éditions du Seuil, 1965.
Ricœur, Paul. 'Discours et communication'. In *Paul Ricœur*, pp. 51–68. Paris: Éditions de l'Herne, 2004.
Ricœur, Paul. 'Droit des cités'. *Le Monde*, 23 August 1991.
Ricœur, Paul. *Du Texte à l'action: essais d'herméneutique II*. Paris: Éditions du Seuil, 1986.
Ricœur, Paul. 'Entre philosophie et théologie: la règle d'or en question'. *Revue d'Histoire et de Philosophie Religieuses* 69 (1989): 3–9.
Ricœur, Paul. 'Entretien'. In *Éthique et Responsabilité: Paul Ricœur*, ed. Jean-Christophe Aeschlimann, pp. 11–34. Neuchâtel: À la Braconnière, 1994.
Ricœur, Paul. 'Ethics and Human Capability: A Response'. In *Paul Ricoeur and Contemporary Moral Thought*, eds J. Wall, W. Schweiker and W. D. Hall, pp. 279–90. London: Routledge, 1999.
Ricœur, Paul. 'Fragility and Responsibility'. In *Ricoeur at 80 – Festschrift: Special Issue of Philosophy and Social Criticism* 21, nos. 5–6 (1995): 15–24.
Ricœur, Paul. *Freud and Philosophy: An Essay on Interpretation*, trans. Denis Savage. New Haven, CT and London: Yale University Press, 1970.
Ricœur, Paul. 'From Metaphysics to Moral Philosophy'. *Philosophy Today* 40, no. 4 (1996): 443–58.
Ricœur, Paul. *From Text to Action*, trans. Kathleen Blamey and John B. Thompson. London: Althone Press, 1991.
Ricœur, Paul. 'Herméneutique de l'idée de révélation'. In *La Révélation*, pp. 15–54. Bruxelles, Bd du Jardin botanique 43: Facultés universitaires Saint-Louis, 1977.
Ricœur, Paul. *Histoire et vérité*. Paris: Éditions du Seuil, 1964.
Ricœur, Paul. *History and Truth*, trans. Charles A. Kelbley. Evanston, IL: Northwestern University Press, 1973.
Ricœur, Paul. 'L'herméneutique du témoignage'. In *Le Témoignage*, ed. E. Castelli, pp. 35–61. Paris: Aubier, 1972.
Ricœur, Paul. 'L'usure de la tolérance et la résistance de l'intolérable'. *Revue Des Deux Mondes*, no. 11/12 (1999): 222–31.
Ricœur, Paul. 'La déclaration des droits de l'homme'. In *Responsables des droits de l'homme*, pp. 79–87. Paris: Bayard, 1998.
Ricœur, Paul. 'La grammaire de Ferry'. *Libération*, 12 March 1992.
Ricœur, Paul. 'La justice, vertu et institution'. In *La Sagesse pratique: autour de l'œuvre de Paul Ricœur*, eds Jeffrey Andrew Barash and Mireille Delbraccio, pp. 11–28. Paris: Centre National de Documentation Pédagogique, 1988.
Ricœur, Paul. *La Mémoire, l'histoire, l'oubli*, L'Ordre philosophique. Paris: Éditions du Seuil, 2000.
Ricœur, Paul. 'La métaphore et le problème central de l'herméneutique'. *Revue Philosophique de Louvain* 70 (1972): 93–112.
Ricœur, Paul. *La Métaphore vive*, L'Ordre philosophique. Paris: Éditions du Seuil, 1975.

Ricœur, Paul. 'La place du politique dans une conception pluraliste des principes de justice'. In *Pluralisme et équité*, eds Joëlle Affichard and Jean-Baptiste de Foucauld, pp. 71–84. Paris: Éditions Esprit, 1995.

Ricœur, Paul. 'La promesse d'avant la promesse'. In *La Philosophie au risque de la promesse*, eds Marc Crépon and Marc de Launay, pp. 25–34. Paris: Bayard, 2004.

Ricœur, Paul. *Le Conflit des interprétations; essais d'herméneutique*. Paris: Éditions du Seuil, 1969.

Ricœur, Paul. 'Le dialogue des cultures: la confrontation des héritages culturels'. In *Aux Sources de la culture française*, pp. 97–105. Paris: Éditions La Découverte, 1997.

Ricœur, Paul. *Le Juste 1*. Philosophie. Paris: Éditions Esprit, 1995.

Ricœur, Paul. *Le Juste 2*. Philosophie. Paris: Éditions Esprit, 2001.

Ricœur, Paul. 'Le juste entre le légal et le bon'. *Esprit* 174 (1991): 5–21.

Ricœur, Paul. 'Le juste, la justice et son échec'. In *Paul Ricœur*, eds Myriam Revault d'Allonnes and François Azouvi, pp. 287–307. Paris: Éditions de l'Herne, 2004.

Ricœur, Paul. 'Le sujet convoqué: à l'école des récits de vocation prophétique'. *Revue de l'Institut Catholique de Paris* 28 (1988): 83–99.

Ricœur, Paul. *Lectures 1: autour du politique*. La Couleur des idées. Paris: Éditions du Seuil, 1991.

Ricœur, Paul. *Lectures 2: la contrée des philosophes*, La Couleur des idées. Paris: Éditions du Seuil, 1994.

Ricœur, Paul. *Lectures 3: aux frontières de la philosophie*, La Couleur des idées. Paris: Éditions du Seuil, 1999.

Ricœur, Paul. *Liebe und Gerechtigkeit = Amour et justice*. Tübingen: Mohr, 1989.

Ricœur, Paul. 'Life in Quest of Narrative'. In *On Paul Ricoeur: Narrative and Interpretation*, ed. David Wood, pp. 20–33. New York: Routledge, 1991.

Ricœur, Paul. 'Love and Justice'. In *Radical Pluralism and Truth: David Tracy and the hermeneutics of religion*, eds Werner G. Jeanrond and Jennifer L. Rike, pp. 187–202. New York: Crossroad, 1991.

Ricœur, Paul. 'Manifestation et proclamation'. In *Le Sacré: études et recherches: actes du colloque*, ed. Enrico Castelli, pp. 57–76. Paris: Aubier, 1974.

Ricœur, Paul. *Oneself as Another*, trans. Kathleen Blamey. London: University of Chicago Press, 1992.

Ricœur, Paul. 'Otherwise: A Reading of Emmanuel Levinas's "Otherwise than Being or beyond Essence" '. In *Yale French Studies* 104 (2004) 82–99.

Ricœur, Paul. *Parcours de la reconnaissance: trois etudes*, Les essais. Paris: Stock, 2004.

Ricœur, Paul. 'Phenomenology and Theory of Literature: An Interview with Paul Ricoeur'. *Modern Language Notes* 96, no. 5 (1981): 1084–90.

Ricœur, Paul. *Philosophie de la volonté. Finitude et culpabilité 2: La Symbolique du mal*. Paris: Aubier-Montaigne, 1968.

Ricœur, Paul. *Reflections on the Just*, trans. David Pellauer. Chicago and London: University of Chicago Press, 2007.
Ricœur, Paul. 'Responsabilité: limitée ou illimitée?' In *Cahiers de l'école de la cathédrale*, pp. 23–30. Paris: Coopérative de l'Enseignement Religieux de Paris, 1997.
Ricœur, Paul. *Soi-même comme un autre*. Paris: Éditions du Seuil, 1990.
Ricœur, Paul. *Sur la Traduction*. Paris: Bayard, 2004.
Ricœur, Paul. *Temps et récit 1: l'intrigue et le récit historique*, L'ordre philosophique. Paris: Éditions du Seuil, 1983.
Ricœur, Paul. *Temps et récit 2: la configuration dans le récit de fiction*. L'ordre philosophique. Paris: Éditions du Seuil, 1984.
Ricœur, Paul. *Temps et récit 3: le temps raconté* L'ordre philosophique. Paris: Éditions du Seuil, 1985.
Ricœur, Paul. *The Conflict of Interpretations*, trans. Don Ihde. Evanston, IL: Northwestern University Press, 1974.
Ricœur, Paul. *The Course of Recognition*, trans. David Pellauer. Cambridge, MA: Harvard University Press, 2005.
Ricœur, Paul. 'The Erosion of Tolerance and the Resistance of the Intolerable'. *Diogenes* (1996): 189–202.
Ricœur, Paul. 'The Human Being as the Subject Matter of Philosophy'. In *The Narrative Path: The Later Works of Paul Ricoeur*, eds T. Peter Kemp and David Rasmussen, pp. 89–101. Cambridge, MA: MIT Press, 1989.
Ricœur, Paul. *The Just*, trans. David Pellauer. Chicago: University of Chicago Press, 2004.
Ricœur, Paul. 'The Plurality of Sources of Law'. *Ratio Juris* 7, no. 3 (1994): 272.
Ricœur, Paul. 'The Problem of the Will and Philosophical Discourse'. In *Patterns of the Life-World. Essays in Honour of J. Wild*, eds James M. Edie, Francis H. Parker and Calvin O. Schrag, pp. 273–89. Evanston, IL: Northwestern University Press, 1970.
Ricœur, Paul. *The Rule of Metaphor*, trans. R. Czerny. London: Routledge, 1986.
Ricœur, Paul. *The Symbolism of Evil*, trans. Emerson Buchanan. Boston: Beacon Press, 1969.
Ricœur, Paul. *Time and Narrative 1*, trans. Kathleen McLaughlin and David Pellauer. Chicago: University of Chicago Press, 1984.
Ricœur, Paul. *What Makes Us Think?*, trans. M. B. DeBevoise. Princeton, NJ: Princeton University Press, 2000.
Ricœur, Paul, and Edmond Blattchen. *L'Unique et le singulier: l'intégrale des entretiens d'Edmond Blattchen*, Noms de dieux. Bruxelles: Alice, 1999.
Ricœur Paul and Richard Kearney. 'Universality and the Power of Difference'. In Richard Kearney, *On Paul Ricœur*, The Owl of Minerva, pp. 145–50. Aldershot: Ashgate, 2004.
Ricœur, Paul and Yvanka B. Raynova. 'All That Gives Us to Think: Conversations with Paul Ricœur'. In *Between Suspicion and Sympathy: Paul*

Ricoeur's Unstable Equilibrium, ed. Andrzej Wierciński, pp. 670–96. Toronto: Hermeneutic Press, 2003.

Ricœur, Paul and Tamás Tóth. 'The Graft, the Residue, and Memory: Two Conversations with Paul Ricœur'. In *Between Suspicion and Sympathy: Paul Ricoeur's Unstable Equilibrium*, ed. Andrzej Wierciński, pp. 642–69. Toronto: Hermeneutic Press, 2003.

Ricœur, Paul and Mark I. Wallace. *Figuring the Sacred: Religion, Narrative, and Imagination*. Minneapolis, MN: Fortress Press, 1995.

Ricœur, Paul, François Azouvi and Marc B. de Launay. *La Critique et la conviction: entretien avec François Azouvi et Marc de Launay*. Paris: Calmann-Levy, 1995.

Ricœur, Paul, Nathalie Crom, Bruno Frappat and Robert Migliorini. 'La conviction et la critique: entretien recueilli à l'occasion de ses 90 ans par Nathalie Crom, Bruno Frappat et Robert Migliorini'. In *Paul Ricœur*, pp. 15–18. Paris: Éditions de l'Herne, 2004.

Rider, Sharon P. *Avoiding the Subject: A Critical Inquiry into Contemporary Theories of Subjectivity*, Library of Theoria 23. Stockholm: Thales, 1998.

Risser, James. 'After the Hermeneutic Turn'. *Research in Phenomenology* (2000): 30 71–88.

Risser, James. 'Communication and the Prose of the World: The Question of Language in Merleau-Ponty and Gadamer'. In *Merleau-Ponty in Contemporary Perspectives*, eds Patrick Burke and Jan Van der Veken, pp. 131–44. Dordrecht and London: Kluwer Academic, 1993.

Robert, Franck. 'Fondement et fondation'. In *Merleau-Ponty: De la nature à l'ontologie*, eds Renaud Barbaras and Patrick Burke, pp. 351–72. Paris: Vrin, 2000.

Robert, Franck. 'Présentation'. In Maurice Merleau-Ponty and Renaud Barbaras, *Notes de cours sur L'Origine de la géométrie de Husserl; suivi de Recherches sur la phénoménologie de Merleau-Ponty*, pp. 5–10. Paris: Presses Universitaires de France, 1998.

Robinet, André. *Merleau-Ponty: sa vie, son œuvre*. Paris: Presses Universitaires de France, 1963.

Robinson, Gillian, and John F. Rundell. *Rethinking Imagination: Culture and Creativity*. London: Routledge, 1994.

Rockmore, Tom. *Heidegger and French Philosophy: Humanism, Antihumanism and Being*. London: Routledge, 1995.

Rogozinski, Jacob, ed. *Le Retrait du politique: travaux du Centre de recherches philosophiques sur le politique*, Cahiers du Centre de recherches philosophiques sur le politique. Paris: Galilée, 1983.

Roman, J. 'Au-delà du structuralisme'. *Magazine Littéraire*, no. 390 (2000): 46–7.

Rorty, Richard. *Consequences of Pragmatism: Essays 1972–1980*. Brighton: Harvester Press, 1982.

Rorty, Richard. *Essays on Heidegger and Others*. Cambridge: Cambridge University Press, 1991.

Rosenthal, Sandra B. *Mead and Merleau-Ponty: Toward a Common Vision*. Albany: State University of New York Press, 1991.
Ross, Stephen David. *Art and its Significance: An Anthology of Aesthetic Theory*. Albany: State University of New York Press, 1994.
Ross, Stephen David. *The Gift of Touch: Embodying the Good*. Albany: State University of New York Press, 1998.
Rouse, Joseph. 'Merleau-Ponty's Existential Conception of Science'. In *The Cambridge Companion to Merleau-Ponty*, ed. Taylor Carman and Mark B. N. Hansen, pp. 265–90. Cambridge: Cambridge University Press, 2005.
Roviello, Anne-Marie. 'Les écarts du sens'. In *Merleau-Ponty, phénoménologie et expériences*, eds Marc Richir and Etienne Tassin, pp. 161–84. Grenoble: Millon, 1992.
Royle, Nicholas. *After Derrida*. Manchester: Manchester University Press, 1995.
Royle, Nicholas. *Jacques Derrida*, Routledge Critical Thinkers. London: Routledge, 2003.
Ruedin, I. 'Bodies of Responsibility: Merleau-Ponty and Derrida'. *Philosophy Today* 46, no. 3 (2002): 243–54.
Saint-Exupéry, Antoine de. *Pilote de guerre*. Paris: Gallimard, 1942.
Salas, D. 'De la philosophie politique à la philosophie du droit'. *Magazine Littéraire*, no. 390 (2000): 65–7.
Sallis, John. *Delimitations: Phenomenology and the End of Metaphysics*. Bloomington: Indiana University Press, 1986.
Sallis, John. *Force of Imagination: The Sense of the Elemental*, Studies in Continental Thought. Bloomington: Indiana University Press, 2000.
Sanders, Carol, ed. *The Cambridge Companion to Saussure*. Cambridge: Cambridge University Press, 2004.
Sandywell, Barry. *Presocratic Reflexivity: The Construction of Philosophical Discourse c. 600–450 BC*, Logological Investigations 3. London: Routledge, 1995.
Saussure, Ferdinand de. *Cours de linguistique générale*. Wiesbaden: Harrassowitz, 1967.
Saussure, Ferdinand de. *Course in General Lingusitics*, eds Charles Bally and Albert Sechehaye, in collaboration with Albert Reidlinger, trans. Wade Baskin. London: Peter Owen, 1960.
Schaeffer, Jean-Marie. *Art of the Modern Age: Philosophy of Art from Kant to Heidegger*, New French Thought. Princeton, NJ: Princeton University Press, 2000.
Schaffer, E. S., ed. *Boundaries of Literature*, Comparative Criticism 7. Cambridge: Cambridge University Press, 1985.
Scharff, Robert C. and Val Dusek. *Philosophy of Technology: The Technological Condition: An Anthology*, Blackwell Philosophy Anthologies 18. Malden, MA: Blackwell, 2003.
Schenk-Mair, Katharina. *Die Kosmologie Eugen Finks: Einführung in das Denken Eugen Finks und Explikation des kosmischen Weltbegriffs an den*

Lebensvollzügen des Schlafens und Wachens. Würzburg: Königshausen & Neumann, 1997.
Schiff, William and Emerson Foulke. *Tactual Perception: A Sourcebook*. Cambridge: Cambridge University Press, 1982.
Schiffrin, Deborah. *Approaches to Discourse*, Blackwell Textbooks in Linguistics. Oxford: Blackwell, 1994.
Schofield, Malcolm, Myles Burnyeat and Jonathan Barnes. *Doubt and Dogmatism: Studies in Hellenistic Epistemology*. Oxford: Clarendon Press, 1980.
Schrag, Calvin O. *Communicative Praxis and the Space of Subjectivity*. Bloomington: Indiana University Press, 1986.
Schrag, Calvin O. *Convergence Amidst Difference: Philosophical Conversations Across National Boundaries*, SUNY Series in the Philosophy of the Social Sciences. Albany: State University of New York Press, 2004.
Schrag, Calvin O. 'John Wild on Contemporary Philosophy'. *Philosophy and Phenomenological Research* 22 (1962): 409–11.
Schrag, Calvin O. 'La récupération du sujet phénoménologique: en dialogue avec Derrida, Ricœur et Lévinas'. In *Life: Phenomenology of Life as the Starting Point of Philosophy*, ed. Anna-Teresa Tymieniecka, pp. 183–92. Paris: Kluwer Academic, 1994.
Schrag, Calvin O. *The Self After Postmodernity*. New Haven, CT: Yale University Press, 1997.
Schrift, Alan D. *Nietzsche's French Legacy: A Genealogy of Poststructuralism*. London: Routledge, 1995.
Schusterman, Richard. 'The Silent, Limping Body of Philosophy'. In *The Cambridge Companion to Merleau-Ponty*, eds Taylor Carman and Mark B. N. Hansen, pp. 151–80. Cambridge: Cambridge University Press, 2005.
Schweiker, W. 'Starry Heavens and Moral Worth: Hope and Responsibility in the Structure of Theological Ethics'. In *Paul Ricoeur and Contemporary Moral Thought*, eds J. Wall, W. Schweiker and W. D. Hall, pp. 117–42. London: Routledge, 1999.
Sebbah, François-David. 'French Phenomenology'. In *A Companion to Phenomenology and Existentialism*, eds Hobert L. Dreyfus and Mark A. Wrathall. London: Blackwell, 2006.
Sedgwick, Peter R. *Descartes to Derrida: An Introduction to European Philosophy*. Oxford: Blackwell, 2001.
Shankman, Steven. *In Search of the Classic: Reconsidering the Greco-Roman tradition, Homer to Valéry and Beyond*. University Park, PA: Pennsylvania State University Press, 1994.
Shapiro, G. 'Jean-Luc Nancy and the Corpus of Philosophy'. In *Thinking Bodies*, eds J. F. MacCannell and L. Zakarin, pp. 52–62. Irvine, CA: Stanford University Press, 1990.
Sheets-Johnstone, Maxine. *Giving the Body Its Due*, SUNY Series: The Body in Culture, History, and Religion. Albany: State University of New York Press, 1992.

Sheppard, Darren, Simon Sparks and Colin Thomas. *On Jean-Luc Nancy: The Sense of Philosophy*. London: Routledge, 1997.
Siegel, Jerrold. 'A Unique Way of Existing: Merleau-Ponty and the Subject'. *Journal of the History of Philosophy* 29, no. 3 (1991): 455–75.
Silverman, Hugh J. *Inscriptions: Between Phenomenology and Structuralism*. London: Routledge, 1987.
Silverman, Hugh J. 'Is Merleau-Ponty Inside or Outside the History of Philosophy?' In *Chiasms: Merleau-Ponty's Notion of Flesh*, ed. Fred Evans, pp. 131–43. Albany: State University of New York Press, 2000.
Silverman, Hugh J. 'Merleau-Ponty and Derrida: Writing on Writing'. In *Ontology and Alterity in Merleau-Ponty*, eds Galen A. Johnson and Michael B. Smith, pp. 130–41. Evanston, IL: Northwestern University Press, 1990.
Silverman, Hugh J., ed. *Philosophy and Non-Philosophy Since Merleau-Ponty*. London: Routledge, 1988.
Silverman, Hugh, J. *Postmodernism and Continental Philosophy*, Selected Studies in Phenomenology and Existential Philosophy 13. Albany: State University of New York Press, 1988.
Silverman, Hugh J. *Questioning Foundations: Truth, Subjectivity, and Culture*. New York: Routledge, 1993.
Silverman, Hugh J. 'Reading Postmodernism as Interruption (between Merleau-Ponty and Derrida)'. In *Écart and Différance: Merleau-Ponty and Derrida on Seeing and Writing*, ed. M. C. Dillon, pp. 208–19. Atlantic Highlands, NJ: Humanities Press, 1997.
Silverman, Hugh J. *Textualities: Between Hermeneutics and Deconstruction*. London: Routledge, 1994.
Silverman, Hugh J. 'Traces of the Sublime: Visibility, Expressivity, and the Unconscious'. In *Merleau-Ponty: Difference, Materiality, Painting*, ed. Véronique M. Fóti. Atlantic Highlands, NJ: Humanities Press, 1996.
Silverman, Hugh J. *Writing the Politics of Difference*, Selected Studies in Phenomenology and Existential Philosophy 14. Albany: State University of New York Press, 1991.
Silverman, Hugh J. and Don Ihde, eds *Hermeneutics and Deconstruction*. Albany: State University of New York Press, 1985.
Simms, Karl. *Paul Ricœur*, Routledge Critical Thinkers. London: Routledge, 2003.
Simon, Claude. *La Route des Flandres*. Paris: Éditions de Minuit, 1975.
Singer, Alan. *Aesthetic Reason: Artworks and the Deliberative Ethos*, Literature and Philosophy. University Park, PA: Pennsylvania State University Press, 2003.
Singer, Linda. 'Merleau-Ponty and the Concept of Style'. *Man and World* 14 (1981): 153–63.
Skinner, Quentin. *The Return of Grand Theory in the Human Sciences*. Cambridge: Cambridge University Press, 1985.
Skúlason, Páll. *Le Cercle du sujet dans la philosophie de Paul Ricœur*. Paris: L'Harmattan, 2001.

Slatman, Jenny. *L'Expression au-delà de la représentation: sur l'aisthêsis et l'esthétique chez Merleau-Ponty*. Leuven and Dudley, MA: Peeters, 2002.
Slatman, Jenny. 'The Psychoanalysis of Nature and the Nature of Expression'. In *Merleau-Ponty: De la nature à l'ontologie*, eds Renaud Barbaras and Patrick Burke, pp. 207–22. Paris: Vrin, 2000.
Slob, Wouter H. *Dialogical Rhetoric: An Essay on Truth and Normativity After Postmodernism*, Argumentation Library 7. Boston: Kluwer Academic, 2002.
Smith, James K. A. 'Between Predication and Silence: Augustine on How (Not) to Speak of God'. *Heythrop Journal* 41, no. 1 (2000): 66–86.
Smith, Joel. 'Merleau-Ponty and the Phenomenological Reduction'. *Inquiry* 48 (2005): 553–71.
Smith, Nicholas H. *Charles Taylor: Meaning, Morals and Modernity*, Key Contemporary Thinkers. Cambridge: Polity Press, 2002.
Smith, Paul and Carolyn Wilde. *A Companion to Art Theory*, Blackwell Companions in Cultural Studies 5. Oxford: Blackwell, 2002.
Sobchack, Vivian Carol. *Carnal Thoughts: Embodiment and Moving Image Culture*. Berkeley: University of California Press, 2004.
Solomon, Robert C. and Kathleen M. Higgins. *A Short History of Philosophy*. Oxford: Oxford University Press, 1996.
Spariosu, Mihai. *The Wreath of Wild Olive: Play, Liminality, and the Study of Literature*. Albany: State University of New York Press, 1997.
Sparks, Simon. 'The Experience of Evil: Kant and Nancy'. In *Theoretical Interpretations of the Holocaust*, ed. Dan Stone, pp. 205–32. Atlanta, GA: Rodopi, 2001.
Sperber, Dan and Deirdre Wilson. *Relevance: Communication and Cognition*. Oxford: Blackwell, 1995.
Spivak, G. C. 'Response to Jean-Luc Nancy'. In *Thinking Bodies*, eds J. F. MacCannell and L. Zakarin, pp. 32–51. Irvine, CA: Stanford Univeristy Press, 1990.
Stafecka, M. 'Where Does Meaning Come From?' In *the Visible and the Invisible in the Interplay Between Philosophy, Literature and Reality*, ed. Anna-Teresa Tymieniecka, pp. 63–70. London: Kluwer Academic, 2002.
Steele, Meili. 'Recognizing Invisibility, Revising Memory'. In *The Visible and the Invisible in the Interplay between Philosophy, Literature and Reality*, ed. Anna-Teresa Tymieniecka, pp. 235–52. London: Kluwer Academic, 2002.
Steinbock, Anthony J. 'Reflections on Earth and World: Merleau-Ponty's Project of Transcendental History and Transcendental Geology'. In *Merleau-Ponty: Difference, Materiality, Painting*, ed. Véronique M. Fóti. Atlantic Highlands, NJ: Humanities Press, 1996.
Stenstad, G. 'Merleau-Ponty's Logos: The Sens-ing of Flesh'. *Philosophy Today* 37, no. 1 (1993): 52.
Stern, Robert. *Transcendental Arguments: Problems and Prospects*, Mind Association Occasional Series. Oxford: Oxford University Press, 1999.

Stewart, John Robert. *Beyond the Symbol Model: Reflections on the Representational Nature of Language*, SUNY Series in Speech Communication. Albany: State University of New York Press, 1996.

Stivale, Charles J. *The Two-fold Thought of Deleuze and Guattari: Intersections and Animations*, Critical Perspectives. New York and London: Guilford Press, 1998.

Strauss, C. 'Partly Fragmented, Partly Integrated: An Anthropological Examination of "Postmodern Fragmented Subjects"'. *Cultural Anthropology* 12, no. 3 (1997): 362–404.

Surprenant, Céline. 'Speaking in Water'. In *The Speculative Remark: One of Hegel's Bons Mots*, ed. Jean-Luc Nancy, pp. ix–xviii. Stanford, CA: Stanford University Press, 2002.

Sweeney, R. D. 'Trace, Testimony, Portrait'. In *Life Truth in Its Various Perspectives: Cognition, Self-Knowledge, Creativity, Scientific Research, Sharing-in-Life, Economics*, ed. A. T. Tymieniecka, pp. 159–70. London: Kluwer Academic, 2002.

Tallis, Raymond. *Why the Mind Is Not a Computer: A Pocket Lexicon of Neuromythology*, Societas: Essays in Political and Cultural Criticism. Exeter: Imprint Academic, 2004.

Taminaux, Jacques. 'Time and the Inner Conflicts of the Mind'. In *The Tract De unitate minori of Petrus Thome*, eds Egbert P. Bos and Thomae Petrus, pp. 43–58. Leuven: Peeters, 2002.

Taylor, Charles. 'Atomism'. In *Powers, Possessions and Freedom*, ed. Alkis Kontos, pp. 39–62. Toronto: University of Toronto Press, 1979.

Taylor, Charles. 'Merleau-Ponty and the Epistemological Picture'. In *The Cambridge Companion to Merleau-Ponty*, eds Taylor Carman and Mark B. N. Hansen, pp. 26–49. Cambridge: Cambridge University Press, 2005.

Taylor, Charles. *Sources of the Self: The Making of the Modern Identity*. Cambridge: Cambridge University Press, 1989.

Taylor, Mark C. *Deconstruction in Context: Literature and Philosophy*. Chicago: University of Chicago Press, 1986.

Taylor, Victor E. and Charles E. Winquist. *Encyclopaedia of Postmodernism*. London: Routledge, 2001.

Thébaud, Jean-Loup. 'La chair et l'infini: J. F. Lyotard et Merleau-Ponty'. *Esprit*, no. 6 (1982): 158–62.

Thibault, Paul J. *Re-reading Saussure: The Dynamics of Signs in Social Life*. London: Routledge, 1997.

Thierry, Yves. 'Le "cogito" comme expérience sensible'. In *Notes de cours sur L'Origine de la géométrie de Husserl; suivi de Recherches sur la phénoménologie de Merleau-Ponty*, eds Maurice Merleau-Ponty and Renaud Barbaras, pp. 255–68. Paris: Presses Universitaires de France, 1998.

Thiselton, Anthony C. *Interpreting God and the Postmodern Self: On Meaning, Manipulation and Promise*, Scottish Journal of Theology: Current Issues in Theology. Edinburgh: T&T Clark, 1995.

Thiselton, Anthony C. *New Horizons in Hermeneutics*. London: HarperCollins, 1992.

Thiselton, Anthony C. *The Two Horizons: New Testament Hermeneutics and Philosophical Description, with Special Reference to Heidegger, Bultmann, Gadamer, and Wittgenstein*. Exeter: Paternoster Press, 1980.

Thomas, Douglas. *Reading Nietzsche Rhetorically*, Revisioning Rhetoric. New York and London: Guilford Press, 1999.

Thommaset, Alain. 'Une éthique à l'école de Paul Ricœur'. *Études* 10 (1996): 351–60.

Thompson, Evan. *Colour Vision: A Study in Cognitive Science and the Philosophy of Perception*, Philosophical Issues in Science. London: Routledge, 1995.

Tillich, Paul and Robert C. Kimball. *Theology of Culture*. London: Oxford University Press, 1964.

Toadville, Ted. 'Singing the World in a New Key: Merleau-Ponty and the Ontology of Sense'. *Janus Head* 7, no. 2 (2004): 273–83.

Tuana, Nancy and Sandra Morgen, eds *Engendering Rationalities*, SUNY Series in Gender Theory. Albany: State University of New York Press, 2001.

Turnbull, William. *Language in Action: Psychological Models of Conversation*, International Series in Social Psychology. London: Routledge, 2002.

Tymieniecka, Anna-Teresa. 'Human Being – Individual and Moral – as the Articulating Factor of the Human Sciences'. In *Foundations of Morality, Human Rights, and the Human Sciences*, pp. ix–xiii. Dordrecht: Kluwer Academic, 2001.

Tymieniecka, Anna-Teresa. *Why Is There Something Rather Than Nothing? Prolegomena to the Phenomenology of Cosmic Creation*. Assen: Van Gorcum, 1966.

Vahabzadeh, Peyman. *Articulated Experiences: Toward a Radical Phenomenology of Contemporary Social Movements*, SUNY Series in the Philosophy of the Social Sciences. Albany: State University of New York Press, 2002.

Vallega, Alejandro A. *Heidegger and the Issue of Space: Thinking on Exilic Grounds*, American and European Philosophy Series. University Park, PA: Pennsylvania State University Press, 2003.

Van den Hengel, John. 'Can There Be a Science of Action?' In *Ricoeur as Another: The Ethics of Subjectivity*, eds Richard A. Cohen and James L. Marsh, pp. 71–92. Albany: State University of New York Press, 2002.

Van Den Hengel, John W. *The Home of Meaning: The Hermeneutics of the Subject of Paul Ricoeur*. Washington, DC: University Press of America, 1982.

Van Leeuwen, Theodoor Marius. *The Surplus of Meaning: Ontology and Eschatology in the Philosophy of Paul Ricoeur*, Amsterdam Studies in Theology 2. Amsterdam: Rodopi, 1981.

Vasseleu, Cathryn. *Textures of Light: Vision and Touch in Irigaray, Levinas and Merleau-Ponty*, Warwick Studies in European Philosophy. London: Routledge, 1998.

Vasterling, Veronica. 'Body and Language: Butler, Merleau-Ponty and Lyotard on the Speaking Embodied Subject'. *International Journal of Philosophical Studies* 11, no. 2 (2003): 205–23.

Venema, Henry Isaac. 'Am I the Text? A Reflection on Paul Ricoeur's Hermeneutic of Selfhood'. *Dialogue* 38, no. 4 (1999): 765–84.

Venema, Henry Isaac. *Identifying Selfhood: Imagination, Narrative, and Hermeneutics in the Thought of Paul Ricœur*, McGill Studies in the History of Religions. Albany: State University of New York Press, 2000.

Venema, Henry Isaac. 'Oneself as Another or Another as Oneself?' *Literature and Theology* 16, no. 4 (2002): 410–26.

Villela-Petit, Maria. 'Le soi incarné: Merleau-Ponty et la question du sujet'. In *Maurice Merleau-Ponty: le philosophe et son langage*, ed. François Heidsieck, pp. 415–47. Grenoble: Groupe de Recherches sur la Philosophie et le Langage, 1993.

Visker, Rudi. 'Raw Being and Violent Discourse: Foucault, Merleau-Ponty and the (Dis-)Order of Things'. In *Merleau-Ponty in Contemporary Perspectives*, eds Patrick Burke and Jan Van der Veken, pp. 109–30. London: Kluwer Academic, 1993.

Visker, Rudi. *Truth and Singularity: Taking Foucault into Phenomenology*, Phenomenologica 155. London: Kluwer Academic, 1999.

Von Herrmann, Friedrich Wilhelm. *Bewusstsein, Zeit und Weltverständnis*, Philosophische Abhandlungen 35. Frankfurt am Main: Vittorio Klostermann, 1971.

Waldenfels, Bernhard. 'Dialogue and Discourses'. In *Writing the Politics of Difference*, ed. Hugh J. Silverman, pp. 165–76. Albany: State University of New York Press, 1991.

Waldenfels, Bernhard. 'Interrogative Thinking: Reflections on Merleau-Ponty's Later Philosophy'. In *Merleau-Ponty in Contemporary Perspectives*, eds Patrick Burke and Jan Van der Veken, pp. 3–12. London: Kluwer Academic, 1993.

Waldenfels, Bernhard. 'Merleau-Ponty'. In *A Companion to Continental Philosophy*, eds Simon Critchley and William Schroeder, pp. 281–91. Oxford: Blackwell, 1998.

Waldenfels, Bernhard. 'The Paradox of Expression'. In *Chiasms: Merleau-Ponty's Notion of Flesh*, ed. Fred Evans. Albany: State University of New York Press, 2000.

Waldenfels, Bernhard. 'Vérité à faire: Merleau-Ponty's question concerning truth'. *Philosophy Today* (1991): 185–94.

Wall, J. 'Moral Meaning: Beyond the Good and the Right'. In *Paul Ricoeur and Contemporary Moral Thought*, eds J. Wall, W. Schweiker and W. D. Hall, pp. 47–63. London: Routledge, 1999.

Wall, John. 'The Economy of the Gift: Paul Ricoeur's Significance for Theological Ethics'. *Journal of Religious Ethics* 29, no. 2 (2001): 235–60.

Wall, J., W. Schweiker and W. D. Hall. 'Introduction: Human Capability and Contemporary Moral Thought'. In *Paul Ricoeur and Contemporary Moral*

Thought, eds J. Wall, W. Schweiker and W. D. Hall, pp. 1–14. London: Routledge, 1999.

Wallace, Mark I. 'The Summoned Self: Ethics and Hermeneutics in Paul Ricoeur in Dialogue with Emmanuel Levinas'. In *Paul Ricoeur and Contemporary Moral Thought*, eds J. Wall, W. Schweiker and W. D. Hall, pp. 80–96. London: Routledge, 1999.

Walzer, Michael. *Spheres of Justice: A Defence of Pluralism and Equality*. Oxford: Blackwell, 1983.

Ward, Graham. *The Blackwell Companion to Postmodern Theology*, Blackwell Companions to Religion. Oxford: Blackwell, 2001.

Ward, Graham. *The Postmodern God: A Theological Reader*, Blackwell Readings in Modern Theology. Oxford: Blackwell, 1997.

Ward, Graham. *Theology and Contemporary Critical Theory*, Studies in Literature and Religion. Basingstoke: Macmillan, 2000.

Watson, J. B. *Behaviorism*. London: Kegan Paul, Trench Trubner, 1930.

Watson, J. B. 'Psychology as the behaviorist views it'. *Psychological Review* 20 (1913).

Watson, Stephen H. 'On How We Are to and How We Are Not to Return to the Things Themselves'. In *Ontology and Alterity in Merleau-Ponty*, eds Galen A. Johnson and Michael B. Smith, pp. 45–8. Evanston, IL: Northwestern University Press, 1990.

Webb, Stephen H. 'The Rhetoric of Ethics as Excess: A Christian Theological Response to Emmanuel Levinas'. *Modern Theology* 15 (1999): 1–16.

Weihe, Edwin. 'Merleau-Ponty's Doubt: The Wild of Nothing'. In *Merleau-Ponty in Contemporary Perspectives*, eds Patrick Burke and Jan Van der Veken, pp. 99–108. London: Kluwer Academic, 1993.

Weiss, Allen S. *Mirrors of Infinity: The French Formal Garden and 17th-century Metaphysics*. New York: Princeton Architectural Press, 1995.

Weiss, Allen S. *The Aesthetics of Excess*. Albany: State University of New York Press, 1988.

Weiss, Gail. 'Écart: The Space of Corporeal Difference'. In *Chiasms: Merleau-Ponty's Notion of Flesh*, ed. Fred Evans, pp. 203–17. Albany: State University of New York Press, 2000.

Welton, Donn. *Body and Flesh: A Philosophical Reader*. Oxford: Blackwell, 1998.

Westphal, Merold. 'Situation and Suspicion in the Thought of Merleau-Ponty: The Question of Phenomenology and Politics'. In *Ontology and Alterity in Merleau-Ponty*, eds Galen A. Johnson and Michael B. Smith, pp. 158–79. Evanston, IL: Northwestern University Press, 1990.

White, Erin. 'Between Suspicion and Hope: Paul Ricoeur's Vital Hermeneutic'. *Literature and Theology* 5 (1991): 311–21.

White, Richard J. 'Autonomy as Foundational'. In *Questioning Foundations*, ed. Hugh J. Silverman. New York: Routledge, 1993.

White, Vernon. *Atonement and Incarnation: An Essay in Universalism and Particularity*. Cambridge: Cambridge University Press, 1991.

White, Vernon. *Identity, Society and Church*. London: SCM, 2002.
Whitehouse, G. 'Ricoeur on Religious Selfhood: A Response to Mark Wallace'. *Modern Theology* 16, no. 3 (2000): 315–24.
Whitehouse, G. 'Veils and Kingdoms: A Ricoeurian Metaphorics of Love and Justice'. In *Paul Ricoeur and Contemporary Moral Thought*, eds J. Wall, W. Schweiker and W. D. Hall, pp. 164–86. London: Routledge, 1999.
Wierciński, Andrzej. *Between Suspicion and Sympathy: Paul Ricoeur's Unstable Equilibrium*. Toronto: Hermeneutic Press, 2003.
Willard, Dallas. 'Is Derrida's View of Ideal Being Rationally Defensible?' In *Derrida and Phenomenology*, eds William R. McKenna and J. Claude Evans, pp. 23–41. Boston: Kluwer Academic, 1995.
Willard, Dallas. *Logic and the Objectivity of Knowledge: A Study in Husserl's Early Philosophy*, Series in Continental Thought. Athens, OH: Ohio University Press, 1984.
Williams, Bernard Arthur Owen. *Problems of the Self; Philosophical Papers 1956–1972*. Cambridge: Cambridge University Press, 1973.
Williams, Raymond. *Keywords: A Vocabulary of Culture and Society*. London: Fontana, 1983.
Williams, Rowan. 'The Suspicion of Suspicion: Wittgenstein and Bonhoeffer'. In *The Grammar of the Heart*, ed. Richard H. Bell, pp. 36–53. San Francisco: Harper & Row, 1988.
Wilson, Raymond J. 'Metaphoric and Metonymic Symbolism: A Development from Paul Ricoeur's Concepts'. In *The Visible and the Invisible in the Interplay between Philosophy, Literature and Reality*, ed. Anna Teresa Tymieniecka, pp. 49–61. London: Kluwer Academic, 2002.
Wirth, Stephen. *Mensch und Welt: Die Anthropo-Kosmologie Eugen Finks*, Philosophie im Gardez! Mainz: Gardez! Verlag, 1995.
Wolfe, Cary. *Critical Environments: Postmodern Theory and the Pragmatics of the 'Outside'*, Theory Out of Bounds 13. Minneapolis: University of Minnesota Press, 1998.
Wolfe, Cary. *Zoontologies: The Question of the Animal*. Minneapolis: University of Minnesota Press, 2003.
Wolfson, Elliott R. *Language, Eros, Being: Kabbalistic Hermeneutics and Poetic Imagination*. New York: Fordham University Press, 2004.
Wolin, Richard. *Heidegger's Children: Hannah Arendt, Karl Löwith, Hans Jonas, and Herbert Marcuse*. Princeton, NJ: Princeton University Press, 2001.
Wolin, Richard. *The Politics of Being: The Political Thought of Martin Heidegger*. New York: Columbia University Press, 1990.
Wolterstorff, Nicholas P. *John Locke and the Ethics of Belief*, Cambridge Studies in Religion and Critical Thought 2. Cambridge: Cambridge University Press, 1996.
Wood, Andrew David. *The Wager of Faith: The Philosophy of Paul Ricoeur and a Theology of Testimony*. Birmingham: University of Birmingham Press, 1993.
Wood, David. 'Interpreting Narrative'. In *On Paul Ricoeur: Narrative and Interpretation*, ed. David Wood, pp. 1–19. London: Routledge, 1991.

Wood, David. *On Paul Ricoeur: Narrative and Interpretation*, Warwick Studies in Philosophy and Literature. London: Routledge, 1991.
Wood, David. *The Step Back: Ethics and Politics after Deconstruction*, SUNY Series in Contemporary Continental Philosophy. Albany: State University of New York Press, 2005.
Worms, Frédéric. 'Entre intuition et réflexion. Le sens de la critique dans la phénoménologie de Merleau-Ponty'. In *Notes de cours sur L'Origine de la géométrie de Husserl; suivi de recherches sur la phénoménologie de Merleau-Ponty*, eds Maurice Merleau-Ponty and Renaud Barbaras, pp. 193–219. Paris: Presses Universitaires de France, 1998.
Wynn, F. 'The early relationship of mother and pre-infant: Merleau-Ponty and pregnancy'. *Nursing Philosophy* 3 (2002): 4–14.
Wyschogrod, Edith. 'Blind Man Seeing: From Chiasm to Hyperreality'. In *Chiasms: Merleau-Ponty's Notion of Flesh*, ed. Fred Evans. Albany: State University of New York Press, 2000.
Wyschogrod, Edith. 'Towards a Postmodern Ethics: Corporeality and Alterity'. In *The Ethical*, eds Edith Wyschogrod and Gerald P. McKenny, pp. 54–65. Oxford: Blackwell, 2003.
Wyschogrod, Edith and Gerald P. McKenny. *The Ethical*, Blackwell Readings in Continental Philosophy 5. Oxford: Blackwell, 2003.
Wyschogrod, Edith, Jean-Joseph Goux and Eric Boynton. *The Enigma of Gift and Sacrifice*, Perspectives in Continental Philosophy 23. New York: Fordham University Press, 2002.
Yeo, Michael Terrence. 'Creative Adequation: Merleau-Ponty's Philosophy of Philosophy'. Dissertation, McMaser University, 1988.
Yount, Mark. 'Two Reversibilities: Merleau-Ponty and Derrida'. *Philosophy Today* (1990): 129–40.
Zaccaria, Giuseppe. 'On Paul Ricœur's Philosophy of Law: Reflections on his Latest Works'. In *Between Suspicion and Sympathy: Paul Ricoeur's Unstable Equilibrium*, ed. Andrzej Wierciński, pp. 539–50. Toronto: Hermeneutic Press, 2003.
Zahavi, Dan, Sara Heinämaa and Hans Ruin. *Metaphysics, Facticity, Interpretation: Phenomenology in the Nordic Countries*, Contributions to Phenomenology 49. London: Kluwer Academic, 2003.
Zarka, Yves Charles. *L'autre Voie de la subjectivité: six études sur le sujet et le droit naturel au XVIIe siècle*. Paris: Beauchesne, 2000.
Ziarek, Ewa Plonowska. *Gombrowicz's Grimaces: Modernism, Gender, Nationality*. Albany: State University of New York Press, 1998.
Ziarek, Ewa Plonowska. *The Rhetoric of Failure: Deconstruction of Skepticism, Reinvention of Modernism*, The Margins of Literature. Albany: State University of New York Press, 1996.
Ziarek, Krzysztof. 'Is all technological?' *New Centennial Review* 2, no. 3 (2002): 139–68.
Zielinski, Agata. 'La notion de « transcendance » dans *Le Visible et l'invisible*: de l'indétermination au désir'. In *Merleau-Ponty: De la nature*

à l'ontologie, eds Renaud Barbaras and Patrick Burke, pp. 415–31. Paris: Vrin, 2000.

Žižek, Slavoj. 'How to Give Body to a Deadlock?' In *Thinking Bodies*. Irvine, CA: Stanford University Press, 1990.

Žižek, Slavoj. *The Ticklish Subject: The Absent Centre of Political Ontology*. London: Verso, 1999.

Zou, Lin. 'Radical Criticism and the Myth of the Split Self'. *Criticism: A Quarterly for Literature and the Arts* 42, no. 1 (2000): 7–30.

Index

agape, 124–5, 127, 128
alterity, 9, 14–15, 29, 64–6, 76, 84, 89–91, 93, 95, 105n90, 106, 128, 136, 173, 180, 181–4, 190, 201n120, 205; *see also* Derrida
Aristotle, 71n48, 85, 108, 110, 113
Augustine of Hippo, 89

Barbaras, Renaud, 7, 18, 37n25, 78
Bataille, Georges, 149
behaviourism, 24, 26, 38n53
Benveniste, Emile, 189
Bergson, Henri, 62
Bernasconi, Robert, 160n6, 181
Blanchot, Maurice, 43n101, 53, 138
Blondel, Maurice, 31
body, 7, 12n42, 14, 15, 16, 19, 20–4, 29, 30, 47, 52, 55, 58, 60, 150–2, 175–7, 206, 209
Boltanski, Luc, 120–1, 122, 123, 124, 129
Bourgeois, Patrick, 90, 96, 105n89

call, 33–4, 51–9, 62, 66–7, 81, 90–1, 93, 128, 140–1, 142, 204
call and response, 45, 52–3, 54, 55, 57, 58–9, 63, 65, 67, 78, 81–3, 95–7, 141, 204, 207
Caputo, John D., 4, 83
Cavell, Stanley, 66–7, 96
Changeux, Jean-Pierre, 84, 86
Chrétien, Jean-Louis, 58–9, 66, 145

cogito, 18, 24, 84, 88, 101n47, 151–3, 165n77, 165n81
Cohen, Richard, 91
community, 9, 109, 111–16, 121–2, 130, 137, 157, 174, 180, 181, 184–5, 190, 192–3
contact, 14–17, 29, 32–4, 45, 49, 51–2, 59, 62, 63–8, 95, 137, 142, 147–53, 173, 179, 204
con-tact, 14, 148, 149, 153, 173, 180, 187
contact sans contact, 187
Cornell, Drucilla, 90, 122, 133n44
Critchely, Simon, 66, 90, 96, 181–2
Cumming, Robert Denoon, 4, 5, 6, 43n102, 99n13

Dennett, Daniel, 101n44
Derrida
 alterity, 14–15, 65, 89–92, 93
 the decision, 22–3, 83, 95, 104n83, 121
 the gift, 123, 126–7, 128, 136
 héritage/inheritance, 94–5
 hospitality, 23, 54, 90–2, 123, 143, 207
 Impossible, the, 23, 50, 93, 94, 114, 117–18, 123, 125, 136, 205
 justice, 94, 92–5, 98, 104n83, 118–19, 123
 and Merleau-Ponty, 7, 13–20, 21–3, 25, 31–2, 33–5, 35n,

263

41n83, 46–8, 52, 53, 55, 61, 186, 203
  and Nancy, 140, 142, 143, 144, 145, 150, 186, 187, 188, 192, 201n120
  narrative, 102n56
  phenomenology, 1–6, 92–3, 130, 159, 193, 203–9
  responsibility, 90, 94, 103n81
  and Ricœur, 76, 77, 80–2, 85, 91–4, 95–7, 108–9, 117, 120, 123–5, 127, 203
  scepticism, 67, 105n90
  subjectivity, 80–1, 95
Descartes, René, 151, 170, 178, 185, 186
Descombes, Vincent, 11n16, 43n102
Devisch, Ignaas, 182, 192
différance, 31, 36n19, 46, 51, 80, 148
Dillon, Martin, 50–1, 59, 60
doubt, 53, 88, 93, 113
  and interrogation, 53
  and suspicion, 103n73
Dreyfus, Hubert and Stuart, 20–1

Edie, James, 45–6
expression, 20, 22, 45–9, 51, 55, 56, 57, 60, 61–3, 64, 82, 147, 204

fact/essence dichotomy, 17–20, 22, 23, 32, 58, 95
figure/ground relation, 24–6, 28, 30, 31, 34, 40n63, 59, 63–4, 82, 144, 170–3
  and language, 47–51, 55, 59
flesh, 21, 47, 84
  of the body, 47, 60
  of language, 47
  of the world, 15, 58
Foucault, Michel, 4, 60
Franck, Didier, 145

Gadamer, Hans-Georg, 107
García-Düttmann, Alexander, 143

Gauchet, Marcel, 31, 70n36
Gestalt, 18, 24, 25, 26, 29, 30, 33, 45
  and language, 47–8, 49, 51, 58, 61, 63
Gifford, Paul, and Johnnie Gratton, 83
Gilbert-Walsh, James, 155
Glendinning, Simon, 37n23
Greisch, Jean, 209

Heidegger, Martin, 37n31, 111, 141, 156, 177–8
  being-with/*Mitsein*, 153, 177–9, 181, 183
  and Derrida, 4, 80, 99n19
Heidsieck, François, 44n106
Hermeneutics, 76–9, 83–6, 87, 93, 98, 106, 107–8, 118, 136, 149, 152
Husserl, Edmund, 1, 3, 77, 108, 124, 179
  and Derrida, 3, 4–6, 14–15, 48, 55
  and Merleau-Ponty, 14–15, 42n105, 46
Hutchens, B. C., 137
Hyppolite, Jean, 60

il y a, 18–19, 52, 53, 174
incarnation, 15–17, 27, 28, 117
incommensurability, 124–5, 130, 148, 169, 185, 186, 189, 190–1
  incommensurability in common, 191–2
information theory, 24
Ingram, David, 156
Irigaray, Luce, 38n55

James, Ian, 12n34, 137, 149, 157–8, 169, 178, 183, 197n60
Jay, Martin, 5
Jervolino, Domenico, 89
justice, 93, 94, 106–30, 136, 155–6, 158, 179, 190–1

and the decision, 107, 117–18, 153–9
and *justesse*, 94, 118
and love, 124–30
and the undecidable, 118
and vengeance, 109, 110
and violence, 117, 126

Kant, Immanuel, 1, 10n1, 108, 115, 117, 138, 155, 159
  fact of reason, 115
Kearney, Richard, 85, 91, 105n89, 119

Langer, Monica, 67
Lawlor, Leonard, 4, 10n, 11n, 36n19, 46–7, 104n88, 131n20
Lefort, Claude, 33, 123
Levin, David Michael, 18–19, 20, 48, 63
Lévinas, Emmanuel, 18, 91, 108, 111, 124, 128, 152, 181
Locke, John, 80, 175
logos, 18–19, 20, 21, 52, 55, 56–7, 67, 145, 176
  logos blanc, 71n50
  logos endiathetos, 29, 55, 57
  logos proforikos, 29, 55
Low, Douglas, 61
Lyotard, Jean-François, 32

MacIntyre, Alistair, 122, 129
Madison, Gary Brent, 60–1
Mauss, Marcel, 126, 128
May, Todd, 174, 192
meaning
  dehiscence of meaning, 16, 39n55, 48, 52, 64, 65, 81
  as excarnational, 26, 32, 59
  and gesture, 49, 51, 56–7, 59
  and meaningfulness, 19, 21, 25, 29, 50, 52, 54, 55, 58, 61, 63, 64–5, 82, 140, 206
  as structure/form, 25, 27–30, 33, 39n57, 52

in the world, 2, 17–20, 25–7, 30, 56, 57–8, 64, 82, 85, 86, 146
Melville, Peter, 154
Merleau-Ponty, Maurice
  attunement, 54, 71n44
  cosmology of the visible, 28–9, 47, 79, 109, 203, 206
  on the decision, 22–3
  hyper-reflection, 31–2
  the interrogative, 45, 53, 54, 61, 67, 70n37, 76, 77, 78, 97, 207
  and language, 32, 34–5, 45–68
  on the *langue/parole* distinction, 48–9, 56
  and ontology, 8, 13, 15–17, 26, 28–32, 45, 53, 60, 65, 67–8
  the *phénomène-enveloppe*, 27, 33, 80, 176
  pregnancy, 12, 19, 28–9, 47, 50, 52, 54, 56, 57, 59, 63, 81, 119, 139–40
  and Ricœur, 76–7, 78, 79, 81, 82, 84, 97–8, 206
  and Sartre, 43n102, 99n13
  singing the world, 56, 63
  the to-be-interpreted, 33, 52, 54, 81
  see also Derrida and Merleau-Ponty; Husserl and Merleau-Ponty; Nancy and Merleau-Ponty; Ricœur and Merleau-Ponty
metaphysics, 3, 4, 14, 18, 25, 50, 145, 150, 181, 145, 177, 181–2
  metaphysics of presence, 8, 14, 15, 17, 30, 32, 50, 83, 85, 144, 150, 207
Morris, David, 40n63
mutuality, 19, 22, 29, 48, 55, 64–5, 76, 112, 123, 126, 127, 129, 130, 133n45, 136, 205, 207

Nancy, Jean-Luc
  the arts, 187–90
  the caress, 150–1

community, 131n17, 137, 157, 174, 180, 184, 185, 190, 192–3
concordia discors, 180, 184, 188, 206
corpus, 151, 152, 159, 170–7, 186, 206
cosmos, 137–8, 142–4, 146, 170, 175, 176, 179, 182, 184, 187, 191, 200n109, 204
and the decision, 153–9, 185–93
excription, 148–9, 157, 172, 173, 174, 189
finite thinking, 144–5, 149, 155, 174, 175, 176, 193, 206
freedom, 153–8
and Merleau-Ponty, 139, 141, 147, 164n57, 165n78, 165n81, 170–2, 173, 174, 183, 188, 196n42, 201n120, 206
on the mouth, 147–8, 151, 153
ontology, 136, 137, 144, 147–53, 155, 174, 178–9, 180, 193
patency, 139, 144, 147, 173, 205
resonance, 71n44, 141–2, 152
rhythm, 141, 176, 188–9, 200n109
and Ricœur, 100n29, 131n17, 133n43, 145, 146, 149–51, 152–3, 158, 162n31, 171, 179, 183, 188, 189, 206
the senses, 186–7, 188–90
sens/signification, 138–40, 141, 142, 144, 146, 147, 154, 179
sharing, 158, 173, 178, 181, 184, 185
singular-plural, 157, 175, 177–85, 206
spacing, 141, 146–7, 150, 170, 171, 174–6, 184, 187, 189, 193, 194
techne, 145–6, 149, 163, 183, 191
on universals, 133n43, 159
on weight/*pesée*, 148, 153, 173, 177

the with/*avec*, 146, 173, 178–9, 182, 183, 192, 201
and the 'yet without'/*'sans pourtant'*, 137, 142, 143–4, 152, 175, 176, 187, 205, 209
nihilism, 50–1, 123, 143–4
Norris, Andrew, 154, 157, 174, 185

ontology
of enunciation, 151–2
indirect, 28–32, 67, 77
ontological diplopia, 31, 60, 95
and presence, 15–16, 76, 77, 207
of relations, 178–9
of the visible, 26
see also Merleau-Ponty and ontology; Nancy and ontology; Ricœur and ontology
other *see* alterity

Pascal, Blaise, 138
presence, 15–17, 21, 28, 34, 45, 52, 53, 77, 79, 80, 83, 143–7, 149, 150–1, 204–5, 207
in contrast to the present, 145–6
as passage, 144, 159, 174, 207
as proximity, 15, 35n6, 45, 76, 204
see also contact; metaphysics; ontology
promise, 79–80, 91, 123
Proust, Marcel, 52
Punday, Daniel, 102n56, 105n89

Rapaport, Hermann, 68n1
Rawls, John, 111, 112–14, 115–17, 120, 122, 123–4, 129
original situation, 112–16, 117, 120, 129, 130n12
Ricœur's critique of, 116–17
and Walzer, 120
Reynolds, Jack, 20, 22–3
Richir, Mark, 44n108, 71n50
Ricœur, Paul
attestation, 87–8, 89, 92, 93, 97, 101, 107, 113, 136

being-demanding-to-be-said, 81
chacun, 111–12
commitment, 88–9, 91, 94, 97, 98, 108, 115–19, 129
democracy, 123
the detour, 77, 78, 79, 83, 86, 87, 96, 98n3, 101n47
discordant concord, 79, 179, 206, 208
fragmentation, 77–87
hermeneutics of the self, 8, 78–9, 82, 85, 95, 106, 151, 152
idem/ipse identity, 79–80, 91, 95, 181, 206
and the interrogative, 78
just distance, 110, 112, 116, 121, 123, 150, 206
logics of equivalence and superabundance, 126, 128
and Merleau-Ponty, 76–7, 78, 79, 81, 82, 84, 97–8, 206
and narrative, 76, 79, 81–3, 84, 96, 109, 110, 113, 129, 136, 146, 189
narrative identity, 79, 82, 91, 106, 153
ontology, 77–8, 82, 84, 85, 87–8, 95, 96–8, 125, 130
polysemy of being, 75, 85, 98
specific plurivocity, 117, 119, 129
tension, 84, 116, 121, 125, 126, 128–9, 131n18, 175
translation, 121
universals, 122
utopia, 77, 114, 205
wager, 87–8, 136

Rodin, Auguste, 34
Rousseau, Jean-Jacques, 117

Sallis, John, 4, 25, 31, 41n79
Saussure, Ferdinand de, 48, 69n20
scepticism, 17, 50, 67–8, 96–7, 105n90, 143
Schapp, Wilhelm, 80
Silverman, Hugh, 4, 11n22, 12n28, 41n83, 53, 54
social contract, 108, 111, 112, 115–16
Spinoza, Baruch de, 83
style, 22, 27, 29–32, 33–4, 54, 59, 62, 141
  and écriture, 41n83
suspicion, 17, 49, 89, 93, 96–7, 98, 103n73, 113; *see also* doubt

thaumazein, 19, 139
Thévenot, Laurent, 120–1, 122, 123, 124, 129
touch, 13–16, 21, 145, 148–50, 184, 186–7, 190, 204
  and *humainisme*, 14, 186

undecidability, 22–3, 90, 118, 122, 157

Venema, Henry Isaac, 82
Visker, Rudi, 64

Waldenfels, Bernhard, 60n37
Walzer, Michael, 111, 120, 186, 190–1
  Ricœur's critique of, 120–1
Wood, David, 53–4, 79, 83, 208